P9-EDK-322

GOD IN CREATION

Also by Jürgen Moltmann

THE CRUCIFIED GOD

THE THEOLOGY OF HOPE

THE CHURCH IN THE POWER OF THE SPIRIT

THE TRINITY AND THE KINGDOM

THE POWER OF THE POWERLESS

JÜRGEN MOLTMANN

God in Creation

A NEW THEOLOGY OF CREATION AND THE SPIRIT OF GOD

The Gifford Lectures
1984–1985

1817

Harper & Row, Publishers, San Francisco

Cambridge, Hagerstown, New York, Philadelphia
London, Mexico City, São Paulo, Singapore, Sydney

Translated by Magaret Kohl from the German *Gott in der Schöpfung: Ökologische Schöpfungslehre* published by Christian Kaiser Verlag, Munich, 1985

FIRST U.S. EDITION

85 86 87 88 89 10 9 8 7 6 5 4 3 2 1

To the University of St Andrews
and
Emory University, Atlanta
in token of gratitude for the
conferring of an honorary doctorate

CONTENTS

PREFACE

The doctrine of creation has not been made a separate theme in German Protestant theology since the dispute between the Confessing Church and the 'German Christians' during the years of dictatorship. The impression left by the alternative presented at that time has been too deep-seated: either 'natural theology', which thought that God's order could be discovered in the natural conditions of nation and race, and that his will could be seen in the event of Hitler's seizure of power; or 'revealed theology', which hears and holds fast to Jesus Christ as 'the one Word of God', as the Barmen Theological Declaration put it in 1934, in its first thesis. The problems that were hammered out then in continental European theology between Karl Barth, Emil Brunner, Friedrich Gogarten and Paul Althaus have by no means become out of date and superseded.

But today new questions have come to the fore which were still completely unknown at that time. Faced as we are with the progressive industrial exploitation of nature and its irreparable destruction, what does it mean to say that we believe in God the Creator, and in this world as his creation? What we call the environmental crisis is not merely a crisis in the natural environment of human beings. It is nothing less than a crisis in human beings themselves. It is a crisis of life on this planet, a crisis so comprehensive and so irreversible that it can not unjustly be described as apocalyptic. It is not a temporary crisis. As far as we can judge, it is the beginning of a life and death struggle for creation on this earth.

In the 1930s, the problem of the doctrine of creation was knowledge of God. Today the problem of the doctrine of God is knowledge of creation. The theological adversary then was the religious and political ideology of 'blood and soil', 'race and nation'. Today the theological adversary is the nihilism practised in our dealings with nature. Both perversions have been evoked by the unnatural will to power, and the inhumane struggle for domination on earth. The inhumanity of this power complex and its perversion manifests the godlessness of our modern world and its terrifying God-forsakenness.

Fifty years ago, discernment of the triune God revealed in Christ brought the church the assurance of faith; and today, in the same way, discernment of the God who is present in creation through his Holy Spirit can bring men and women to reconciliation and peace with nature. The salutary 'christological concentration' in Protestant theology then, must be matched today by an extension of theology's horizon to cosmic breadth, so that it takes in the whole of God's creation.

By the title 'God in Creation' I mean God the Holy Spirit. God is 'the lover of life' and his Spirit is *in* all created beings. In order to understand this, I have dropped the earlier divisions of theology, which followed the pattern of the three articles of the Apostles' Creed. Instead I have interwoven these three articles together in a trinitarian sense so that I was able to develop a pneumatological doctrine of creation. This doctrine of creation, that is to say, takes as its starting point the indwelling divine Spirit of creation; and I hope that it may therefore also provide points of departure for a discussion with the old and new non-mechanistic, holistic philosophies of nature.

Chapter One describes this doctrine of creation as an '*ecological doctrine*'. This is of course intended first of all to point to the ecological crisis of our time, and the ecological thinking which we have to learn. But in a deeper sense it is also a reference to the symbolism of 'home' and 'dwelling' which I have employed in this book. According to its Greek derivation, the word 'ecology' means 'the doctrine of the house' (οἶκος). What does the Christian doctrine of creation have to do with 'a doctrine of the house'? If we see only a Creator and his work, there is no connection. But if we understand the Creator, his creation, and the goal of that creation in a trinitarian sense, then the Creator, through his Spirit, *dwells in* his creation as a whole, and in every individual created being, by virtue of his Spirit holding them together and keeping them in life. The inner secret of creation is this *indwelling of God*, just as the inner secret of the sabbath of creation is *God's rest*. If we ask about creation's goal and future, we ultimately arrive at the transfiguring indwelling of the triune God in his creation, which through that indwelling becomes a new heaven and a new earth (Rev. 21), and at God's eternal sabbath, in which the whole creation will find bliss. The divine secret of creation is the Shekinah, God's indwelling; and the purpose of the Shekinah is to make the whole creation the house of God.

If this is the theological side of the ecological doctrine of creation, the anthropological side must correspond to it. Existence can only become a home if the relationship between nature and human beings is without stresses and strains – if it can be described in terms of reconciliation, peace and a viable symbiosis. The indwelling of human beings in the natural system of the earth corresponds, for its part, to the indwelling of the Spirit in the soul and body of the human being, which puts an end to the alienation of human beings from themselves.

As in earlier books, I have followed an ecumenical method. I have tried to draw on both Protestant and Catholic sources, and to enter into discussion with theologians from both sides, so that what the churches have in common emerges, both in the impasses that still exist and in our hopeful approaches to one another. I have also continued to seek a dialogue between the churches of East and West, and have discovered that Orthodox theology has preserved a creation wisdom which was pushed aside and lost in the West, in the wake of modern developments in science, technology and industry. It is the earliest traditions of Christian theology which frequently offer the most pregnant ideas for the revolution in our attitude to nature which is so vitally necessary today.

I have devoted not the least part of my attention to Christian and Jewish sources. Christianity took over the doctrine of creation from Israel's Scripture, and will therefore do well to listen attentively to what Jewish interpretations of these common traditions have to tell us. The best creation wisdom is to be found in the Jewish theology and practice of the sabbath. In abandoning the sabbath, the Gentile Christian churches have lost this means of access, and we generally overlook it altogether.

Outside Christianity, Judaism, in its kabbalistic tradition, developed ideas about the divine *zimsum* (God's self-limitation) and the divine Shekinah. These concepts have always influenced Christian thinking beneath the surface, but today it is important for us to take them up quite deliberately and in open dialogue – important for the understanding of nature as creation, and of considerable influence for the Jewish-Christian dialogue.

The ecumenical method does not merely extend to different theologies in a single period. It also reaches out to the different periods of theology. I have therefore taken up long-term problems in the Christian doctrine of creation, and have tried to enter into discussion with Augustine and Aquinas, Calvin and Newton, and other of our theological and scientific forebears. That explains the digressions into the history of theology. These do not merely provide illustrative material and offer us intellectual models. They are also intended as contributions to theological discussion beyond the frontiers of the times.

Finally, the ecumenical method is open for the secular *oikoumene*, which literally means 'the inhabited globe', and in this case the sciences, technologies and economics which today determine the relationship between human beings, machines and nature. It is the doctrine of creation particularly which will work out points of approach for a theological discussion with scientific findings, hypotheses and theories. I have tried here to take account of the upheaval which the sciences are undergoing today wherever they are pursued in awareness of the ecological crisis.

With this book I am continuing the series of systematic contributions to theology which I began in 1980 with *The Trinity and the Kingdom of God* (ET 1981). I intended to confine myself here to my own contribution to the doctrine of creation, but have discovered that it has turned out to be more comprehensive, and rather more of a textbook, than I originally planned. I wished to present everything in a single volume, from creation to the sabbath, in order to make the connection between these things as clear as possible; so I have not followed the common practice of dividing the doctrine of creation from anthropology. This means that the anthropology has had to be curtailed. The sections on the individual and society, societies and humanity, and humanity and nature, have deliberately been omitted. I shall come back to these problems at a later point. Nor have I been able to carry the discussion foward as far as I had intended at a number of points. This is particularly evident in the chapter on 'The Space of Creation'. I hope to be able to develop this subject further elsewhere in the light of new scientific conceptions about the space-time continuum.

The time has now come for me to offer readers the total plan of these systematic contributions to theology. Changes are of course possible; but the reader should know in what context a book was written and to what limitations it is therefore subject.

Volume I: The Trinity and the Kingdom of God, 1980 (ET 1981)
Volume II: God in Creation, 1985 (ET 1985)
Volume III: Christology
Volume IV: Eschatology
Volume V: The Foundations and Methods of Christian Theology.

As I have already indicated from time to time, these contributions are not designed to be summed up under the heading of 'systematic theology', 'church dogmatics' or 'the doctrine of faith'. Their overall title is: *Messianic Theology*. The justice and scope of this title will be explained in detail and defended against misunderstandings and criticism in the next volume, on christology.

I put forward the main ideas of this doctrine of creation in lectures held in Tübingen in the summer semester of 1973, in the winter semester of 1980/81, and in the winter semester of 1984/85, and in the Candler School of Theology, Emory University, Atlanta, in the autumn semester of 1983. An initial draft appeared in the Festschrift for Thomas F. Torrance, *Creation, Christ and Culture* (ed. R. W. A. McKinney, Edinburgh 1976, pp. 119–34), under the title 'Creation and Redemption'. Another section from the present book appeared under the title 'Schöpfung aus nichts' in the Festschrift for Hans-Joachim Kraus, *Wenn nicht jetzt, wann dann*? (ed. H.-G. Geyer, Neukirchen 1983, pp. 259–69). The section on 'The Alienation and Liberation of Nature' was published in English in the collection *On Nature*, issued by the Boston University Institute for Philosophy and Religion (ed. L. Rouner, Notre Dame 1984).

I have to thank the University of Edinburgh for inviting me three years ago to give the Gifford Lectures for 1984–85. This is not only a great honour. It was also a serious challenge to thorough work on a Christian doctrine of creation for the problems of our time.

I have been greatly helped by discussions with my assistants Dr Michael Welker, Dr Konrad Stock and Adelbert Schloz. I am also particularly grateful to Helmut Kirschstein and André Schmalz for their laborious work on the proofs.

15 October 1984 Jürgen Moltmann

ABBREVIATIONS

AV	Authorized Version of the Bible
BoA	M. Luther, *Werke*, 4 Vol. selection, Bonn 1912–13
CD	K. Barth, *Church Dogmatics*, ET Edinburgh and Grand Rapids 1936–69
ET	English translation
EvTh	*Evangelische Theologie*, Munich
FRLANT	Forschungen zur Religion und Literatur des Alten und Neuen Testaments, Göttingen
HTR	*Harvard Theological Review*, Cambridge, Mass.
KuD	*Kerygma und Dogma*, Göttingen
PG	J. P. Migne, Patrologia Graeca, Paris 1857ff.
PL	J. P. Migne, Patrologia Latina, Paris 1878ff.
RGG[3]	*Religion in Geschichte und Gegenwart*, 3rd ed., Tübingen 1957–65
RSV	Revised Standard Version of the Bible
SJT	*Scottish Journal of Theology*, Edinburgh
TDNT	*Theological Dictionary of the New Testament*, ET Grand Rapids 1964–76
TRE	*Theologische Realenzyklopädie*, Berlin and New York1976ff.
WA	M. Luther, *Werke*, Weimarer Ausgabe, Weimar 1883ff.
ZThK	*Zeitschrift für Theologie und Kirche*

Translator's Note

Biblical quotations are normally from the RSV, except where changes of wording were necessary to bring out the author's point. Modern authors are cited from English translations when these are available, but with some minor changes of wording to harmonize with the context. (In particular, 'human beings' has been used in preference to 'man' as a translation of *Mensch*.)

I

God in Creation

SOME GUIDING IDEAS FOR AN ECOLOGICAL DOCTRINE OF CREATION

With this doctrine of creation I am taking a further step along the road on which I started out with *The Trinity and the Kingdom of God* (1980; ET 1981). In that book I developed a social doctrine of the Trinity. Here my subject is the corresponding ecological doctrine of creation.

It is easy to see the connection between the two.

As long as God was thought of as the absolute subject, the world had to be viewed as the object of his creation, preservation and redemption. The more transcendent the conception of God became, the more immanent were the terms in which the world was interpreted. Through the monotheism of the absolute subject, God was increasingly stripped of his connection with the world, and the world was increasingly secularized. As a result, the human being – since he was God's image on earth – had to see himself as the subject of cognition and will, and was bound to confront his world as its ruler. For it was only through his rule over the earth that he could correspond to his God, the Lord of the world. God is the Creator, Lord and owner of the world; and in the same way the human being had to endeavour to become the lord and owner of the earth. This was the idea behind the centralistic theologies, and the foundation of the hierarchical doctrines of sovereignty.

Our standpoint is a different one. We have begun to understand God, in the awareness of his Spirit, for Christ's sake, as the triune God, the God who in himself constitutes the unique and perfect fellowship of the Father and the Son and the Holy Spirit. If we cease to understand God monotheistically as the one, absolute subject, but instead see him in a trinitarian sense as the unity of the Father, the Son and the Spirit, we can then no longer, either, conceive his relationship to the world he has created as a one-sided relationship of domination. We are bound to understand it as an intricate relationship of community – many-layered, many-faceted and at many levels. This is the fundamental idea behind non-hierarchical, decentralized, confederate theology. In this introduction we shall formulate a few guiding ideas which will provide the points of reference for this doctrine of creation.

1. *Knowledge of Nature as God's Creation is Participating Knowledge*

If a doctrine of creation is to be ecological, it must try to get away from analytical thinking, with its distinctions between subject and object, and must strive to learn a new, communicative and integrating way of thought. This means that it will have to revert to the pre-modern concept of reason as the organ of perception and participation (methexis).

Modern thinking has developed by way of an objectifying, analytical, particularizing and reductionalistic approach. The aim is to reduce an object or fact to its smallest possible, no-longer-divisible components, and from that point to reconstruct it. This is a trend in all modern disciplines which are designed to be what are called 'exact' sciences, on the model of physics. It is therefore quite true to say that we know more and more about less and less; and it is not without reason that people deplore the domination of the specialists. The concern and the methods of this kind of thinking are directed towards the domination of objects and facts. The old Roman principle for successful rule, *divide et impera*, also provides the guideline for modern methods of dominating nature.

Yet modern sciences, especially nuclear physics and biology, have now proved that these forms and methods of thinking do not do full justice to reality, and hardly bring any further advances in knowledge. On the contrary, objects can be known and understood very much better if they are seen in their relationships and co-ordinations with their particular environments and surroundings (which include the human observer) – if, that is to say, they are integrated, not isolated; perceived in their totality, not split up. This perception of things-as-a-whole is inevitably less sharply defined than the segmenting knowledge which aims to dominate; but it is richer in connections and relationships.

To be alive means existing in relationship with other people and things. Life is communication in communion. And, conversely, isolation and lack of relationship means death for all living things, and dissolution even for elementary particles. So if we want to understand what is real *as* real, and what is living *as* living, we have to know it in its own primal and individual community, in its relationships, interconnections and surroundings.

But we shall then have to conceive of the inversion of this as well. We shall have to understand that everything real and everything living is simply a concentration and manifestation of its relationships, interconnections and surroundings. Integrating, and integral, thinking moves purposefully in this social direction towards the goal of an inclusiveness that is many-sided, and ultimately fully comprehensive.

When this happens, of course, the concern that motivates cognition changes. We no longer desire to know in order to dominate, or analyse and reduce in order to reconstruct. Our purpose is now to perceive in order to participate, and to enter into the mutual relationships of the living thing.

Integrating and integral thinking serves to generate the community between human beings and nature which is necessary and promotes life. And here 'nature' means both the natural world in which we share, and our own bodily nature. As a network and interplay of relationships is built up, a symbiotic life comes into being. This life has to be differently defined on its different levels.

On the legal and political level, we have to see it as a 'covenant with nature', in which the rights of human beings and the rights of the earth are respected and balanced out. Nature must no longer be viewed as 'unclaimed property'.

On the medical level, this symbiotic life must be defined as 'the psychosomatic totality' of the human being who stands over against himself. The body must no longer be seen as something which we 'possess'.

On the religious level, it has to be interpreted as 'a community of creation'. Creation is certainly not the world which human beings are supposed to 'subdue'.

Integrating and integral thinking is impelled by the will to find a way into this covenant, this totality, this community; to arrive at an awareness of these things, to deepen them after they have been ignored for so long, and to restore them when they have been destroyed.

In this sense, a theological doctrine of creation in our own time is also guided by the will to find a way into the community of creation, to reawaken the awareness of that community and to restore it.

The methods of an ecological doctrine of creation of this kind cannot be one-dimensional. It must use multifarious ways of access to the community of creation, and make people aware of them. We find these approaches in both tradition and experience, in science as well as in wisdom, in intuition but also in deduction. We shall try to look critically at theological traditions in the doctrine of creation. But I should also like to take up new, post-critical scientific methods and ways of thinking. And the approaches of poetic perception and intuition must be integrated as well. The doctrine of creation that emerges will not be one that merely builds up concepts and tries to find definitions, on the philosophical model, important though that is. It will also take up and use symbols, which mould the unconscious and guide awareness in a way which is unknown to the conscious mind. Finally, there is an expectant and creative imagination in the spheres of the potential and the future which we have to call poetic. If we were to exclude this from a doctrine of creation, we could not talk about 'the future of creation' at all. Theology always includes the imagination, fantasy for God and his kingdom. If we were to ban the images of the imagination from theology, we should be robbing it of its best possession. Eschatologically orientated theology is dependent on a messianic imagination of the future, and sets this imagination free.

2. *Creation for Glory*

It is my intention to present a deliberately and emphatically Christian doctrine of creation. In this context I understand the word 'Christian' in its original sense, as 'messianic'; but messianic as the word has been moulded by Jesus' proclamation and his history. So a Christian doctrine of creation is a view of the world in the light of

Jesus the Messiah; and it will be determined by the points of view of the messianic time which has begun with him and which he defines. It is directed towards the liberation of men and women, peace with nature, and the redemption of the community of human beings and nature from negative powers, and from the forces of death.

This messianic doctrine of creation therefore sees creation together with its future – the future for which it was made and in which it will be perfected. Ever since ancient times, 'the future of creation' has been termed 'the kingdom of glory'.[1] This symbol of cosmic hope is supposed to indicate that 'creation in the beginning' is an open creation, and that its consummation will be to become the home and dwelling place of God's glory. Human beings already experience the indwellings of God in the Spirit here in history, even if as yet only partially and provisionally. That is why they hope that in the kingdom of glory God will dwell entirely and wholly and for ever in his creation, and will allow all the beings he has created to participate in the fullness of his eternal life.

The embodiment of the messianic promises to the poor and the quintessence of the hopes of the alienated is that the world should be 'home'. This means being at home in existence – that the relationships between God, human beings and nature lose their tension and are resolved into peace and repose.[2]

If the creative God himself dwells in his creation, then he is making it his own home, 'on earth as it is in heaven'. All created beings then find in nearness to him the inexhaustible wellspring of their life, and for their part find home and rest in God.

Then at last the true community of created beings with one another also begins: a community which Jewish and Christian messianic traditions have called 'the sympathy of all things'. The bond of love, participation, communication and the whole complex warp and weft of interrelationships determines the life of the one, single creation, united in the cosmic Spirit.[3] A many-faceted community of creation comes into being.

3. *The Sabbath of Creation*

According to the biblical traditions, creation is aligned towards its redemption from the very beginning; for the creation of the world points forward to the sabbath, 'the feast of creation'. 'Sabbath is one-sixtieth part of the world to come.'[4] On the sabbath the creation is completed. The sabbath is the prefiguration of the world to come. So when we present creation in the light of its future – 'the glory of God', 'existence as home' and the general 'sympathy of all things' – then we are developing *a sabbath doctrine of creation*. What this means, factually and practically, is the aspect and prospect of creation which is perceived on the sabbath, and only then. The sabbath is the true hallmark of every biblical – every Jewish and also every Christian – doctrine of creation. The completion of creation through the peace of the sabbath distinguishes the view of the world as creation from the view of the world as nature; for nature is unremittingly fruitful and, though it has seasons and rhythms, knows no sabbath. It is the sabbath which blesses, sanctifies and reveals the world as God's creation.

Curiously enough, in the theological traditions of the Western churches creation is generally presented merely as 'the six days' work'. The seventh day, the sabbath, was often overlooked. Consequently God was presented throughout merely as the creative God: *Deus non est otiosus*. The resting God, the celebrating God, the God who rejoices over his creation, receded into the background. And yet it is only the sabbath which completes and crowns creation. It is only in his sabbath rest that the creative God comes to his goal, which means coming to himself and to his glory. When people celebrate the sabbath they perceive the world as God's creation, for in the sabbath quiet it is God's creation that they are permitting the world to be.[5]

Israel celebrates the sabbath in the time and context of her own history. But the sabbath which is repeated week by week does not merely interrupt the time for work and the time for living. It points beyond itself to the sabbatical year, in which the primordial conditions between human beings, and between human beings and nature, are supposed to be restored, according to the righteousness of the covenant of Israel's God. And this sabbatical year, in its turn, points in history beyond itself to the future of the messianic era. Every sabbath is a sacred anticipation of the world's redemption. It was with the proclamation of the messianic sabbath that the public ministry of Jesus of Nazareth began (Luke 4.18ff.) Through his giving of himself to death on the cross, and through his resurrection from the dead, the messianic era which he proclaimed was actually initiated, according to the Christian view. That is why Christians celebrate the first day of the week as the feast of the resurrection: it is the first day of the new creation. They are therefore perceiving creation in the light of the resurrection and discerning reality in the light of its new creation.

The light of the resurrection is a light that fills even times past and the dead with hope for their coming redemption. The light of Christ's resurrection is the light of the Christian sabbath. But it is more than that. It shines as messianic light on the whole sighing creation, giving it, in its transience, an eternal hope that it will be created anew as the 'world without end'.

4. *The Messianic Preparation of Creation to be the Kingdom*

This doctrine of creation does not belong within the context of a two-term, dual dogmatics. It has a multiple, dialectical and process orientation. Theological tradition has hitherto given preference to the two-term, dual structure, talking about 'creation and redemption', 'creation and convenant', 'nature and super-nature', 'necessity and freedom'. These dualities were the context in which the famous principle of mediaeval theology was coined:

gratia non destruit, sed praesupponit et perfecit naturam.

This maxim starts from the assumption that the grace of God is to be seen in the incarnation of the eternal Logos in Christ, and concludes that this incarnation presupposes and perfects creation. It also follows from this tenet that the christology presupposes the anthropology, and – to adopt Karl Rahner's epigrammatic phraseology – that anthropology is 'deficient christology' and christology is 'realized anthropology'.[6] Being a Christian, that is to say, presupposes being a person first of all, and completes and perfects that initial condition.

In my view, the second term of this proposition is incorrect, because it fails to distinguish between grace and glory, history and new creation, being a Christian and being perfected. Because the second distinction is not made sufficiently clear, the mediaeval tenet has continually led to triumphalism: the glory which perfects nature is supposed already to be inherent in the grace; the kingdom which is the inner foundation of creation is thought already to exist in the covenant; and the perfection of the human condition is considered to be already integral to being a Christian.

I would therefore like to reformulate the second part of the theological tenet in the sense of a three-term dialectic, and say:

> *gratia non perfecit, sed praeparat naturam ad gloriam aeternam; gratia non est perfectio naturae, sed praeparatio messianica mundi ad regnum Dei.*

This principle proceeds from the assumption that the grace of God can be seen in the raising of Christ, and concludes that Christ's resurrection is the beginning of the new creation of the world. It follows from this that we have to talk about nature and grace, and the relationship between nature and grace, in a forward perspective, in the light of the coming glory, which will complete both nature and grace, and hence already determines the relationship between the two here and now. It also follows that God's covenant in history cannot already be called 'the inner foundation' of creation. We can give this name only to the coming kingdom of God's glory, which his covenant in history promises and guarantees. And the third and last conclusion is that being a Christian is not yet in itself the completion, but represents only a messianic path towards a possible future consummation of the condition of being human. On this path Jewish existence runs parallel to the Christian life, as a way and witness to the same hope for a humanity that will be finally liberated, glorified and united in righteousness. Christian existence does not displace or supersede Jewish existence. It is dependent on that existence, and is its companion along the same road.

In mediaeval Judaism, the Christian church in its evangelization of the nations was often viewed and valued as the divinely willed *praeparatio messianica* of the Gentile peoples. We shall take up this Jewish assessment of Christian existence and extend it beyond the world of the Gentiles to nature itself. For Christianity is intended to be the *praeparatio messianica naturae* as well.

If we think in terms of this messianic movement, then the great theological dualities will be freed from their position as mere antitheses. They will be relativized. In the messianic movement they will be understood as complementary. They will no longer be defined over against one another, by way of mutual negation; they will be determined in all their complex interconnections in relation to a third, common to them both. The structure of the terms, which has become petrified into an antithesis, will be brought into movement, once the two sides of the antithesis are understood as complementary aspects of a common process. This makes it possible to discern and define more precisely the possible reconciliation between freedom and necessity, grace and nature, covenant and creation, being a Christian and being a human being.

5. Creation in the Spirit

According to the Christian interpretation, creation is a trinitarian process: the Father creates through the Son in the Holy Spirit. The created world is therefore created 'by God', formed 'through God' and exists 'in God'. Basil wrote in this connection:

> Behold in the creation of these beings the Father as the preceding cause, the Son as the One who createth, and the Spirit as the perfecter; so that the ministering spirits have their beginning in the will of the Father, are brought into being through the efficacy of the Son, and are perfected through the aid of the Spirit.[7]

For a long time theological tradition stressed only the first aspect of this process, so as to place God the Father, as Creator and Lord, over against his creation, in a monotheistic way. Attempts have also continually been made to develop a specifically christological doctrine of creation. Here we shall proceed differently, and shall present the trinitarian understanding of creation by developing the third aspect, creation in the Spirit.

According to the biblical traditions, all divine activity is pneumatic in its efficacy. It is always the Spirit who first brings the activity of the Father and the Son to its goal. It follows that the triune God also unremittingly breathes the Spirit into his creation. Everything that is, exists and lives in the unceasing inflow of the energies and potentialities of the cosmic Spirit. This means that we have to understand every created reality in terms of energy, grasping it as the realized potentiality of the divine Spirit. Through the energies and potentialities of the Spirit, the Creator is himself present in his creation. He does not merely confront it in his transcendence; entering into it, he is also immanent in it.

The biblical foundation for this interpretation of creation in the Spirit is Psalm 104. 29–30:

> When thou hidest thy face, they are dismayed;
> when thou takest away their breath, they die and return to their dust.

When thou sendest forth thy breath, they are created;
and thou renewest the face of the ground.

From the continual inflow of the divine Spirit (*ruach*) created things are formed (*bara'*). They exist in the Spirit, and they are 'renewed' (*hadash*) through the Spirit. This presupposes that God always creates through and in the power of his Spirit, and that the presence of his Spirit therefore conditions the potentiality and realities of his creation. The further assumption is that this Spirit is poured out on everything that exists, and that the Spirit preserves it, makes it live and renews it. And because, to the Hebrew mind, the Spirit (*ruach*) is feminine, this divine life of creation must be apprehended through feminine metaphors, not merely with masculine ones.

The same may be said about the Hebrew interpretation of the Wisdom of creation, the daughter of God:

The Lord possessed me in the beginning of his way; before his works, I was there.
I was set up from everlasting, from the beginning, or ever the earth was.
When there were still no depths, I was already brought forth; when there were no springs abounding with water.
Before the mountains had been shaped, before the hills, I was brought forth;
before he had made the earth with its fields, or the first of the dust of the world.
When he prepared the heavens, I was there: when he laid a compass upon the face of the deep.
When he made firm the skies above, when he established the fountains of the deep,
when he assigned to the sea its limits, so that the water might not transgress his command,
when he marked out the foundations of the earth:
then I was beside him, like a master workman, and I was daily his delight, playing before him always,
rejoicing in his inhabited world and delighting in the sons of men
(Prov. 8.22–31).

Yet this Wisdom of creation and the concept of creation in the Spirit are still awaiting theological development even today. John

Calvin was one of the few people to take up and maintain this conception: '*Spiritus Sanctus enim est, qui ubique diffusus omnia sustinet, vegetat et vivificat.*'[8]

The Holy Spirit, 'the giver of life' of the Nicene Creed, is for Calvin 'the fountain of life' (*fons vitae*). If the Holy Spirit is 'poured out' on all created beings, then 'the fountain of life' is present in everything that exists and is alive. Everything that is, and lives, manifests the presence of this divine wellspring.

If the Holy Spirit is 'poured out' on the whole creation, then he creates the community of all created things with God and with each other, making it that fellowship of creation in which all created things communicate with one another and with God, each in its own way. The existence, the life, and the warp and weft of interrelationships subsist in the Spirit: '*In him* we live and move and have our being' (Acts 17.28). But that means that the interrelations of the world cannot be traced back to any components, or universal foundations (or whatever name we may give to 'elementary particles'). According to the mechanistic theory, things are primary, and their relations to one another are determined secondarily, through 'natural laws'. But in reality relationships are just as primal as the things themselves. 'Thing' and 'relation' are complementary modes of appearance, in the same way as particle and wave in the nuclear sector. For nothing in the world exists, lives and moves *of itself*. Everything exists, lives and moves *in others*, in one another, with one another, for one another, in the cosmic interrelations of the divine Spirit. So it is only the community of creation in the Spirit itself that can be called 'fundamental'. For only the Spirit of God exists *ex se*; and it is therefore the Spirit who has to be seen as the sustaining foundation of everything else, which does not exist *ex se* but *ab alio et in aliis*. The patterns and the symmetries, the movements and the rhythms, the fields and the material conglomerations of cosmic energy all come into being out of the community, and in the community, of the divine Spirit. The 'essential being' of creation in the Spirit is therefore the co-activity; and the interrelations manifest the presence of the Spirit because they show the 'overall consistency'.[9] 'In the beginning was relation,' writes Martin Buber.

With his idea of the immanence of God the Spirit in creation, Calvin came very close to the Stoic notion of the divine universe, and the indwelling of the World Soul in the one Universal Body. But he distinguished his doctrine of the cosmic Spirit from Stoic pantheism by way of the Christian doctrine of the Trinity: 'God's Spirit acts into and penetrates the world, effecting and fashioning the world's coherence' without himself becoming merged in it. The cosmic Spirit remains God's Spirit, and becomes our Spirit since he acts in us as the power that makes us live.

With this differentiation, and in awareness of the divine immanence in the world, it is also possible to conceive of the self-transcendence of the world into its open future. How are we to think of this self-transcendence? The presence of the divine Spirit in creation makes the universe an eccentric double world of earth and heaven which points beyond itself. It is open for the future of the kingdom of glory, which is to renew, unite, fill and *ful*fil heaven and earth.

But the *presence* of the divine Spirit in creation must be further differentiated, theologically; for we have to distinguish between his cosmic, his reconciling and his redeeming indwelling.

The way the Spirit in his indwelling *acts* will have to be differentiated in each given case according to the mode of his self-manifestation as subject, as energy, or as potentiality.

The *efficacy* of the Spirit can then be differentiated into his creating, his preserving, his renewing and his consummating activity.

Creation in the Spirit is the theological concept which corresponds best to the ecological doctrine of creation which we are looking for and need today. With this concept we are cutting loose the theological doctrine of creation from the age of subjectivity and the mechanistic domination of the world, and are leading it in the direction in which we have to look for the future of an ecological world-community.[10] The progressive destruction of nature by the industrial nations, and the progressive threat to humanity through the pile-up of nuclear armaments, have brought the age of subjectivity and the mechanistic domination of the world up against their definitive limits. Faced with these limits, we have only one realistic alternative to universal annihilation: the non-violent, peaceful, ecological world-wide community in solidarity.

This transition to a totally new era does not merely confront the theological traditions of Christianity with problems of adaptation. These traditions are faced to an even stronger degree with the need to rediscover their own original truth, which was distorted or suppressed in the age that is now drawing to a close, when the world was dominated by means of the subjection of nature and the accumulated potential for military annihilation. We shall therefore deliberately refrain from drawing a dividing line between the theological doctrine of creation and the sciences and their scientific theories – a line prompted by an anxious attempt to preserve theology's own identity. What we are seeking is *a community* of scientific and theological insights. It is only in our common recognition of the danger of universal ecological and nuclear catastrophes, and only in our common search for a world capable of surviving, that we shall also then be able to put forward the particular contribution of the Christian traditions and the hope of the Christian faith.

6. *God's Immanence in the World*

An ecological doctrine of creation implies a new kind of thinking about God. The centre of this thinking is no longer the distinction between God and the world. The centre is the recognition of the presence of God *in* the world and the presence of the world *in* God.

Because it grew up in an environment moulded by pantheistic, matriarchal, animist religions, the belief in Yahweh to which the Old Testament testifies, laboriously and perseveringly taught *the difference* between God and the world: God is not to be understood in wordly terms, and the world must not be interpreted as divine. God does not manifest himself in the forces and rhythms of nature; he reveals himself in human history, which is determined by his covenant and his promise. This means that the forces of fertility must not be worshipped as divine forces. The fertility cults in Canaan were rejected as 'idolatry', and the transformation of Yahweh into a 'Baal', a divine natural power, was persecuted as the worst form of blasphemy. The basis of the enduring distinction between God in the world was belief in creation, for this set God over against the world. God's context is transcendence, and the world, as 'the work of his hands', is turned into immanence. Nature is stripped of her divinity, politics become profane, history is divested of fate. The world is turned into passive matter.

This distinction between God and the world was also seized on by modern theological apologetics as a way of adapting the biblical traditions to the secularizing processes of modern European times. The ruthless conquest and exploitation of nature which fascinated

Europe during this period found its appropriate religious legitimation in that ancient distinction between God and the world.

But of course this was a falsification of the critical truth of the Old Testament distinction. It is a truth that must not be surrendered; but an ecological doctrine of creation today must perceive and teach God's *immanence* in the world. This does not mean departing from the biblical traditions. On the contrary, it means a return to their original truth: through his cosmic Spirit, God the Creator of heaven and earth is present *in* each of his creatures and *in* the fellowship of creation which they share. '*Deus penetrat praesentia sua totum universum.*'[11] God is not merely the Creator of the world. He is also the Spirit of the universe. Through the powers and potentialities of the Spirit, the Creator indwells the creatures he has made, animates them, holds them in life, and leads them into the future of his kingdom. In this sense the history of creation is the history of the efficacy of the divine Spirit. So even when we consider the original biblical traditions, it is one-sided to view creation only as the work of 'God's hands' and, as his 'work', something that has simply and solely to be distinguished from God himself. Creation is also the differentiated presence of God the Spirit, the presence of the One *in* the many.

If we are to follow the concept of God's transcendence in relation to the world with an understanding of this divine world-immanence, it is advisable to eliminate the concept of causality from the doctrine of creation, and indeed we have to stop thinking in terms of causes at all; for the causality approach allows us to conceive only of the transcendence of the divine *causa prima* which, since it is divine, must also be *causa sui*. But creating the world is something different from causing it. If the Creator is himself present in his creation by virtue of the Spirit, then his relationship to creation must rather be viewed as an intricate web of unilateral, reciprocal and many-sided relationships. In this network of relationships, 'making', 'preserving', 'maintaining' and 'perfecting' are certainly the great *one-sided* relationships; but 'indwelling', 'sym-pathizing', 'participating', 'accompanying', 'enduring', 'delighting' and 'glorifying' are relationships *of mutuality* which describe a cosmic community of living between God the Spirit and all his created beings.

The trinitarian doctrine of creation therefore does not start from an antithesis between God and the world, so that it can then go on to define God and the world over against one another ('God is not-worldly and the world is not-divine'). It proceeds differently, starting from an immanent *tension* in God himself: God creates the world, and at the same time enters into it. He calls it into existence, and at the same time manifests himself through its being. It lives from his creative power, and yet he lives in it. So if God as Creator stands over against his creation, he also stands over against himself. If the creation stands over against its Creator, God again stands over against himself. The God who is transcendent in relation to the world, and the God who is immanent in that world are one and the same God. So in God's creation of the world we can perceive a self-differentiation and a self-identification on God's part. God is in himself, and yet he is at the same time outside himself. He is outside himself in his creation, and is yet at the same time in himself, in his sabbath.

There are two great concepts which can be used to help us to comprehend this self-differentiation and tension of God's in his creation.

1. The rabbinic and kabbalistic *doctrine of the Shekinah*. 'The Shekinah, the descent of God to human beings and his dwelling among them, is conceived of as a division which takes place in God himself. God cuts himself off from himself. He gives himself away to his people. He suffers with their sufferings, he goes with them through the misery of the foreign land. . . .' This is the way Franz Rosenzweig describes God's Shekinah among the people of his choice.[12] But the same thing is true in its own degree of the indwelling of God in the creation of his love: he gives himself away to the beings he has created, he suffers with their sufferings, he goes with them through the misery of the foreign land. The God who in the Spirit dwells in his creation is present to every one of his creatures and remains bound to each of them, in joy and sorrow.

2. The Christian *doctrine of the Trinity*. In the free, overflowing rapture of his love the eternal God goes out of himself and makes a creation, a reality, which is there as he is there, and is yet different from himself. Through the Son, God creates, reconciles and redeems his creation. In the power of the Spirit, God is himself present in his creation – present in his reconciliation and his redemption of that creation. The overflowing love from which everything comes that is from God, is also the implicit ground for God's readiness to endure the contradictions of the beings he has created. And here too

is already the source of his will towards reconciliation and the redemption of the world through the suffering patience of his hope.

The Son, the eternal counterpart within God himself, becomes the Wisdom, the pattern, through which creation is made. The Son in whom the world is created becomes flesh, and himself enters into the world in order to redeem it. He suffers the self-destruction of creation in order through his sufferings to heal it. What is not assumed by God in this way in his creation cannot, either, be healed.

God the Spirit is also the Spirit of the universe, its total cohesion, its structure, its information, its energy. The Spirit of the universe is the Spirit who proceeds from the Father and shines forth in the Son. The evolutions and the catastrophes of the universe are also the movements and experiences of the Spirit of creation. That is why Paul tells us that the divine Spirit 'sighs' in all created things under the power of futility. That is why the divine Spirit transcends himself in all created beings. This is manifested in the self-organization and the self-transcendence of all living things.

7. *The Principle of Mutual Interpenetration*

The archetype of this dialectical movement is to be found in the Godhead itself. The doctrine of the Trinity is the formulation for the distinctions and the unity in God. Through the concept of perichoresis, the social doctrine of the Trinity formulates the mutual indwellings of the Father, the Son and the Holy Spirit, and the eternal community that is manifested through these indwellings.[13] In God is the eternal community of the different Persons, by virtue of their reciprocal indwelling and their mutual interpenetration, as the Johannine Jesus tells us: 'I am *in* the Father and the Father is *in* me' (14.11); 'I and the Father are one' (10.30). The trinitarian perichoresis manifests that highest intensity of living which we call divine life and eternal love; and, conversely, God's infinite intensity of life is manifested in the eternal perichoresis of the divine Persons. We must not view the trinitarian perichoresis as a rigid pattern. We should see it as at once the most intense excitement and the absolute rest of the love which is the wellspring of everything that lives, the keynote of all resonances, and the source of the rhythmically dancing and vibrating worlds.

In God there is no one-sided relationship of superiority and subordination, command and obedience, master and servant, as

Karl Barth maintained in his theological doctrine of sovereignty, making this the starting point for his account of all analogously antithetical relationships: God and the world; heaven and earth; soul and body; and, not least, man and woman too.[14] In the triune God is the mutuality and the reciprocity of love.

Our starting point here is that all relationships which are analogous to God reflect the primal, reciprocal indwelling and mutual interpenetration of the trinitarian perichoresis: God *in* the world and the world *in* God; heaven and earth *in* the kingdom of God, pervaded by his glory; soul and body united *in* the life-giving Spirit to a human whole; woman and man *in* the kingdom of unconditional and unconditioned love, freed to be true and complete human beings. There is no such thing as solitary life. Contrary to Leibniz's view, every monad has many windows. In actual fact it consists only of windows. All living things – each in its own specific way – live in one another and with one another, from one another and for one another.

Everything that lives
Lives not alone, nor for itself.[15]

It is this trinitarian concept of life as interpenetration or perichoresis which will therefore determine this ecological doctrine of creation.

8. *The Cosmic Spirit and Human Consciousness*

When we are considering nature, we give the name of spirit to the forms of organization and modes of communication in open systems. We can begin with informed matter, move up through the forms of living systems, the many strata of living symbioses, human beings and human populations, and end with the ecosystem 'earth', the solar system, our Milky Way galaxy and the whole complex of galaxies in the universe.

The organizational principles of spirit on all these levels are the same:

1. synchronically: self-assertion and integration;
2. diachronically: self-preservation and self-transcendence.[16]

Moreover spirit shows a recognizable tendency to develop into more and more complex open systems (*a*) by amalgamating open life systems into symbiotic foms of life, and (*b*) by developing ever richer forms of life in the virgin territory of the possible, the future.

Consciousness is reflective and reflected spirit. By postulating this we are repudiating the Augustinian and Cartesian identification of consciousness and spirit. We are interpreting the spirit realistically, as the biblical traditions suggest we should do, not idealistically. If consciousness is reflected spirit, then for us a large domain of the human spirit is also still unconscious; for the human being is a highly complex life system, with many strata, a system which is open in its many relationships and dependencies. Spirit is the quintessence of the human being's self-organisation and his self-transcendence, his inner and his outward symbioses:

— If spirit is the human being's comprehensive organizational principle, then we have to talk about a spirit-soul and a spirit-body, and about a unity of body and soul *in* the spirit. Yet the human being's spirit is not identical with the conscious subjectivity of his reason and his will; it comprehends the whole unified structure of his body and his soul.

— Through the spirit we are bound together with other people socially and culturally. This interlocking association is again an organized open system (i.e., spirit) which can in this sense be described as the common spirit of the human community.

— Through the spirit we are bound together with the natural environment. This association is a system comprising human beings and nature. We might describe it as a spiritual ecosystem. Through the spirit, human societies as part-systems are bound up with the ecosystem 'earth' (Gaia); for human societies live in and from the recurring cycles of earth and sun, air and water, day and night, summer and winter. So human beings are participants and sub-systems of the cosmic life system, and of the divine Spirit that lives in it.

The important thing is therefore to extend the human consciousness *of* the spirit to as many formations of the spirit as possible, and to expand the individual consciousness according to the organizational principles of the spirit which we have named (self-assertion and integration, self-preservation and self-transcendence), so that it reaches out to the social, the ecological, the cosmic and the divine consciousness. In this way the individual consciousness enters into the higher, more complex and more stratified organizational forms of the spirit and arrives at a more differentiated and higher interchange of life. And in this way the divine, the cosmic, the social and the individual spirit also arrives at a further and higher awareness of its self in the human being.

The conception 'God in creation' in the shape of the idea of creation in the Spirit is well suited to help us to stop thinking of creation and evolution as opposing concepts, and instead to link them with one another as complements: there is a creation of evolution, because evolution is not explicable simply in terms of itself; there is an evolution of creation, because the creation of the world has been so designed that it points in the direction of the kingdom of glory, and therefore transcends itself in time. We have to see the concept of evolution as a basic concept of the self-movement of the divine Spirit of creation.

> For thou lovest all things that exist,
> and hast loathing for none of the things which thou hast made,
> for thou wouldst not have made anything if thou hadst hated it.
> How could anything endure if thou didst not will it?
> Or how could anything not called by thee be preserved?
> Thou sparest all things, for they are thine,
> O Lord who lovest the living,
> and thy immortal spirit is in all things
> (The Wisdom of Solomon, 11.24–12.1).

II

In the Ecological Crisis

We shall not begin this theological doctrine of creation with an exploration and interpretation of the origin of the Jewish and Christian belief in creation. Instead I should like first to survey and analyse the critical situation in which this belief finds itself today wherever it is maintained – a critical situation to whose problems and perplexities faith in creation has itself contributed.

Our situation today is determined by the ecological crisis of our whole scientific and technological civilization, and by the exhaustion of nature through human beings. This crisis is deadly, and not for human beings alone. For a very long time now it has meant death for other living things and for the natural environment as well. Unless there is a radical reversal in the fundamental orientation of our human societies, and unless we succeed in finding an alternative way of living and dealing with other living things and with nature, this crisis is going to end in a wholesale catastrophe.

The ecological crisis of the modern world has its starting point in the modern industrial countries. These grew up in the midst of civilizations which had been shaped by Christianity. We cannot ignore the historical effects of the Christian belief in creation. Those effects throw a light of their own on the belief itself, and today require us to criticize the developments which we know have gone wrong and to interpret belief in creation in a new way, in the light of its true beginnings.

The crisis of the modern world is not due merely to the technologies for the exploitation of nature; nor can we put it down to the sciences which made human beings the lords of nature. It is based much more profoundly on the striving of human beings for power and domination. In the sphere of Christian civilization, this striving was set free from its earlier religious inhibitions and actually reinforced by a misunderstood and misused biblical belief in creation; for 'subdue the earth' was viewed as a divine command given to human beings – a command to dominate nature, to conquer the world and to rule over it. Unbridled striving for power was to make human beings like their God, 'the Almighty'; so these human beings invoked God's almighty power in order to furnish a religious justification for their own. The Christian belief in creation as it has been maintained in the European and American Christianity of the Western churches is therefore not guiltless of the crisis in the world today.

If we turn back from the ideas and behaviour which are leading to a foreseeable universal death, and move towards a future for all the living in the common survival of human beings and nature, what does this change of direction look like? It is here that the really serious questions are put to the Christian belief in creation today. A new theological doctrine of creation must take up these questions, and try to find an answer to them.

How must the Christian belief in creation be interpreted and reformulated, if it is no longer to be itself one factor in the ecological crisis and the destruction of nature, but is instead to become a ferment working towards the peace with nature which we seek?

For centuries, men and women have tried to understand God's creation *as nature*, so that they can exploit it in accordance with the laws science has discovered. Today the essential point is to understand this knowable, controllable and usable nature *as God's creation*, and to learn to respect it as such. The limited sphere of reality which we call 'nature' must be lifted into the totality of being which is termed 'God's creation'.

What does this reversal of thinking mean for the natural sciences? What does it mean for the liberation of nature from its subjugation by human beings? What does it mean for the liberation of the human being from his unnatural pursuit of power, a liberation which will set him free for natural community with God's other created beings?

Today a theological doctrine of creation which can responsibly be maintained must first of all come to terms critically with its own tradition and the history of its own influence, before it can face up to the dialogue with the modern natural sciences and the contemporary philosophy of nature.

If we deliberately place the starting point of this doctrine of creation in the context of the present world situation, this does not mean that we want to adapt the doctrine apologetically to that situation, as a way of rescuing it from attack. Nor does it mean that the doctrine of creation has to be subjected to the laws and limitations of the present situation. But it must be exposed to the criticism of the present day, so that it may arrive at its own origins. The *text* of a Christian doctrine of creation speaks its own language, develops its own visions, and asks its own questions. But this text can only be heard in the particular *context* of the present, at any given time. The more clearly the experiences and recognitions, questions and impasses of the present situation are recognized and accepted, the more clearly and unequivocally belief in creation can speak.

We shall not, therefore, choose the way out taken by the 'creationists', who want to confront the present day, and the modern natural sciences and their theories, with the alternative of a biblicist cosmology. That would be nothing but a retreat to the doctrine of creation of a past era. It would not be an interpretation of the belief in creation today, in the light of its true origins.

On the other hand, we are also unable to follow those theologians who accept the cosmological theories that are under discussion at the moment, sanctioning them by making them the basis of their own religious cosmologies. That would merely be to dissolve the specifically Jewish and Christian belief in creation in a generally religious elevation of a world view which happens to be the subject of debate at the present time.

Here we shall take a different approach, and shall pursue the model of identity and relevance. The *identity* of the Christian belief in creation has become questionable in today's ecological crisis and must therefore be given a new definition in that context; while the *relevance* of belief in creation must prove itself in ideas about the present ecological crisis and in suggested ways of escape from that crisis.

In this introductory chapter, we shall first of all try to estimate the extent of the ecological crisis, viewing it as the crisis of man's rule over nature, and enquiring into the contribution made to it by science and technology, and by Christian theology. The second part of this chapter will be devoted to a critical discussion of the relation between theology and the sciences, with a view to a 'theology of nature' still to be developed. Finally, on the basis of a philosophy of nature, we shall look at ideas for ending the estrangement of nature, and for a viable attitude and behaviour towards the natural environment and the physical nature of human beings themselves. In this opening chapter we shall merely be trying to find initial points of reference for a contemporary doctrine of creation. I shall not attempt here to give a comprehensive account of all the problems raised.

§1 THE CRISIS OF DOMINATION

The ecological crisis (also familiar to us under the palliating heading of 'environmental pollution') makes it obvious today that theology and the sciences, together with many other disciplines, share a common destiny. But of course the phrase 'ecological crisis' is a feeble and also an inaccurate description of the real facts. This is really a crisis of the whole life system of the modern industrial world. It is a crisis which human beings have brought on themselves and their natural environment, and into which they are driving both themselves and the environment more and more deeply.[1]

The living relationship of human societies to the natural environment has been lastingly – if not already irreparably – destroyed by human technologies for exploiting nature. But the sciences are involved in these exploitative technologies as well. Technologies are nothing but applied sciences. And the sciences, together with the technologies, have grown up out of particular human concerns. Human concerns are bound up with them, precede them and utilize them. These concerns are governed by the basic values and convictions of human societies. And the values and convictions which prevail in human societies, and regulate public life, themselves derive from fundamental human convictions about the meaning and purpose of life. So when we talk about the ecological crisis of modern civilization, we can only mean a crisis of the whole system with all its part-systems, from the dying of the forests to the spread of neuroses, from the pollution of the seas and rivers to the nihilistic feeling about life which dominates so many people in our mass cities.[2]

This means that the natural environment of human beings cannot be understood apart from the social environment. The processes which intervene destructively in the natural environment originate in the economic and the social processes. So if the destruction of nature is to be halted, the economic and social conditions of human society must be changed. Societies which are primarily out to develop production, and increase the efficiency of human labour, and make further strides in already existing technologies, can neither restrict nor overcome the progressive destruction of the environment which they are causing.[3]

The norms which regulate a society derive from its cultural traditions. These traditions have emerged from the interplay between the meaning of life as the society sees it, and the social and economic form of that life. Over a long period of history, systems of value and meaning have become very deeply rooted in the human subconscious. Changing them is painful, and usually takes a very long time. Societies which are unable fundamentally to alter their systems of value and meaning, so as to adapt themselves to the new situation, are unable to change as a whole. This means that they cannot end the destruction which they are causing. On the contrary, the destruction of the natural environment which they have brought about has, in its turn, a destructive retroactive effect on the societies themselves, evoking a loss of values and crises of meaning.

As we know, the strain on the environment grows in proportion to the density of the human population. If the concentration of human populations in our mass cities becomes the general destiny of mankind, then it is only a question of time before patterns of emotional behaviour, moral codes and convictions about life are deeply disturbed. Anxieties and aggressions will increase. The ecological crisis therefore brings with it social crises – crises of value and significance in human society, and a growing instability in the crises of personal life.[4]

Individual living things can react ambivalently to a crisis of this kind; and the same is true of a human society. The defence measures that are undertaken can even serve to spread and deepen the crisis. For example, if foreign bodies penetrate an organism, the organism often initiates a process of self-immunization. The defence mechanism provides protection for a time, but in the long run it destroys the organism itself. Self-immunization is therefore often the cause of a fatal illness.[5] In a similar way, there is often a resistance to the ecological crisis in our society which actually contributes to the spread and deepening of that very crisis: people make light of it, talking about 'strains on the environment' and the regrettable 'side-effects' of modern technologies. The airy assumption is that the ecological crisis can be solved by technological means. But minimizing the crisis does not merely suppress the pain crisis causes; it is also a way of pushing aside the necessary transformation of the whole system of living. The result is that people are becoming increasingly apathetic about the slow death of nature. Even the human will to live is threatening to swing over into a death wish, since in this crisis of the whole system, human affirmation of life is not possible without a complete change of direction. Only life systems that are capable of suffering are capable of surviving, because they are the only ones that are prepared to learn and are open to change and renewal.[6]

Here we shall first of all investigate the interactions of science and values in modern civilization, and shall then go on to show the connection between the Christian belief in creation and these values. We shall not be looking at science and theology *per se*, on the purely theoretical level. We shall be considering them both in the context of the human usurpation of power over nature. Consequently it is not the theoretical conceptions in themselves that we shall be investigating here; our concern is with their structures of power. We are presupposing the work that has already been done on the relationship between theology and science on the purely theoretical level.[7]

1. The modern sciences originated in the context of certain human ideals, values and convictions. Particular concerns lent impetus to scientific development. Definable claims were to be satisfied by exploitable scientific results.[8] It is true that scientific curiosity in itself can be described as pure, detached pleasure in knowledge. Not every piece of scientific work has been commissioned for a particular purpose. But in the social context of the sciences, non-scientific interests are always and everywhere involved. In the struggle for existence, scientific and technological progress is not used merely for the enhancement of living; it is also utilized by the political will to achieve or secure power. In terms of social reality, there is no such thing as 'value-free science'. Today many scientific projects have become so expensive that ministries of science are set up to deal with the politics involved. And if science is linked with politics, then science and the scientists belong within the political context, whether they like it or not. The criteria for assessing scientific projects are then political criteria. If scientists

want to remain the controlling agents of their own work, then the inescapable consequence is their political responsibility, both for their work and for its results.

The political context of science and technology is determined by the sum total of the claims from which the collective behaviour of a society takes its bearings. The sum total of these prevailing wishes, demands and ideas are what we call the accepted values. Through the judgments to which they give rise, these values regulate the way people act, and give practical life its orientation. What values have guided the development of modern civilization? If modern scientific and technological civilizations are compared with earlier cultures, before modern times, the essential difference becomes clear: it is the difference between societies based on growth, and societies based on equilibrium. The earlier civilizations were by no means 'primitive', let alone 'under-developed'. They were highly complicated systems of equilibrium – equilibrium in the relationship between human beings and nature, equilibrium in the relationship between human being and human being, and equilibrium in the relationship between human beings and 'the gods'. It is only modern civilizations which, for the first time, have set their sights on development, expansion and conquest. The acquisition of power, the increase of power, and the securing of power: these, together with 'the pursuit of happiness', may be termed the values that actually prevail in modern civilizations.[9]

The Jewish-Christian tradition is often made responsible for man's usurpation of power over nature and for his unbridled will to power. It was this tradition, we are told, which decreed that human beings should rule the earth. In return that same tradition has stripped the world of nature of its demons and its gods, and has made it the profane world of human beings.[10] Yet this allegedly 'anthropocentric' view of the world found in the Bible is more than three thousand years old, whereas modern scientific and technological civilization only began to develop in Europe four hundred years ago at the earliest. So there must have been other, more important factors in its development. Whatever the economic, social and political chances that may require mention, another factor was more important still in determining the way people four hundred years ago saw themselves. This was the new picture of God offered by the Renaissance and by nominalism: God is almighty, and *potentia absoluta* is the pre-eminent attribute of his divinity. Consequently

God's image on earth, the human being (which in actual practice meant the man) had to strive for power and domination so that he might acquire *his* divinity.[11] Power became the foremost predicate of the deity, not goodness and truth. But how can the human being acquire power, so that he may resemble his God? Through science and technology; for 'knowledge is power', as Francis Bacon exultantly proclaimed. The goal of the scientific knowledge of natural laws is power over nature, and with that the restoration of the human being's resemblance to God and his hegemony.[12] In his theory of science, *Discours de la méthode*, Descartes also declared that the aim of the exact sciences was to make men 'maîtres et possesseurs de la nature'.[13]

As long as the acquisition of power is the concern prompting the scientific search for knowledge, power will be the very mould in which the sciences are cast: power will be the actual form they take.[14] And this will be true of them, not merely in their technological application, but even in their basic methodological principles. The method whereby the natural life systems are analysed and objectified is the method by which these systems are subjected to the will of human beings: *divide et impera,* divide and conquer! Moreover, through this method the human being confronts nature from the outset and in principle as its ruler. He is no longer one member of the community of creation; he confronts creation as its lord and owner. Consequently he can no longer identify himself in terms of body and nature. He becomes merely the subject of cognition and will. The reduction of the natural environment to the status of mere objects corresponds to this subjectification of the human being.[15] The Cartesian dualism of *res cogitans* and *res extensa* is the theory that prompts this modern process of differentiation between man and nature, and the purposes behind that process. Yet to identify the human being as *res cogitans* is just as hostile to his humanity as the subjection of nature to the geometrical notion of extension is hostile to nature. 'The non-spiritual view of nature which Descartes especially brought into vogue was bound to result in the non-natural view of the mind and spirit, and the godless view of both': this was already Franz Baader's critical comment.[16]

The scientific objectification of nature leads to the technological exploitation of nature by human beings. In the modern industrial countries, the relationship between society and nature is wholly determined by the appropriation of the forces of nature and by the exploitation of mineral resources – what German calls *Bodenschätze* – the treasures of the earth. 'The idea spanning the whole of human society is exploitation', writes Alexander Mitscherlich. 'Our relationship to "Mother Nature" has hitherto been an undisturbedly infantile, predatory one. Our capacities for exploitation have grown to gigantic proportions; but the same is by no means true of our capacity for controlling our own emotional reactions as human beings, and our own desires.'[17]

Although Marxism criticizes capitalist 'exploitation of human beings by human beings', where nature is concerned it too has retained the language of exploitation.[18] The destruction of the environment by the socialist industrial states does not fall behind the environmental destruction of the capitalist industrial countries. Towards the different political systems, the ecological crisis is apparently neutral. Whether nature is destroyed by capitalist expansion or by socialist increased productivity makes no difference to nature. For the victim nature, scientific and technological civilization is undoubtedly the most terrible monster ever to appear on earth.

The results are so familiar that there is no need to describe them at any length. Everywhere uncontrollable processes of growth have sprung up: growing populations, industrial growth, growing pollution, a growing use of energy, a growing exposure to stimuli, and growing mental and spiritual instability among men and women. These processes are interdependent and mutally accelerating. 'Progress' is no longer an expression of hope, as it was in the nineteenth-century; it is a fate to which people in the industrial countries feel themselves condemned. When ancient civilized nations are assessed as 'under-developed' or 'developing', this merely shows the mindless imperialism of this ideology of progress, which judges everything on the basis of its own condition, and which aims merely at its own hegemony.[19]

As needs are fulfilled, demands grow. Growing demands are the driving force for rising production. But this race between rising demands and the compulsion to fulfil them cannot be won. There cannot be unlimited progress with limited resources, and a limited potentiality cannot satisfy unlimited demands. Even if mankind discovers new sources of energy and produces new kinds of food by way of genetic techniques, this race is forcing humanity into a global crisis, if demands continue to be as totally unrestrained as they are at present.

'Progress' itself seems to be caught up in a vicious circle, in which it ministers to death, not life. A critical question is therefore being inexorably forced on our scientific and technological civilization: is nature really nothing but a free-for-all? Unclaimed property which human beings can appropriate and do with whatever they like?

2. Christian theology is no less affected by the ecological crisis than the sciences and technologies. The modern industrial countries developed in those parts of the world which were under Christian influence. Here the prevailing systems of value and significance were for a long time determined by the Bible and the church. Even modern secular forms of culture and atheistical philosophies of life still belong to the sphere of influence of the biblical and Christian traditions, even if they dissociate themselves critically from those traditions. The theological dilemma can be seen in the following points:

Modern critics of the Jewish-Christian tradition point out that the biblical charge given at creation, 'Be fruitful and multiply and subdue the earth' (Gen. 1.28), lays the intellectual foundations for today's ecological crisis: unlimited reproduction, over-population of the earth, and the subjugation of nature.[20] But can a legitimation of human rule over the world really be found in this commission? Is the triumphal progress of the modern subjugation of nature a realization of that biblical designation of the human being? Here there are several misunderstandings, which have regrettably often been promoted by theology and the church, for apologetic reasons.

The specific biblical concept of 'subduing the earth' has nothing to do with the charge to rule over the world which theological tradition taught for centuries as the *dominium terrae*. The biblical charge is a dietary commandment: human beings and animals alike are to live from the fruits which *the earth* brings forth in the form of plants and trees.[21] A seizure of power over nature is not intended. A charge 'to rule' can be found only in Gen. 1.26: 'Then God said, "Let us make man in our image, after our likeness; and let them have dominion over the fish of the sea, and over the birds of the air, and over the cattle, and over all the earth." ' But here 'having dominion' is linked with the correspondence between human beings and God, the creator and preserver of the world – the correspondence which is meant when the human being is described as being the image of God. Because human beings and animals are to live from the fruits of the earth, the rule of human beings over the animals can only be a rule of peace, without any 'power over life and death'. The role which human beings are meant to play is the role of a 'justice of the peace'.

It always causes misunderstanding when biblical texts are torn out of their proper context in the biblical tradition, and are used to legitimate other concerns. It is therefore important to remember the Yahwist's account of creation too: Genesis 2.15 talks about 'the Garden of Eden' which human beings are 'to till and keep'. So human mastery over the earth is intended to resemble the cultivating and protective work of a gardener. Nothing is said about predatory exploitation. It is true that the will to achieve power, to expand and to progress, which is the hallmark of modern civilization, has often been theologically legitimated with the help of the biblical doctrine of creation; but this subsequent legitimation has no foundation in the Bible itself. 'Human independence' towards the world and the resulting 'possession of the world by the human mind' which this independence made possible, and which Friedrich Gogarten extolled, was not a deduction by way of the Christian faith.[22] If theology is to develop its own critical potential, it must free itself from apologetic adaptations of this kind, and from retrospective claims to ideas which are really alien property.

But is it not at least true that the biblical belief in creation has stripped the world of its gods and demons? Has it not, after all, broken pagan taboos and so 'set the world free' for human beings? Has the sharp differentiation between God and the world, as 'the work of his hands', not de-sacralized the world and thrown it open for unbiased investigation by human beings? Surely it was through the biblical belief in creation that the world of mysterious powers became the world of human beings? Because the second creation account gives the impression that the world was created for the sake of men and women, people believed that the modern conquest of the world by human beings proved that the ancient anthropocentric view of the world was the true one. The negation in this apologetic thesis is certainly correct enough: it is true that belief in creation views the world as neither divine nor demonic. But the logical position is a false one. Interpreting the world as God's creation means precisely *not* viewing it as the world of human beings, and taking possession of it accordingly. If the world is God's creation, then it remains his property and cannot be claimed by men and women. It can only be accepted as a loan and administered as a trust. It has to be treated according to the standards of the divine righteousness, not according to the values that are bound up with human aggrandisement.

According to the anthropocentric world view, heaven and earth were made for the sake of human beings, and the human being is the crown of creation; and this is certainly what is claimed by both its supporters and its critics as 'biblical tradition'.[23] But it is unbiblical; for according to the biblical Jewish and Christian traditions, God created the world for his glory, out of love; and the crown of creation is not the human being; it is the sabbath. It is true that, as the image of God, the human being has his special position in creation. But he stands together with all other earthly and heavenly beings in the same hymn of praise of God's glory, and in the enjoyment of God's sabbath pleasure over creation, as he saw that it was good. Even without human beings, the heavens declare the glory of God. This *theocentric* biblical world picture gives the human being, with his special position in the cosmos, the chance to understand himself as a member of the community of creation. So if Christian theology wants to find the wisdom in dealing with creation which accords with belief in creation, it must free that belief from the modern anthropocentric view of the world.

Finally, theology has often enough responded to the triumphal progress of science by withdrawing to the field of history, leaving nature to the sciences.[24] The theology of history seemed an appropriate way of assimilating and interpreting the historical traditions of biblical promise and future hope. The theology of history was also able to evaluate the practical behaviour of men and women in history. Whereas 'nature' took on the overtones of what is timeless, static and continually recurring, 'history' was filled with remembrance and hope and the real meaning of human life. History became the symbol for the world when the notion 'cosmos' ceased to fulfil this function, because it had been superseded by the concept of nature as the object of the sciences. The study of history became 'the universal science', both theologically and atheistically.[25] Yet this modern notion of 'the world caught up in the process of history' also leaves theology still bounded by the dualism of modern European times, which defines nature and history over against one another. The history of human beings in their relation to nature is not seen as a part of natural history. On the contrary, nature is interpreted as part of human history. Contingency, openess to the future, and the wealth of potentiality are historical elements which are denied to nature but appropriated to human history.

But theology must free belief in creation from this overvaluation of history also. A contemplation of the history of nature[26] is one of the perspectives which make this possible. But another viewpoint is lacking: the perspective of the character of the earth in which history takes place. And a final perspective is missing also: the vista of that creation which overrides and overreaches history in both time and space. Is there not a natural limitation of the historical world of men and women? Is there not a perception of God's creation which embraces the human history of salvation and disaster precisely because it is not totally engrossed by that history? What meaning does heaven have in God's creation?

As long as theological discernment is concerned merely to imitate scientific discernment of nature and to emulate it, there will be at most *belief* in creation, but no adequate *concept* of creation, in dealing with the world. What kind of understanding is it, if we understand the world as God's creation?

If science sets its sights on the acquisition of power, then scientific knowledge is dominating knowledge.[27] We know something to the extent in which we can dominate it. We understand something if we can 'grasp' it. Through scientific terms we define, and through definitions we pin things down and make objects identifiable.

But *belief* in creation only arrives at the understanding of creation when it recollects the alternative forms of *meditative* knowledge. 'We know to the extent to which we love', said Augustine. Through this form of astonished, wondering and loving knowledge, we do not appropriate things. We recognize their independence and participate in their life. We do not wish to know so that we can dominate. We desire to know in order to participate. This kind of knowledge confers community, and can be termed communicative knowledge, as compared with dominating knowledge.[28] It lets life be life and cherishes its livingness. Christian theology must remember this, its own wisdom, if it wants to make its contribution to the conquest of the ecological crisis of scientific and technological civilization.[29]

§2 ON THE WAY TO AN ECOLOGICAL THEOLOGY OF NATURE

In the history of the theological doctrine of creation, three stages can be distinguished. These have been determined by the relationship between theology and science at any given time.[30]

1. In the first stage, the biblical traditions and the ancient world's picture of the universe were fused into a religious cosmology. In this fusion, pantheistic elements which glorified the cosmos and gnostic elements which disparaged it were both excluded. The theological idea of the transcendence of the Creator in relation to his creation evoked the cosmological notion of a temporally and spatially limited, contingent and immanent world. At the same time, the indwelling of the Spirit of the transcendent Creator in his creation allowed this world to appear as the divinely ordered world, which is filled with God's glory and is guided by his wisdom.[31] Mediaeval theological cosmology was always a cosmological exposition of the six days' work according to Genesis 1, with the help of the ancient Ptolemaic world picture. From this cosmology the modern sciences have successively freed themselves, although the physico-theology of the Enlightenment (which Newton also supported) again offered the developing sciences the framework of a religious cosmology.

2. In the second stage, the sciences emancipated themselves from this cosmology, while theology detached its doctrine of creation from cosmology altogether, and reduced it to personal belief in creation. The world view of ancient and mediaeval times was rejected as unscientific, and the biblical creation narratives were written off by historical criticism as myths. So all that remained was the reduction of the doctrine of creation to the personal faith which says that human beings have to put their trust in God the Creator, not in his creatures. In order to protect it from scientific attack, the Protestant theology of modern times liked to explain faith in creation as an expression of the feeling of absolute dependence. That is to say, it was interpreted as an existential truth, or a truth about life. In this second stage science and theology were busy with their mutual demarcation. Only the definition of the borderline between them seemed to offer the liberty they both required. After the severe conflicts that gathered round the trials of Giordano Bruno and Galileo Galiei, and after the public disputes about Charles Darwin and Sigmund Freud, mutual demarcation did indeed confer peace. But it was peaceful co-existence on the basis of mutual irrelevance.

3. Today theology and science have entered a third stage in their relationship. Now they have become companions in tribulation, under the pressure of the ecological crisis and the search for the new direction which both must work for, if human beings and nature are to survive at all on this earth. It is only slowly that theologians are beginning to see that their continual attempts to draw dividing lines between theology and the sciences are no longer necessary, because science's earlier unquestioning faith in itself has disappeared. Scientists are also slowly beginning to discover that Christian theology is not conserving antiquated world views, but that it is a partner that deserves to be taken seriously, both in the sphere of cosmology and in the realm of social practice. In a global situation where it is a case of 'one world or none', science and theology cannot afford to divide up the one, single reality. On the contrary, theology and the sciences will arrive together at the ecological awareness of the world.[32]

Because the transition from the second stage to the third is only just beginning, I should like to give a critical account of the theological retreat from cosmology into personal faith in creation, so that from there we may find the ways of approach for the ecological shaping, and the ecological responsibility, of the theological doctrine of creation.

After Nicolaus Copernicus had completed his book *De revolutionibus orbium coelestium*, it was first published in 1543 by the Nuremberg Reformer Andreas Osiander.[33] In his preface, in order to explain the significance of the new Copernican world view, the theologian draws on the rhetorical term *hypothesis*: hypotheses are not *articuli fidei*; they are *fundamenta calculi*. Consequently the hypotheses on which the new world picture rests do not contradict the articles of the Christian faith. It is true that Copernicus later repudiated this preface of Osiander's; but the distinction became an influential one none the less.[34] The faith that is directed towards God himself does not tie reason down to a particular world picture. It sets the sciences free to arrive at knowledge of the world against the open horizon of variable hypothetical working drafts. Belief in God frees reason from dogmatism, and the sciences from idols and idolatries. If it is here that faith's critical power is to be found outwardly, then it must be asked what its own personal alignment is.

Johannes Kepler, like Galileo after him, maintained the view that

God's intention in the Bible was not to correct erroneous opinions about *the world*, or to save people the effort of investigation. His sole purpose was to reveal to human beings everything that was necessary for their *salvation*.[35] This Reformation tendency to interpret the biblical traditions in the light of human – and indeed personal – questions of salvation was subsequently felt to be liberating, and is occasionally still seen as such today. For it is thought to be a way of maintaining the validity of the Bible in the scientific age on the one hand and, on the other, as a possible way of studying nature in the light of reason, unprejudiced by the dogmas of faith. But this concentration on the salvation of the individual person also cut theology off from human ways of knowing and mastering the world. Theology's domain became the soul's assurance of salvation in the inner citadel of the heart. The earthly, bodily and cosmic dimensions of the salvation of the whole world were overlooked. The universality and totality of salvation were surrendered. But when personal salvation came to be thought of as something that had nothing to do with the world, in the same degree the knowledge and fashioning of the world ceased to have any reference to salvation and disaster. This meant that the calamitous dichotomy between the subjectivity of human beings and the objective world of 'mere things' was deepened. The truth of faith and the truth of reason split apart. Now theology could only present belief in creation in the context of human existence, but not in the context of nature and the relationship between human beings and nature. But if God is no longer 'the all-determining power', truth is no longer a single truth and salvation is no longer the redemption of the whole.

With only a few exceptions, Protestant theology accepted the dichotomy of the modern world. Many people even saw in it the Reformation distinction between law and gospel, person and works – and also the distinction between the spiritual and the worldly kingdom. It was only later that it became clear that here theology's influence was far from salutary, and that it had in fact deepened the divisions. 'Faith had now set reason free' was the formula that was used. The Reformation, it was claimed, had instituted an 'eternal contract' between 'the living Christian faith' and 'research, which was now free in every direction to work on its own and for itself'. By 'emancipating' science, the Reformation had done enough 'for the needs of our time', wrote Friedrich Schleiermacher.[36] Friedrich Gogarten,[37] Rudolf Bultmann[38] and Emil Brunner[39] then intensified the difference between person and nature to such an extent that it was no longer possible to detect any positive connection between personal and scientific knowledge at all. Even Gerhard Ebeling, when he is considering 'science and belief in creation', still takes as his first subject 'the emancipation of science'.[40]

Karl Barth also defined limits: 'There is free scope for natural science beyond what theology describes as the work of the Creator. And theology can and must move freely where science which really is science and not secretly a pagan *Gnosis* or religion, has its appointed limits.' He did not say anything more precise about the topography of these boundaries; he merely prophesied that 'future workers . . . will find many problems worth pondering in defining the point and manner of this shared boundary.'[41] Happily he himself did not abide by these limits, but often drew on scientific insights in his doctrine of creation.

From the point of view of the modern sciences themselves, the legitimation formula 'emancipation of the sciences' is derived from the myth that theology was the ruling party. But, historically speaking, the sciences were never 'set free' by the church and faith; they laboriously emancipated themselves from the authority of the state churches. Nor can theology, in a process of hindsight, claim to have performed any such services for the development of the sciences.

After its retreat from cosmology, theology concentrated on personal faith. 'I believe that God created *me*. . . .' as Luther's Short Catechism says. Of course all belief in creation includes that personal conviction. But this personal confession of faith was now increasingly interpreted in an exclusive sense, although it was meant inclusively: for Luther goes on ' . . . together with all other creatures.' 'The statement about the creation of the world is not theory – not a hypothesis to explain the world. It is personal, existential knowledge.' For 'the assurance about the world as creation is based on God's encounter with me', explained Paul Althaus.[42] For Emil Brunner as well, belief in God the Creator was 'truth-as-encounter'. He too wanted to teach 'creation, not a theory about the way in which the world came into existence'.[43] But no theological doctrine of creation must be allowed to reduce the understanding of belief in creation to the existential self-understanding of the person. It must mean the whole knowable world. If God is not the Creator of the world, he cannot be my Creator either.

The continual confrontation between world view and belief in creation which we can observe here, still shows the marks of the slow transition from the first stage to the second. If today the division of reality into person and nature proves to be fictitious, both scientifically and theologically, this criticism does not mean that theology ought to return to the religious cosmologies of its past, whether they be biblical, patristic or mediaeval. It cannot be the aim of the ecological theology of nature, which is so necessary today, to satisfy the ideological need for a closed outlook on the world. Its aim ought to be to offer points of reference in the ecological world crisis. In the disputed relationship between theology and the sciences, silenced and dying nature has, so to speak, in her own way become the third partner. Consequently the separation between theology and science is only to a secondary degree the point at issue. The primary requirement is to fit theology and the sciences ecologically into the natural surroundings which are the framework providing their conditions.

Scientific information is rapidly increasing; and once this information has been examined and ordered, it must be interlocked into theories, if it is to be capable of practical application. The development of ever new individual theories requires points of orientation in wider theories about the universe as a whole. It is not wise to tie down comprehensive theories of this kind by way of a hard and fast world view. Nor does it take us any further if we give these world views an ideological backing and impose them through political authority. The store of knowledge is increasing so rapidly that individual theories and their total orientations will also be more ephemeral and more readily superseded than they were earlier. They are acquiring the character of the provisional draft, which must be kept variable and be itself creative inasmuch as it must make new working sketches possible. And a theological theory of nature will also be both variable and provisional.

In the second stage of theology and the sciences, all the various ways of thinking started from the subjectivity of the person, and from this standpoint gathered the surveyable world together under the headings of nature and history. Thinking in terms of subjectivity is objectifying, particularizing, defining and identifying thinking. Entry into the ecological stage means that this way of thinking changes. The subjectivity that has been arrived at, and the possibilities it offers for objectifying the world, are not obliterated; but we begin to understand a life system in the light of its own special environment. Things are no longer merely objects for the human subject. They are at the same time seen in their own environmental structure and their own environmental communication. The human being as the cognitive subject also begins to understand himself, and his ways of knowing and working, in the context, and in the light, of his closer and more remote surroundings. This means that objectifying thinking is absorbed into integrative thinking. The particularizing way of looking at things is transformed into a comprehensive one.[44] The cognition which is related to the perceiving subject is replaced by participating knowing. In the second stage the prevailing method was to isolate objects. In this third stage the integration of objects into their living worlds is more important.

4. What tasks emerge from this for theology?

The sciences have shown us how to understand creation as nature. Now theology must show how nature is to be understood as God's creation.

(*a*) Understanding nature as God's creation means seeing it as neither divine nor demonic, but viewing it as 'the world'. If this world has been *created* by God, then it is not necessarily existent; it is contingent. Its very being is contingent, and so is everything that happens in it. But if it is contingent, it cannot be deduced from the idea of God. It can be known merely through observation. The rational order in which and through which we comprehend and know worldly happenings is therefore in itself contingent, temporal and open to change. This is true of 'natural laws' as well.[45]

(*b*) Everything which can be made the object of scientific knowledge must in this context be seen as 'nature'. But the concept of creation goes beyond this, because it views as created, not merely the reality that has been turned into the object, but also the human subjectivity which confronts that reality, and the finite human spirit itself. In every modern scientific division between subject and object, belief in creation perceives a created community – a divided one perhaps, but none the less a community of creation that has not been revoked. Even the human subjectivity of reason and will which confronts nature, remains creaturely and contingent, and never becomes absolute.

(*c*) But the concept of creation goes beyond even this tension-laden history between human beings and the nature which is accessible to them. According to the Christian creeds, God is the Creator of heaven and earth, and of 'all things visible and invisible'. So the visible, scientifically knowable reality accessible to human beings is only part of creation. The 'nature' that men and women can make the object of their cognition and domination is for theology only the visible part of creation. Understanding nature as God's creation therefore means putting together in a wider context the known sector of reality and the sector that is not yet known (but is in principle knowable), and hence seeing the known sector as relative – as not existing of itself but as pointing beyond itself. Theologically speaking, 'visible' nature cannot be adequately understood as creation unless what is in principle invisible is believed in as creation also. Theologically, knowledge of earthly reality cannot be lifted and gathered up into the assumption of a wider creation unless belief in heaven, as the other side of God's creation, is restored.

(*d*) Finally, a fourth idea is important for an understanding of nature as God's creation. It is not possible for a biblically determined Christian theology to see the present condition of the world as pure divine 'creation', and to join in the Creator's original verdict: 'Behold, it was very good' (Gen. 1.31). Much more applicable to the present condition of the created world is Paul's recognition of the 'anxious waiting' and the 'longing' of creation, which is 'subjected to futility, not of its own will, but by the will of him who subjected it, on the strength of hope' (Rom. 8. 19–21). Enslavement through the bondage of transience, and a yearning openness for the future of the kingdom of God's glory, determine the present condition of the world. And this is not only true of the world of men and women; it applies to the whole creation. Anyone who perceives 'creation' in the present condition of the world begins to suffer with that creation, and also to hope for it. In this condition, what is termed 'nature' is neither a pure primordial state, a paradisal Garden of Eden, nor is it the end of all things – perfection. It is a destiny to which creation is subjected: a continual process of annihilation, an all-embracing fellowship of suffering, and a tense and anxious openness for a different future. To understand 'nature' as creation therefore means discerning 'nature' as the enslaved creation that hopes for liberty. So by 'nature' we can only mean a single act in the great drama of the creation of the world on the way to the kingdom of glory – the act that is being played out at the present time. It is only seldom that theology has perceived the ordering of nature into this history of disaster and redemption, or that it has brought this concept to bear; and yet it is only with this that the programme 'understanding nature as God's creation' becomes realistic. In the seventeenth-century Gottfried Arnold brought out the point in his hymn 'O Durchbrecher aller Banden . . .', where he speaks of 'fettered' human beings, together with the rest of creation,

> 'sighing, struggling,
> crying, praying'

for deliverance from nature.[46] In the same century Henry Vaughan also saw humanity as part of a universal 'tarrying expectation in hope'. He headed his poem 'For the earnest expectation of the creature waiteth for the manifestation of the sons of God':

> And do they so? Have they a sense
> Of ought but influence?
> Can they their heads lift, and expect,
>   And groan too? Why th'Elect
> Can do no more . . .

§3 THE ALIENATION AND LIBERATION OF NATURE

1. *Karl Marx and the Estrangement of Nature*

The sciences and technologies are based on a particular fundamental relationship between the human being and nature.[47] In the sciences nature is encountered as the embodiment or synthesis of the objects which the human subject is capable of knowing methodically. In the world of work and in the technologies, nature is encountered as the embodiment or synthesis of the materials over which the human subject disposes, and which he can appropriate and form. In science and technology the human being experiences himself as the subject of his world. 'Subject' does not mean merely that he is the centre of his world, and the point of reference for everything in it. He is also its ontological basis, its first and all-determining being.[48] Through science and technology, nature is turned into an object. It comes into view to the extent in which it can be made available to the human subject. The human being perceives nature by way of his seizure of power. He dominates nature through his labour. Nature encounters him in this labour as the embodiment of the objects which he has to handle and process.

Philosophy has made many attempts to overcome the division of the world into subjectivity and objective things, *res cogitans* and *res extensa*. This division does not have to be petrified into a hard and fast ontological dualism. It is also quite possible to see the subjectification of the human being and the objectification of nature as a historical relationship of mutual condition. In this case the actual subject is history. It is differentiated into the human subject and the natural object, but it remains the unity within this difference. If historical dialectic replaces ontological dualism as the interpretative framework for understanding the difference between subject and object, we have then to ask whether there can be a future in which this difference is absorbed into a higher unity, so that the tensions and contradictions which are present in the antithesis may give way to a peaceful resolution. The philosophies of history which belonged to German Idealism were devoted to this problem. But the dialectical conception of the difference between subject and object only covers the human relationship to nature, not nature itself. Even in historical dialectic, nature appears merely as object of the human being. It receives attention to the extent in which it is made part of human history through knowledge and labour. This approach does not permit nature to be apprehended in its independent character.

Karl Marx tried to overcome Idealist subjectivism by way of the model of dialectical materialism, hoping thereby to resolve the conflict between man and nature at the same time. According to the vision of his early writings, communism does not merely overcome the alienation of the human being. It also vanquishes the alienation of nature, and brings not only humanity but also nature to its true, essential being. In this respect communism is supposed to be 'perfected naturalism'.

> Only here has his natural existence become his human existence; and nature become man for him. Society is therefore the perfected unity in essence of man with nature, the true resurrection of nature, the realized naturalism of man and the realized humanism of nature.[49]

If a person has become human in the true sense, because private property has been abolished and the alienation of his labour has been overcome, he will also discover 'the human essence of nature', for he will then have found the natural essence of the human being. So human beings and nature will overcome their mutual estrangement and become a living unity. In this living unity, Marx, following Goethe, conceived of the person as 'natural human being' in the following terms: 'The true, bodily human being, who stands on firm, solidly established earth, inhaling and exhaling all the powers of nature . . .' The logical figure in this picture of inhaling and exhaling is the dialectical identity. It derives from Schelling's philosophy of nature.[50]

> This communism, as fully developed naturalism, equals humanism, and as fully developed humanism equals naturalism; it is the genuine resolution of the conflict between man and nature, and between man and man – the true resolution of the conflict between existence and being, between objectification and self-affirmation, between freedom and necessity, between individual and species. It is the solution of the riddle of history, and knows itself to be the solution.[51]

2. *Ernst Bloch: 'Nature as Subject'*

Ernst Bloch took up the idea of the naturalization of the human being, in order to link Marx's dialectical materialism even more closely with Schelling's philosophy of nature.[52] Bloch starts from a correspondence between the human being and nature: the counterpart of the creative person is productive matter, while the counterpart of the hoping person is the material sphere of the really-possible. Consequently Bloch assumes that there is a subject 'nature' which corresponds as partner to the human subject. It is only when nature ceases to appear merely as 'nature for the human being' – that is to say, his object and raw material – but is recognized in its individual character as a 'subject' of its own that the history of nature can be perceived as something on its own, independent of human beings: and it is only then that nature's own independent future can be heeded. And only then, too, can a community between human beings and nature come into being in which both can find their 'home country'. By using the expression 'nature as subject', Bloch is not remystifying nature into 'the Great Mother', although he recognized quite early on the elements of truth in the matriarchal pattern. What he means is 'the not-yet-manifest driving power in reality as a whole of the "That" (the most immanent efficient cause in matter).'[53] In nature herself there is a 'matrix of fecundity'. Nature is always *natura naturans* (Spinoza's phrase). In the human being she certainly concentrates all her energies into what Bloch poetically calls her 'supreme flowering'. But she none the less remains the subject, and never becomes the object of the subject 'human being'.

From this Bloch goes on to the idea of 'alliance technology', through which the human being and nature are mediated to one another in their respective subjectivities. 'In place of the technician as mere trickster or exploiter, we have quite specifically the subject mediated to himself through society, who increasingly mediates himself to the problem of nature as subject.'[54] Alliance technology – or, as we say today, soft technology – accepts the co-productivity of nature as subject. In this alliance, it is not only the person who desires to bring forth and manifest his true essential being. Nature too is to manifest herself in the alliance, in her own individual character.

According to Bloch, Spinoza's idea of *natura naturans* presupposes the profounder idea (which probably derives from the Kabbala) of the *natura abscondita*, which thrusts towards its manifestation. Consequently 'the nature that is finally manifested' is to be found in the context of the future – the future of the alliances which mediate between human beings and nature: 'The more an alliance technology becomes possible, in place of a technology applied from outside – an alliance technology mediated through the co-productivity of nature – the more surely the engendering energies of a frozen nature will be once more set free.'[55] 'Our previous technology stands in the midst of nature like an army of occupation in enemy country, which knows nothing of the country's interior: the material on which technology works transcends it.'[56] Bloch was able to formulate these ideas only by drawing on Romantic concepts of nature; but with their help he none the less anticipated important ecological principles. Both the notion of the subjectivity of complex life systems, and the methods of communicative cognition assimilate his ideas.

With this philosophy of nature Bloch of course departed widely from orthodox contemporary Marxism. In 1957 he was condemned by Marxist philosophers and reproached for 'an anti-Marxist doctrine of earthly redemption'. Bloch's thesis about the appearance of 'nature as subject' was castigated as an idealistically mystical dogma: nature had no subject except the working human being. Bloch's conception was not merely *un*scientific; it was actually antiscientific. His dogmas were in contradiction to socialist practice. 'In reality, the development of the human being and the whole history of mankind is a process in which nature is exploited by human beings in material production . . . Even in socialism and communism, there is no "identity" in the sense of a marriage between the human being and the subject "nature" in their "home country".'[57] The only subject of nature is the human being. Nature's creative character may not yet have been exploited to the full in the human being; but this disposition will find its fuller development, not side by side with human beings, but only within them. Liberty is for human beings only, not for nature.

If we consult Karl Marx himself at this juncture, we are forced to discover that in *Capital* he departed from the visions of his early writings, where these were inspired by the philosophy of nature. Now there is no more talk about 'the naturalization of the human being'. 'The resurrection of nature' has been struck off the programme. 'The new society is designed for the benefit of men and women only – and, moreover, quite unequivocally at nature's expense. Nature is to be subjugated through gigantic technological devices and with the least possible expenditure of labour and time; and – as material substratum for providing every conceivable kind and quantity of consumer goods – its function is to serve all human beings.'[58] Now nature only crops up in the sense of 'natural resources', and as 'the object of labour', which the human being is going to transform into consumer goods. In this way the working man or woman 'subdues' the play of natural forces. But this means that for the later Marx the conflict between human beings and nature remains, and cannot be resolved. Natural necessity and human liberty remain ultimately unmediated and unreconciled, in all mediations and reconciliations.

Yet fundamentally the seeds of the ideas which Marx propagated in *Capital* are already present in the early writings. There too he was really only aware of nature in the form of 'natural forces', and objects were for him merely the 'products' of objective activity on the part of the human being. He never described the relationship between human beings and nature as 'home', or 'a home country'. He always saw this relationship merely as a necessary 'metabolic process'. This concept of the metabolism between the human being and nature (a concept borrowed from Jacob Moleschott) offers no ground for the greater hope for the future which Bloch cherished.

Marx therefore only conceived of the abolition of human self-alienation at nature's expense. The alienation of nature brought about by human beings was for him recognizable only in the predatory exploitation of the capitalism which had to be overcome. Yet even in communism nature remains the human being's subjugated slave. An end to this estrangement of nature was not yet part of Marx's viewpoint. But this simply means that where the relationship between human beings and nature was concerned, Marx remained confined to the framework offered by the concepts of Bacon and Descartes, so that his dialectical materialism is nothing more than another version of modern Idealism. Why?

The reason is that Marx, and orthodox Marxism, can only conceive of a practical relationship to nature. This practical relationship is *work*. Under the aspect of work, the human being can perceive nature in no other way than as the object that has to be worked *on*, and as raw material for his own purposes. In addition, the viewpoint and aims of work have made even reason operational to such an extent that the human being can discern only what he himself brings forth according to his own concepts, as Kant already pointed out. The substantiality of nature, in the sense of its independence, escapes the objectifying gaze that is focused only on production.

It was only insight into the ecological crisis of modern industrial societies which could lead to a conversion, among Marxists also. Thus Alfred Schmidt writes in the *Postscriptum 1971* to his book on the concept of nature in Marx, which first appeared in 1962: '"The resurrection of nature" and "the humanization of man" – today these are no longer the chimaera of an eschatological fantasy. Their success or failure is going to determine whether or not humanity arrives at a reasonable condition – or indeed survives at all.'[59] This is a subsequent justification of Ernst Bloch, about whose philosophy of nature Schmidt still writes in the same book: 'It is a matter of indifference how many of these ideas of Bloch's go back to the Renaissance philosophy of Jakob Böhme or to Schelling's romantic speculations about nature. They are as a whole incompatible with a materialist position.'[60] So either the ecological understanding of the world is 'incompatible' with materialist positions, or materialism in the form it has hitherto taken is 'incompatible' with the reasonable condition in which humanity and nature together acquire chances of survival.

3. *The Home Country in Nature*

The relationship of the human being to the natural environment is evidently determined by at least two concerns of a fundamental kind. The one is the concern of work, which we have already described. People work on nature so as to acquire food, and in order to build up their own world. Under the aspect of work, the human being is always the active agent, while nature is always passive. Man is the master, and nature is his slave. Has the human being no other elemental need which inevitably determines his relationship to nature? There is a need of this kind. It has hitherto been theoretically overlooked, and was given a back seat when the huge industrial cities were built up – to the detriment of human beings and nature alike. This concern is *the interest of habitation*. The human being does not only have to work on nature. He also has to be able to dwell in nature. The interests of habitation are different from the interests of work. We can sum up the interests of habitation under the concept of 'home' or – in Bloch's phrase – 'home country'. The idea of a 'home country' is not primarily an appeal to a regressive dream of origin, composed of 'fatherland' and 'mother tongue' and childish security. There can only be a home country in liberty, not in slavery.

In this connection we are using the phrase 'home country' to designate a network of social relationships without stresses and strains. I am 'at home' where people know me, and where I find recognition without having to struggle for it. Relaxed social relationships of this kind allow the person to live in an equilibrium which sustains him, and relieves him of struggle and anxiety. The home of the natural environment is just such a network of tranquillized social relationships. Human society must be adapted to the natural environment. That means that it must observe nature's capacity for regeneration and adjust itself to nature's cycles. Nature is not in itself a home for human beings. On the contrary, the human being's natural constitution shows that he is an unfinished being who is not adjusted to the environment at all. It is only when nature has been moulded into an environment that it can become the home in which men and women can live and dwell. Nature is certainly capable of being a home for human beings, but only if they use it without destroying it. Predatory exploitation is practised only by alien and homeless groups of people. To use nature without destruction also preserves it by allowing it to be experienced for what it is. The development of ecological horticulture and the preservation of the countryside are obvious examples of possible symbioses between human beings and nature. They also show how senseless the violation of nature is.

The previous forms of industrialization were all centralized on major industries and industrial combines. This meant a concentrated strain on the natural world which caused irreparable havoc. This is becoming evident to people in the congested industrial centres, because their surroundings are becoming uninhabitable. So if the industrial societies are to be humanized, must not the interest of capital and labour in production be counterbalanced by the interests of men and women in the habitability of the region in which they live? Today this is the starting point for citizens' action groups and for the conflicts about the further development of environmentally harmful industries; for decline in habitability means the destruction of human opportunities for living. But international corporations and outside capital are apparently simply not interested.

The human being has not merely a right to work; he has a right to habitation. The two interests must be balanced out. This is not merely a requirement in the context of social policy. It is also a demand for a radical change of direction in the relation between human beings and nature. The ecological attitude to the natural environment must surmount the one-sided, pragmatic and utilitarian approach.

But the rediscovery of external nature will remain incomplete if it is not accompanied by a simultaneous rediscovery of nature 'within' – the nature which the human being is himself, in his bodily make-up.

4. *Soul and Body*

Are there any models and prototypes for this in other sectors of life? In the sphere of European ideas, the new ecological attitude to nature is intellectually rooted in psychosomatic medicine, among other things.[61]

As we know, even Descartes was unable to apply the strict distinction between subject and object to human life itself. He was unable to discover the link between *res cogitans* and *res extensa* in the human being. His assumption that the pineal gland links soul and body fell disappointingly short of his own definitions. The rise of modern medicine, and its enormous successes, were due to the introduction and application of scientific methods. But the awareness that the object of medical research and treatment is the subject 'human being' was something that could not be obliterated. In medicine, the man or woman who is the subject undertaking the treatment confronts the man or woman who is the subject undergoing that treatment. The patient remains a person. In medicine, the hard and fast distinction between the human being and nature cannot be applied to the human being himself.

The human being exists in his body as long as he lives. He can certainly stand back from himself, and objectify the bodily existence which he *is* into the body which he *has*. But for all that, he is still his body, and his body is still himself. The human being is never wholly an object to himself – never something which he has completely at his disposal. If that were possible he would stop being a human being. Even the person who is ill is, as a sick person, always still a subject, however much he is also made to become the object of therapeutic treatment.

Psychosomatic medicine began when 'the spell of scientific objectivism was broken' by the introduction into pathology of the subject, the sick person himself. Psychosomatic medicine recognized the extent to which a person can form and regulate the processes of his illness through his own physical and mental influence – what can best be described as his 'human' influence.[62] Once human subjectivity has been recognized, it becomes possible to enter medically as well into the way the sick person 'processes' and assimilates his illness. Human medicine in the true sense cannot be founded on a subject-object relationship. It has to presuppose a relationship between subject and subject. Its tendency is to abolish the alienation of the body which results from purely physical medicine. It supplements the concepts of 'having' by the concepts of 'being'.[63] It comprehends the totality of the human person.

The alienation of the human being from his bodily existence must be viewed as the inner aspect of the external ecological crisis of modern industrial society. Religion and upbringing made people identify themselves as the subjects merely of cognition and will; their bodily existence was something that had to be objectified and subdued. Men and women became the masters of themselves – and their own possession. They learnt to 'control' themselves, and to keep their bodily feelings and needs 'under command'. They became their own slaves and property. Self-command and self-control were the moral maxims of the industrial societies.[64] It was only with the help of these principles that people could be kept continually available, because they had to proffer themselves as workers and as consumers. Functionally rational behaviour in work, in personal dealings, and in consumption is the prerequisite for the efficient functioning of an industrial society. The clock reduces living time – time as we experience it – to mechanical time. The clock became the key machine of the modern industrial age.[65] As a result, human beings have become alienated from the rhythms and cycles of their bodies. And this is especially true of the woman. The body is turned into an instrument for labour and for enjoyment. People are only conscious of it when it stops performing its proper service and falls ill. As a medium for the instinctive, emotional impulses of the whole person, it is becoming unknown. Receptivity, spontaneity and wholeness of being are lost to the person who is increasingly turned into the subject and object of his own self.

The discovery by medicine of the psychosomatic wholeness of the person – his totality of soul and body – and the acceptance of the bodily experience of the self in the life of the individual and the community, are first approaches towards overcoming the ecological crisis in the human being's relationship to his own bodily nature. If human society is to find a home in the natural environment, the human soul must correspondingly find a home in the bodily existence of the human person. Unless the person's own physical nature is liberated from its subjugation by the subject, nature in the environmental sense will not be liberated from the estrangement brought about by the subjection and exploitation imposed on it. And the reverse is equally true. To dwell in nature as a home belongs together with the quickening of one's own bodily existence through the soul and spirit.

5. *The Naturalization of the Human Being*

It is inconceivable that the alienation of nature brought about by human beings can ever be overcome without the naturalization of the human being himself. This naturalization should not be seen in terms of a romantic 'return to nature'. What it means is that men and women should find a new understanding of themselves, and a new interpretation of their world in the framework of nature.

If the modern metaphysics of subjectivity is to be made responsible for the estranging objectification of nature, then the new self-interpretation of men and women must be founded on a non-subjectivistic metaphysics. If the centralistic build-up of modern industries has a destructive effect on the environment, then the new interpretation of the world of human beings must provide the foundation for a non-centralistic culture. The Cartesian 'subject' metaphysics was just as centralistic a theory about the world as the Aristotelian metaphysics of substance. Both can only be done away with by means of a relational metaphysics, based on the mutual relativity of human beings and the world. And more recent theories which enter into the ecological situation of the modern world seem in fact to be pointing in this direction.[66]

In the German discussion, there have been first of all new discoveries and concepts which move in the direction of a humanization of nature.[67] With the help of 'the theory of open systems' and more modern information theories, it became possible to concede a certain subjectivity, on their own individual levels, to the systems of matter and life in the natural environment. The growing indeterminacy of behaviour in complex open systems, their temporal structure, and the scope of the possibilities open to them provide reasonable grounds for assuming that they possess a subjectivity of their own which is not objectifiable by the human subject. This means that knowledge through domination must be replaced by communicative knowledge: knowledge itself becomes a cognitive living relationship. The 'object' becomes the recipient and the sender of information, reacts as its own kind of subject, and is perceived as such. But in this model for overcoming the estrangement of nature, the human being remains for nature itself the great and central subject.

The other direction which an ecological theory can take, aims at the naturalization of the human being.[68] It assumes that, fundamentally speaking, the human being does not *confront* nature: he himself is nothing other than one of nature's products. Nature is the great subject which unremittingly brings forth new forms and manifestations of life, last of all the human being. The human being is therefore the object, since he is the product of productive nature. This is not merely true for the genesis and development of the human species from 'the transitional field "animal to man" '. It applies equally to the rise and development of 'the world of human beings' in modern industrial societies. 'Nature', as the quintessence of all systems of matter and life, has developed its relatively most complex form in the growth of human societies. In human societies, 'nature' has found a relative concentration and a relative centralization, if by nature we mean all those sectors which for human societies make up the ecosystem 'earth'. But this means that in human knowledge of nature, nature really recognizes itself, and that in the human objectification of nature, nature itself becomes objective.[69] According to this model, in the subject-object relationship between human beings and nature the subject is really nature itself. If this is accepted, then in those sectors of nature which he can objectify, the human subject must accept the fundamental subjectivity of nature; and he must continually fit his own world into the over-riding cohesions of nature and its evolution.

In this sense, it is important for the way the human being understands himself that he should not see himself initially as subject over against nature, and theologically as the image of God; but that he should first of all view himself as the product of nature and – theologically too – as *imago mundi*.[70]

This then gives rise to a different concept of natural experience as well. It is not we who '*have* experiences', or 'experience' something. Experiences happen to us. We receive impressions, and register them, and take them in. They crystallize into our perception. Out of perceptions we go on to build up concepts, with which we order and identify the flux of happening. There are several starting-points for this reversal of the modern, subjectivistic concept of the human being, which is so hostile to nature. Let me here point merely to two German philosophical anthropologies.

In his influential treatise on *Die Stellung des Menschen im Kosmos* Max Scheler lays great stress on the special position of the human being. But he does at least ask: 'Is it not as if there were a ladder on which some primordial being, in building the world, continually turns back on himself, so that on ever higher steps and in ever higher dimensions, he pauses and reflects, in order finally in the human being to possess and understand himself fully?'[71]

The conceptual figure of 'eccentric positionality' which Helmut Plessner has introduced into modern philosophical anthropology points in the same direction. The human being exists in himself, and yet confronts himself at the same time. He always experiences himself simultaneously in the mode of being and in the mode of having. He is not fully absorbed by either of them: 'He neither *is* solely body nor *has* he solely a body. Every demand made by physical existence requires a balance between being and having, the outward and the inward.'[72]

In the modern world of human beings, science and technology has continually extended the 'having' of nature. Modern medicine has achieved its successes in the sector which might be described as the human being's 'having a body'. At the same time, the human being *is* nature, and the body which he has objectified into his property *is* also he himself, in his bodily existence. Localizing the world of human beings once more in the history of nature, and rediscovering nature in the 'being' body, are not romantic flights from the responsibility which has devolved on modern men and women through the power which they have acquired. These things mean discovering dimensions of life which have been suppressed and repressed, and in their light overcoming the inhumanity and unnaturalness of the modern world.

The 'being nature' of the human being is the primary given fact. His domination of nature and his possession of nature are secondary. They remain dependent on the primary fact, because it is this on which they build and from which they live.

III

The Knowledge of Creation

Having described the dimensions of a Christian doctrine of creation in the ecological crisis of the present day, we must now go on to investigate its special theological basis. Where can we find the foundation for knowledge of the world as God's creation? With what objective theological right is nature (*physis*) seen and treated as creation (*ktisis*)? Under what subjective conditions is the world in its present condition experienced as creation? Does nature actually disclose itself as God's creation? Or is it only experienced as creation in the light of the self-revelation of the creative God?

Every natural theology proceeds from the self-evidence of nature as God's creation. On the other hand, every theology of nature interprets nature in the light of the self-revelation of the creative God. So what is the relation between natural theology and the theology of nature? By asking this question we are turning the traditional interest in natural theology upside down: the aim of our investigation is not what nature can contribute to our knowledge of God, but what the concept of God contributes to our knowledge of nature. By reversing the question put to the natural theology in this way, we are also compelled to define revealed theology differently, where this has a bearing on nature.

§1 COVENANT, CREATION AND THE KINGDOM OF GOD

For a *biblical* doctrine of creation we have to draw on the whole testimony of Scripture, not merely on Genesis 1 and 2. By 'biblical', we mean here Jewish and Christian, not fundamentalist. The starting point for a *Christian* doctrine of creation can only be an interpretation of the biblical creation narratives in the light of the gospel of Christ. This means that a Christian doctrine of creation cannot be biblicist.

In the biblical traditions of the Old and New Testaments, experience of the world as creation is determined by belief in the revelation of the creative God in Israel's history.[1] The world does not disclose itself as God's creation just by itself. It is only because he reveals himself as its creator, preserver and saviour that God manifests the world as his creation. It was only on the strength of this revelation that Israel came to experience the world as creation and to deal with it accordingly, in the way reflected in the Wisdom literature. Israel learnt to understand the world as God's good creation in the light of the saving events of the exodus, the covenant and the settlement in the Promised Land. But of course the genus 'natural theology' was unknown to Israel. It derives from Greek philosophy.[2]

The *special* experience of God which emerged from 'God the Lord's' revelation of himself moulded and interpreted Israel's *general* experience of the world. Saving events and the experience of creation have a double relationship to one another. On the one hand, the experience of creation shows that the God of the covenant with Israel is the Lord and Creator of the whole world; so it reveals the universality of the one, sole God. On the other hand, this in its turn means that the whole universe, all human beings and all nations enter into the redeeming light of the salvation which Israel has experienced and for which Israel hopes. Creation is the universal horizon of Israel's special experience of God in history. This horizon embraces on the one hand 'creation in the beginning' and, on the other, 'the creation of the End-time'. It takes its definition from the creation of the heavens and the earth 'in the beginning' (Gen. 1.1), and from the creation of 'the new heavens and the new earth' (Isa. 65.17) at the end. But this means that Israel did not merely develop a *protological* understanding of creation; in the process of so doing it also arrived at an *eschatological* view of creation. Both dimensions are necessarily present in 'the soteriological understanding of creation'.[3] They therefore belong to every biblical theology of nature.

The final syllable of the German word for creation, Schöp*fung*, means the *completed* process of creation, and its result. And when we talk about creation, we think involuntarily about the beginning of all things, and imagine the genesis of the world as a condition which was brought about and completed once and for all. That is why 'creation in the beginning' was also delineated through a wealth of symbols of origin: paradise, the primordial condition, innocence, the Garden of Eden, and the unscathed world. Ever since Thomas Aquinas, the Christian doctrine of creation too, in its theological account, has always expounded 'the six days' work' (*hexaemeron*).[4] It was not sufficiently noticed that the stories about creation in the Priestly Writing and in the Yahwist's account do not as yet present a *Christian* doctrine of creation,[5] for the messianic orientation is here not yet overtly present. The specifically Christian revelation of God was therefore only discussed under the doctrine of redemption. But this is one-sided, in a number of different ways. One cannot simply detach the Israelite belief in creation from Israel's own particular experience of salvation, and assign it instead to the experience of salvation which is specifically Christian, without thereby changing and reinterpreting it. But one cannot, either, reduce belief in creation to a certain view about the origin of the world without marring it fundamentally.

The different biblical traditions talk about God's creation in the perspective of the beginning of time, in the perspective of historical time, and in the perspective of eschatological time. So if 'creation' is to be the quintessence of the whole divine creative activity, the corresponding doctrine of creation must then embrace creation in the beginning, creation in history, and the creation of the End-time: *creatio originalis – creatio continua – creatio nova*. 'Creation' is the term for God's initial creation, his historical creation, and his perfected creation. The idea of God's unity is preserved only through the concept of creation as a meaningfully coherent process. This process acquires its significance from its eschatological goal. The symbols 'the kingdom of God', 'eternal life' and 'glory' are ways of describing this eschatological goal of God's creation. It is not the historical covenant which is already 'the inner ground of creation', as Karl Barth maintained: this is true only of the kingdom of glory; for this eternal kingdom is the inner ground of the historical covenant as well.[6]

Creation in the beginning points beyond itself to the history of promise given with Abraham, Isaac and Jacob. This history of promise points to the messianic history of the gospel of Christ, and both point to the coming kingdom which will renew heaven and earth, filling everything with the divine radiance. In this process of creation, which is consistently and coherently aligned towards the kingdom of God, we can none the less (in accordance with the different conditions of being and time) distinguish between creation in the beginning, the creations of history, and the eschatological new creation.

If we keep in view the goal of creation's history, we can discern in the created world the real promises of the kingdom of glory. The present world is a real symbol of its future. By virtue of its self-transcendence, all created things point beyond themselves. Because of its non-identity, created beings are open for their future truth. We therefore perceive that creation is aligned towards history, but that, all the same, its ultimate meaning is not that it provides a theatre for God's history with men and women; for the ultimate meaning of history itself is to be found in the new, consummated creation. Creation in the beginning is therefore certainly open for salvation history; but salvation history, for its part, exists for the sake of the new creation. Consequently even creation in the beginning already points beyond salvation history towards its own perfected completion in the kingdom of glory. In this respect history is not the framework of creation; creation is the framework of history. This sets limits to the 'historization of the world'.[7] Creation is more than merely a stage for God's history with men and women. The goal of this history is the consummation of creation in its glorification.

At this juncture let us establish the following points:

1. Knowledge of the world as divine creation is made possible through the historical revelation of God the Lord. It does not emerge from the mere observation of the world in itself.

2. Through knowledge of the world as creation, the revelation of God the Lord becomes universal.

3. If it is understood as God's creation, the universe is caught up into the history of God's rule. Creation in the beginning prepares for this history, and the history itself is consummated in the new creation in the kingdom of God.

4. But in what situation is creation, if it is perceived historically in this way? This is the central question of a theology of nature. We are replying with the thesis: the time of the Christian perception of creation is the time of Jesus the Messiah. Under the presupposition of faith in Jesus the Christ, the world is revealed in the messianic light as a creation that is both in bondage, and open for the future.

§2 'NATURAL THEOLOGY'

The expression *theologia naturalis* is taken from Stoic philosophy.[8] The *genus physikon* meant the doctrine about the forces of nature, which were conceived of as persons. In Roman Stoicism too, *theologia naturalis* was the term used for knowledge about the essence of things, not for a theology of empirically experienceable nature. It was only when it was taken over by Christian theologians that the concept of nature was altered. It now meant the reality which was theologically termed 'creation'. *Natura* was no longer understood as the eternal essence of experienceable things, but as their finite, dependent and contingent reality. What kind of knowledge of God (*theologia*) does this understanding of nature presuppose?

Theological traditions talk about a twofold knowledge of God: the knowledge derived from creation, and the knowledge derived from Scripture.[9] God is only imperfectly knowable 'by the light of nature', or 'from the book of nature'. All knowledge confers community or fellowship; but the natural knowledge of God, being imperfect, does not lead to perfect fellowship with him. This natural knowledge of God consists of an *innate* knowledge (*notitia insita*), which is to be found in every human being in the inner testimony of the conscience, and an *acquired* knowledge, derived from knowledge of nature (*notitia acquisita*). The first is direct knowledge of God; the second is mediated knowledge, but generally accessible. Both are imperfect revelations of the God manifested in nature, and in the light of nature. Both lack final validity in the perspective of the supernatural mystery of faith. Natural knowledge of God certainly confers wisdom, but it does not confer salvation and blessedness. The knowledge of God that confers blessedness comes solely from the 'supernatural' revelation of God in Jesus Christ, because it is this which leads to perfect fellowship with God.

The place given theologically to *theologia naturalis* has always been determined by salvation history: the natural knowledge of God which is now given and possible is a 'remainder' left over from the knowledge of God that existed in paradise. In the unmarred pristine condition of the world, there was a direct, general and perfect knowledge of God. But under the conditions of human sin and corrupted nature, this now only exists in rudimentary form. The *theologia naturalis* that is accessible in the history of sin and death is a recollection of the primordial knowledge of God.

If natural theology is defined in this way, what function does it have in the framework of Christian theology?

The relationship between natural and revealed theology has been defined in many different ways in theological history. Natural theology was the preparation for revealed theology; or its confirmation; or its goal; or its substitute; or its rival; or its enemy. We shall pick out three functions here, and exclude the other possibilities.

1. *An educative function:* it makes people ask where the revelation of the true God is to be found. In this sense, according to Thomas Aquinas, it belongs among the *praeambula ad articulos fidei.*

2. *A hermeneutical function:* it helps people to understand what they believe. In this sense it belongs to the *intellectus fidei.* It is not a proof of faith, but it makes faith comprehensible. It presents the universal claim which is bound up with the word 'God'.[10]

Whether natural theology is used as a preparation for faith, or in order to give a comprehensible account of faith, in both cases it is Christian belief that defines what it presupposes is natural, direct and general knowledge of God.[11] But for the Christian faith, natural knowledge of God has another, completely different meaning namely

3. *An eschatological function.* If natural theology is a 'remainder' left over from the paradisal knowledge of God, it is then at the same time an anticipation of knowledge of God in glory.

Christian knowledge of God is not in itself direct. It is mediated through Christ, through word and sacrament. Nor is Christian knowledge of God general. It is limited to the open circle of the proclamation and of believers. Christian knowledge of God is knowledge of God in parable. But for that very reason, this knowledge thrusts forward from faith in the word in parable, to the seeing of God face to face (I Cor. 13.12) – that is to say, from mediation to the unmediated, and hence also from particularity to universality. On this path of hope, recollections of the beginning stir and wake, so that through the anticipation of direct knowledge of God in the Spirit, the 'remnants' of the direct knowledge of God left over from paradise are also apprehended and absorbed.[12] The reality of the world that can be experienced conceals and shelters within itself traces of creation-in-the-beginning. These traces are at the same time a reflection of the coming glory. All knowledge of the world 'as' creation is hence a metaphorical knowledge of this world as parable of the world to come. In this function, natural knowledge of God belongs to pneumatology: 'the light of nature' is a pre-reflection of the light of glory.[13] Nature does not shine of itself; it reflects the light of future glory. This pre-reflection has the character of the messianic light which makes the present world manifest in its neediness, and alive in its yearning for liberty, and allows it to be perceived as true and real parable and promise of the kingdom.

The distinction between 'natural theology' and 'revealed theology' is misleading. There are not two different theologies. There is only one, because God is one. But this one single theology exists in varying circumstances and temporal conditions. These circumstances and temporal conditions are determined by the particular *modus praesentiae Dei*.

Theologia naturalis is the one, single theology under the conditions of the *regnum naturae*. In its pure form, nature is creation-in-the-beginning. So pure *theologia naturalis* is theology under the conditions of the pristine creation, and of the human being as the pure image of God – in paradise, to put it symbolically. In history we talk about 'nature', as distinct from creation, in order to include the conditions of sin and corruption; and we talk about 'nature', as distinct from sin, in order to include its creaturely aspect.[14] So nature means the reality of that world which is no longer God's good creation and is not yet God's kingdom.

Theologia revelata is the one, single theology in the *regnum gratiae*. It presupposes the self-revelation of God in the history which is determined by human sin and death. Consequently the full concentration and expression of this theology is the *theologia crucis*: in the cross of Christ God reveals himself to the godless. Here knowledge of God and the event of the justification of the godless coincide. Because grace presupposes creation, and points beyond itself to glory, theology in the *regnum gratiae* is historical theology – *theologia messianica* or, as it used to be called, *theologia viatorum*.

Theologia gloriae, finally, is the one single theology in the *regnum gloriae*. It subsists in the enraptured gaze upon the unveiled glory of God, face to face. This presupposes judgment, and the radical new creation of the created being; for otherwise no one can 'look upon God' and live. This is direct knowledge of God, without the mediation of images and parables. It is a universal fellowship with God which knows no limits, but embraces all human beings and, in its own way, the whole universe: 'the whole earth is full of his glory' (Isa. 6.3).

If what we are considering is a single theology under the different conditions of being and time which we have described, then it is obvious that the second form of theology in each given case absorbs the preceding one. Theology in the kingdom of glory fulfils the promises and beginnings of natural and historical theology. But it also means that the theology which is possible at any given time is *the whole of theology*. Revealed theology is natural theology in the conditions of history, just as theology in paradise was revealed theology in the conditions of the pristine creation. The theology of glory is then true natural theology and perfected revealed theology in the condition of a consummated creation and history.

We have defined the theology which is given and possible at the present time as revealed theology; and we have called revealed theology, in the Christian sense, messianic theology. Messianic theology is theology under the presupposition of the presence of the Messiah and the beginning of the messianic era. On this presupposition, the messianic understanding of the world is the true natural theology. In the messianic light, all earthly things and all living beings can be discerned in their forfeiture to transience and in their hope for liberation to eternity. In Romans 8.19ff., Paul presented especially clearly this perception of the world as creation in the messianic light; and it is from this perception of creation in the present era of the world that the Christian doctrine of creation will have to proceed.

§3 THE WORLD AS PROMISE AND ANTICIPATION

The first possible way of understanding creation in our present era in the light of its redeeming and glorifying future is to interpret the world as a parable. When Karl Barth developed his ideas about the world's capacity for being a parable of the kingdom of heaven, and its need to be just such a parable,[15] he was taking up the concern of natural theology, though not its methods or its modern claim. In Jesus' parables in the New Testament Barth found 'as it were the prototype of the order in which there can also be other true words alongside the *one* Word of God, created and determined by it, exactly corresponding to it, and therefore enjoying its power and authority.'[16] These parables pick up everyday worldly experiences and turn them into signs and present realizations of 'the kingdom of heaven'.[17] The experiences become pointers to something different. The kingdom of heaven is hidden in the parable of everyday experience and, as parable, becomes a present realization. It is communicated in an indirect way. Religious, cultural and political experience are not the only sectors which are capable of acting as parable; the same may be said of the experience of nature. Here Barth uses a theatrical metaphor: the drama is the history of Christ, which reveals God and reconciles the world; 'the theatre and setting, the location and background', are provided by the world of created things, which is different from God, but which God brings into being.[18] Barth picks up Calvin's metaphor about the world as *theatrum gloriae Dei*, distinguishing sharply between the stage of creation and the divine drama of salvation. To the cosmic stage Barth ascribes only the characteristics of constancy, of rotation and of persistence. In these attributes creation is designed to correspond to the faithfulness of its Creator.[19] But the drama of salvation has a different character – the character of something unexpectedly new, which comes from outside. It is the light of revelation which makes the footlights on the stage of the world light up; for the world of created things is 'only' the theatre, 'only' the space in which God's own glory shines forth in the work of reconciliation.[20] The creaturely lights and truths point to the one light from which they derive, and to the one truth to which they correspond. They are the lights and truths of the *theatrum gloria Dei*, and it is there alone that their meaning and the justification for their existence are to be found.

Here the world as parable means its correspondence to the kingdom of heaven, which it does not *per se* resemble at all. It means a similarity in unmistakable dissimilarity. The difference between the thing compared and the image is not the difference in creation between heaven and earth; it is the difference between the Creator himself and his creation. The analogy only comes into being at all in the Creator's condescending descent into his creation, and in the approach of the kingdom of heaven to the world of everyday experience which we find demonstrated in the parables of the incarnate Son of God. Here we can find a critical affirmation of the lights and truths of this world by the light and the truth of God himself.

Barth certainly tries to 'see together' things that are in fact incomparable: the *gloria Dei* and the *theatrum mundi*; the eternal light and the little created lights. But this is only possible if (to keep the stage metaphor) the theatre itself is part of the play that is being performed. It is impossible if the theatre is declared to be merely the 'setting and background' for the drama. But in the theological context, the theatre and the play are one and the same, because the drama of salvation is only played out once – once and for all. In this theatre no other dramas are conceivable for which creation could also be 'the setting and background'.[21]

Barth stressed the distinction so strongly, first because in thinking of 'the creaturely world', he had in mind only creation in the beginning and its preservation, not the continuing and contingent history of creation; and because, secondly, he extols 'the revelation of reconciliation' as being already 'the triumph of . . . glory'.[22]

But what the New Testament parables of the kingdom of God demonstrate is the hidden *presence of the future* of the coming kingdom. They are to be interpreted eschatologically, as historical parables of the future world, not ontologically, as earthly parables of heavenly glory.[23] The world as creation can be and has to be a parable of its own future, the kingdom of God; but it is not a parable of God himself. It is only in the kingdom of glory that the world will become God's image and likeness, because it will become his own dwelling. In parables, the eschatological future of the kingdom creates for itself provisional designs, preparations and attempts, in the midst of the experiences of this world. Barth does not give enough emphasis to this idea of creation as a sketch or design for the kingdom of God. His parable theory bridges the duality of covenant and creation, but covenant and creation are not themselves in their turn grasped as parables of the coming glory. But then does not everything passing remain merely a parable of what is immortal, so that

> 'Earth
> [Is] but the shadow of heaven, and things therein
> Each to other like'?[24]

If we understand the parable as the hidden presence of a qualitatively new, redeeming future in the everyday experiences of this world, then the parable becomes the promise.[25] The parables are then anticipations of what is promised in the indadequate field of experience of this present time. What the kingdom of God itself is, certainly exceeds the boundaries of experience in the time of this world and our own comprehension. But it is like 'a man who went out . . .' and like 'a woman who has ten silver coins and loses one . . .' The future of the kingdom which is made present in the parable bursts apart everyday experience and through this 'alienation effect' shocks us into a new awareness.

If we transfer this understanding of the parable to the experience of the natural world, we still experience individual things as they appear to us, but they then appear to us in the pre-reflection of their own true future. This is not due to our own ideas and hopes. It is a result of their real self-differentiation and their objective capacity for anticipation. Material structures and complex systems of life have scope for possibility, and in that context are capable of anticipation – and are also actually in need of anticipation, where communication with other living things is concerned. Constancy, persistence and rotation were the characteristics that struck Barth about nature. But this is a one-sided impression. If all systems of life have a temporal structure, then they are all – each in its own way – open to the future. It is this temporal structure that gives them their character as pointers. It is therefore realistic to talk about 'genuine cyphers' of the world.

It is theologically necessary to view created things as real promises of the kingdom; and it is equally necessary, conversely, to understand the kingdom of God as the fulfilment, not merely of the historical promises of the world, but of its natural promises as well.[26] There is more than merely a parable here. A parable points to something different, and presents the other thing by way of 'the pointer', the image. But a promise points towards its own fulfilment and anticipates a future still to come. The promise is caught up and absorbed in its fulfilment: when what has been promised is realized, the promise is discarded. If the world as creation is the real promise of the kingdom of God, it then itself belongs to the history of the kingdom and is not merely its 'stage and backcloth'; for at the end of this history it is destined to be revealed in its eternal transfiguration.

In this connection it is also useful to take up again the ancient theological doctrine of the *vestigia Dei*. Anyone who understands nature as God's creation sees in nature, not merely God's 'works', but also 'traces of God', ciphers and hidden tokens of his presence. 'God's signature is on the whole of nature. All creatures are love letters from God to us.'[27] Nature is not the revelation of God. Nor is it God's image. But it shows 'traces of God' everywhere, if we are able to perceive in it a mirror and reflection of God's beauty. The key to the interpretation of this world of divine cyphers has always been thought to lie in the revelation of God; for only the person who knows God because God reveals himself to him is capable of recognizing and interpreting the traces of God in nature. Consequently the doctrine of the *vestigia Dei* has to be further developed in two different ways: (*a*) since God reveals himself in a trinitarian sense, as the triune God, the *vestigia Dei* in nature are *vestigia trinitatis*; (*b*) since God reveals himself as the God who promises the coming kingdom of glory, the *vestigia Dei* in nature are *vestigia regni Dei*. They are the traces of the creative Spirit by whom the coming kingdom of glory is prepared. We shall therefore be able to interpret the world of nature as bearing the prints of the triune God and as being the real promise of the coming kingdom.

The interpretation of natural experience as an anticipation of the future widens out in the history of promise. As long as nature and human history represent promises of future glory, without as yet being that future glory itself, all knowledge of God and the world is parabolic, figurative knowledge. But then how are we to conceive of knowledge of God and the world in the kingdom of glory? The idea that comes to mind is at first surprising: a divine existence will appear in the world which can no longer be expressed in images, and is no longer in need of image. Images make present what is absent. When what was absent is present, the image is no longer necessary; it is even detrimental. In the kingdom of glory, the Old Testament commandment 'You need not make for yourself an image, or any likeness . . .' (Exod. 20.4–6) will find universal fulfilment. According to kabbalistic tradition, the messianic world will be a world without pictures and parables.[28] The parable and the thing compared will no longer be distinguished from one another, and no longer related to one another, because God will be directly and universally manifest through himself, and creation with all created things will participate directly and without any mediation in his eternal life. The Creator's distance from those he has created will be ended through his own indwelling in his creation; though the difference between Creator and creature will not disappear. The difference between faith and experience will be overcome in the contemplation of glory. 'When that which is perfect is come, then that which is in part shall be done away' (I Cor. 13.10, AV). Knowing and perceiving in parables are, in the Pauline sense, knowledge 'in part'. Prophecies and promises are also 'in part'. When distances in space and time end, this also means an end of the world which we can only lay hold of through its 'double', in the form of symbols, metaphors and the concepts of the imagination. The double itself then disappears. What will also pass away is theology, which – on the basis of the divine revelation – reduces God to language in the inadequate material of this world, which is imprisoned in futility. In the *theologia patriae* the *theologia viatorum* will be fulfilled and laid aside. In the song of praise in the eternal home country 'the Lord's song in a foreign land' (Ps. 137.4) dies away – the song which still echoes with the rough tones and the bitter cry of exile. The kingdom of glory, which fulfils all promises and hopes, will shine forth in a light which has never hitherto issued from its source, says Jewish messianism. According to the Christian faith, it is this light which we see pre-reflected and mirrored in the light of God's reconciliation with the world in Jesus, the Messiah.

§4 MESSIANIC KNOWLEDGE OF THE WORLD

At first sight, the New Testament does not seem to add anything new to the understanding of the world as creation. Jesus and the apostles presupposed the Old Testament and contemporary Jewish belief in creation as a matter of course. The gospel of the kingdom of God which they proclaimed made no difference to this. Paul too has seldom anything to say about this subject. So the New Testament is not supposed to have paid any particular attention to questions about the *dominium terrae* and human dealings with nature either.[29] But this impression is deceptive. It only arises if we understand by 'creation' a myth about origins, and therefore look at the wrong passages. The New Testament testimony about creation is to be found in *the resurrection kerygma* and in *the experience of the Holy Spirit*, who is the energy of the new creation. Eschatological christology and pneumatology does in fact involve a fundamentally new interpretation of the divine creative activity. It is not the protological creation of the world that is presented here. It is the eschatological creation, as might be expected of testimonies belonging to the messianic era. God's eschatological creation is put into language through the groups of words ἐγείρειν (raise), ζωοποιοῦν (make alive) and καλεῖν (call to life).

In Romans 4.17, Paul calls Abraham the father of faith, because he believed the God 'who gives life to the dead and calls into existence the things that do not exist'.[30] The faith in the promise which alone justifies, is put on the same level as creation out of nothing and the raising of the dead; for the God of the promise is the Creator of all things and the One by whom the dead are raised. Just as Deutero-Isaiah sees the miracle of the Red Sea and the miracle of creation in a single vista, so in this passage Paul gathers into one perspective the justification of the sinner, the raising of the dead, and creation out of nothing. The beginning of the world and its consummation are both inherent in the present experience of justification. The experience of justification is the subjective approach to the objective process of the new creation of the world, which will make it the kingdom of the eternal God.

For Paul, the raising of the crucified Jesus is the beginning of the End-time process of the raising of the dead, and with that the new creation of the world. Out of the perfect tense of Jesus' resurrection, he justifies the future of this hope (Rom. 8.11; I Cor. 6.14; II Cor. 4.14, and frequently). If eternal life has appeared in the raising of Jesus, then this living energy is manifested in the presence of his Spirit. Mortal bodies will finally be made to live when the resurrection life overcomes, not merely sin, but death as well. In I Cor. 15.20–24, Paul sees this process in a particular temporal order: first of all Christ; then – at his coming – those who belong to Christ; and then the end. He uses the words ἀπαρχή and ἀρραβών to describe this process as a process of successive anticipations, where in each given case the parts stand for the whole, as beginnings pointing towards the completion. Because eschatological creation proceeds from the process of the resurrection and the creation of life, in the New Testament the Creator God is given the new messianic name of ὁ ἐγείρας Ἰησοῦν, the Father of Jesus Christ, the God who raises the dead, the God of hope (Rom. 15.13). Faith in the resurrection is therefore the Christian form of belief in creation. It is belief in creation under the conditions of this life, which is subject to death.

But faith in the resurrection is not merely belief in the raising of Christ; it is itself creative liberty and a rising up in the Spirit.[31] In II Cor. 4.6, Paul sees the enlightenment of faith through knowledge of Christ in the same, single perspective as creation in the beginning:

the person who believes will be irradiated by the light of the new creation. He stands in the sunrise of the new day of creation. He participates in the new creation. Paul develops this idea in the doctrine of the charismata of the Holy Spirit (I Cor. 12; I Cor. 14; Rom. 12.3ff.). The Holy Spirit is the power of the resurrection. The power of the resurrection is the life-giving Spirit. It is *ruach*, the creative power of God, through which God communicates his energies to his creation. That is why Paul presents the community of the risen Jesus as the place where the Spirit is manifested (Eph. 1.19f.; Eph. 4). The gifts of the Spirit are the energies of the new eternal life. It is in these that the grace of God takes on specific form. Through them men and women, with all their powers and potentialities, are committed for the kingdom of God. The reception, the ministry and the spread of the living energies of the creative Spirit belong within the universal context of the End-time. In the last days 'I will pour out my spirit on all flesh' (Joel 2.28). The bodily character of the gifts of the Spirit is always emphasized, because it is in the new bodily obedience that they are experienced. But if the vital energies of the Spirit are experienced in bodily terms, this is the foundation for the hope for 'the redemption of the body' from death to that embodiment of eternal life which is described as 'the spiritual body' (σῶμα πνευματικόν). The process of the new creation of the world through the power of the eternal life which overcomes death, is not merely universally directed towards the whole breadth of creation; it is also aligned towards the depths of the human being's real bodily existence, which it pervades.

This is brought out by Paul in Romans 8.19ff. in the connection he makes between the believer's experience of unredeemed bodily nature, his recognition of the whole enslaved creation, and the listening to the sighs of the Spirit.[32] He starts from the hope for the glory 'that is to be revealed to us'. But it is this very hope which makes us conscious of 'the sufferings of this present time'. That is the double effect of hope. That is why according to Paul 'we have' the first fruits of the Spirit and yet 'wait' for the redemption of the body. That is why 'we are' children of God and call God, 'Abba, beloved Father', and yet 'long' for our 'adoption' as children, and do not know what we should pray for. The point where the liberty of the children of God has come so close that we revive in hope is the very point where we become painfully aware of the chains of bondage. This inner dialectic brings believers into profound solidarity with the whole enslaved creation. Paul describes this in three concentric circles:

1. The children of God, who *have already* been seized by the first energies of the Spirit, long for liberty. They are saved, but as yet only in hope. So their faith is simultaneously assurance and pain.

2. They long for the redemption of the body. They are already freed from 'the body of sin', but because of that they suffer all the more under 'the body of death' from which they have not yet been released. 'Who will deliver me from this body of death?' sighs the person who has been liberated from the power of sin and who has been justified through grace (Rom. 7.24).

3. In physical terms, believers are bound together in a common destiny with the whole world and all earthly creatures. So what they experience in their own body applies to all other created things. The unredeemed character of the body which believers sense in themselves corresponds to the tragedy of non-human creation, which is subject to futility. Nature has fallen victim to transience and death. It has not fallen through its own sin, like human beings. To talk about 'a fallen nature' is therefore highly dubious. And yet a sadness lies over nature which is the expression of its tragic fate and its messianic yearning.[33] It is enslaved and wishes to be free, for it is transitory and wishes for 'an abiding habitation'.

The transitoriness of earthly things is the general experience of this world. It has been metaphysically interpreted again and again. But Paul's interpretation is not metaphysical; it is messianic. The creature is subject to transience, but for the sake of the one who has subjected it, and on the strength of hope (Rom. 8.20). The coming kingdom of God is destined to be the kingdom of freedom for those who believe; and through their perfected liberty non-human creation is destined to be free also. The liberty which believers lay hold of in germ through the Spirit is not an exclusive liberty from created being and from the body. It is an inclusive liberty, for these things too. 'Their very faith makes them one with unredeemed creation, in so far as faith is in its very nature hope and therefore a looking for the redemption of the body.'[34] Creation in the beginning started with nature and ended with the human being. The eschatological creation reverses this order: it starts with the liberation of the human being and ends with the redemption of nature. Its history is the mirror-image of the protological order of creation. Consequently the enslaved creation does not wait for the appearance of Christ in glory in the direct sense; it waits for the revelation of the liberty of the children of God in Christ's appearance. Creation is to be redeemed through human liberty.

Finally, the Spirit of God himself represents believers and creation in their sighs for liberty through his 'sighs too deep for words' (Rom. 8.26). The dumb sighs of nature and the uttered cry of human beings for liberty are gathered up by the Spirit into his own sighing. In the bondage of creation, in the pains of the body and in the yearning of believers, the Spirit is co-imprisoned and co-suffering, and keeps the waiting and the hoping alive through his own wordless and inexpressible sighs. We can surely understand this as meaning that God the Creator, who has entered into his creation through his Spirit, himself holds created being in life (Ps. 104. 30), and therefore also suffers with its sufferings. The messianic era does not merely bring an *outpouring* of the gifts of the Spirit on men and women. It also *awakens* the Spirit itself in the whole enslaved creation.

The messianic knowledge of the world starts from the expressed hope of faith in the raised Christ and sees a correspondence to this in the sadness and longing for liberty of imprisoned creation. Because in human beings faith brings liberation from the closed-in isolation which is sin, in nature too the isolation of the life systems can be seen as their 'bondage' to transience, and 'openness' is recognizably their living character. The human being who is closed in upon himself finds his correspondence in the nature that is sealed off and therefore dies. The person who has been opened up for a new hope for life finds his correspondence in the nature which has been thrown open for its own future. In human beings this new orientation is to be apprehended in hope; in nature it can be identified as unrest, as a drive and thrust towards higher complexity and a more prodigal fullness of life. Human beings and nature have their own destinies on their own particular levels; but in their enslavement and their liberty they share a common history.

§5 THE EUCHARISTIC COMMUNITY OF CREATION

True knowing does not desire to dominate what is known in order to possess it. It wants to arrive at community with the object of its knowledge. True knowing is communicative knowing. It extends as far as the love which respects the independence of others, and loves them in their very difference, for their own sake. The highest form of communicative knowing is loving union (Gen. 4.1).

Communicative knowing is bound up with joy in existence and with the expression of an exulting gratitude for the community experienced. The process of knowledge is consciously realized when it itself finds expression in spontaneous joy and explicit delight. In the shared expression of the knowing and the giving-oneself-to-be-known, a third dimension is arrived at. And where this is accomplished, the result is not merely an *esse* but a *bene esse*.

In perceiving the world as creation, the human being discerns and enters into a community of creation. This community becomes a dialogue before the common Creator. Knowledge of the world as creation is in its primal form thanksgiving for the gift of creation and for the community found in it, and adoring praise of the Creator. The 'creation' psalms in the Old Testament (Pss. 8, 19, 104, etc.) are hymns of gratitude and praise to the Creator. They have a eucharistic character. That is a form-critical comment, but it is by no means intended to relegate the recognition of the world as creation to the realm of religious poetry. The purpose is to draw attention to the fact that gratitude and praise are the appropriate and irrelinquishable elements in the communicative knowledge of creation. Perceiving the world as creation is not 'a matter of opinion' – an intellectual tenet. It implies a particular attitude towards the world and a way of dealing with it which touches the existence of the perceiving person and draws him into a wider fellowship. Perception of the world as creation confers felicity in existence. Offering the world to God in thanksgiving confers freedom in existence.

There are very many and very various definitions of the essential character of the human being. In the present context we may define him by saying that he is destined to be the eucharistic being.[35] To express the experience of creation in thanksgiving and praise is his designation from the very beginning, and it is also the content of his life in its consummated form. The human being does not merely live in the world like other living things. He does not merely dominate the world and use it. He is also able to discern the world in full awareness as God's creation, to understand it as a sacrament of God's hidden presence, and to apprehend it as a communication of God's fellowship. That is why the human being is able consciously to accept creation in thanksgiving, and consciously to bring creation before God again in praise.

Early sacrificial cults in human history show an awareness that this world is the property of the gods, not of men and women. That is why the first-fruits were sacrificed to the gods – often even the first-born child. In the biblical traditions these sacrificial cults were increasingly replaced by thanksgiving. But these acts of thanksgiving still expressed the awareness that the world is God's creation and his gift. The person who thanks, lays the given and accepted gift before the giver.

As God's gifts, all his creatures are fundamentally eucharistic beings also; but the human being is able – and designated – to express the praise of all created things before God. In his own praise he acts as representative for the whole of creation. His thanksgiving, as it were, looses the dumb tongue of nature. It is here that the priestly dimension of his designation is to be found. So when in the 'creation' psalms thanks are offered *for* the sun and the light, *for* the heavens and the fertility of the earth, the human being is thanking God, not merely on his own behalf, but also in the name of heaven and earth and all created beings in them. Through human beings the sun and moon also glorify the Creator. Through human beings plants and animals adore the Creator too. That is why in the praise of creation the human being sings the cosmic liturgy, and through him the cosmos sings before its Creator the eternal song of creation. This is not meant anthropocentrically; for in the community of creation 'everything that has breath' praises the Lord, and 'the heavens declare the glory of God' even without human beings – indeed as the representatives of human beings too, in their own way. The monastic traditions of the Orthodox church and the Hasidic traditions of Judaism have preserved these splendid concepts. Today they must be rediscovered and translated into the practical dealings of human beings with created nature. They are well suited to overcome the one-sided and impoverished attitudes of people living in the modern industrial world.

IV

God the Creator

Theological doctrines of creation often confine themselves to the question: what does God mean for the world which he creates and sustains, and what does it mean for the world to be God's creation? But before we turn to this cosmological enquiry, I should like to look at the theological question: what does it mean for God to be the Creator of a world which is different from him, and is yet designed to correspond to him? What does this creation mean for God? What is his purpose with it? How does he experience it? How does he participate in it? Let us begin by analysing the actual circumstances of creation, according to the accounts we find in the Old Testament.

§1 'IN THE BEGINNING GOD CREATED THE HEAVENS AND THE EARTH'

The first sentence in the Priestly Writing's creation narrative is the summing up of a long process of reflection by Israel's faith.[1] Because this thinking belonged within the framework of the dispute between belief in Yahweh and the cosmogonies of the religious cults from Egypt to Babylon, this opening sentence reflects a deliberate confrontation. The world, we are told here, is not the result of a struggle between the gods, as the Enuma Elish epic says. Nor was it born from a cosmic egg, or from some primordial matter. To say that God 'created' the world indicates God's self-distinction from that world, and emphasizes that God desired it. This means that the world is not in itself divine; nor is it an emanation from God's eternal being. It is the specific outcome of his decision of will. Since they are the result of God's creative activity, heaven and earth are neither divine nor demonic, neither eternal like God himself, nor meaningless and futile. They are contingent. They are his goodly work in which he has pleasure – no more than that, but no less than that either. They take their reality from their affirmation by their Creator.

In the tradition of the Priestly Writing, the verb *bara'* is used exclusively as a term for the divine bringing forth, for which there is no corresponding human analogy. The word means a bringing forth in the sphere of history, nature and spirit, through which something comes into existence which was not there previously (Exod. 34.10; Num. 16.30; Ps. 51.10; and frequently). *Bara'* is never used with the accusative of a material out of which something is to be made. This shows that the divine creativity has no conditions or premises. Creation is something absolutely new. It is neither actually nor potentially inherent or present in anything else.

The text makes a clear distinction between 'creating' (*bara'*) and 'making' (*'asah*). In Gen. 1.1, the word 'create' is used for creation as a whole. The 'making' begins in v. 2, as it were, and is completed with the sabbath: 'So on the seventh day God finished his work which he had made' (Gen. 2.2). 'Making' is the term for the purposeful 'manufacture' of a work, in which something is given its particular character and aptitude. The divine making of the 'works' of creation finds its analogy in the work of human beings. 'The reason given for the sabbath commandment is that God *made* heaven and earth in six days (Exod. 20.11; 31.17), not that he created them. For only his "making" can be a model for this human work, since it is a forming and producing; but the divine creativity and human activity are not comparable with one another.'[2]

Because God's creative activity has no analogy, it is also unimaginable. The divine act of creation is never described in differentiated terms. Nor is it dissected into a number of different processes. It is unified and unique. This means among other things that time is excluded from the act of creation, for time always requires duration, and creation takes place suddenly, as it were – in a moment. Does this mean that the act of creation is outside time? Is it timeless? And if we call it timeless, is it then eternal like God himself?

How are we supposed to understand the phrase 'in the beginning'? The absolute way it is used suggests that what is meant is the sheer, unqualified precondition for all happening in time, rather than the beginning of time itself. Created time only begins when light and the rhythm of day and night comes into being. All the works which the Creator makes in his creation follow one another consecutively; the phrases 'and God said . . .', 'and God separated . . .' make this evident. Only creation itself cannot have any preceding condition of this kind; it cannot follow on anything else. In its uniqueness it is in every respect 'for the first time'. The beginning has no presuppositions at all.

The later theological interpretation of creation as *creatio ex nihilo* is therefore unquestionably an apt paraphrase of what the Bible means by 'creation'.[3] Wherever and whatever God creates is without any preconditions. There is no external necessity which occasions his creativity, and no inner compulsion which could determine it. Nor is there any primordial matter whose potentiality is pre-given to his creative activity, and which would set him material limits.

The formula *creatio ex nihilo* is an exclusive formula. The word *nihil* is a limit-concept: out of nothing – that is to say out of pure Nothingness. The preposition 'out of' does not point to any pre-given thing; it excludes matter of any kind whatsoever. Actually the phrase is misleading: the preposition 'out of' points the gaze in a direction where there is 'nothing' to be seen, and 'nothing' to be found. The formula is intended to negate the alternative, 'out of something'; so the words 'out of' ought really to be eliminated too. But the formula *ex nihilo* denies only the 'something'. This prompts still other questions. How are we to define this *nihil*, which is supposed to deny and exclude everything that has definition?

The distinction between μὴ ὄν, relative negation of being, and οὐκ ὄν, absolute negation of being (Latin *nihil privativum* and *nihil negativum*) derives from Platonic philosophy.[4] It is impossible ever to define 'nothing' except over against 'being', as being's negation, non-being; for 'nothing' has no substance of its own. It demonstrates its nature in the negation of something that is. In time it appears as the no-longer-existing of present being. However, it can also appear in time in the making-possible of something that will be. Not-yet-being can contain the potentiality for being in its becoming. What Ernst Bloch calls 'The ontology of Not-yet-being' is in this sense the complementary counterpart to the Platonic philosophy of No-longer-being. In this ontology, the negative is interpreted as productive.[5] But both interpretations of non-being in time work with the μὴ ὄν concept. Neither of them arrives at the limit-concept of 'Nothingness': 'nothing comes of nothing.'

What is really being denied through the expression 'nothing'? The fundamental ontological question asked by Leibniz and Heidegger was: 'Why is there something at all, rather than nothing?' If we pick up this question, we arrive at the following ambiguity. If the expression 'nothing' is a denial that there is anything at all, then the fundamental question, if it is precise, ought really to be: why is there something at all, rather than not-something? But in Leibniz's question the negation in the 'Nothing' apparently goes beyond the negation of the 'something at all'. What is meant can be the negation of being as a whole – everything, 'everything or nothing'. But the intention can also be to negate absolute Being. Absolute Nothingness would then be a counter term to absolute Being, and could then as such also be understood as a negative delineation of absolute Being. In this case the formula *ex nihilo* would be a shadowy pointer to a *de Deo*. In order to exclude this mystical reversion to pantheism as well, the formula, ever since Augustine, has been: *non de Deo, sed ex nihilo*. We shall have to come back to the mystical interpretations of the *ex nihilo* formula at a later point. At the moment it will be sufficient if we establish that this formula describes the unique meaning of the Old Testament verb for creation, *bara'*. But what does it mean in positive terms?

The world was created neither out of pre-existent matter, nor out of the divine Being itself. It was called into existence by the free will of God: *creatio e libertate Dei*. If it is created through God's free will, and is not an emanation from God's essential nature, then the act of creation must be based on a divine resolve of the will to create. God determines that he will be the Creator of a world, before he calls creation into existence. Creation cannot be conceived of as an emanation from the supreme Being; but neither must it be thought of as 'the work' of an arbitrary, capricious Demiurge. Did God have a choice? Did God throw dice? asked Albert Einstein sceptically, seeing this as calling in question the reasonableness of the world and his confidence in it. This criticism of an arbitrary God is justified. So when we say that God created the world 'out of freedom', we must immediately add 'out of love'.

God's freedom is not the almighty power for which everything is possible. It is love, which means the self-communication of the good. If God creates the world out of freedom, then he creates it out of love.[6] Creation is not a demonstration of his boundless power; it is the communication of his love, which knows neither premises nor preconditions: *creatio ex amore Dei.* In Dante's words,

> From the Creator's love came forth in glory
> the world . . .[7]

In his love God can choose; but he chooses only that which corresponds to his essential goodness, in order to communicate that goodness as his creation and in his creation. God's almighty power is demonstrated only inasmuch as all the operations of that power are determined by his eternal nature itself. God therefore does what for him is axiomatic – what is divine. In doing this he is entirely free, and in this freedom he is entirely himself. This excludes all forms of duresse. But it also does away with any apparent arbitrariness. In his free love God confers his goodness: that is the work of his creation. Out of his free love he conveys and communicates his goodness: that is the work of sustaining his creation. His love is literally ecstatic love: it leads him to go out of himself and to create something which is different from himself but which none the less corresponds to him.[8] The delight with which the Creator celebrates the feast of creation – the sabbath – makes it unequivocally plain that creation was called into being out of the inner love which the eternal God himself *is*.

The event of creation is depicted as creation through the Word: 'And God said "Let there be light"; and there was light' (Gen. 1.3). A series of other acts are named as well: God saw, God separated, God called, God made, God blessed, and others. But at the decisive points God 'makes' his creation through the Word which he utters. The word of creation is the continuum joining the Creator and his creation.[9] The Creator and the creation are united first of all by his command, his injunction, his behest and his decision. If God creates his work through what he says, this again underlines his freedom towards what he has created.

What is called forth is of course in its existence response to the creating word; but it is not linked with that word through causality, or in a 'final', or operative, sense, so that the cause could be deduced from the effect. According to Aristotelian and mediaeval ontology, the cause actually communicates its own being to the effect. To call God 'the cause of the world' (*causa efficiens prima*) is then to imply that there is a graduated participation of all things effected by God in the divine cause that effects them. But there is no ontological link of this kind between the word of creation and created things. There is no *analogia entis* in creation by way of the divine Word that calls into being out of Nothingness. The analogy in which God's creatures 'correspond' to him and give him delight, only comes into being when God blesses what he has created.

The act whereby God introduces order through separation belongs to the event of God's creative utterance. God confers order on his creation by dividing light from darkness, heaven from earth, day from night. Through this separation the works of his creation acquire identifiable form, rhythm and symmetry. This separation is not identical with the divine 'making', but is the concrete form which the making takes. Even less can it be called the divine creative activity; for it is only the result of that activity.

The Priestly Writing again uses the expression 'create' in connection with the creation of human beings (Gen. 1.27); and here it is introduced by a solemn divine proclamation (v.26). The reason for this new creative act on God's part is given as the desire to create God's image on earth. It is not the soul which is the hallmark of human beings, for the animals are 'living souls' as well. What distinguishes human beings is that they are ordained to be the image of God. Whatever this may mean for human beings and their position in creation (and we shall be considering this in detail in the chapter on anthropology), what it means for God is that in creation he does not merely want to recognize his work; he also wants in his work to recognize himself. The creation of God's image on earth means that in his work God finds, as it were, the mirror in which he recognizes his own countenance – a correspondence which resembles him. As God's *work*, creation is not essentially similar to the Creator; it is the expression of his will. But as *image*, men and women correspond to the Creator in their very essence, because in these created beings God corresponds to himself. It is here that the supreme analogy in creation is created. It is an *analogia relationis*. As the image of God on earth, human beings correspond first of all to the relationship of God to themselves and to the whole of creation. But they also correspond to the inner relationships of God to himself – to the eternal, inner love of God which expresses and manifests itself in creation. As God's image, men and women are beings who correspond to God, beings who can give the seeking love of God the sought-for response, and who are intended to do just that. As God's image, men and women are his counterpart in the work of creation. The human being is the Other who resembles God (Ps. 8.5).

We can perceive that this relationship of God's to his image on earth is already more intimate that the *vis-à-vis* relationship of the Creator to the work he has created. In a certain sense God enters into the creatures whom he has designated to be his image. In the context of the messianic traditions about the likeness to God, we can at all events say that the creatures who are destined to be the image of God are also destined for the becoming human of the Son of God; and it is in this that they will find the fulfilment of their designation. The 'image of the invisible God' created in the beginning is destined to be 'the image of the Son of God incarnate'. So the initial designation of human beings is revealed in the messianic light. This means that the very creation of God's image on earth in itself implies an unheard of condescension, self-limitation and humiliation on the part of the God who is without compare.

Having distinguished exegetically between God's 'creating' and his 'making', between his 'creating' and his 'separating', and finally between his work and his image, we must go on to carry these distinctions through systematically as well.

In a modern theology of nature, it is neither wise nor appropriate to reduce the fact of the divine creation to the process of God's separating activity; for to do so calls in question the theological character of this 'theology of nature' itself. But if we call in question the 'theology' in the theology of nature, the natural character of nature is threatened too. A danger of this kind is inherent in the process thinking of A. N. Whitehead, and in the process theology which was built up on his ideas.[10] If the idea of the *creatio ex nihilo* is excluded, or reduced to the formation of a not-yet-actualized primordial matter 'no-thing', then the world process must be just as eternal and without any beginning as God himself. But if it is eternal and without any beginning like God himself, the process must itself be one of God's natures. And in this case we have to talk about 'the divinization of the world'. God and nature are fused into a unified world process, so that the theology of nature becomes a divinization of nature: God is turned into the comprehensive ordering factor in the flux of happening.

> Process theology rejects the notion of *creatio ex nihilo*, if that means creation out of *absolute* nothingness. That doctrine is part

> and parcel of the doctrine of God as absolute controller. Process theology affirms instead a doctrine of creation out of chaos . . . A state of absolute chaos would be one in which there is nothing but very lowgrade actual occasions happening at random, i.e., without being ordered into enduring individuals.[11]

Here God's creativity is quite evidently equated with his dividing and ordering of the flux of happening into 'enduring individuals'. But this means that process theology of this kind has no doctrine of creation. It is conversant only with a doctrine about the preservation and ordering of the world. The correct viewpoints in the processive doctrine of order should not be surrendered; but the creation of heaven and earth must none the less be maintained, if this is to be theology, and is to preserve the fundamental distinction between creation and Creator.

It is not wise or appropriate either to do as Schleiermacher did first of all, and to allow God's creative relationship to the world to be made wholly congruent with, and wholly absorbed by, his relationship as its preserver.[12] For if the creation of the world is reduced to God's general and present rule over that world, the world will once more cease to be a finite creation, and will be turned into a world without a beginning, eternal as God is eternal. Just as there can be no time without eternity, there is then no eternity without time; for there is 'no God without a world, and no world without God'. God's efficacy can then only be conceived of within the world; the world cannot be thought of as within the efficacy of God. But if there is no creation in the beginning, there cannot be a new creation either. The 'new creation' has to be reinterpreted as the moral creation of a new humanity. And if there is no new creation of all things, there is nothing that can withstand the Nothingness that annihilates the world.[13]

§2 GOD'S DETERMINATION OF HIMSELF TO BE CREATOR

If God *creates* heaven and earth, he has then determined that he will be *the Creator* of heaven and earth. Creation is founded on his creative resolve, and his creative resolve touches both God himself and his creation. It is an act of will that is directed both outwards and inwards, whereby the act that is directed inwards objectively precedes the divine act that is turned outwards: before God creates the world he determines that he will be the world's Creator. This self-designation can be seen from the reflexive structure of the existential resolve of will and the personal decision: *God* commits *himself* to create a world.[14]

If creation is viewed under the aspect of a divine resolve of will, God's determination that he will be the Creator of a world could already imply a self-limitation on God's part in favour of this particular one of his innumerable possibilities. The Reformed doctrine of decrees presented creation under the aspect of the creative resolve, and Karl Barth developed this.

Another possibility is to infer the creative God from the creation of heaven and earth. Is a particular resolve on God's part to become Creator then required at all? Surely his divine life is itself eternally creative? Is it in any way possible to conceive of a condition in which God is not creatively active? For his creative activity is simply and exclusively an expression of his own inner life itself. God is not creative because he has decided to be so; he is creative because he is God. So he requires no decree in order to create. All created things are rooted in the creative ground of the divine life from which they have sprung. This doctrine of the creative emanation of the divine life again picks up earlier Neoplatonic ideas. It was maintained by Paul Tillich. Does creation originate in God's creative decree, or in the eternally creative divine life? Can the doctrine of decrees and the doctrine of emanation be reconciled?

According to the Reformed doctrine of decrees, God is pure and absolute life (*actus purissimus*).[15] He cannot be conceived of without the activity which is essential to his nature and which is at the same time the absolute cause of the divine efficacy in creation. The activity which is immanent to God and essential to his nature *is* the eternal, unchangeable resolve of his essential nature. The result of this resolve is the creative decree. It is only notionally that it is distinguished from the resolve itself, just as this divine resolve can only be distinguished notionally, and not substantially, from the nature of God. It is through the identification of God's efficacy and his nature that the Reformed doctrine of decrees differs from Nominalist speculations about the *potentia Dei absoluta*: God's nature *is* his eternal efficacy. His resolve to create is therefore an 'essential' resolve, not an arbitrary one. Consequently God's resolve bears all the essential characteristics of God: it is absolute, eternal, unchangeable. So it cannot either be or not be. In his essential resolve, God has 'no choice'. God's resolve is 'an activity or tendency of the divine will in accordance with the nature of God, to do in the course of time that which can and should serve the revelation of God's glory.'[16] This shows the goal of the divine resolve: God determines to reveal his own glory. In that glory his own eternal life and nature are manifested. The creation of a world different from himself is the first step towards realizing this eternal resolution to reveal the glory that is the essence of his nature. God decides for the kingdom first of all, and then for creation. Consequently it is the kingdom that determines creation, and creation is the real promise of the kingdom. So although it is certainly true that a revelation of God's will is present in creation first of all, creation's goal and end is the eschatological revelation of God's nature in glory. According to this view, God's almighty power is entirely and wholly determined by 'the holy character of the divine nature itself'. God's will expresses nothing other than the glory of his eternal Being. Because the concept of the eternal decree implies the unity of God's nature and his will, the Reformed doctrine of decrees excluded every idea of an arbitrary God, or a heavenly tyrant, without falling victim to naturalistic ideas about the manifold emanations of the Ultimate or The One. Nor do we find any speculation in orthodox Reformed theology about what God might have done but did not do. God's liberty is his essential activity. But in this case, is a finite creation, created 'in the beginning', still conceivable at all? Does the idea of the essential resolve of God's nature not make of him the eternally creative God? But the Reformed doctrine of decrees never had only creation in the beginning in mind; it always simultaneously had in view the eternal kingdom of glory, for whose sake God created heaven and earth.[17] Consequently creation certainly has a beginning, but its consummation in the glory of God has no end. So in this respect God is not 'the eternally creative God'; he is the God who glorifies himself in both time and eternity.

Karl Barth picked up this tradition. He emended it brilliantly in his christological doctrine of election, but in his doctrine of creation he did not always do it justice, because he did not take over the Reformed *ordo decretorum*, but made 'the covenant', not 'glory', the inner ground of creation. Like the Reformed tradition, Barth rejected the Nominalist doctrine of the *potentia Dei absoluta*, and joined issue with it wherever he met it. And yet in his doctrine about God's primal resolve he retained a 'Nominalist fringe', so that he could show that God's decision was a free resolve of grace.[18] 'God . . . could have remained satisfied with Himself and with the impassible glory and blessedness of His own inner life. But He did not do so. He elected man . . .'[19] The background of what the infinite God *might have done* is intended to bring out the character of grace in the decision which he in fact made. But of course Barth thereby again turns the resolve of God's being into a resolve of his will. In formulating the resolve as a resolve of God's essential nature, the Reformed tradition had no need of a background belonging to the sphere of what God might have done, or might also have done, or might have done otherwise; and it never reasoned so speculatively.

If the essential resolve is viewed as a decision of will, this means introducing into the essential nature of God the before-after structure which belongs to every decision of this kind. 'Before' the resolve, the nature of God exists 'in impassible glory'; 'after' that resolve, the divine nature is one which is most profoundly touched by love, suffering and the cross. Even if this resolve is presented as having been formed 'from eternity', so that only what is decided through this resolve has reality, speculation about 'possibilities' open to God (which are then completely and utterly unreal) is still bound to endanger the actual reality. 'Could God' really 'have remained satisfied' with his inner glory and blessedness? What is fundamentally in question here is whether the concept of freedom of choice can really be applied to God's eternal and essential liberty.[20] The quintessence of freedom of choice is almighty power. The formal concept of freedom means an absolute right of disposition over property. But without the substantial notion of freedom, freedom of choice is an empty concept. And in the substantial sense the truth of freedom is love. But love is the self-communication of the good. This self-communication of the good can only take place in freedom. In this sense freedom and love are synonymous.[21]

What concept of freedom is appropriate to God? If we start from thh point of view of the created being, the Creator appears as almighty and gracious. His freedom has no limits, and his commitment to what he has created is without obligation. But if we start from the Creator himself, the self-communication of his goodness in love to his creation is not a matter of his free will. It is the self-evident operation of his eternal nature. The essential activity of God *is* the eternal resolve of his will, and the eternal resolve of his will *is* his essential activity. In other words, God is not entirely free when he can do and leave undone what he likes; he is entirely free when he is entirely himself. In his creative activity he is wholly and entirely himself. He loves the world in the surrender of his Son with the very same love which he *is*, from eternity to eternity (John 3.16; I John 4.16). The glory with which he glorifies himself is simply and solely the glory of his own eternal, divine life.

The doctrine of decrees starts from the assumption that God is the absolute subject. It therefore begins with his will. The doctrine of emanation takes the other approach. It assumes that God is the supreme substance. Consequently it begins with his essential nature. Where the doctrine of decrees sees the creations of the divine will, the doctrine of emanation sees the overflow of the divine nature. Because the doctrine of emanation is gnostic and Neoplatonic in origin, it was condemned by the church's theology, or only employed with the greatest caution. And yet it contains elements of truth which are indispensable for a full understanding of God's creation. We shall consider it here only in the form in which it was maintained by Paul Tillich.

For Tillich, 'divine life' and 'divine creativity' are one and the same thing.[22] The divine life is essentially creative and actualizes itself in inexhaustible abundance. God is therefore the Creator to all eternity. This means that God did not 'decide' for creation 'once upon a time'. It is not an event *within* the life of God. It is 'identical' with his life. Creation is neither chance nor necessity. It is God's 'destiny'. It follows from this that the doctrine of creation cannot properly talk about a beginning in time. All it can do is to offer statements about the fundamental relationships between God and the world. The meaning of the human being's finitude is to be found in his creatureliness. The theological correlative of this is to be found in the divine creativity. Because the divine life is creative by reason of its eternal nature, human beings require all three modes of time in order to symbolize this eternal creativity. That is why we say that God *has created* the world, *creates* the world in the present moment, and *will fulfil* it. But these are merely creaturely ways of regarding 'the creative process of the divine life'. 'Being a creature means both to be rooted in the creative ground of the divine life and to actualize one's self through freedom.'[23] Here Tillich evidently concentrates the statements of the doctrine of creation on a timeless situation. In this situation, God stands in the relation of Creator to all finite beings, and these beings understand their finitude as creatureliness.

Creation as a unique act, and creation as the outcome of that act, then vanish behind the eternal correlation of Creator and creature.

If God does not merely create, but *is* in his divine nature eternally creative, then his creation is eternal as well. This undoubtedly applies to Tillich's statement that 'God eternally creates himself'. But it must also apply to the extra-divine creations of the creative, divine Life-process. Has not Tillich here simply carried over into the doctrine of Creator and creation the earlier metaphysical statement about the *causa prima* which in relation to itself has to be described as *causa sui*? And if God does not merely create, but if he is 'eternally creative' how can we understand his sabbath rest?

If the eternally creative divine life and the divine creativity are one and the same, it becomes difficult to distinguish between God's creatures and God's eternal creation of himself. If creation is said to be 'identical' with the divine life, how can there be beings who are not *God* and yet *are*? By identifying the divine creativity with the divine life itself, Tillich is really abolishing God's self-differentiation from the world which he has created.

Moreover, because for Tillich the eternal origin of God and creation are identical, he is bound to conceive of the return to this origin in equally monistic terms. But in this case the differentiations between God and the world have to be ascribed, not to creation but to 'the Fall'. The abolition of the alienations of nature and existence which are 'given' with the Fall is bound to lead to the concept of an all-resolving, all-dissolving Universal One, in which everything that has been separated finds itself again. But can the doctrine described in this way still be considered a doctrine of creation? What distinguishes it from the pantheism of *natura naturans*?

In spite of these critical comments, it is important to maintain the identity of the divine life and the divine creative activity. But this identity can be preserved even if the divine life is not seen as in itself creative. The idea of God's eternal self-creation leads in the wrong direction, because it introduces a differentiation into God which would be better excluded: if God is supposed to be his own Creator, then he would also have to be his own creature. It is more appropriate if we view the eternal divine life as a life of eternal, infinite love, which in the creative process issues in its overflowing rapture from its trinitarian perfection and completeness, and comes to itself in the eternal rest of the sabbath. It is the same love, but it operates in different ways in the divine life and in the divine creativity. This distinction in God makes it possible to preserve the distinction between God and the world in all the different forms which the communion between them takes. In his creative activity, God employs his inner, divine life. Consequently he also communicates his love to the creatures of that love. This gives human beings a share, not merely in the productivity of his will, but also in his 'nature' (II Peter 1.4). The beings who are created to be his image are also 'of his race'; they are 'his offspring' (Acts 17.28f.). This suggests a fellowship with God which really does go beyond mere creatureliness, even if the expression 'emanation of the divine Being' is an inappropriate way of describing it. To be God's creature and his image means being more than merely a work of his hands. It means being actually 'rooted' in the creative ground of the divine life. This becomes especially clear if we understand creation pneumatologically, in the light of the Creator Spirit who dwells in his creation.

When, finally, we compare the doctrine of decrees and the doctrine of emanation, our aim should not be to arrive at a well-balanced and harmonious synthesis of the two doctrines. Our purpose should be to find a deeper understanding of the creative God. According to the doctrine of decrees, God's creation is the outcome of his *de*cision; according to the doctrine of emanation, the divine life *dis*closes itself. If the resolve to create is 'an essential resolve' on God's part, we must then say that God *dis*closes himself in the *de*cision he makes. His divine life flows into his resolve, and from that resolve overflows to his creatures. Through the resolve, the divine life is communicated to created beings. Whereas the doctrine of decrees ought really to formulate God's decision as being an '*essential* resolve', so as to be able to talk about creation in a way that is appropriate to God, the doctrine of emanantion, conversely, ought to talk about 'the resolved essence' of God, so as to avoid the misleading naturalistic analogies of 'source' and 'overflow'. Through its resolve, the divine life becomes creative; and in its creativity it is wholly and entirely itself, and is itself wholly and entirely.

The unity of will and nature in God can be appropriately grasped through the concept of love. God loves the world with the very same love which he eternally *is*. This does not mean that he cannot but love the world eternally; nor that he could either love it, or not. The supreme New Testament statement 'God is love' can only be understood if God is thought of not merely as supreme substance but also as subject; and, again, not merely as absolute subject, but also as supreme substance. Both possible metaphysical ways of thinking are integrated and excelled by the trinitarian justification and interpretation of this 'practical definition' of God: *Deus est caritas*. The doctrine of decrees and the doctrine of emanation do no more than lead us to the threshold of an all-embracing trinitarian doctrine of creation.

§3 CREATION OUT OF NOTHING

The creation of the world is founded on God's determination that he will be the Creator. Before God issues creatively out of himself, he acts inwardly on himself, resolving *for himself*, committing *himself*, determining *himself*. Let me go a little more deeply into this idea with the help of the Jewish kabbalistic doctrine of God's 'self-limitation' (*zimsum*).[24] This may help us to deepen the interpretation of the doctrine of the *creatio ex nihilo*. But we shall take up and employ the doctrine about God's self-limitation, and about Nothingness, in the messianic light of faith in the crucified Son of God.

Ever since Augustine, Christian theology has called God's work of creation an act of God outwards: *operatio Dei ad extra, opus trinitatis ad extra, actio Dei externa*. It distinguished this from an act of God inwards, which takes place in the divine relationships within the Trinity. Theologians have made this distinction between God's 'inward' and his 'outward' aspect so much as matter of course that no one has even asked the critical question: can the omnipotent God have an 'outward' aspect at all? If we assume an *extra Deum*, does this not set God a limit? And who can set limits to God? If there were a realm outside God, God would not be omnipresent. This space 'outside' God would have to be co-eternal with God. But an 'outside God' of this kind would then have to be 'counter' to God.

However, there is in fact one possible way of conceiving an *extra Deum*. But it is only the assumption of a self-limitation by God himself preceding his creation which can be reconciled with God's divinity without contradiction. In order to create a world 'outside' himself, the infinite God must have made room beforehand for a finitude in himself. It is only a withdrawal by God into himself that can free the space into which God can act creatively. The *nihil* for his *creatio ex nihilo* only comes into being because – and in as far as – the omnipotent and omnipresent God withdraws his presence and restricts his power.

It was Isaac Luria who first of all developed these ideas in his doctrine of *zimsum*.[25] *Zimsum* means concentration and contraction, and signifies a withdrawing of oneself into oneself. Luria was taking up the ancient Jewish doctrine of the Shekinah, according to which the infinite God can so contract his presence that he dwells in the temple. But Luria applied it to God and creation. The existence of a world outside God is made possible by an inversion of God. This sets free a kind of 'mystical primordial space' into which God – issuing out of himself – can enter and in which he can manifest himself. 'Where God withdraws himself from himself to himself, he can call something forth which is not divine essence or divine being.'[26] The Creator is not an 'unmoved mover' of the universe. On the contrary, creation is preceded by this self-movement on God's part, a movement which allows creation the space for its own being. God withdraws into himself in order to go out of himself. He 'creates' the preconditions for the existence of his creation by withdrawing his presence and his power. 'In the self-limitation of the divine Being which, instead of acting outwardly in its initial act, turns inwards towards itself, Nothingness emerges. Here we have an act in which Nothingness is called forth.'[27] It is the affirmative force of God's self-negation which becomes the creative force in creation and salvation.

The kabbalistic doctrine of the self-limitation of God has also found a place in Christian theology. Nicholas of Cusa, J. G. Hamann, Friedrich Oetinger, F. W. J. Schelling, A. von Oettingen, Emil Brunner and others all saw that when God permitted creation, this was the first act in the divine self-humiliation which reached its profoundest point in the cross of Christ.[28] Let us take up the idea at this point and think it through further.

1. God makes room for his creation by withdrawing his presence. What comes into being is a *nihil* which does not contain the negation of creaturely being (since creation is not yet existent), but which represents the partial negation of the divine Being, inasmuch as God is not yet Creator. The space which comes into being and is set free by God's self-limitation is a literally God-forsaken space.[29] The *nihil* in which God creates his creation is God-forsakenness, hell, absolute death; and it is against the threat of this that he maintains his

creation in life. Admittedly the *nihil* only acquires this menacing character through the self-isolation of created beings to which we give the name of sin and godlessness. Creation is therefore threatened, not merely by its own non-being, but also by the non-being of God its Creator – that is to say, by Nothingness itself. The character of the negative that threatens it goes beyond creation itself. This is what constitutes its demonic power. Nothingness contradicts, not merely creation but God too, since he is creation's Creator. Its negations lead into that primordial space which God freed within himself before creation. As a self-limitation that makes creation possible, the *nihil* does not yet have this annihilating character; for it was conceded in order to make an independent creation 'outside' God possible. But this implies the possibility of the annihilating Nothingness. It emerges from this that in a doctrine of Nothingness, a distinction has to be made between the non-being of a creature, the non-being of creation, and the non-being of the Creator. It is only in connection with the last of these that we can talk about Nothingness.

2. God 'withdraws himself from himself to himself' in order to make creation possible. His creative activity outwards is preceded by this humble divine self-restriction. In this sense God's self-humiliation does not begin merely with creation, inasmuch as God commits himself to this world: it begins beforehand, and is the presupposition that makes creation possible. God's creative love is grounded in his humble, self-humiliating love. This self-restricting love is the beginning of that self-emptying of God which Philippians 2 sees as the divine mystery of the Messiah. Even in order to create heaven and earth, God emptied himself of his all-plenishing omnipotence, and as Creator took upon himself the form of a servant.

This points to a necessary correction in the interpretation of creation: God does not create merely by calling something into existence, or by setting something afoot. In a more profound sense he 'creates' by letting-be, by making room, and by withdrawing himself. The creative making is expressed in masculine metaphors. But the creative letting-be is better brought out through motherly categories.

3. If God is creatively active into that 'primordial space' which he himself has ceded and conceded, does he then create 'outwards'? Of course it is only through the yielding up of the *nihil* that a *creatio ex nihilo* is conceivable at all. But if creation *ad extra* takes place in the

space freed by God himself, then in this case the reality outside God still remains *in* the God who has yielded up that 'outwards' in himself. Without the difference between Creator and creature, creation cannot be conceived of at all; but this difference is embraced and comprehended by the greater truth which is what the creation narrative really comes down to, because it is the truth from which it springs: the truth that God is all in all. This does not imply a pantheistic dissolution of creation in God; it means the final form which creation is to find in God. Then the initial self-limitation of God's which makes creation possible assumes the glorifying, derestricted boundlessness in which the whole creation is transfigured. In Dante's words:

> His glory, in whose being all things move,
> pervades Creation . . .[30]

The movement from God's initial self-limitation to his eschatological delimitation in respect of his creation can best be grasped if we compare the process of the original creation with the process of the new creation. According to the tradition of the Priestly Writing, creation in the beginning is a creation through the word. As such it is for the Creator effortless. It is not from *the labour* of his creative work that the Creator rests on the sabbath. But the divine creation of salvation in the midst of humanity's history of disaster looks very different; for this is anything but effortless. Talking about the obliteration of the sins of God's people, Isa. 43.24f. says: 'You have burdened me with your sins, you have wearied me with your iniquities. But I will blot out your transgressions for my own sake and I will not remember your sins.' The Chosen One who, according to Isaiah 53, will bring salvation to the lost, is called *ebed Yahweh*, the Servant of God. His soul has 'travailed' (Isa. 53.11). He carries sins and sicknesses like a man who carries a heavy load (Isa. 53.4). That is why and that is how he is going to be victorious (Isa. 53.11,12). In the hymn in Philippians 2, the mystery of the Messiah is seen as his emptying of himself and humbling of himself in 'the form of a servant'. The new creation of salvation comes into being out of God's 'labour and travail'.[31] Through his self-emptying he creates liberation, through his self-humiliation he exalts, and through his vicarious suffering the redemption of sinners is achieved. It is these 'works' that John means when he passes down to us as Jesus' last word on the cross: 'It is finished' (John 19.30). Even the vital energies of the Holy Spirit always operate only in 'the fellowship of Christ's sufferings', according to Paul (Phil. 3.10). It is in the fellowship of Christ's sufferings that the powers of the resurrection and the new creation are experienced and are efficacious (II Cor. 4.7ff.; 6.4ff.). This power is perfected in the weak (II Cor. 12.9). The new creation of heaven and earth is destined finally to emerge from the history of God's suffering, and to have this suffering at its centre. This new creation is to be the kingdom of the crucified Christ: 'Worthy is the Lamb that was slain, to receive power and riches and wisdom and strength and honour and glory and blessing' (Rev. 5.12; also 7.14ff.; 11.15; 12.10f.; 21.23). It is from the apotheosis of the Lamb that the kingdom of glory comes into being, as we see in the picture of the mystic Lamb which is to be found in the domes or apses of many Christian churches. The crucified one becomes the foundation and centre of the kingdom of glory which renews heaven and earth – the kingdom which already begins with his resurrection and glorification.

If we compare the processes of creation as they are described, we can see *initial creation* as the divine creation that is without any prior conditions: *creatio ex nihilo*; while *creation in history* is the laborious creation of salvation out of the overcoming of disaster. The *eschatological creation* of the kingdom of glory, finally, proceeds from the vanquishing of sin and death, that is to say, the annihilating Nothingness. God overcomes sin and the death of his creatures by taking their destiny on himself; and he overcomes in his own eternal Being the Nothingness which lies heavy over sin and death.

If God's creativity goes back to a creative resolve, this already implies the Creator's openness for redeeming suffering and his readiness for his own self-humiliation. Because of the self-isolation of his creatures through sin and the consequence of sin, death, God's adherence to his resolve *to create* also means a resolve *to save*. *Creatio ex nihilo* in the beginning is the preparation and promise of the redeeming *annihilatio nihili*, from which the eternal being of creation proceeds. The creation of the world is itself a promise of resurrection, and the overcoming of death in the victory of eternal life (I Cor. 15.26, 55–57). So the resurrection and the kingdom of glory are the fulfilment of the promise which creation itself represents.

This brings us to a final interpretation of the statement about the *creatio ex nihilo*, from the standpoint of the cross of Christ. If God creates his creation out of nothing, if he affirms it and is faithful to it in spite of sin, and if he desires its salvation, then in the sending and surrender of his own Son he exposes himself to the annihilating Nothingness, so that he may overcome it in himself and through himself, and in that way give his creation existence, salvation and liberty. In this sense, by yielding up the Son to death in God-forsakenness on the cross, and by surrendering him to hell, the eternal God enters the Nothingness out of which he created the world. God enters that 'primordial space' which he himself conceded through his initial self-limitation. He pervades the space of God-forsakenness with his presence. It is the presence of his self-humiliating, suffering love for his creation, in which he experiences death itself. That is why God's presence in the crucified Christ gives creation eternal life, and does not annihilate it. In the path of the Son into self-emptying and bondage, to the point of the death he died, and in the path of his exaltation and glorification by the whole creation, God becomes omnipresent. By entering into the God-forsakenness of sin and death (which is Nothingness), God overcomes it and makes it part of his eternal life: 'If I make my bed in hell, thou art there' (Ps. 139.8).

In the light of the cross of Christ, *creatio ex nihilo* means forgiveness of sins through Christ's suffering, justification of the godless through Christ's death, and the resurrection of the dead and eternal life through the lordship of the Lamb.

In the light of creation, the cross of Christ means the true consolidation of the universe. Because from the very beginning the Creator is prepared to suffer in this way for his creation, his creation endures to eternity. The cross is the mystery of creation and the promise of its future.

Does the resurrection of the crucified Christ also bring the Nothingness of world history into the light of the resurrection? Here the experiences of Auschwitz and Hiroshima raise questions for which no answers are endurable, because the questions are fundamentally protests. Even Hegel found that there was a Negative which could not 'be turned to good' in any dialectic. He therefore left the 'unresolved contradiction' – the Peloponnesian and the Thirty Years' War, and other mass annihilations – out of his dialectic altogether. Ernst Bloch too was able to see nothing in the incinerators of Maidanek except the hard, meaningless, annihilating

Nothingness: 'There is undoubtedly a grain of wheat that dies without bringing any fruit, a grain of wheat that is trampled into the ground, without there being truly – let alone necessarily – any positive negation of this negation afterwards.'[32] Only the militant hope that is associated with objectively real possibilities, he believes, can keep at bay the fields of of annihilating Nothingness; but even the passion for life cannot completely do away with the death that is utterly meaningless. This idea of the negative is really Manichaean. It can do no more than 'keep Nothingness at bay'. It cannot abolish or overcome it.

Is Christian faith in the resurrection in a position to go any further than this? Certainly not in the practical struggle against war and mass annihilation. But where it can go further is in its hope in the God who raises the dead. Belief in the resurrection looks towards God at the very point where humanly speaking there is nothing to hope for and nothing to be done. This was already the situation in Israel's resurrection faith. In 'the valley full of dry bones' Ezekiel heard 'the word of the Lord': 'Behold I will cause breath to enter you and you shall live' (Ezek. 37.1ff.) Even the resurrection of Christ after his execution was not for Christians a potentiality for Being which was still inherent in his Non-being. It was the miracle of God's new creation. The hope of resurrection therefore brings even the Nothingness of world history into the light of the new creation.

Does this have practical consequences? It does not lead to the kind of optimism that overlooks the negative. But it does offer the strength to hold fast to what is dead, and to remain mindful of those who have died. The hope of resurrection brings the living and the dead into a single fellowship of hope. In this fellowship death is not suppressed, nor are the dead given over to oblivion. The messianic community of the church of the risen Christ has always been understood as a community of the living *and the dead* (Rom. 14.7–9; Luke 20.38). This hope, which binds the living and the dead together, can be expressed in negative terms: 'Even the dead will not be safe from the enemy once he is victorious.[33] But the protest against senseless murder, with which no one can come to terms, can only retain its staying power if it is borne up by a hope for the victims of that senseless murder. The protest against the annihilating Nothingness must not lead to the suppression and forgetfulness of the annihilated; and equally, hope for the annihilated must not permit us to come to terms with their annihilation.

The first is obviously the danger for revolutionaries; the second is the danger of the religious.

Will the eschatological Nothingness be brought into the light of the new creation as well, through the raising of the crucified Christ? This question hangs together with the previous one, because experience of the Nothingness of world history is a foretaste of the apocalyptic annihilation of the world. This makes it a difficult question to answer, because the apocalyptic situation which we call 'the end of the world' has not yet come about, although human beings have at their disposal all the necessary means for destroying 'their world', at least, and all life on earth. But the answer cannot be any different from the answer to the previous question. Even 'the end of the world' can set no limits to the God who created the world out of nothing, the God who in his Son exposed his own self to annihilating Nothingness on the cross, in order to gather that Nothingness into his eternal being. And this is true whether the end of the world is brought about by natural catastrophe or human crime. How should the Creator-out-of-nothing be diverted from his intention and his love through any devastations in what he has created? Anyone who expects 'the end of the world', is denying the world's Creator, whatever may prompt his apocalyptic anxiety. Faith in God the Creator cannot be reconciled with the apocalyptic expectation of a total *annihilatio mundi*.[34] What accords with this faith is the expectation and active anticipation of the *transformatio mundi*. The expectation of 'the end of the world' is a vulgar error. Like the expectation of the *annihilatio mundi*, it is gnostic in origin, not biblical. It is the means by which many people would like God to win acceptance at the world's expense. But eschatology is nothing other than faith in the Creator with its eyes turned towards the future. Anyone who believes in the God who created being out of nothing, also believes in the God who gives life to the dead. This means that he hopes for the new creation of heaven and earth. His faith makes him prepared to withstand annihilation, even when there is nothing left to hope for, humanly speaking. His hope in God commits him to faithfulness to the earth.

§4 THE TRINITARIAN DOCTRINE OF CREATION

Is there a specifically Christian doctrine of creation? What can the Christian faith add to the interpretation of the Old Testament traditions about creation?

The Israelite understanding of the world as creation was moulded by the revelation of God's redemption in the exodus, the covenant, and the promise of the land; and, in the same way, the Christian understanding of the world as God's creation is shaped by the revelation of his redemption in the history of Jesus Christ. This Christian understanding does not contradict the statements about creation which were arrived at through Israel's experience of salvation. The Christian understanding is the messianic interpretation of these earlier statements. Christian, or messianic, belief in creation does not 'go one better' than Israel's faith; not does it push this faith aside. It is an acknowledgment of it. If, in the Christian interpretation, concepts about the protological creation which the Old Testament has passed down to us are further defined by ideas about the eschatological creation, this is due to Christianity's messianic orientation. That is also the reason why Christian understanding proclaims the Creator of heaven and earth as 'the Father of Jesus Christ', and develops Old Testament monotheism in a trinitarian sense: the Father created heaven and earth through the Son in the Spirit.[35] How did Christian theology arrive at this conclusion in its doctrine of creation?

1. The Cosmic Christ. If Christ is the ground of salvation for the whole creation, for sinful men and women, and for 'enslaved' non-human creatures, he is then also the ground for the existence of the whole creation, human beings and nature alike.[36] A discernment of the eschatological redemption of the whole creation through Christ was the premise which led to the deduction that the protological creation had its foundation in Christ. This conclusion underlies the New Testament statements about Christ as 'the mediator in creation'. We find the beginnings of this idea in Paul. He bases the liberty of believers in all sectors of life on the fact that everything is subjected to the sovereignty of Christ, but bases the universality of Christ's sovereignty on the fact that everything has been created through him: 'For us there is only one God, the Father, from whom are all things and for whom we exist, and one Lord, Jesus Christ, through whom are all things and through whom we exist' (I Cor. 8.6). In the epistles to the Ephesians and Colossians too, awareness of the universality of salvation in and through Christ leads to the insight that 'in him all things were created' (Eph. 1.9ff.; Col. 1.15ff.). 'The first-born from the dead' (Col. 1.18) is also 'the first-born of all creation' (1.15).

Hebrews 1.2 then presents the Christian vista of the universal lordship of Jesus, the Son of the eternal Father, and his mediatory function in creation, together with his preservation of the world and the purification of our sins through him. 'The Son' is called 'the brightness of his glory' and 'the express image of his (God's) person' (Heb. 1.3 AV). These are symbols which Israel's wisdom literature used to describe the eternal Wisdom of God through whom God created the world, still sustains it, and will one day glorify it (Prov. 8.22–31). The New Testament idea of Christ as mediator in creation in based on a *sophia* christology, according to which Jesus is both God's Son and his eternal Wisdom. The Logos christology of the Gospel of John goes back to this when it declares: 'In the beginning was the Word, and the Word was with God, and the Word was God . . . All things were made through him, and without him was not anything made that was made' (John 1.1, 3).

It is the eschatological experience of salvation that leads Christians to say that God's eternal Wisdom and his eternal creative Word have been revealed 'last' and finally (Heb. 1.2) in Jesus, the crucified Lord who has been raised from the dead; and when they deduce from this that the Father of Jesus Christ and no other God created and still sustains this world *through the eternal Son*. The trinitarian doctrine of creation is determined by the revelation of Christ: because Jesus was revealed as the Son of the eternal Father, the Wisdom and the creative Word which are identified with the Son also take on a personal and hypostatic character which they lack in the Old Testament testimonies, although those testimonies also show tendencies in this direction, or are at least open for hypostases of this kind.

2. *The Spirit as Creator*. According to the New Testament testimonies, the outpouring of the Spirit and the experience of the energies of the Holy Spirit in the community of Christ belong to the eschatological experience of salvation. The gift of the Spirit is the

guarantee or 'earnest' – the advance payment – of glory (II Cor. 1.22; 5.5; Eph.1.14). The powers of the Spirit are the powers of the new creation. They therefore possess men and women, soul and body. They are the powers of the resurrection of the dead which proceed from the risen Christ and are testified to the world through the church, which is charismatically wakened to eternal life. According to Joel 2.28, the era of the Spirit is the promised End-time. The power of the Spirit is the creative power of God, which justifies sinners and gives life to the dead. The gift of the Holy Spirit is therefore eternal life.

In the gift and through the powers of the Holy Spirit a new divine presence is experienced in creation. God the Creator takes up his dwelling in his creation and makes it his home. The experience of the Spirit is the experience of the Shekinah, the indwelling of God: men and women become in their bodies 'the temple of the Holy Spirit' (I Cor. 6.13–20). The new Jerusalem will become God's tabernacle or dwelling among human beings (Rev. 21.3). In the life-giving operations of the Spirit and in his indwelling influence, the whole trinitarian efficacy of God finds full expression. In the operation and indwelling of the Spirit, the creation of the Father through the Son, and the reconciliation of the world with God through Christ, arrive at their goal. The presence and the efficacy of the Spirit is the eschatological goal of creation and reconciliation. All the works of God end in the presence of the Spirit.

The experience of the eschatological reality of the Spirit leads to the conclusion that this is the same Spirit in whose power the Father, through the Son, has created the world, and preserves it against annihilating Nothingness: 'When thou takest away their breath, they die and return to their dust. When thou sendest forth thy breath, they are created; and thou renewest the face of the ground' (Ps. 104. 29–30). This means that the Spirit is the efficacious power of the Creator and the power that quickens created beings. It also means that this power is itself creative, not created, and that it has been 'breathed forth' by the Creator, that is to say, emanated. And this, in its turn, means that in the Spirit the Creator himself is present in his creation. Through the presence of his own being, God preserves his creation against the annihilating Nothingness. 'Si . . . Dominus spiritum subtrahit, omnia in nihilum rediguntur.'[37]

But through the presence of his own being, God also participates in the destiny of his own creation. Through the Spirit he suffers with the sufferings of his creatures. In his Spirit he experiences their annihilations. In his Spirit he sighs with the enslaved creation for redemption and liberty. What is true of the Shekinah which dwells in Israel and wanders with Israel into exile, is in its own way true also of the Shekinah of the Creator in his creation. Through his Spirit the Creator is himself involved in his creation. The Spirit is capable of suffering. He can be 'quenched' and 'grieved' (I Thess. 5.19; Eph. 4.30). For he is the power of the love from which creation has issued and through which it is sustained.

Is the Holy Spirit 'the third Person of the Trinity', according to the testimonies of the eschatological revelation in the New Testament? In most passages the mode of efficacy of the Spirit is described as the operation of a divine energy. But what is special about the efficacy of the Spirit cannot be assigned to the attributes or powers of God. The Spirit also acts as an independent subject, and he does so not merely towards men and women; in the glorification of the Son and the Father, he acts on the Son and the Father as well. We have to see the Holy Spirit as a divine subject wherever he is named together with the divine subjects of the Father and the Son but is distinguished from them, as is the case in the benedictory and baptismal formulas. And yet the Spirit always points away from himself towards the Son and the Father. To say this does not mean that we should give up the personal character of the Spirit, as this was later defined in the trinitarian doctrine of the patristic church. But it does mean that we cannot apply the concept of person to the Father, the Son and the Spirit in exactly the same way. It is precisely the experience of the unique character of the Spirit which makes it evident that each subject of the Trinity possesses his own unique personality, so that no single, univocal concept of person is applicable to the Father, the Son and the Spirit. None the less, the Holy Spirit is God himself: God in a unique character which can be differentiated from the character of God the Father and God the Son.

The Christian doctrine of creation takes its impress from the revelation of Christ and the experience of the Spirit. The One who sends the Son and the Spirit is the Creator – the Father. The One who gathers the world under his liberating lordship, and redeems it, is the Word of creation – the Son. The One who gives life to the world and allows it to participate in God's eternal life is the creative

Energy – the Spirit. The Father is the creating origin of creation, the Son its shaping origin, and the Spirit its life-giving origin.

Creation exists in the Spirit, is moulded by the Son and is created by the Father. It is therefore from God, through God and in God.

The trinitarian concept of creation binds together God's transcendence and his immanence. The one-sided stress on God's transcendence in relation to the world led to deism, as with Newton. The one-sided stress on God's immanence in the world led to pantheism, as with Spinoza. The trinitarian concept of creation integrates the elements of truth in monotheism and pantheism. In the panentheistic view, God, having created the world, also dwells in it, and conversely the world which he has created exists in him. This is a concept which can really only be thought and described in trinitarian terms.

When the divinization of the creature in the fertility cults determined the relationship of the human being to nature, the critical distinction between God the Creator and the world as his creation had a liberating effect on men and women. But in the meantime the de-divinization of the world has progressed so far that the prevailing view of nature is totally godless, and the relationship of human beings to nature is a disastrous one. This means that today we have to find an integrating view of God and nature which will draw them both into the same vista. It is only this that can exert a liberating influence on nature and human beings alike.

§5 THE COSMIC SPIRIT

The earlier theological idea of the Creator Spirit who interpenetrates, quickens and animates the world was pushed out by the modern mechanistic world picture. In terms of theology, the masculine idea of the lordship of God superseded the earlier feminine idea of 'the World Soul'. God rules everything, not like a World Soul but like the master of the universe, said Isaac Newton.[38] In terms of cosmology, the symbol of the world machine supplanted the earlier symbol of the world organism. Both these new concepts made the world calculable, and open to the subjection of human beings. But if the world immanence of God the Spirit is surrendered in favour of the world transcendence of God the ruler, the result is a view of nature which is dead and spiritless as well as godless.

In modern times, Christian theology has tried again and again to break the spell of the mechanistic world view, and the doctrine of domination which underlies it. But the organic cosmologies put forward by Oetinger, Schleiermacher, Rothe, Heim and others have remained marginal. The triumphal progress of the 'exact' sciences did not permit these alternatives. Moreover, the danger of pantheism, on Spinoza's model, also made many theologians shrink from attempts of this kind. And yet it is essential to take up the old ideas again – and essential for theological reasons, first of all: for without a pneumatological doctrine of creation there cannot be a Christian doctrine of creation at all. But cosmological reasons are cogent also: for without a perception of the Creator Spirit in the world there cannot be a peaceful community of creation in which human beings and nature share.

The biblical creation narrative begins by elucidating the initial statement about God's creation of heaven and earth, explaining that 'The Spirit of God hovered (i.e., brooded) over the waters' (Gen.1.2). The explanation was seldom heeded in theological interpretation. But it is intended to point out that the divine Spirit (*ruach*) is the creative power and the presence of God in his creation.[39] The whole creation is a fabric woven by the Spirit, and is therefore a reality to which the Spirit gives form. What does God's immanence in the world through the Spirit mean for our understanding of the world as God's creation? What are the criteria for perceiving the Creator Spirit in nature? In order to distinguish the idea of creation in the Spirit from all 'spiritualist' and animist notions, we must start theologically from the revelation and experience of 'the Holy Spirit' in the church of Christ, and from this deduce the presence and the mode of efficacy of 'the Spirit' in creation.[40]

(*a*) The first experience of the Holy Spirit in Christian faith is the experience of 'the power of the Spirit': the believer is born again of the Spirit (John 3.5); in Christ he is a new creature (II Cor. 5.17).

(*b*) The second experience of the Holy Spirit is equally primal. It is the experience of community in the social, religious and natural limitations which are otherwise insurmountable; in the Spirit, Jews and Gentiles, Greeks and barbarians, masters and slaves, women and men, become 'one' (Gal. 3.28); that is to say, they are 'one heart and soul' and have 'everything in common' (Acts 4.31–35).

(*c*) Again, just as primary as this experience of community is the experience of the individuation of each personal calling and each personal gift of the Spirit: to everyone his own. There are many gifts of the Spirit, but only one Spirit (I Cor. 12).

(*d*) Finally, in these experiences of the presence of the Holy Spirit, hope is assured, because future is anticipated – the future of the new creation: the rebirth of the cosmos to glory, the blessed community of creation which joins all separated creatures, and the direct fellowship with God of the creation united in Christ and renewed in the Spirit.

In the mechanistic world view, conclusions about complex systems are generally drawn from simple ones; relationships in complex systems are reduced to conditions in simpler systems and are then reconstructed from there. Here we shall take the reverse course. Taking certain human experiences of God and complex relationships to God, we shall draw certain conclusions about human and natural conditions. Our premise is the principle that the more complex system explains the simpler one, because it is capable of integrating it; not vice versa.

If we start from this principle, we discover the following ways in which the cosmic Spirit operates in nature.

(*a*) The Spirit is the principle of creativity on all levels of matter and life. He creates new possibilities, and in these anticipates the new designs and 'blueprints' for material and living organisms. In this sense the Spirit is the principle of evolution.

(*b*) The Spirit is the holistic principle. At every evolutionary stage he creates interactions, harmony in these interactions, mutual perichoreses, and therefore a life of co-operation and community. The Spirit of God is the 'common Spirit' of creation.

(*c*) This means that in an equally primal sense the Spirit is the principle of inidividuation, the principle which differentiates particular 'working sketches' of matter and life on their various levels. Self-assertion and integration, self-preservation and self-transcendence are the two sides of the process in which life evolves. They are not mutual contradictions. They complement one another.

(*d*) Finally, all creations in the Spirit are in intention 'open'. They are directed towards their common future, because they are all, each in its own way, aligned towards their potentialities. The principle of intentionality is inherent in all open systems of matter and life.

When we say that the Creator Spirit pervades the world, we mean that we see each individual as part of the whole, and everything limited as a representative of what is infinite.[41] All created things are individuations of the community of creation and manifestations of the divine Spirit.

When we say that the creation's Creator Spirit indwells both every individual creature and the community of creation, we mean that the presence of the infinite in the finite imbues every finite thing, and the community of all finite beings, with self-transcendence. There is no other way of conceiving the presence of the infinite in the finite, if the infinite is not to destroy the finite, or the finite the infinite.

Can we find any clues in the Christian traditions for this transference of the perception of the Holy Spirit in faith to the Spirit of creation?

Paul uses the word *pneuma* in a double sense, both for the Spirit of God and for the human spirit: 'It is the Spirit himself bearing witness with our spirit that we are children of God' (Rom. 8.16). 'The human spirit' does not mean some higher spiritual principle, or some mystical summit of the soul. It means the centre of the whole personal, bodily and spiritual being – the psychosomatic totality of the person. This can already be perceived in the human self, inasmuch as this self is 'the living I' in the mind and in the direction of the will. By the expression *pneuma*, Paul means a 'self' that 'can become an object to himself, [has] a relationship to himself [and] live in his intentionality.'[42]

Paul expresses this structure of self-differentiation and intention towards self-transcendence in the term 'longing', or 'yearning' (ἀποκαραδοκία). He finds it first of all among believers, who 'have the first-fruits of the Spirit' (Rom. 8.23). They long to be the children of God and wait for the redemption of the body. Secondly, he finds it in the whole anxiously waiting creation (Rom. 8.19ff.). Creation waits for 'the revealing of the sons of God' and therefore longs together 'with us' (Rom. 8.22). Finally, he perceives in the Holy Spirit himself 'an inexpressible sighing' (Rom. 8.26). So what believers experience and perceive in the Holy Spirit reveals the structure of the Spirit of creation, the human spirit, and the Spirit in the whole non-human creation; because it is to this that their experience corresponds. What believers experience in the Holy Spirit leads them into solidarity with all other created things. They suffer *with* nature under the power of transience, and they hope *for* nature, waiting for the manifestation of liberty.[43]

If the Spirit is God's immanent presence in the world, do we not then also have to talk about a *kenosis* of the Spirit?[44]

The history of the Logos and the history of God's Spirit were often seen parallel to one another in theology, and were even viewed as interwoven with one another. But a clear distinction was made between the incarnation of the Logos and the inhabitation of the Spirit. The Word 'becomes flesh' but the Spirit 'indwells'. If we keep this dogmatically useful distinction in mind, we can – and indeed must – talk about a *kenosis* of the Spirit. The Spirit is not one of the powers of God. According to the Christian and trinitarian understanding he is God himself. If God commits himself to his limited creation, and if he himself dwells in it as 'the giver of life', this presupposes a self-limitation, a self-humiliation and a self-surrender of the Spirit. The history of suffering creation, which is subject to transience, then brings with it a history of suffering by the Spirit who dwells in creation. But the Spirit who dwells in creation turns creation's history of suffering into a history of hope. 'The presence of the Spirit of creation generates the hope of created things in the difference between life and suffering.'[45]

Is this theological view of the history of nature and the history of humanity as the divine history of the Spirit tenable at all, in view of the aberrations of evolution, and the history of human crimes and catastrophes? If the world were completely and wholly godless and forsaken by the Spirit, it would have become nothing (Ps. 104.29); it would have ceased to exist. But the world does exist, even if it is not in a condition that could be said to be in accordance with God. So in the suffering history of the world of nature and human beings, we have to discern the inexpressible sighings of the indwelling Spirit, and the suffering presence of God.[46] This perception is at the same time a perception of the self-transcendence of the indwelling Spirit, his torment and his yearning in matter. It is therefore also the perception of the cosmic dimensions of the world's hope.

Does the idea of the indwelling Creator Spirit lead to the pantheism of the 'all-pervading' World soul?

If all created being is the warp and weft of the same divine Spirit, then is not everything 'at heart related', as the German Romantics claimed? Does this not mean that everything is equally divine? Is pantheism – whether in the philosophical form maintained by Spinoza, or in the mysticism of the Chinese Tao – a real help in combating the destruction of nature today?

Heinrich Heine put forward a pertinent judgment on the questionability of the pantheism of the Goethe era: 'It is unfortunately true', he wrote, 'and we have to admit it, that pantheism has turned people into indifferentists. They have come to think that if everything is God, then one's personal concerns are surely a matter of indifference. It does not matter whether a man busies himself with clouds or antique gems, with folk songs or the anatomy of apes, with ordinary people or comic actors. *But this is where the error lies: everything is not God; God is everything.* God does not manifest himself to an equal degree in everything. On the contrary, he manifests himself to a varying extent in different things, and the drive to achieve a higher degree of infinity is inherent in everything; that is the great law of progress in nature.'[47]

In saying this Heine was pointing to the difference between pan-entheism and pantheism. Whereas simple pantheism makes everything a matter of indifference, panentheism is capable of differentiation. Whereas simple pantheism sees merely eternal, divine presence, panentheism is able to discern future transcendence, evolution and intentionality.

But differentiated panentheism is not capable of linking God's immanence in the world with his transcendence in relation to it. This is the benefit of the trinitarian doctrine of creation in the Spirit and of the Creator Spirit who indwells creation. This doctrine views creation as a dynamic web of interconnected processes. The Spirit differentiates and binds together. The Spirit preserves and leads living things and their communities beyond themselves. This indwelling Creator Spirit is fundamental for the community of creation. It is not the elementary particles that are basic, as the mechanistic world view maintains, but the overriding harmony of the relations and of the self-transcending movements, in which the longing of the Spirit for a still unattained consummation finds expression.[48] If the cosmic Spirit is the Spirit of God, the universe cannot be viewed as a closed system. It has to be understood as a system that is open – open for God and for his future.[49]

V

The Time of Creation

Everything that happens is temporal and takes place in time. So what is time? Does it precede all happening? Is it constituted through happening? Is it a condition of possible experience, or do we experience time itself? Does it make any difference to the way we experience time whether we view reality as creation, or whether we understand it as nature? Augustine long ago admitted that he found it difficult to define what time really is: 'What then is time?' he enquires. 'I know well enough what it is, provided that nobody asks me; but if I am asked what it is and try to explain, I am baffled.'[1]

§1 TIME AS THE REPETITION OF ETERNITY

Mircea Eliade has looked at time in the context of the history of religion, and has shown that in the archaic stage of their development, human beings do not really experience reality as history at all, if by history we mean the progressive march of contingent events and individual acts.[2] All happening is seen as the reflection and repetition of mythical, primordial happening, and it is only the primordial which is real. The early history of humanity is dominated by myth and by the notion of 'the eternal return'. Human experience and human acts must find their foundation and their form in their correspondence to what is primal and divine if they are to be meaningful and in this sense 'real'. It is true that new things are continually happening, but the archaic human being responds to these new events through ritual. The whole world in which he lives is ritualized; for it is only ritual which confers safety in a mysterious and chaotic world. Ritual mirrors the divine, and through ritual men and women come under divine protection. And if life is experienced as ritual, and if ritual is the means of mastering the world, then the experience of time belongs within the same framework.

There is a pure, primordial time. This is the time which *was* at the moment when the world came into being. It is the time which can in principle be repeated. In the greater and lesser feasts, this primordial time is actualized – made present – and the transient, workaday time of everyday life is regenerated. The 'archaic human being' is aware of two different times: there is daily, transitory time; and there are festal times. In everyday existence time passes away, becomes bygone time, degenerates. In the festival it is born anew from its origins. In everyday life chaos is experienced in the experience of transience. In the festival the eternal birth of the cosmos out of chaos is repeated. The song of creation, *Enuma elish*, was recited in the temple of Marduk, and in the recitation Marduk's mythical struggle with the monster Tiamat was actualized and became a present reality. Of course the struggle out of which the world came into being took place 'once upon a time' – which is to say in the mythical beginnings. But it is repeated in the festival, so that it is experienced as an event that is present here and now. 'The struggle and the victory of creation takes place at this very moment', as Mircea Eliade says.[3]

Eliade sums up the mythical experience of time in the feast like this:

1. The first act of the ceremony represents the vanquishing of Tiamat, and signifies the regression into the mythical, primordial time which preceded creation.
2. The creation of the world which took place 'once upon a time' is reactualized in the New Year festival.
3. In the festal ritual, human beings participate in the creation of the world. In the ecstasy of the feast, they are translated into primordial time.
4. In the feast, human beings experience the rebirth of time and its periodic, recurring new creation.

The periodically recurring festival of origin has two functions. It divides up time into weeks, months, years, and so forth. And it also infuses into transitory time fresh life from its eternal origins. The mythical time of the festival, by breaking into everyday time, abolishes its transience. This experience of time in the feast of renewal displays an anti-historical tendency. It is not the experience of history. On the contrary, it dissolves the experience of history in the eternal return of the same thing.[4]

The church year, with its annually recurring Christian festivals, has a similar character in its neutralization of history. The unique events of the history of revelation are transported and transformed into 'the eternal return of the same thing', so that they can be pressed into the service of archaic human religious feeling. That is why one of our hymns begins: 'Again the Lord's own day is here.' And at the festival that celebrates the birth of Christ we can even sing about 'the ever-circling years' that will 'bring round the age of gold'. The remembrance days of our political and private religion have the same function. Events that were once epoch-making or seminal in national history are turned into days which recur annually. The unique birth of a human being is celebrated in yearly birthdays. In this way the contingent experience of history is transformed into repeatable ritual.

Conversely, it is evidently difficult for people to comprehend unusual or unique events without the help of archetypal patterns. Yet if they are apprehended with the help of these patterns, they immediately lose their individuality, and are transferred to the level of general and recurring experiences. Anything that does not fit into the accustomed pattern is generally already screened out from the very beginning by the organs of perception themselves. If it is perceived at all, it is simply felt to be disturbing and disconcerting. The appropriate attitudes with which to meet an event like this have first of all to be discovered. But normally people react to events of this kind according to particular rituals. It was religion first of all which accompanied with special ritual forms the unique events which touch our existence deeply. Birth, marriage and death were declared 'occasional' or extraordinary happenings by the ruling religions; and these happenings were met by particular rituals, laid down in the appropriate office books. The individual character of these events is dissolved into what is general and continually repeated. The answer to an individual death is a general answer, given in the burial ceremony. Anything that cannot find a response through religious ritual is seen as a disturbance of life in general, and as disconcerting for the individual person; for the individual event as such demands the individual creation of a new, unusual action. But the perception that an event is individual is difficult, and so is the creation of an individual attitude to meet that event, even when it has been perceived. So both the perception and the attitude required are screened out and by-passed. It is not merely the 'archaic' human being who is inclined to perceive only what is repeatable, recurring and general, so that he celebrates history through rituals, instead of determining history through his own individual decisions. The same may be said of men and women as 'religious' beings too. The vague generality of religious language, among other things, makes this evident. If we were to put the matter in slightly exaggerated form, we might in this context define the nature of religion as myth and ritual, and see its function as the abolition of history. Myth eradicates the experience of history, and ritual blots out history's decision.

It is the human being belonging to prehistoric cultures who is generally termed 'archaic'. But as a type he is present in historical human beings too; and in post-historical society he is going to play a dominating role as 'post-historic man'.[5] In the *post-histoire* of the total administrative state, all historical 'events' will be robbed of their singularity, individuality and irreversibility. Instead they will be turned into 'cases', which will either be judged according to precedents or made into precedents themselves. All cases are then in principle the same, and receive the same treatment under the law. There is no such thing as 'a special case', and there is no such thing as 'individual treatment'. On the level of the rational administration of a society's total concerns, the individuality of events is eradicated, and the creative achievement of decisions eliminated. Once life in the administrative state has become totally bureaucratized, the result in actual practice is 'the end of history'. Because the growing power of human beings means that the terrors and perils of history are growing to immeasurable proportions also, many people actually desire a transition to a 'post-historic age', regarding this as humanity's sole chance of survival. But this 'farewell to history' also requires that politics be transformed into administration, and that all possible events be reduced to happenings that can be poured into a generally accepted mould. Or permissible events will be restricted to cases that can be registered; individual decisions will be renounced, or reduced to a choice between the possible variations of ritual observances. The individual historical person will be resolved into an example of what is general and calculable. In 'the post-historic age' – if it should come about – the historical era's experience of time will be surmounted. Instead the archaic sense of time will return on new levels. It is therefore important for us to be clear about the structure of this archaic awareness of time, and for us not to see the archaic as something that has been superseded.

The archaic human being lives in the eternal presence of particular divine archtetypes, which pre-form his ideas and experiences, and his perceptions of reality. He lives in particular divine rituals, which mould all his actions. He experiences time as the continual repetition of what is identical with itself. It is only this repetition that gives his life permanence. He exists in an eternal present which we have to call timeless. Through the continually recurring suspension of time in the feast, he is able to annul time's irreversibility, which he very well perceives. For him, time acquires a cyclical structure. His life runs its course within time's circular flow. So no event is unique, and no past is final. Everything comes round again. Every moment, everything begins again from the beginning. So nothing new ever happens in this world, and nothing in the world can ever really pass away either. It is true that things appear and pass away in time. But because time is conceived of in terms of the eternal return, everything really abides. The eternal return keeps the universe alive, quickening it anew out of its eternal origins. To experience time like this is not to experience the individuality of events and the irreversibility of their happening. The very opposite is true. This experience of time is the experience of repetition. But the experience of repetition is nothing other than the experience of eternity.

In this context, we have to see Plato's doctrine of Ideas as the rational representation of the archaic archetypes of perception. That is why he calls time 'the everlasting likeness, moving according to number, of the eternity that abides in unity'.[6] But time can only be understood as the image of eternity if its course is circular. Only the circle can be the image of the infinite in the finite, because its orbit is endless, and every point on the periphery is equidistant from the centre.

For Aristotle too 'time itself appears to be something like a circle'.[7] If the course of time is represented by the image of a circular path, time must periodically recur on itself. If it periodically recurs on itself, then it also restores all conditions in the world at periodic intervals. But this is only conceivable if we proceed from the immutable unity of being, while at the same time perceiving the finitude of the world. The immutable unity of being then becomes manifest in the finitude of the world. The medium through which infinite being is manifested in finite being is then time; for it is in its temporality that the finitude of the world is shown. Its becoming and its passing away is what distinguishes it from infinite, eternal and immutable being. But if the one immutable being is to find expression and manifestation in the temporality of the finite world, the flux of time must be represented as a circle on which every point is equidistant from the centre, so that eternal being is equally near to – and far from – all times. Eternity shows itself in finite being through the circulation of time, since in this it is contemporaneous with all times. In the image of time's orbit, eternity is eternal simultaneity. In its circular course, time is the extensity of eternity, just as eternity is the intensity of time. From time immemorial, the eternity of the gods was therefore depicted through their presence in all three modes of time: Zeus was, Zeus is, Zeus will be, Zeus is eternal.

§2 TIME AS THE ETERNAL PRESENT

Everything that happens, happens in time. What is now, was in the past not-yet, and will one day be no more. But does not time itself remain, in the becoming of things and their passing away? Is there any way in which we can distinguish future, present and past except by presupposing the unity of time, and by assuming that time itself is eternal? If we perceive the becoming of things and their passing away as being part of 'the flux of time', are we not then assuming that time is a continuum and, as such, homogeneous? And are we not therefore supposing that future and past are in principle the same in kind? Unless there is something that is permanent, we should be unable to understand what is transient *as* transient. Without the transient, we should be unable to apprehend the permanent. Can we discern temporal events as temporal if we do not have eternity as abiding 'point'? But where is this abiding 'point' of eternity to be found? Is it beyond time, or in the stationary present, or in the form of time itself?

'We must, then, in my judgment first make this distinction', says Plato in the *Timaeus:* 'What is that which is always real and has no becoming, and what is that which is always becoming and is never real?'[8] That which is always real, he goes on, is apprehended through *noesis*. But we can hold fast merely to fleeting impressions of what is always becoming, and can only arrive at uncertain opinions about it. What is always real is truly perceived through the *logos*. But we have no more than uncertain impressions about the world of fleeting appearances. We find truth only in what is permanent and always present. No truth is to be found in fortuitous events and sensory perceptions, which come and pass away. Truth is not to be found in the individual experience of a unique event. It can only be discovered through the knowledge of what is universal.

Plato took over this fundamental differentiation from Parmenides. His distinction was this: 'The one (way) shows that being is, and that it is impossible for it not to be. That is the way of persuasion, for persuasion attends on truth. But the other way maintains that it is not, and that this non-being must necessarily exist. This path is totally unexplorable; for thou couldst not know that which is not, nor utter it.'[9] But this means that there cannot be any true knowledge or assertions about the future and past of anything – either about its not-yet-being, or about its no-longer-being. The present is the only time in which we can perceive a thing, or say anything about it. And in fact this is what Parmenides asserts in the famous Eighth Fragment:

> There thus remains only evidence of this one way: that being exists. There are many signs along this way: because it is unborn, it is also imperishable, whole, unique, unshakeable and without end. It never was, nor will it ever be, since it is now simultaneously a unified, continuous whole . . . So how could what is, ever be in the future? How could it ever have become? For if it came into being once, it *is* not; nor *is* it, if it is at some time in the future going to be. Thus becoming is extinguished and perishing is disposed of.[10]

Here Parmenides is evidently talking about Being itself, the divine, the eternal. But he does not conceive of it as something in the beyond. Being is what is always present. The present becomes being's epiphany. This removes the present from the flux of time, making it 'the eternal present'. In the presence of eternity, 'becoming' really is 'extinguished and perishing is disposed of'. The eternal present cuts off being from non-being, whether that non-being is being-that-is-not-yet or being-that-is-no-longer.

So Parmenides does not put eternal being at the centre (as it is in the image of time as a circular path), so as to make it contemporaneous with all three modes of time. Instead he designates the present as the time of eternal being, and confronts it with the other times in such a way that these others disappear completely. Only the divine, eternal being is present. Only what is present *is*. What comes into being in time and passes away again can never be truly present, because it 'is' only in the transition from being-that-is-not-yet to being-that-is-no-longer. So in the strict sense it never *is* at all. This means that the 'now' of the eternal present of being has itself no temporal extension: 'It never was and never will be.' But it is not 'always' either, because this 'always' would have to be expressed through its presence in the three different modes of time. The eternal present of being extinguishes the experience of history.

But does it make sense to measure future and past being only against present being, and to define them as being-that-is-not-yet or being-that-is-no-longer? Is not future being also potential being, and a being-that-can-exist? Is not past being also real being – being which, since it is being that has once truly come into existence, is also being that abides? We cannot experience the history of being in the eternal present of being. For the history of being is always an experience of non-being as well, and an experience of being-that-is-not-yet and being-that-is-no-longer. The experience of being in time makes it possible to comprehend, not merely what *is*, but also, in this sense, what is not.

Georg Picht has shown from Kant's concept of time how much the interpretation of time as the eternal present has moulded the scientific thinking of modern times.[11] Like Aristotle, Kant sees time as belonging to *aisthesis*, and he therefore discusses it in his *Transcendental Aesthetic*. Time is 'pure intuition': *pure* because it is *a priori*, preceding all possible phenomena; and *intuition* because it determines the form in which anything can arrive at being a phenomenon at all. This makes time a transcendental condition required for perception in general. But this means: 'Time, therefore, in which all changes of phenomena must be thought, remains and changes not; because it is that in which succession and simultaneity can be conceived of only as determinations thereof.'[12] Kant says more or less the same thing in his chapter on 'The Schematism of the Pure Conceptions of the Understanding':

> Time passes not, but in it passes the existence of the changeable. To time, therefore, which is itself unchangeable and permanent, corresponds that which in the phenomenon is unchangeable in

existence, that is substance, and it is only by it that the succession and simultaneity of phenomena can be determined in regard to time.[13]

If all happening takes place *in* time, time itself cannot happen. Nor can it be subject to change. It is not time itself that 'passes', as we say; it is everything that happens which 'passes' in time. So time itself is timeless and continually present, and endures eternally. Time, understood as the transcendental condition which makes all experience possible, is therefore a category of eternity, if eternity is taken to mean the immutable and purely present. As 'pure intuition', time is a category of the transcendental self, which Kant puts in the place of Parmenides' pure being.

Seen as pure intuition, the meaning of time is not the perception of history. It is the making-present of the past and future in the eternal, enduring present of the understanding and of the understanding subject. Temporal intuition is an observation of all events *sub specie aeternitatis*, as it were. This understanding of time therefore means that the distinction between 'future' time and 'past' time also ceases to be valid and becomes irrelevant. The categorial concept of time brings future and past on to the same line. The concept does not take in time's irreversibility. But this presupposes that all temporal events are in principle the same in kind. For it is only if they are the same in kind that they can all be intuited in the same time.

But does everything that happens really happen in the same time? Are the modes of time the same in kind ontologically? Is time a category of eternity, or is it constituted through particular happenings and processes?

§3 THE TIME OF CREATION

Augustine devoted the whole of the eleventh book of his *Confessions* to a meditation on time and the awareness of time.[14] Prayers alternate with explanations for the reader, and define the point where time is to be experienced. Augustine begins with a prayer: 'O Lord, since you are outside time in eternity, are you unaware of the things that I tell you? Or do you see in time the things that occur in it?' It is only after this that he asks himself the question: '*Quid est tempus?*' That is to say, he puts the question about the nature of time in the realized presence of eternity, which is God's mode of being, not man's. He takes up the same ontological question about the being of time as Parmenides, Plato and Aristotle; but he puts it in another 'divine situation': the divine Being himself is not experienced in the epiphany of the eternal present. God confronts the world and time as their Creator. So Augustine does not ask about the One Being, or about the unity of time. He begins with a reflection on the act of creation: '*In principio fecisti coelum et terram.*' The confrontation with the Creator God, and his distance from created being, determines Augustine's experience of time and its interpretation.

For him, the unity of eternity and time is not to be found in the eternal present; it lies in the creative Word of God, from which everything proceeds that is. This means that time cannot be a category of eternity. It has to become a definition of created being in its difference from the eternal being of God. But if this is the starting point, then we are faced with the question: 'What was God doing before he made heaven and earth?'[15] Augustine does not reply to this with the jesting response that 'He was preparing hell for people who pry into mysteries'. He earlier writes in *The City of God*: without movement and change there is no such thing as time. Eternity knows no change. So time does not happen unless creation happens, and unless from creation there issues forth a being that changes. 'Of course the world is not created *in* time, but *with* time', he says. 'For what happens in time happens after something and before something else. The time that lies behind is the past, the time that is ahead the future . . . But the world was created with time when once the movement of change was included in its creation.'[16]

He develops this idea further in the *Confessions*. Time is part of creation. If God did not create the world *in* time but *with* time, then he made time together *with* creation. Only the Creator is 'before' created being, and 'before' time is only eternity.

> No, although you are before time, it is not in time that you precede it. If this were so, you would not be before all time. It is in eternity, which is supreme over time because it is a never-ending present, that you are at once before all past time and after all future time.[17]

Here Augustine too uses the idea of the eternal present for the concept of eternity: 'Your today is Eternity, for your today does not give place to any tomorrow, nor does it take the place of any yesterday.'[18] Time is therefore a characteristic of created being. Time only exists as created time.

But how, then, are we to understand the point of coincidence of time and eternity in the act of creation which took place *in principio*? Is time's point of inception to be found in time itself, or in eternity? Augustine thinks that the beginning of time is an absolute, and is therefore in eternity, not in time. If there is no time without creation, then God must be 'before all time the eternal Creator of all time' (XI, 30). But if creation is in time, how can the Creator be an eternal Creator? If God is *creator aeternus*, surely his creation must be eternal too? If God is eternally creative, he can never '*have created*' at any time, so he has 'never' created.[19]

In considering God's creative act, how can we think of God's eternity and the temporality of the creature simultaneously, without the one's cancelling out the other? There is no transition and no mediation between eternity and time if time and eternity are defined over against one another. We therefore have to proceed from the assumption that it was only a self-alteration of eternity which made created time possible and made room for it. This is what the doctrine of God's essential creative resolve says. The question: what was God doing before he created the world and time? is not a pointless question. It has to be answered by saying that before the creation of the world, God resolved to be its Creator in order to be glorified in his kingdom. The unique transition from eternity to time is to be found in this self-determination of God's. In this essential resolve, God withdrew his eternity into himself in order to take time for his creation and to leave his creation its own particular time. Between God's essential eternity and the time of creation stands *God's time* for creation – the time appointed through his resolve to create.

For Augustine, the creaturely difference that marks time off from eternity means that time is not a category of eternity, but takes its definition from the alteration and movement of created reality. Time is the creaturely form of happening. Creation is experienced as the flux of time, which flows from the being-that-is-not-yet of the future through the being of the present into the being-that-is-no-longer of the past. Unlike the pure Being of God, created being is always bound together with non-being. And this makes future and past, predicates of created being. Augustine rejects the Eleatic argument, according to which non-being is unknowable and inconceivable, so that future and past do not exist, in the strict sense. He therefore also has to reject the Eleatic elevation of the present into the present of eternity. 'How can we say that even the present *is*, when the reason why it *is*, is that it is *not to be*?'[20] So he understands the present as temporal, not eternal: 'Rightly, we can only say that time *is*, by reason of its impending state of *not being*.' But then there is obviously no fixed point in time. Even prolonged time is no more than a succession of fleeting moments. The experience of the transience of all things in time deprives human beings of any fixed point in time at all, and fills their hearts with 'restlessness'.[21] It is this restlessness which makes them enquire about the eternity of God, which alone can give them continuance.

Yet although we ourselves are temporal beings, we compare and measure out the times. We perceive the times in our souls:

> Neither future nor past 'is'; nor can it properly be said that there 'are' three times, past, present and to come: yet it may perhaps be properly said that there 'are' three times; a present of things past, a present of things present, and a present of things future. For these three do exist as a kind of triad in the soul, though nowhere else that I can see. For in the soul is the present of things past, that is memory (*memoria*); the present of things present, that is sight (*contuitus*); the present of things future, that is expectation (*expectatio*).[22]

Through memory, sight and expectation, the soul has the ability to unite the times in itself, to keep them present and to make them contemporaneous. Admittedly the soul can only do this imperfectly, and merely in a spiritual way: memory does not call back the past; it merely 're-presents' it by way of impressions and images.[23] Expectation does not anticipate the future itself, in a proleptic sense; it only anticipates experiences and acts by means of inadequate images and preconceptions. And yet memory does represent a certain re-creation of the past in the present; and expectation does in a sense represent the new creation of the future in the present mind. For by means of memory and expectation, the soul intervenes in non-being and calls it into present existence. The soul's power of remembrance and hope must in its own way be termed 'creative'. The created mind of man reaches out through time, penetrating past, present and future being, through remembrance, sight (or present perception) and expectation; and in this way it partakes of the eternal Creator Spirit and engenders in the soul of human beings a relative eternity, in the sense of a relative simultaneity of past, present and future being. Human beings are made in the image of God; and this means that in the flux of time they are able to mirror the unity of time in the soul. Augustine rightly introduced into the naive enumeration of the different modes of time *the subject* of the experience of time – the human soul. There is no such thing as past, present and future *per se*. There is only present past, present present and present future. The remembering, perceiving and expecting *soul* is the common point of reference, and the unity of the times.

So much for Augustine's position. But before leaving him we have to consider two questions which he himself raises.

1. Does *the beginning* of time belong in time or in eternity? If it belongs within time, then there was time before time; if it belongs to eternity, time itself is eternal. Augustine inclines to the view of 'eternal creation', as he shows by calling God 'the eternal Creator of all times'. Karl Barth tried to find a way out of Augustine's logical impasse. His suggestion is as follows. There was no time before creation. Before creation there was only God's eternity. But 'His eternity is itself revealed in the act of creation as his readiness for time, as pre-temporal, supra-temporal (or co-temporal) and post-temporal, and therefore as the source of time, of superior and absolute time'.[24] In the act of creation God's eternity 'unfurls' its 'pre-temporal, co-temporal and post-temporal being'. This idea of a 'preparedness of eternity for time' is helpful if it means that the eternal God permits a time different from himself. But it loses its force if it simply means the interpretation of eternity as eternity in relation to time – as is indicated by the words pre-, co- and post-. The suggestion has its roots solely in the concept of the essential creative resolve. For through this resolve time is already constituted. Augustine certainly saw a logical difficulty here too; for if this is a resolve of the will, it cannot be essential and eternal; and if it is essential and eternal, it cannot be an act of will. But if eternity is not also supposed to exclude the self-movement of the Absolute, then the idea of the eternal God's designation of himself to be Creator can take us a step further: by designating himself to be the Creator of a temporal world, God declares himself 'prepared' for time. He takes time for his creation and allows it time. He withdraws his eternity into himself in order to give his creation its time. Between his essential eternity on the one hand and creaturely temporality on the other, there is therefore *God's own time* which he designated

for his creation through his creative resolve, and the temporal era of creation which is thereby inaugurated. The Augustinian statement about *creatio cum tempore* refers only to the temporal being of the creature. The proposition *creatio in tempore* cannot, in contrast, refer to created time. It can only refer to the time established and inaugurated by God with his creative resolve. If we make this distinction, we can quite well talk about *creatio cum tempore – in tempore*, understanding this in the sense that God created the world with *its* time – in *his* time. *Mundus factus cum tempore creato in tempore Dei.*

2. Karl Barth called time as distinct from eternity 'this division into present, past and future, this flux of that which is from the past through the present, and into the future'.[25] The direction of time which Barth gives here is the opposite of Augustine's. This draws our attention to an important problem. According to our everyday feelings, our lifetime flows from the future into the past. That is the vector of transience. Yet at the same time we count the years in the reverse direction, from a temporal beginning or centre of time in the direction of an endless future.

Augustine's view raises a question: if every future changes into the past by way of the present, does not *the past* have ontological precedence in time? What comes, passes away; expectation becomes remembrance; remembrance turns into forgetting; and the end of every becoming is death. The irreversibility of time's flow from the future into the past really makes everything past: there is a past past, a present past and a future past. So if any one time is supposed to be particularly close to eternity, then in this respect it is the past, not the present. The past is the end of all things.

But if this is the character of time, are we then to suppose that God made his creation for death? Is the time of creation the time of death? Surely created time belongs within God's time, the time of its Creator? What meaning can the creation of transience have? If death is already the destiny of creation itself, not only the destiny of sin, then created existence is not anything we can possibly affirm. All that remains for the soul is the yearning, searching glance for its home beyond, in the eternity of God. The inescapable transitoriness of all things in the flux of time can only be countered by a religious flight from the world into the divine eternity.

Augustine's experience of God is the experience of the distance between Creator and creature, and between eternity and time. In this distance he discovers the temporality of created being, and the creatureliness of time. Because it is made in the image of God, the soul conforms to the divine eternity, making the past present through remembrance, and the future present through expectation. In this way it confers on time a relative unity. It is this that makes the experience of history possible. Non-being in future and past is perceived and experienced in the Being of the present. But the fundamental distance between the time of created being and the eternal Being of God makes Augustine identify time with transience, and describe the time of created being as the time of death. Yet this is not the only possible way of characterizing time by what happens in it.

§4 EXPERIENCES OF TIME IN THE HISTORY OF GOD

The biblical traditions tell us about experiences of life and time in God's history with the world, a history which is determined by promise, covenant, deliverance, redemption and other divine acts. We shall look now at the development of biblical concepts of time, so as to show from them that the experience of time is determined by whatever is fundamentally experienced in time – that is to say, experienced about God. Time is not a formal category which can be applied in the same way to everything, and therefore behaves towards everything with equal indifference. Time is never empty. It is always 'ful(l)-filled' time. We have to talk about the event itself if we want to understand its time.

1. Israel was familiar first of all with the *kairological* understanding of time. Concepts about an endless, linear, temporal continuum, and ideas about time in the absolute sense, were alien to her. On the contrary, every happening had 'its own time'. There is seedtime, and the time of harvest; the time to give birth, and the time to die (Eccles. 3.1–8). Every event has its particular moment in time, and this moment in time is the event's own, proper setting. 'The event is inconceivable without its time', says von Rad, 'and *vice versa*.'[26] That is why Israel talked about 'times' in the plural. She was not conscious of time as a unity, because she did not see world events as homogeneous. Time is determined by happening, not happening by time. The time of the event is the appropriate, the favourable time – the only time in which it can take place. It is true that this was also in accord with the astrological notions of the

ancient East at that time, in which the times of all events were seen as being ordered through the stars. But in the story of the covenant with Noah, Israel already bound these times for seedtime and harvest, frost and heat, day and night, not to the constellations of the stars, but to the covenant and faithfulness of her God. 'While the earth remains . . . .' guarantees the rhythm of the times and the kairos of every event through God's faithfulness to the covenant. It is God's covenant with his creation, conferred once and for all, which establishes the times of created being.

2. In a second stratum, Israel developed an interpretation of time drawn from *the history of the promise*. The One who is Ever-Being, the Eternally Abiding and the Continually Present may be manifested in the experience of the eternal return of the same thing, in the perception of recurring regularities, and in the concept of the timeless and universal. But Israel experienced her God in unique, historical happenings. The events of the promise to Abraham, Isaac and Jacob are followed by the event of the Exodus, in which God reveals himself, and out of which Israel emerges as God's people. The Exodus is understood as a *unique* event, never repeated in this form. But it is understood at the same time as an event that is also in the literal sense *once-and-for-all* – an event determing every succeeding generation in Israel as it determined the Exodus generation itself. The Exodus event is therefore an event in the past but not a past event. As an event in the past, it determines the times that follow. It is an event that initiates history. It establishes the time of God's covenant with Israel, and discloses for Israel God's future.

Later on, the Israelites proceeded to relate, not merely this one, unique event, but a whole series of similar events. The so-called 'brief historical creeds' (Deut. 26.5; Josh. 24.3ff.), with their summaries of saving events, describe a coherent divine history. In this way Israel acquires the conception of history as *a succession*. History is inaugurated by the promise and is fulfilled through the people's history with that divine promise. 'Israel's history existed only in so far as God accompanied her', writes von Rad.' It was God who established the continuity between the various separate events and who ordained their direction as they followed one another in time.'[27] Every individual incident is astoundingly new. The cohesion of these incidents and the direction in which they tend is revealed by the divine promise.

The form which this knowledge takes, and the way in which the history of God's promise is communicated, can only be narrative, not a systematic and generalizing concept. The story makes the past present, in order to proclaim the future. It awakes remembrance in order to justify hope. The story tells of the divine faithfulness which has been experienced, in order to awaken new trust in God in the future. The promise that has gone forth, and the divine faithfulness that has been experienced, point to the future; and it is the future that has precedence in the different modes of time.[28]

3. The *prophetic* experience of history can be described, in von Rad's words, as 'the eschatologizing of historical thinking': the prophets also belong within the tradition of the election of their people and the history of the promise. But what sets them apart from the historical writings is their present experience of the rupture of this salvation history through the destruction of Jerusalem and the new enslavement of the people. For them, this meant experiencing the discontinuity of history. It is only this experience of the present which, for the first time, allows the history of the past to become *a past history*. On the other hand, if there is a future at all for the nation in the history of God, this future cannot be the prolongation of tradition, or the continuing development of the past. In von Rad's words: 'The new element which in a certain respect differentiates them from all previous spokesmen of Jahwism is – to use the controversial but unavoidable term – the eschatological element.'[29] The eschatological is therefore defined by the promise of something totally new in quality, as we see from Isaiah 43.18f.: 'Remember not the former things, nor consider the things of old. For behold, I will create a new thing; now it shall spring up.' The future is God's new creation. It is not a return of primordial days, nor is it a prolongation of the past. Past history and the new future which is prophetically promised no longer belong within the same temporal continuum. They are contrasted as 'old and new'. They become two separate times which are different in quality. Their unity is to be found solely in the faithfulness of God, who lets the old become obsolete and creates what is new.

Against the transcendent background of God's faithfulness, the prophets then discover the analogies through which they herald God's new creation. The new creation will bring 'the new Exodus' (Deutero-Isaiah), 'the new covenant' (Jeremiah), 'the new Servant of God' (Deutero-Isaiah), 'the new settlement of the promised land' and 'the new Jerusalem'; finally, it will bring 'the new heaven and the new earth' (Trito-Isaiah). It is true that the prophets describe God's new creation with the images of times belonging to the faraway past, which cannot be brought back again. But they paint this new creation in incandescent colours: the new Exodus will be a festal procession, not a nocturnal flight, and there will be more splendour in the new Jerusalem than ever there was in the old. God's saving acts in the past turn into promises of his deeds in the future. Von Rad puts it as follows: The prophetic proclamation only became eschatological 'when the prophets expelled Israel from the safety of the old saving actions and suddenly shifted the basis of salvation to a future action of God'.[30] God's acts of old and his new acts no longer belong to one and the same time. The new acts of God belong to 'his time', 'the new time'. The hoped-for future makes of the remembered past its own prehistory, and confers retroactive continuity, as it were. By creating what is new, God reverts in faithfulness to what is old.

4. A glance at *apocalyptic* literature shows that this present experience of the severance of all the bridges to the past divine history can heighten the difference between past and future to cosmic dimensions. Present and past become 'this age of unrighteousness and death'; the future becomes 'the coming age of righteousness and life'. The two world times confront one another as two powers, each of which determines whatever is in their own temporal sphere. They are defined exclusively, one against the other, so that they confront one another as death and life, perdition and salvation, hell and heaven. It is only the revealed Torah – revealed 'now already' in this age of perdition – which communicates the life of the new age in the old, or forms a communicative bond between the righteous in this wicked world and their saving future in the other. It is a person's attitude towards the Law which decides whether he will be saved from this world's time and will participate in the time of the future. But apart from that, 'there is no true life in the life that is false', as Adorno says. Apart from that, all the good that is done serves merely to stabilize the evil system. Apart from personal observance of the Torah, all that remains to the apocalyptist is what Marcuse calls 'the great refusal'; he can only watch the worsening of conditions and wait for the coming of the new world time.

5. *The New Testament's* understanding of time is *messianic* throughout, and its premise is therefore the apocalyptic doctrine of time. Its background is the idea of the two aeons; and against this

background the Christ event – Jesus' death and resurrection – is viewed and proclaimed as the decisive turn of the age. Here too, time is defined through the experienced event of God himself. Jesus' crucifixion and death mark the end of the old age. The raising of Jesus 'from the dead' manifests the dawn of the new age of resurrection and eternal life, even if initially it is only for this one person and the people who believe in him. In this sense Christ really is 'the end of history' – the end, that is, of the history that is dominated by sin, law and death. But his resurrection ushers in the new, enduring world time. 'If anyone is in Christ he is a new creation; the old has passed away. Behold, everything has become new' (II Cor. 5.17). The old existence of men and women, which was dominated by the power of sin and the fate of death, now dies and, in faith, is buried with Christ into his death (Rom. 6.4ff.). New human existence is born under the power of righteousness and the prospect of eternal life. The qualitative difference between a past determined by sin, law and death, and the future determined by grace, love and eternal life, is stressed so emphatically that there is no continuity between the one and the other. The difference between this and the apocalyptic understanding of time lies solely in the fact that with Christ and in the fellowship of his people this qualitatively new future has already begun, in the very midst of this present age. The new world time thrusts itself into this world time, making it a time that passes away.

With the coming of the Messiah, the messianic time begins. But Jesus, the Messiah, was crucified in powerlessness and, as the risen One, only appeared initially to the women and men who were his disciples; so this messianic time is only the beginning of the new era, under the still-enduring effects of the old. This delineation of time is expressed in the New Testament through the phrase 'at hand'. Jesus proclaims the nearness of the kingdom that is 'at hand' (Mark 1.15). For Paul, 'the night is far gone, the day is at hand' (Rom. 13.12). According to the First Epistle of Peter, 'the end of all things is at hand' (I Peter 4.7). Through the coming of Christ the new age has been heralded – has dawned – has begun. But it has not yet appeared in its full force. We call this daybreak of a new creation the *messianic* time because it is the time of a well-founded hope, even if it is not yet the time of universal fulfilment, to which we give the name the *eschatological* time.

So what is new about the messianic time is not entirely new. The messianic gospel which Paul proclaims picks up 'what was promised before' (Rom. 15.4) and goes back to Israel's history of promise. In the past history of disaster there was always the scarlet thread of promise and hope for salvation. In this sense there is future in the past. The messianic gospel takes up the promises and the experiences of Israel's hope and spreads them throughout the world. With faith in Jesus the Messiah it therefore evokes among the Gentiles hope for the messianic kingdom of the God of Israel. From the other side, it can be said that in the gospel the coming Lord hastens ahead of his own kingdom and gathers his people. The future of the new world is already present, but as yet only as its own beginning, in the form of Word and faith.

What Paul expounds through the messianic gospel is presented by Matthew and Luke through the messianic Torah in Jesus' Sermon on the Mount: in the fellowship of Jesus the Messiah and in his Spirit, and with the beginning of the messianic era, the righteousness of the kingdom of God is manifested and implemented. It is no longer an unendurable burden for men and women. It is a matter of course, and a joy. It no longer belongs to the exile of a hostile world. It stands in the daybreak colours of its own world, the kingdom of God. That is why it no longer merely suffers injustice, but enters into its own home country.

On the foundation of its experience of the Messiah who is already present, messianic faith divides up the times according to the powers that dominate them:

To *the past* belongs everything which, in the presence of Jesus the Messiah, is *no longer* valid and no longer efficacious: sin, 'the Law' and death.

To *the present* belongs everything which, in the presence of Jesus the Messiah, is *now already* valid and efficacious: grace, reconciliation and liberty.

To *the future* belongs everything which, although it is *not yet* experienced, is none the less *already* to be hoped for: the resurrection of the dead, the redemption of the body, and eternal life.

But this means that *the present time* of believers is no longer determined by the past. It takes its definition from the future. The believer's present is free from the past and open for the future of the Messiah. It is the present of the One who is to come. So it is by no means true that the Christian faith replaces the archaic, cyclical interpretation of time by a modern, linear one. What it puts at this point is its own messianic understanding of time, which distinguishes between the quality of past and future – which is the very opposite of setting them on a single line.

6. Summing up this brief survey of the biblical traditions, we can say the following:

(*a*) *The time of the right and opportune moment* is determined by the event itself. Every event has its time.

(*b*) *Historical time* is determined by the sending-forth of God's promise and by the events of God's faithfulness.

(*c*) *The messianic time* is determined by the coming of the Messiah and the dawn of the new creation in the midst of the transient time of this world.

(*d*) *Eschatological time* is determined by the universal fulfilment of what was promised in historical time and what has dawned in the messianic time.

(*e*) *Eternal time*, finally, will be the time of the new eternal creation in the kingdom of the divine glory.

If we look back at these qualitatively different experiences and concepts of time, we can discover continuity in them, inasmuch as in each given case the experience of the coming time fulfils the earlier time and gathers it into itself. So, looking back, we can also say that what was earlier points to what comes afterwards. In the history of God, the different times and the different experiences of time are determined by what happens from God's side. Whatever happens from God's side has a certain direction, pointing from creation at the beginning to the eternal kingdom. For God did not create the world for transience and death. He created it for his glory, and therefore for its own eternal life. Augustine evidently did not take this dimension of time into account.

§5 THE INTERLACED TIMES OF HISTORY

History, as a general concept, and without the addition of any special subject, is undoubtedly one of the fundamental symbols for the world of modern European times. It is also one of the almost untranslatable mysteries of the German mind in particular. In our present context we shall confine ourselves to some dimensions of time and the historical experience of time, so that we can comprehend both the value and the limitations of this modern world symbol.

The modern symbol 'history' is often interpreted through the picture of progress. We human beings take steps and advance, and when we have a clear goal in front of us, our progress is like a straight line. The human being who advances towards a particular goal sees the past as what he leaves behind him with every step; the future is that which opens up ahead of him in a new way with every fresh step; and the present is no more than the transition from the past to the future. Through the power of memory, he can still hold fast to the past – sometimes and to some degree; but the more the past recedes, the more it escapes him. He anticipates the future with every step that brings him nearer to his goal. But he hardly experiences the present at all, because he knows no rest and can never linger anywhere. There is always only one goal and one way and one progression. Consequently, for the advancing man or woman there is always merely *one* past and *one* future. Whether it is he himself who 'hastens' through the different modes of time, or whether it is time that 'passes him by', as we say, may remain an open question. We can make this clear to ourselves by considering the 'advancing' person; but the same thing can also be transferred to modern society, inasmuch as it too is involved in a single and common progress and in a process which can be defined in unified terms.

But does this idea fit the community in which we live, or does it violate that community? Does it do justice to the men and women of past generations? Does it respect the rights and the dignity of the generations of the future? Isn't history, pictured as progress, always at the same time an instrument of domination – the domination of one society, one class and the one, present generation, an instrument used to suppress all the others and take possession of them? And isn't history, pictured as progress, also an instrument for subjecting nature to the will and intentions of human beings?

Today we are coming up against the limits of this modern world symbol at a whole number of different points. Consequently we have to differentiate within the concept of history itself, and have to integrate that concept into the wider concept of nature. I shall try to do the first by way of a complex modalization of the tenses: past, present and future; and shall then go on to point to the limitations of history through the synchronization of human time with the natural time of the ecosystem 'earth'. In both cases, what is at issue is a perichoretic understanding of the different modes of time, which interpenetrate one another qualitatively, and cannot simply be quantitatively separated from one another.

1. The experience of reality as history becomes meaningful and endurable in the eschatological context of 'the future of history'.

2. Historical awareness differentiates between the present past and the past present, and puts us in a position to discover the future in the past, to pick up past possibilities again, and to link them with the present future.

3. Awareness of the future differentiates between the present future and the future present, and puts us in a position to distinguish between future past and future future. This then gives rise to the theologically important distinction between historical future and eschatological future.

4. Present future is aligned towards the synchronization of the different historical times or tenses: the different human histories fuse into a single history because, through growing interdependencies and growing conflicts, either 'a single humanity' will come into being as the subject of a common history, or the hostile groups will all perish together in the one, single catastrophe.

5. Present future is aligned towards the synchronization of human historical time with the rhythms of natural time – the rhythms of the ecosystem earth, and the bio-rhythms of the human body. Either human history and the history of nature will arrive at a co-ordinated harmony, or human history will find its irrevocable end in ecological death.

These theses do more than merely describe a function of history, as a paradigm of modern theology. They also indicate certain changes of function which this paradigm has to undergo today.

1. *The Experience of History against the Horizon of its Future*

The modern experience of reality as history apparently grew up out of the industrial and political revolutions of European and American modern times.[31] The 'philosophy of history', as a genre of its own, began in the eighteenth century, with Bossuet and Voltaire. The nineteenth century then tried to comprehend the crises of the French Revolution and the opportunities of the industrial revolution with continually new outlines of a 'universal history' or 'history of the world'. The development of these ideas has been described often enough. In our present context the following elements are important.

1. Once a human world, made by human beings and modifiable by human beings, cuts itself off from the world of nature, that human world, to the same degree, loses its orientation towards the laws of the cosmos and the rhythms of nature.[32] The Becoming of human history no longer corresponds to the Becoming of nature. Human beings take their bearings, not from nature, but from their own human hopes and purposes. People no longer seek to live 'in accordance with nature', as the Stoics taught. They now live in accordance with their own notions of what they want *to effect* through their actions, and what they can *expect from* the effects of those actions. The more human beings experience themselves as the subject of history, the more they require an answer to Kant's question: What can I hope for?[33] The question about the future of history therefore also becomes the question about the meaning which an event experienced and caused by human beings can have on human hopes and purposes. History is experienced as meaningless when the horizon of hopes and purposes is dark and obscure. On the other hand, the horizon of human hopes and purposes becomes dim and uncertain if the history experienced and caused by human beings can no longer be related to it.

2. As the world of human beings becomes detached from the natural environment, the old ideas about the cycles and rhythms of time are lost. The linear series of points-in-time takes their place. The different experiences and traditions about times of living can be related to their abstract form, into which they can be integrated. Time as it is measured by the clock quantifies everything in exactly the same way. The clock therefore has become the omnipresent and omnipotent time-keeper in modern industrial society.

3. As the human world became detached from the world of nature, 'modern times' began – that experiment which Hegel was still able to welcome as 'the glorious dawn which stands man on his head, that is to say on his own ideas, and forms reality accordingly'.[34] Yet even then, conservative critics branded this 'experiment' as 'the most abominable beast from the abyss'.[35] If scientific and technological civilization is an experiment carried out by human beings, then we must also view it as a human *project*.[36] But a project is only pursued as long as the hopes which prompt it are not fundamentally disappointed by the experiences to which it gives rise. These experiences can interpret the hopes in a new way, and changes of direction within the general orientation can seem called

for on the basis of new experiences. But this hermeneutical process still preserves the continuity. It presupposes that there is no alternative to the way that has been chosen. But the visions of the future which accompany the experiment of modern times are so ambivalent that they already display doubt even here. Nor is it by any means certain, even today, how long the chance to turn back will still be open to us, in the crises to which the experiment of modern times is exposed, or when these crises will become the foretokens of the experiment's inexorable catastrophe. So by making history the fundamental symbol of the world, we have not made the world situation progressively better. On the contrary, it has become increasingly critical.

This is already evident from the theoretical contradictions within the actual concept of history. How can history be thought of as a unity, if history does not have a subject – or at least not a single subject? How can history be thought of as a whole, if the future is unknown, so that the whole is either incomplete or, at least, not yet present? How can the world be conceived of as history at all if we ourselves exist as historical beings *in* history, and do not confront it from outside?

These general problems in the experiment history also emerge in the individual dimensions of time and the experiences of time within this experiment. History means temporal differentiation. It is perceived in the differences between present and future, present and past, and future and past. But the modern linearization of time – in order to reduce these differences to the relationship 'before – after' – has depicted them as lying along a single temporal line, P – Pr – F.

Yet the historical concept of time cannot work with a one-dimensional idea of time like this; for history is not a matter of a single process. There is not just a single past, present and future, with varying content, as the idea of a universal history would like to suggest. There are in fact different pasts, presents and futures of individual historical events.[37] We cannot consider the past merely as the preliminary history to our own present. We must view it as a past present, with its own past and its own future. We must then distinguish between the future of that past present, and the present which has grown out of it. Present present has as its presupposition, not merely past present, but also the future of the past present. What is called present today came into being out of the hopes and multifarious possibilities of the past present.

Analogously, we must distinguish between the present future (as an imaginative field of hopes, fears and diverging aims, with a forecourt of already definable and as yet undefinable possibilities) and a future present (which is the reality that develops out of these). The present present is not identical with the future of the past present; nor will the future present be congruent with the present future.

Augustine already thought in this way about the different tenses or modes of time, talking about the present past (PrP) in terms of *memoria*, the present present (PrPr) in terms of *contuitus*, and the present future (PrF) in terms of *expectatio*.[38] Georg Picht,[39] A. M. Klaus Müller,[40] Arthur Prior,[41] Niklas Luhmann,[42] Reinhart Koselleck[43] and Erich Jantsch[44] have differentiated these modes of time even further. The concept of linear time covers only simple series of events. But if these series of events are woven into a network of interrelations and multiple effects, networks of time have to be developed, in which linear and cyclical temporal concepts are combined. In feedback processes, for example, the present comes back to the past future, in order to make its own future comprehensible:

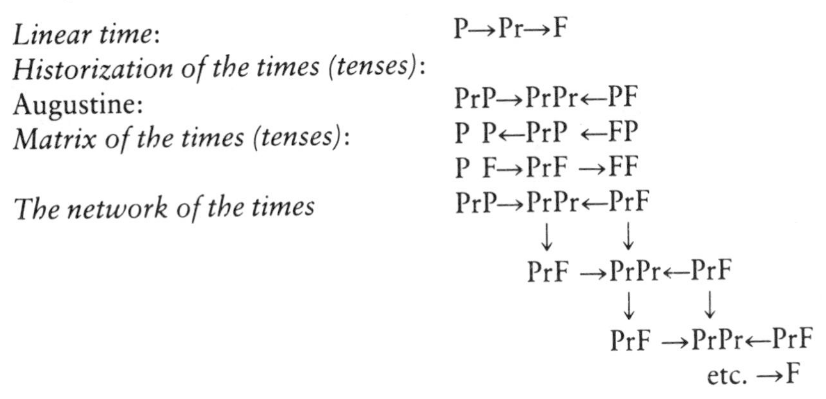

What moves in history, therefore, is the temporal present with its past and its future. But what moves it? We can see that the shifts only continue as long as the present in any given cases does not fulfil the future of the past present; and we can then perceive that *the future as project* always goes beyond *the future as experience*. This future that transcends all remembered, experienced and still-to-be experienced presents is what we call the eschatological future. We have to understand it, not as future history, but as the future *of*

history. As the future of history, it is the future of the past, as well as the future of the present and the future. In this sense it is the source and fountain of historical time. 'The primary phenomenon of primordial and authentic temporality is the future.'[45]

2. *The Historicization of the Present Past*

History encounters us in two forms: as the event which actually took place, and as the description and reconstruction of that event. German has tried to find a way out of this ambiguity by sometimes using two different words: *Geschichte*, for the past events; *Historie* for the account of these events. But the ambiguity suggests the further inherent equivocality of history as a concept: it can be the event, the past experience of the event, the actualization of the experienced event through memory, and the scholarly investigation of the past present 'as it really was', to use Leopold von Ranke's words. We are familiar with history in at least these four different senses – as event, as experience, as tradition, and as an account of the past.

What is of interest to us in our present context is the connection between tradition and history as historical account; for the historical investigation of the past present has always been, and still is, critically related to the actualization – the re-presentation, in the literal sense – of this past through traditions. Historical criticism breaks through the matter-of-course continuity of past and present, as tradition depicts it, by showing the difference between the past and its 're-presentation', and by making the connections between present and past contingent, and a matter for decision.[46]

Historical criticism began with the investigation of the origins of the legends through which the religious and political powers consolidated their rule, and with the consequent exposure of these legends for what they are. 'The true criticism of dogma [is] its history.'[47] Through recognition of the historical relativity and contingency of tradition, people living in the present acquire liberty from the traditions of their origins, and the freedom to form their own future. 'The pressure which tradition exerts upon our behaviour, on a preconscious level, is increasingly reduced by the advances made in the historical sciences.'[48] 'The historical sense breaks the last chains which philosophy and science were unable to break. Now the human being stands there on his own, completely free.'[49]

But if this liberation of men and women from the tutelage of the past and from its prejudices and prejudgments is the concern which at present guides the historically critical attitude to the past, this must not be allowed to lead to an unhistorical understanding of the present.

As we can see from Ernst Troeltsch, historical relativism always has the absolutism of the present subject as its precondition and its consequence. Historical criticism may certainly demolish the absolutist claims of the forces of tradition, but it apparently has difficulty in abolishing the absolutism of the present. Relativism in respect of history and subjective pluralism go hand in hand.

In addition, if historical criticism declares the past things which the different traditions actualize to be 'the past', then this past is assigned to the *one* past of the present present. This implies a kind of imperialism on the part of the present present towards earlier presents. Not least, the vista of the future which is already implicit, or in germ, in the past itself, is lost. The past is more than merely a prologue to the present.

These deadlocks in modern historicism can be solved to a certain degree if, on the one hand, the present past (tradition, both conscious and unconscious) is confronted critically with the past present, identified – with the help of historical reconstruction – as 'things as they really were'; and if, on the other hand, this present past is compared with its own future and its own possibility, which were already implicit or in germ in that past present. Then traditions and dogmas can be critically relativized, and the hopes which they preserve and the hopes which they suppress can be taken up again. Then the possibilities of the past present which were cut short or suppressed or merely neglected, can be picked up once more and integrated into the future of the present present. The future in the past inescapably brings a prospective into the historical retrospective.[50]

A good example is the role which Thomas Müntzer and the German Peasants' Revolt of 1525 have played in the German historical consciousness. For three hundred years, remembrance of this sombre chapter in the history of the Lutheran Reformation and German feudalism was stifled and repressed. It was only when, with the French Revolution, hope for 'liberty, equality and fraternity' dawned on the horizon of the present future, that Friedrich Schiller wrote his play *Wilhelm Tell*, taking over from the struggle of the

Swiss confederates the idea of 'A free people on free land'. When, in the Year of Revolutions (1848), popular sovereignty and democracy became a real possibility in Germany, people remembered the shattered hopes of the peasants in 1525 and took them up again. In 1848/49 Friedrich Engels wrote the first history of the Peasants' Revolt. And in 1921 Ernst Bloch hailed Müntzer – who had for so long been damned as a rebel and agitator – as the first 'theologian of revolution'.

Historical consciousness therefore has at least these two components: historical criticism is critically related to the actualization of the past in traditions and institutions, comparing these with the past present which is open to historical investigation; but historical research also enquires about the future of that past present which was interrupted, suppressed or simply forgotten. The concern prompting the historical criticism of tradition is the liberty of those living in the present. The concern behind the historical investigation of the future in the past is always prompted by questions about the present future. But can then 'the historicism of our modern society' be described as 'a reflection of its future'?[51]

The demolition of the absolute claims of tradition and the abolition of the absolute claims of those living in the present do not end in a general sceptical relativism. They lead to a living relationalism in an intricate fabric of interconnections. The concern that determines these relationships will undoubtedly be stamped by the hopes and fears, the purposes and tasks of the present future. For these will decide the future of the past as well – that is to say, the future of the dead. Eschatological hope for the future always also confers retroactive historical community. The biblical symbol of the eschatological hope for the future is the resurrection of the dead; and this is an expression of hope for those who have gone. The inscription at Yad Vashem in Jerusalem rightly reminds us that

> Forgetfulness leads to exile,
> while remembrance is the secret of redemption.

3. *The Futurization of the Present Future*

Like history, the future is equivocal. Most European languages have two possible ways of talking about the future. *Futurum*, or its equivalent, is used for what *will be*; *adventus*, or its cognates, for that which *is coming*. But English and German have only one possibility open to them. The English word 'future' comes from the Latin *futurum*, while the German *Zukunft* is related to the Latin *adventus* (Greek *parousia*).[52]

If the future is understood in the sense of *futurum*, it means what *will be* out of past and present. It is one form in the process of becoming of *physis*. In this sense, the future offers no occasion for a hope which could communicate enduring certainty. For what is *not yet* will sometime or other *no longer* be. In this sense, the future offers nothing but future past. The process is irreversible: the future will become the past, but the past will never again be future. The future of becoming certainly offers a reason and occasion for development and planning, prediction and programmes; but not for enduring hope.

On the other hand, if we understand future as *adventus*, it means what is coming – what is on the way towards the present. What we describe as a 'coming' event is not something that develops out of the present. It confronts the present with something new, whether it be good or evil. In Greek, *parousia* means presence or arrival. But in the New Testament the word is never applied to Christ's past or his presence here and now. It is always and exclusively kept for his promised and expected coming in glory. In this way the word 'advent' became the quintessence of the messianic hope. When the word *adventus* was translated into German by *Zukunft*, the German word acquired a messianic, advent note. What is meant is something that is coming and which will never go or pass away; something which remains. It is the moment to which we can say, with Goethe's Faust, 'Tarry awhile, thou art so fair'. This is the new, enduring world of the Jewish and Christian hope.

What happens when this 'coming' takes the place of 'the future'? Revelation 1.4 does in fact replace the one by the other: 'Peace to you', says the writer, 'from him who is and who was and who is to come.' We would expect as third term the words '. . . and who will be'. But the future tense of the verb 'to be' is replaced by the future of the verb 'to come'. This alters the third term in the traditional concept of time quite decisively. God's being is in his coming, not in his *be*coming. So his being does not pass away when once it comes. If God and the future are linked together theologically in this way, God's being has to be thought of eschatologically; and then the future has to be understood theologically. But if 'future' is thought of theologically, it acquires a continual transcendence compared with every present, and makes of every present a provisional transcendence. In this way the future becomes the paradigm of transcendence. Of course past and future can then no longer be reduced to the same linear temporal concept, for their relation to one another is now one of qualitative difference. It is the difference between 'old' and 'new'.

This future is not merely the temporal forecourt of any given present. It is the transcending forecourt of past presents as well. This then means that there is a past future, a present future and a future future. The eschatological future determines all three modes of time.

The theoretical distinction between 'the future' and 'the coming' leads to the distinction between extrapolation and anticipation in our practical dealings with what is ahead. There are trends and lines of development in past and present which we can extrapolate into the future.[53] But these extrapolations turn the future into a prolongation of the present. These prolongations of the present are always used to stabilize present conditions of ownership and power; for only the person who has the power to implement his purposes can plan, and has any interest in extrapolation. But the prolongations and extensions of present conditions do not create a real future. On the contrary, they suppress the alternative possibilities the future holds. Extrapolations do not treat the future as an open field of the possible; they see it as a reality already determined by past and present. But this is illusory: it leads to a dangerous blindness to the apocalypse among men and women in the modern system.[54]

On the other hand, the understanding of the future as what is to come, corresponds to the anticipation through which men and women attune themselves to something ahead, whether through their fear of something terrible, or through their hope for happiness. These foretastes, search images and attunements are part of every perception of the unknown. Without anticipatory awareness we should not discern something that is still in the future at all.[55] But in anticipatory awareness, we always align ourselves to what is last and final – to happiness or unhappiness, life or death. The last thing to penetrate our experience is the first in our expectation.[56] It is in the light of this that we then perceive and judge what can come upon us, and what actually does come.

In actual practice we always combine anticipation and extrapolation in a single act, because we link what we hope for, or fear, with what we consider possible. On the levels of planning and programmes, we also link the future we desire with the future we consider possible and achievable.

The content of the future we hope for and consider desirable, or the future we dread and wish to avoid, always has to do with our fundamental concerns, the things towards which our whole existence is aligned and on which it depends. These are the symbols of the eschatological future.

The traces of this eschatological future can be discerned in the different prospective futures of the present – whether it is one's own past present, or the present of someone or something else. The reason is apparently that time is itself a real symbol of the future-eternal. It is this which puts its impress on human experiences of time. No present prospect of the future is identical or identifiable with 'the future' itself. Eschatological future cannot be reduced to a dogma. The critical distinction between the present future in any given case, and the historically always-future future preserves these differences.

4. *The Synchronization of Historical Times*

In a limited and provisional way, the present future always determines the hope and the functions or tasks of history. We must look here at two of these tasks, because unless they are implemented in future there will be no more future for human beings at all.

We might call one of them the synchronization of the different historical times in which human beings have lived and are still living. Earlier, the different nations all had their 'histories', in the plural. Every people, every civilization and every religion had its own past and its own future, and it was these that gave their particular present its form and colouring. In reality there has never been any such thing as 'universal history' in the singular. Up to now there have only been different human histories in our world. When people talked about 'world history', the idea was always associated with an inclusive claim to power. The notion was an instrument for the imperialism of *one* nation, *one* culture or *one* religion, which tried to bring the rest of the world under the dictatorship of its own time. The concept of 'history' *per se* is also an instrument of European, American and Russian domination.

But apart from this, a singular subject of history is coming into existence today, because of the growing danger that humanity will destroy itself.[57] In the face of the nuclear annihilation of the world, the inexorable alternative is 'one world or none'. And if this is so, then we are standing on a cultural threshold of a very special kind. If we today enter a common world – initially for merely negative reasons, because of the mutual threat of global annihilation – then we shall continue to have plural pasts and traditions, but we shall have hope and future only in the singular. For us human beings there is only a common future, for we can now only survive in peace. World peace is the fundamental condition for the survival of humanity. But what will this community of all humanity look like? And who is going to determine its character?

To say that the threatening danger of mutual nuclear annihilation through the super-powers makes the unity of humanity essential, is a negative way of describing that unity; it shows that a united humanity is necessary, but not that it is possible. Because of the shared peril, humanity is really being described as a common object of annihilation, not yet as a common subject of survival. We therefore have to discover the saving element in the apocalyptic peril. But deliverance can come only from the community of hope for life, and out of the solidarity of the will to build a peaceful world. By virtue of the will which this hope inspires, an ever-denser web of interrelations must be created on all levels, between the political blocks and the nations on earth. Forms of communication must be built up at higher and higher stages, so that one day humanity will be so organized that it can become the author of its own history, and can determine its own future. The category of danger in which the future is perceived here is only the framework for the category of hope in which we have to act.

What interests us in this context is the transition from thinking in terms of one's own history to a consideration of one's own history in terms of the necessary community of humanity. It is the transition from particularist to universal thinking. In the present situation of the world, particularist thinking is merely schismatic thinking, because it refuses the community which is necessary and also possible. Thinking like this is aggressively concerned with determining its own particular identity by way of separation from other and alien traditions. In theology, this profile-neurosis was for centuries represented by 'controversial' theology. The transition from controversial to ecumenical theology is the way from the demarcation line drawn against other people to the distinctive, individual contribution to the common future life.

If we choose this path, we no longer read the testimonies of other histories and traditions with an eye for their particularity. We read them with a view to the coming ecumenical community. It is possible to read the testimonies of the different traditions in order to see whether they are Protestant or Catholic or Orthodox. But we shall have to read them in the light of what they contribute to an ecumenical community of the Christian faith. The person who thinks schismatically considers his own part to be the whole. The person who thinks ecumenically considers his own whole to be one part of the coming community. What happens within the ecumenical community of Christians in this way can also have an exemplary effect on the ecumenical community of religions and cultures, and on the ecological and political habitability of our globe.

5. *The Synchronization of Historical Time and Natural Time*

Ever since the beginning of the experiment we know as modern times, history and nature have continually been defined over against one another. This gave people the impression that nature was static, recurring and cyclical; while the experiences of time, change, contingency and the possible were all reserved for human history. A view of nature without history grew up, and with it a view of history without nature. In the great modern conceptions of world history, nature plays at most a marginal role.

Ever since Francis Bacon, the relationship between human beings and nature has been continually described as the relationship of a master to a slave.[58] The modern experiment 'history' has largely been built up on this attitude of mind. We need not describe here the appalling consequences – in the form of 'the ecological crisis' – of the dissociation of human history from the nature which is outside human beings and within them. Up to now, the creations of human history have led only to nature's depletion.

If the common catastrophe of human beings and the earth is still to be avertible at all, then it is certainly only by synchronizing human history with the history of nature, and if the experiment of modern times is carried out 'in accordance with nature' and not in opposition to nature, or at nature's expense.

In order to arrive at viable symbioses between human society and natural environments, it is essential to 'cool off' human history, and to slow down its one-sided varieties of progress. Its concept of time must be brought into harmony with the laws of life and the rhythms of nature, in the environment and in the bodily nature of human beings themselves. This is especially necessary, since among human beings the progress of one group is always at the cost of other groups. If technological progress is achieved at the expense of nature or the coming generations, this progress is merely a seeming, fictitious progress. We need more systems of equilibrium, in order to keep the advancing processes of history within bounds and to make them endurable. The relationship between progress and equilibrium in the human and natural systems must be brought into a co-ordinated, fluid equilibrium if the cost-utility accounts are to be set up realistically and honestly, and if the sum is to come out right.

In order to determine the necessary ethical limitations of human history, it is helpful to make the natural limitations of the history of human beings clear to ourselves.

Human history runs its course within the great, comprehensive ecosystem 'earth'.[59] The continual and unremitting influx of solar energy, the circulation of air and water, the seasons, the phases of the moon and the regular alternation of day and night constitute the unshakable natural environment for the times, the epochs and the goals of human history. And this comprehensive ecosystem earth, which can be endangered by human history and must therefore be respected, is in its turn a part-system in the ecosystem 'sun'; and so on. Every gaze into the immeasurable spaces of the stellar systems and galaxies cuts human history down to scale, showing it to be a small and limited phenomenon in the evolution of life on this one, single planet 'earth'.

Human history itself is not completely delivered over to the arbitrary despotism of present-day human beings. People may be in a position to oppress, exploit and kill other people living at the present day, to burden their children, to ruin the lives of their descendants, and to annihilate the future of coming generations. But they are not capable of destroying the life that has already been lived and the past delight in living of the dead. There is what Whitehead called 'an objective immortality of the dead'. I should like to take up his idea and modify it in our present context by saying that we can be robbed of our future, but not of our past. The dead are safe from us, even if what they lived for and what they hoped for depends on our decisions, because it has not yet been fulfilled. The life which has still to be lived is exposed to danger and annihilation; but the life that has already been lived has been saved from annihilation and is kept safe in eternity from the perils of time.

Every gaze into the cosmic world and every glance into the human past allows us to perceive the limits of our present history, the limits of its mortal dangers and the limits of its unique chances. History, as a general concept, and without the addition of any subject, was and is a fascinating conception of the experiment 'modern times'. It has hence also become the fundamental paradigm of Christian theology in those times. But if we look at the cost and the limits of this experiment, then it is a terrifying concept as well. The necessary circumscription of human history will only become possible when people learn to look beyond history. History became the paradigm of modern theology in the age in which the anthropocentric view of the world prevailed. Human beings were supposed to be 'the crown of creation' and the centre of the world. Everything was supposed to have been created for the human being and his use.

We shall only be able to reduce history to human and natural dimensions if this anthropocentrism is replaced by a new cosmological theocentrism. The creatures of the natural world are not there for the sake of human beings. Human beings are there for the sake of the glory of God, which the whole community of creation extols. The more human beings discover the meaning of their lives in joy in existence, instead of in doing and achieving, the better they will be able to keep their economic, social and political history within bounds. The stress of modern history is making people nervous and ill. They will only recover health if they learn natural serenity in the midst of all their activities.

The 'crown of history' is the sabbath. Without the sabbath quiet, history becomes the self-destruction of humanity. Through the sabbath rest, history is sanctified with the divine measure and blessed with the measure of a true humanity.

VI

The Space of Creation

Ever since Augustine, there have been many theological meditations on time. But meditations on space are rare. In modern times, theology's particular emphasis has been the experience of history. The categories of space have been left to the scientists. For apologetic reasons, a distinction was generally made between the Jewish and Christian experience of the divine in time, and Greek and Roman experience of the divine in space. And this differentiation led to the fruitless dichotomy between history and nature.

The last great discussion on the theological and scientific problem of space was carried on in the seventeenth century, between Newton and Leibniz. Is absolute space, in which all finite things co-exist, an attribute of the omnipresent God? Or is space nothing more than the extension of objects, and total space therefore the warp and weft of relationships between all conceivable extended things? This classic discussion belonging to the early period of the European Enlightenment provides a useful starting point for a new theological discussion about the problem of space.

The problem of space has a scientific aspect and an existential one. Let us look at the existential one first of all.

The metaphysical cosmology of earlier times saw the world as finite and self-contained, conceiving of it in the image of 'the globe'. In the history of science, the transition from this world-picture to the mathematical concept of space as the open, 'infinite' universe is one of the most important developments of the modern mind, and also one of the most astonishing.[1]

It was a transition which took place between the fifteenth and the seventeenth century. But if space itself is now termed 'infinite', unlimited and eternal, is it not thereby given divine attributes? Is 'the infinite universe' a pantheistic name for the divine? If space itself is unlimited and infinite, then the divine cannot be conceived of as anything more than its outermost 'frontier'. If space is merely thought of as a co-ordinate of extension, then – thinking in terms of Euclidean geometry – we see it as the figure of an infinite straight line. The spatial world can then no longer have any centre, unless we take the straight line to be an infinitely large orbit, whose centre is shifted into the infinite as well. This concept suggests that the cosmos is a limitless emptiness. Because this cosmos has lost its centre, it no longer offers any points of orientation either. Can its unity still be maintained at all, as the expression 'universe' would seem to suggest? Doesn't the one, infinite universe dissolve into a multiplicity of relative worlds?

Existentially, once the transition has been made from the closed cosmos to the endless universe, a new feeling about life comes into being. It is not the triumph of the pantheistic assurance that human beings are at home in the harmony of the world. On the contrary, it is the nihilistic sense of being lost, without anything to cling to, in the world's boundless emptiness: *horror vacui*. Pascal was one of the first to express this feeling: 'The eternal silence of these infinite spaces frightens me.'[2] He answered the question: 'What is a human being in the Infinite?' with the unresolved, equivocal definition: 'A Nothing in comparison with the Infinite; an All in comparison with the Nothing; a mean between nothing and everything.'[3] But how can human beings be the middle point between nothingness and everything? For every position – and none – is the middle between nothingness and everything. Nietzsche explained the same feeling about life by 'the death of God', and saw its effect in the loss of every metaphysical orientation:

> What did we do when we unchained the earth from its sun? Where is it moving to now? Where are we moving to? Away from all the suns? Do we not continually stumble and fall? Backwards, sideways, forwards, in all directions? Is there still an above and a below? Are we not wandering through an infinite nothingness? Do we not feel the breath of empty space?[4]

Up to now, no one has found an answer which would deliver modern men and women from this metaphysical homelessness. Generally, people and civilizations think that the point where they are at any given moment is 'the centre of the world'. But in the infinite universe there is no fixed centre, and no steady position. Every position is a relative one.

The theological problems presented by space are to some extent analogous to the problems about the time of creation. Was space brought into being *together with* creation, or was creation brought into being *in* space? Does creation have its space outside God, or within him? If God is the frontier of his creation's space, can he at the same time dwell within his creation? What mediates between the absolute space of God and the relative space of his creation?

Ultimately, these are really questions about the different concepts of space itself. Does space mean a kind of empty container, or vacuum, for a number of possible objects? Or is space identical with the extension of objects? Is it a category through which we apprehend the simultaneity of different objects? Is space always determined and ordered by the subjectivity of the object itself, as the expressions 'living space' and 'room to live in' suggest?

§1 THE ECOLOGICAL CONCEPT OF SPACE

'For the religious man, space is *not homogeneous*', says Eliade.[5] This is the early human experience of space, which we can still find in the history of religion. Spaces are always the spaces lived in and dominated by particular subjects, whether these subjects be animals, human beings, gods, spirits or demons. A particular space is the environment and field of force of this subject – the place which it fills and dominates, and in which it dwells, and which therefore has to be respected as the sphere of that particular life. When Moses takes his father-in-law's sheep into the mountains, he unconsciously enters the space of a God unknown to him. That is why the Voice says to him: 'Do not come near; put off your shoes from your feet, for the place on which you are standing is holy ground' (Exod. 3.5). Sacred space is always enclosed space. The *temenos* cuts it off from spaces that are profane. The holy territory is secured against the unholy and hostile world through magic and ritual. Purificatory rites are required at the doors of the sanctuary before the holy place may be entered.

Shut off in this way against the profane and chaotic world, and at the same time shut out of it, the holy space is nevertheless open 'upwards' for the coming of the gods. Jacob's ladder is a biblical example (Gen. 28.12–19). In his dream, Jacob hears a voice saying, 'I am the Lord, the God of Abraham your father.' Jacob responds: 'How awesome is this place! This is none other than the house of God, and this is the gate of heaven.' He thereupon establishes the sanctuary of Bethel at this sacred place. As the spaces shutting out the world, holy spaces are the gates of heaven. They are points of transition from earthly to heavenly being, from the quality of being that is divine to the quality of being that is human. The religious non-homogeneity of space is based on the religious experience of Being that is different in kind. Consequently it sees the earth as defined and determined Being, while heaven, in contrast, is undetermined Being. It is only when this religious experience of 'the other' – i.e., heaven – has lost its force that the idea of a homogeneous space can arise – a space spreading out equally in all directions, undetermined in its definition, unfixed and boundless in its dimensions.

The religious experience of the holy space is associated with the symbolism of the *genesis* of the world, and the world's *central point*.[6] In early times, land was always occupied and cultivated as a cosmogony. The inhabited and cultivated land had to be enclosed, whether by a wall or by a furrow. In this way it was removed from virgin nature and subjected to the order of human civilization. By occupying the land, parcelling it out and putting it in order, human beings repeat and celebrate the primordial act of the creation of the world. That is why the centre of human civilization is the cult, which justifies and sanctifies human activity on earth. There are many symbols for the centre of the world. The *axis mundi* can be represented by the tent pole or the pillar of the earth, the mountain of the world or the holy city. It is always a perpendicular, because it corresponds to the human being's standing position on earth, and to the earth's gravitation. When, even today, the papal blessing goes out '*urbi et orbi*', this is a continual declaration that Rome is the centre of the world.

Really, every temple represents the world's centre. It is a reflection of the dwelling of the gods in heaven. Solomon's temple was supposed to be designed according to a heavenly blueprint (I Chron. 28.19). Jerusalem was viewed as the earthly image of a heavenly Jerusalem. The Christian basilicas, the Romanesque and Gothic cathedrals were all supposed to be images of paradise and the heavenly city. In this sense they are *imago coeli*.

We saw that, in the experience of time, the ritual of 'the eternal return' of the same thing orders the flux of what is transitory, and exorcizes 'the terrors of history'. In the same way, in the experience of space, the order of the holy space wards off nature's unformed, hostile chaos. Space for human living is made possible, and is stabilized, round the centre of the holy space. Where the divine appears in earthly form, the world is made the environment in which men and women can dwell.

Human beings cannot live in limitless space. It is true that, unlike animals, they have no fixed environment proper to their species. But even a human being cannot live in a purely open world. He always creates his own environment wherever he is. It is only in this environment that he finds peace and feels 'at home'. In this sense all human civilizations are dwellings for human beings. The human subject defines his own space by enclosing it. It is significant that one of the words in German for a fenced-in enclosure is '*Umfriedung*' which is related to the word meaning 'peace'.[7] Within these limits is the territory that is home; outside is whatever is foreign and strange. Within the frontier, domestic peace rules; outside it, life can be hostile. Within, it is homely, and there is a sense of 'rightness'; outside it is sinister. In the dwelling place it is comfort-able; outside it is comfort-less. Nowadays all these words are expressions of feeling. But they really indicate the boundaries within which human life is possible at all. The space of the living person is always enclosed space. Enclosed space is part of human life, just as physical extension belongs to the definition of the body. The original space of the human being is the body. But the enclosure of the space moulded by human life does not merely protect, and does not only repulse. At the same time it means the possibility of communication with neighbouring beings and their environments. It evokes neighbourliness. The frontier is always at the same time the opportunity for communication and contact. It is on this frontier that forms of life acquire their definition. That is why the limits of the human environment can no more be exclusive than they are in the case of other living things. Every frontier enclosing the living space of a living thing is an open frontier. If it is closed, the living thing dies. The ownership of any given space, and the community of the living in the universal cohesion of communication, are not mutually exclusive. On the contrary, they are the very conditions which make one another possible.

'Everything has its time.' And everything produces and forms its space. Every living thing acquires and moulds the environment which belongs to it and is in accordance with its nature.[8] *The ecological concept of space* corresponds to *the kairological concept of time*. Neither time nor space are homogeneous. Both are individual, and are created and determined by what happens 'within' them. Without happening they do not exist at all. There is neither an empty time without events, nor an empty space without objects.[9] But then how did people arrive at the concept of homogenous space in an infinite universe?

§2 THE CONCEPT OF HOMOGENEOUS SPACE

If we are looking at the history of religion, we may no doubt see the extension of sacred space to all being as a preparation for the notion of a unified, homogenous space. A saying of Thales has been passed down to us which maintains that 'everything is full of the gods' (πάντα πλήρη θεῶν).[10] And by saying this he abolished the frontier between sacred and profane space. Everything that is, exists in the divine space. We find the same idea in Parmenides: 'Nor is Being divisible, since it is all alike; nor is there something stronger here than there, that might hinder it from holding together, nor some part weaker; for it is all full of Being. Therefore it is continuous throughout; for Being touches upon Being.'[11] Being is a homogeneous whole. Its extension is the space of being. But there is no space in which Being is *not*, or Non-being *is*. Consequently Parmenides takes the image of the sphere, as a way of conceiving the unified whole of being: 'But since Being has a furthest limit, it is complete on every side, like the mass of a well-rounded sphere, equally poised from the centre to every side.'[12] Just as the circular course of time is the image of eternity, so the spherical form of space is the image of perfection or completeness. Its even and uninterrupted circumscription (πεῖρας) on the one hand, and its centre (κέντρον) on the other, make a symbol of the closed and self-contained sphere. Because its centre is equidistant from every point on the circumference, the symmetry of perfect space is preserved in the sphere in the best conceivable way.

The notion of space as the empty, limitless vessel for objects that are visible and perceptible by the senses was developed by Plato:

> For this reason the mother and receptacle of what has come to be visible and otherwise sensible must not be called earth or air or fire or water, not any of their compounds or components; but we shall not go astray if we call it a nature invisible and characterless, all-receiving, partaking in some very perplexing way of the intelligible, and very hard to apprehend.[13]

For Plato, space is a universal form 'which receives all things into itself'. It is always and everywhere the same. It receives everything into itself, and yet does not take on the character of any of the things that it receives. It is for everything 'the matrix, changed and diversified by the things that enter it; and because of them appearing now in one form and now in another.'[14]

On the one hand it is important to notice here that the metaphor which is associated with the notion of space as a vessel or receptacle is a *feminine* metaphor. 'Mother space', 'the recipient', 'the all-receiving', 'the matrix', are ancient, mythical symbols for the maternal character of Being, in whose great complex and cohesion everything is in safe-keeping. Thus the gods too come forth from the one, ineffable, divine essence, and take on form. Thus 'Mother Earth' takes all living beings into herself, allowing them to exist in her. Plato evidently equated receptive space with primordial matter.

But, on the other hand, if space receives all objects into itself, it cannot itself be an object. Consequently Plato also distinguishes space from the four elements. Space itself can neither become nor pass away, as do all the things contained within it. It is the invisible premise for everything visible. And it is therefore at the same time the invisible presupposition for every perception. Plato attributed divine characteristics to space. To be all-receiving is one of these divine attributes, for Plato compares the Whence of all things with the Father, and that which receives and gathers everything into itself with the Mother. He transfers the ancient mythical images of Father Heaven and Mother Earth to the Ideas from which visible things derive, and to the space in which visible things exist.

Aristotle, on the other hand, discussed the concept of space in an almost cursory fashion in his doctrine of categories.[15] For him, space belongs to the category of quantity. It is nothing other than continuous quantity. Quantity can only be measured by the extension of bodies, or solids. Space therefore extends as far as solids extend. 'The parts of space which are occupied by the parts of the solid have the same common boundary as the parts of the solid.' If every solid, or body, has 'its own space', by virtue of its extension, then 'space' has to be viewed as the total sum of all extended bodies. In his *Physics* Aristotle no longer employs the concept of space, but instead uses the concept of *place* (*topos*). Place is the term used to indicate the position of an object in relation to other objects. His *Physics* does not contain a theory of space, but has instead a topography, with which objects and parts of objects are fixed and located in their relation to others. We might conclude from this that 'space' is the sum total of all places which are occupied by bodies.[16] It is only in his *De caelo* that Aristotle seems to have taken over Parmenides' 'sphere' theory; for there he describes the universe as having a centre, and talks about the space of the universe which represents the inward side of the all-embracing, all-surrounding, divine essence. We do not find the concept of empty space here either.

It is noticeable that the geometrical concept of space and the ontological concept of space evidently part company quite early on, and cease to be connected with one another. Euclid's concept of space only recognizes quantifiable dimensions on parameters which are in principle endless. But it would seem that the ontological concept has to fulfil other requirements: the idea of the globe fulfils the demand for perfection; the idea of the all-receptive space which bears everything within itself fulfils the religious need for divine safe-keeping; the idea of the central point and the circumscription of the world gives to human beings the bearings which the dimensions of geometry cannot give.

§3 THE CREATION OF SPACES AND THE SPACE OF CREATION

The modern Cartesian division between an incorporeal mental subject and a world of extended bodies in geometrical space is alien to the biblical traditions about creation. We come nearer to these traditions if we employ the *ecological* concept of space we have described: every living thing has its own world in which to live, a world to which it is adapted and which suits it. The Cartesian objectification of the world destroys the natural environments of living things in order to incorporate them in the environment of the dominating human subject, which is everywhere the same in kind, the aim being to make living things the objects of the human being's world. Dimensions are then the only essential characteristics of *res extensae*, whether these are stones, plants, animals, other people, or one's own body. The reduction of natural environments to these geometrical structures means at the same time their reduction to utilitarian values. Here we shall be taking a different view, and assuming that space is primarily *living space*. That is to say, it is the environment to which a particular life is related, because it accords that life the conditions in which it can live. The structure of the environment and the structure of perception correspond, and form the two hemispheres of the one, circumscribed sphere of existence.[17]

If we read the traditions about creation with this ecological concept of space in mind, the ways in which they distinguish between the different worlds become significant.[18] Among the works of creation, Psalm 104 names first of all the great cosmic spaces of air, earth and sea. They are perceived and described from the angle of what God does in them, and what lives there. When the Psalmist describes the heavens, we are told that in them the clouds are made God's chariots and the winds his messengers, and that God has restrained the waters. When he is talking about the earth, the Psalmist tells us that the springs and rivers provide drink for all the plants and animals, that the sun and moon order the times, and that plants and trees give food to all the beasts. The sea, finally, is the living space for innumerable animals, among them the giant Leviathan, whom God has created for play. What the poet of Psalm 104 perceives in the world is 'the milieu of the conditions that make existence possible for all life, man and beast alike', 'the basic equipment . . . which is . . . given together with life itself', 'the separate sectors of existence' and 'the elemental needs' of living things.[19]

The creation account in the Priestly Writing is built up in such a way that the different worlds are arranged in a certain order, which begins at their furthest circumference and ends with the milieu closest to human beings. The space of being called heaven is the home of the stars, with their functions for other created things (Gen. 1.6–8). The 'living spaces' sea, air and earth (vv. 9–12) are related to the beings which live in them and which are created for them (vv. 20–22): earth is the environment for plants, sea the environment for fish, air the environment for birds. It is only when all the environmental conditions have been created that animals and human beings are made (vv. 24–28), these being supposed to nourish themselves from the plants.

If we think in terms of environment and biotopes, the construction of the first creation account is astonishingly clear and logical. Modern reproaches that it is the mere outcome of mythical speculation, or that it displays a naive knowledge of nature, are quite wide of the mark.

Let us start from the ecological interpretation of the creation story, and go on to enquire systematically about the relationship of the Creator to his creation. The first thing that strikes the reader is the ambiguity in the concept of *heaven*. On the one hand it is the atomosphere above the earth; but on the other, it is transcendent compared with everything visible. Creation in the beginning was the creation of a double world of heaven and earth. How is heaven to be interpreted, in the transcendent sense? We shall be considering this in detail in the next chapter. In our present context it is enough to remember the other biblical use of the term: heaven is the 'place' of God's glory, and his 'dwelling'. It is 'from heaven' that God acts on earth. In heaven his name is hallowed, his will done, and his kingdom prepared. So in this sense – even though it eludes all our concepts and imaginings – we have to interpret heaven as the dwelling space, the creaturely surroundings and the environment that is closest to God and entirely corresponds to him. Heaven is the milieu nearest to God, his direct environment. The earth, together with the atmosphere and the seas, are the outskirts of his existence, his less immediate environment.

That is why the eschatological hope looks for the time when 'the kingdom of heaven' will come on earth, and God's glory will transfigure his earth as it transfigures his heaven. In this sense it would seem obvious to think of creation as built up in concentric circles of gradated divine environments. This idea was only pushed out because God, the active Creator, came to be placed so much in the centre of the picture that the God who rested on the sabbath came to be overlooked.

But if we apply the image of creation as the dwelling place of God in this second sense, we are faced with the question: can heaven and earth in their finitude ever become the dwelling of the Infinite One? Ought we not rather to say the very reverse – that God is the dwelling place of the world created by him, and that this world remains eternal because it finds space *in him* and is permitted to partake of his eternal life? *Finitum capax* or *non capax infiniti*? 'We do not know whether God is the space of his world, or whether his world is his space', says a Jewish midrash.[20] The Jewish answer to the question is: 'The Lord is the place of his world, but his world is not his place.' But if we follow the doctrine of the Shekinah and the Christian doctrine of the incarnation, we have to speak of the marvel that the infinite God himself should dwell in his finite creation, making it his own environment.[21]

There is no inherent contradiction in these theological ideas. The God who created the world and sustains it, and who invites it to the repose of his sabbath feast, also allows the world to exist before, with and *in* the presence of his infinite Being.[22] In this respect God is the eternal dwelling place of his creation. But the God who has made the world through his wisdom, and keeps it in existence through his Spirit, has always entered into it as well. *God the Spirit* dwells in creation, preparing it to be the place of glorification. We must only distinguish between the one indwelling and the other. They are not the same, and they do not take place on the same level. So the alternative postulated in the midrash I have quoted does not in fact exist. God and the world are related to one another through the relationship of their mutual indwelling and participation: God's indwelling in the world is divine in kind; the world's indwelling in God is worldly in kind. There is no other way of conceiving the continual communication between God and the world.

At the beginning of this part of our reflections we started from the difference between the two concepts of space: the ecological concept and the geometrical one. Before we end the section, let us try to relate the two concepts to one another. The ecological concept of space perceives 'the world' only as a particular *surrounding* world, or environment. The concept of environment has developed out of research into the environment of animals. It can only be applied to the relationship of human beings to the world within certain limits. The ecological concept characterizes space as the particular environment of living things. It does not permit the quantification of space. So how do human beings come to look beyond their specific environment, and to perceive the world as the embodiment of a multiplicity of different environments, and then to quantify this world spatially as well?

Here we shall look first of all at the anthropological ideas of Max Scheler. Scheler was one of the first to give detailed consideration to the implications of research into animal environment. 'Animals only notice and grasp those things which fall into the secure boundaries of their environmental structure.' A human being, in contrast, 'is the X who can exhibit, to an unlimited degree, behaviour which is open to the world. To become human is to acquire this openness towards the world by virtue of the spirit.'[23] It is the peculiar detachment between environment and world which distinguishes human beings from animals, even though animals too are capable of adaptation. Through his power of reflection and the imagination of the spirit, the human being shakes off the spell of the environment, as it were, and perceives 'the world'. He is capable of discerning objects as such; he does not merely evaluate them according to their utility and functional value. He is capable of interrupting his instinctive reactions and acting deliberately. He is not tied to a single environment. He has developed 'empty forms' of space and time, with which he is able to perceive a multiplicity of objects and to build up a number of different environments. According to Max Scheler, these empty forms of space and time in perception are derived from the surplus of human drives. Our instinctual expectation remains unfulfilled, and this is what we originally call empty. 'The first emptiness of all is, as it were, the emptiness of our hearts.'[24]

We are interpreting these phenomenological observations of Max Scheler's theologically when we say that human beings, as beings created by God, are destined for a particular environment – just like the animals together with which they are created; but that, by virtue of their creation in the image of God, in which they are unique, they are open to the world, beyond their own particular environment. In their correspondence to God, the Creator of all the environments of living things, human beings also participate in God's relation to the world, and in God's environment. God's environment is his creation, 'the world'. As God's representative and plenipotentiary on earth, human beings are open for the world as the quintessence of all the environments of living things.

What Max Scheler called 'the infinite emptiness of our hearts' is *the openness of human beings for God* – Augustine's *cor inquietum*. It is not identical with human openness towards the world, and is not merely a theological interpretation of that; it is in itself the very reason for this openness towards the world.[25] Because human beings are at once God's creation and his image, they are also both related to their environment, and open to the world. The simultaneity of the two designations is evident in the ambivalence of the human being's eccentric position in relation to the environment.

§4 THE PROBLEM OF ABSOLUTE SPACE

Alexandre Koyré has shown that the decisive revolution in the thinking of modern European times is to be found in the transition from 'the closed world' to 'the infinite universe'.[26] This transformation of the world picture has destroyed the cosmos in which human beings could feel at home; and with what Koyré calls 'the infinitization of the universe', the world became open for its conquest by human beings. It is also true that the immeasurable world, open on every side, has awakened that sense of alienation in modern men and women which has led to nihilism. The tremendous change in the world picture came about in the hundred years from Copernicus (whose revolutionary work appeared in 1543) to Newton (whose discovery of the law of gravity is dated 1666). Here we shall only look at the dispute about God and space, which was pursued in the seventeenth century between Descartes and Henry More first of all, and later on between Leibniz and Newton.[27]

Copernicus had declared that the visible world of the stars was 'immense' and 'immeasurable', and Giordano Bruno therefore considered them to be 'infinite', pantheistically attributing to them divine predicates; and this then led to the theological and philosophical problem of the spatial *infinity* of the world. People asked whether there was really an indefinite extension of matter, or an infinite space? This question again put up for discussion the two concepts of space which we found postulated from the very beginnings of Greek philosophy. Is space, as Plato thought, 'the receptacle' for all objects? Or is it what Aristotle believed it to be: the extension of objects themselves? Is there any such thing as space *per se*, or is there only 'spatiality', as a characteristic of extended objects?

Theologically, the problem acquired a keener edge when the modern concept of infinity developed: if matter is infinitely extended, what is to prevent us from considering matter to be divine, as Spinoza did? But if space has to be distinguished from the material objects within it, can infinite space be viewed as a characteristic of the transcendent God? Theologically, therefore, the modern problem of space throws open for discussion the controversy between theism and pantheism.

The reduction of science to mathematics is generally ascribed to Descartes. Descartes distinguished strictly between *res cogitans* and *res extensa*, and related the concept of God to the soul alone, no longer to nature. This meant that with the help of his ontology the visible world could be objectified, without any religious scruples, and its objects could be understood solely in terms of mathematics. Basically, this was made possible because he equated matter with extension, as his definition of the *res extensa* shows. Material substance is characterized solely by extension, in length, breadth and depth. From this it follows, first, that matter has no other characteristic; second, that there can be no such thing as empty space without material substances; and third, that it is not possible to conceive of the material universe as being spatially limited. Yet the world of the *res extensa* is not 'infinite', in the metaphysical sense; it is merely, in the mensurable sense, 'endless', or indefinite. The Euclidean space which was Descartes' assumption cannot be limited. The lines of its three dimensions stretch to 'infinity', to use the mathematical term for the indefinite. But at no point did Descartes maintain the metaphysical infinity of the world. Only God is 'infinite'. He did, however, maintain that the extension of matter was limitless: the world is indefinite.[28]

Henry More first of all criticized the strict Cartesian dichotomy of spirit and matter. He then found fault with the reduction of being to matter; and he finally castigated the reduction of matter to extension. Extension cannot be restricted to matter; the spirit has extension too. If, in addition, the *res* is defined solely in terms of *extensio*, it is impossible to talk in the literal sense about a *res cogitans*. Matter is not merely extended; it is also movable. It is only movable in space. So matter is not conceivable without a space from which it can be differentiated. A space of this kind is the very premise of matter. But how, then, are we to define the space in which all objects move, but which is not identical with their extension? In his closer definition of space More starts with Plato and picks up Jewish-kabbalistic ideas. Space is not merely real. It is even *divine*, for it is infinite, immovable, homogeneous, indivisible, simple (that is, uncompounded) and unique. Plato used motherly attributes to describe space because, being in itself distinguishable from things, it 'receives' them. But there is also a Jewish-kabbalistic tradition, according to which one of the names of God is MAKOM, which means the infinite, pure and primary place or, as More interprets it, absolute space. The MAKOM tradition probably goes back to Esther 4.14: 'Enlargement and deliverance will arise for the Jews from another place.' The cryptic paraphrase 'from another place' means 'from God'. Max Jammer has investigated this Jewish tradition,[29] finding that MAKOM KADOSH – 'the holy space' – was applied to the divine Shekinah, the indwelling presence of God in the Temple and in Israel. It is only one step further, following Psalm 139, to describe the omnipresence of God as his spatial presence, and to understand the space *in* which all created things exist and move as 'absolute space' – that is to say, as the spatial dimension of the divine Being. If space is interpreted as the dimension of God's omnipresence, pantheistic conclusions are impossible. 'Absolute space' means the direct presence of God in the whole material world and in every individual thing within it.

This reflection ends up by making a distinction between space and object: absolute space is infinite, immovable, homogeneous, indivisible and unique. But the things in this space, on the other hand, are finite, movable, various, divisible and manifold.[30] It is only by making this distinction between space and matter that it is possible to maintain the distinction between the contingent, created world and the eternal, omnipresent God.[31] If space were equated with the extension of objects, it would be difficult to evade the notion of an eternal and infinite world, existing of its own self. Giordano Bruno did in fact imply a pantheistic notion of this kind and Spinoza developed it further. But any such idea would be the end of the biblical faith in creation. Isaac Newton took over from Henry More the idea of absolute space and the distinction between space and matter: they provide the foundation for his cosmology[32] – though he distinguishes the *absolute* space in which all things exist and move from the *relative* space of the different localizations and relations of bodies to one another. And in the same way he differentiates between relative movement and absolute movement.

What is interesting in this connection is Newton's controversial theory that 'absolute space' is an attribute of the eternal, divine Being. As a dimension of the divine omnipresence, space is 'God's sensorium', through which he perceives all things and all the movement of things:

> . . . Does it not appear from Phaenomena that there is a Being incorporeal, living, intelligent, omnipresent, who in infinite space

– as it were in his sensory – sees the things themselves intimately, and thoroughly perceives them, and comprehends them wholly by their immediate presence to himself?[33]

If God perceives everything immediately and directly through his omnipresence, this presupposes that God's eternal, uncreated omnipresence is the same as the omnipresence of space. But can we then divide up space without dividing God himself? This was Leibniz's counter-argument; but Leibniz misunderstood Newton's phrase about 'God's sensorium' when he objected that God cannot be immediately present to all things if he needs the medium of a sensorium. In fact Newton merely used sensory or 'sensorium' in a figurative sense.

The argument about the divisibility of space was more important. Leibniz himself took Descartes's idea further and defined space as the description of the position of extended things in their relation to one another. This of course compelled him to accept the fundamental relativity of all spatial relations and dimensions. 'Space' can then only be the 'distillation', as it were, of all the mensurable extensions and relations of bodies. There would be no space if there were no bodies. The concept of absolute space requires the idea of 'an empty space'; but according to Leibniz, the notion of 'empty space' is impossible.

In this seventeenth-century discussion, we find, first, two different concepts of space: space as the object in space, and space as the object's spatial extension. Secondly, we find two different concepts of God; the spatially omnipresent God, and God as spirit, confronting his spatial creation in the mind and spirit of human beings. Consequently we find, thirdly, two different 'allocations' of space: according to the first, space is an attribute of the object; according to the second, space is an attribute of God.

There was no serious danger of pantheism as long as a clear distinction was made between the end-lessness of space and the infinity of God, or between infinity as a quantitative concept and as a qualitative one. On the other hand, it was quite possible to preserve the distinction between God and the world with the help of the distinction between absolute space (God) and the finite world of things in space. But even this did not involve any idea of creation, of whatever kind. The theology of nature held by Henry More and Isaac Newton was not theistic; it was pan-entheistic. With the help of the idea of absolute space they could certainly conceive of the world in God; but this did not permit them to think of God as the Creator of the world, and the world as contingent creation. For Leibniz, the real problem was this: if objects did not exist there would be no space either; so if there were no creation there would be neither space nor time. Newton's problem was: if the finite world exists in the eternal space of God, does it not partake of his eternity? And is it not then as eternal as God himself?

The problem which was discussed between Leibniz and Newton can, in my view, only be solved if we think of creation as the mediation between the relative space of objects and the eternal space of God. It is only the concept of creation which distinguishes the space of God from the space of the created world; for with creation, a space for the created world comes into being which is neither the uncreated omnipresence of God nor, as yet, the relative space of objects. Although Max Jammer discussed this 'Jewish-Christian idea of space', he failed to perceive the possible solution it essentially offers for the dispute between Leibniz and Newton. 'According to the Cabala', he writes, 'the Infinite Holy One, whose light originally occupied the whole universe, withdrew his light and concentrated it on his own substance, thereby creating empty space.'[34] This is the doctrine of the divine *zimsum: 'Deus creaturus mundos contraxit praesentiam suam.'* Kabbalistic interpreters surmised that this is why Genesis does not talk about the creation of space; for it is rather that creation is fashioned *in* the emptiness God ceded for it through his creative resolve. So the space of creation precedes both creation and the spaces fashioned within creation, yet without being identical with the uncreated, eternal omnipresence of God. 'After God, in his resolve to create the world, had completed the *zimsum*, he created "vessels". He set them in "the place" which he had made free for them through his withdrawal. These vessels were destined to receive the light in which the world was to spring to life.'[35]

The created world does not exist in 'the absolute space' of the divine Being; it exists in the space God yielded up for it through his creative resolve. The world does not exist in itself. It exists in 'the ceded space' of God's world-presence. It is not the eternal God himself who is the boundary of the world, as Newton seems to think. It is God the Creator. In the doctrine about the world as God's creation we therefore distinguish between three things: first, the essential omnipresence of God, or *absolute space*; second, *the space of creation* in the world-presence of God conceded to it; and third, *relative places*, relationships and movements in the created world. The space of the world corresponds to God's world-presence, which initiates this space, limits it and interpenetrates it.

VII

Heaven and Earth

§1 WHY IS CREATION A DUAL WORLD?

'In the beginning God created the heavens and the earth' (Gen. 1.1). There is no single, unified term in the biblical traditions for the reality created by God. The concepts 'world', 'outer space' or 'universe' are known but seldom used. The biblical writers prefer the dual expression 'heaven and earth' – and almost always in that order.[1] Is this because the Hebrew loves to see totalities as divided into two, and to express them in polarized contrasts? Or does reality as God's creation have to be this dual world of heaven and earth?

According to Hebrew etymology, 'heaven' probably means 'the heights', and 'earth' 'the lower regions, what is below'. In using the term 'heaven', the direct sense and the symbolic one can be distinguished. In the biblical traditions, 'heaven' means the sky – the region of the air, the sphere of clouds and winged beasts, 'the birds of the air'. If it is this region that is meant, a triple term is normally used: heaven, earth and sea.[2] Heaven also means the region of 'the stars of the heavens'. The astral world was thought of as a semi-spherical, heavenly vault, reaching down to the earth on every side. If this region is meant, the writers generally talk about 'heaven and earth', the earth then also including the air and the sea.[3] Finally, heaven can have a symbolic meaning. It can be the higher world beyond this one – the world of the angels, which is invisible and beyond our reach, and which is the space of God's throne and his indwelling glory.[4] When the transcendence of this heaven is considered, the heavens of the air and the stars come together with the earth, closing up to 'this visible world'.

Heaven as the sphere of the angels and the divine throne can be talked about either in the singular or in the plural: 'Behold, to the Lord your God belong heaven and the heaven of heavens, and the earth with all that is in it' (Deut. 10.14; cf. also I Kings 8.27; Neh. 9.6; and frequently elsewhere). 'The heaven of heavens' is evidently supposed to sum up the plurality of the invisible and unknowable spheres of creation in their relation to God. Paul once talks about 'the third heaven' (II Cor. 12.2); but it is not clear whether by this he means the angelic heaven beyond the heaven of the air and the stars. Under the influence of Jewish conceptions, some of the church Fathers talked about 'seven heavens'. Matthew likes to talk about the kingdom of God, in reticent circumlocution, as 'the kingdom of heaven (βασιλεία τῶν οὐρανῶν, first in Matt. 3.2). But we also find the phrase 'the heavenly kingdom' (βασιλεία ἐπουράνιον, II Tim. 4.18).

On the one hand, the variety of the phrases used for heaven brings out the fundamental indefinability for human beings of this whole area of creation.[5] The earth is the sphere which is familiar and with which the human being has been entrusted. He gives the animals their names, and they are to be called by the names he gives them (Gen. 2. 19–20). But heaven – and even more the heavens – are for him the sphere of reality which is inaccessible and unknowable.

'The heavens' is also a circumlocution used for the openness of the visible world, which reaches beyond all frontiers and limitations. If we consider the different phrases 'heaven', 'the heavens' and 'the heaven of heavens', and if we leave all the fantasies aside, it also becomes plain that the world as God's creation does not have its unity within itself; so it cannot be a unified, self-contained universe. If God is its Creator, then his creation has its unity in him, not in itself. Consequently there can be a multiplicity of heavens about which human beings have no idea. At the same time, the point to remember in the context of belief in creation is that heaven is neither God nor is it divine; it is a part of the created world. But as part of the created world it has to be distinguished from the visible world; for it is only if we make this distinction that the visible world can be understood as a created world existing from God, and open for him who dwells in heaven. 'He who dwells in heaven' is the Creator who indwells his creation. The world-immanence of God therefore makes the world an eccentric world, and divides it into heaven and earth.

Just as the expression 'heaven' has both direct meanings and symbolic ones, so has the term 'earth'. The earth signifies the living space of human beings and terrestrial animals, as distinct from the sky and the sea. But 'earth' also means the lower regions, including the air and the sea, as distinct from the starry heavens, the firmament. Finally, compared with the invisible heaven in which the glory of God dwells, the earth means the whole visible and temporal world in which God does not dwell – or not as yet. In this symbolic sense, the earth is not merely this planet. It is the whole material world of which this planet is a part. The earth is then the quintessence of all the systems of life and matter which we know. The early Christian creeds therefore – following Colossians 1.16 – extended the creation of 'heaven and earth' to the creation of 'all things visible and invisible' (Symbolum Apostolici forma orientalis, Symbolum Niceaeno-Constantinopolitanum, Symbolum Quicunque).

How are we to understand the duality of 'heaven and earth'? Attention has often been drawn to the bipolar unity of the world which we find in the history of religion and which, presented as sexual polarity, presses towards fruitful union.[6] 'Father Heaven' and 'Mother Earth' are early patriarchal symbols. It is true that 'Father Heaven' rules over 'Mother Earth', but they are none the less both divine. All life issues from their sacred union. This sexual polarity of the world may have been absorbed into the Israelite view of the double creation, as I Kings 17, Isaiah 45.8 and Hosea 2.21f. show. But systematically the one has nothing to do with the other, since heaven and earth are God's creation, and are not, therefore, themselves divine. In the psalms the fertility of the earth is praised; and in the first creation account the earth is the one that brings forth, at the Creator's command. But there are hardly any echoes of the fertility symbolism of heaven and earth. In the biblical traditions heaven and earth are no longer sexually determined. Consequently the analogy of man and wife is no longer used to describe the relation between them, and the analogy of heaven and earth is no longer applied to the relationship of man and wife, as is usual elsewhere in the ancient world.

In the history of philosophy, the analogy of the relation between soul and body is presented as an obvious one. Plato already talked about 'the body of the world' and 'the world soul':

> In the centre he set the soul and caused it to extend throughout the whole, and further wrapped the body round with soul on the outside; and so he established one single heaven alone, round and revolving in a circle, solitary but able by reason of its energy to fertilize itself, needing no other, but sufficient to itself as acquaintance or friend. For all these reasons the world he brought into being was a blessed god.[7]

If the earth is the body of heaven, and if heaven is the soul of the earth, the result is the image of the macranthropos, a self-sufficient, divine-human entity which revolves within itself. It is true that later the Fathers of the church also took over this picture of the world from Plato's *Timaeus*; but in the biblical traditions the analogy of soul and body is never used to describe the relationship between heaven and earth; and the reverse is also true: the analogy of heaven and earth is never drawn upon to interpret the relations between soul and body. The notion of the divine cosmos which either rests in itself or revolves within itself cannot be combined with the idea of God's creation.

Theologically, we should more readily think of the Creator's relationship to his creation, which finds its analogy in the relationship of heaven to earth. 'There is a correspondence, a similarity, of the relationship between heaven and earth to that between the Creator and the creature', declared Karl Barth in his *Doctrine of Creation*.[8] 'Heaven and earth' are the parable and parallel of God and the human being. In what is this analogy supposed to consist? According to Barth, it consists in the fact that 'Here too and already there is an above and below, an earlier and later, a more and less'.[9] The distinction between the upper and the lower cosmos reflects the real and true above and below of the Creator and the being he creates. It would seem that what underlies this reflection is the reality of the gradated presence of God: God is closer to heaven than the earth.[10] God 'dwells' in heaven and 'acts' on earth from heaven. His will is done 'on earth as it is in heaven'.

It is of course true that in the biblical traditions heaven is always used to described the place *where* God is, *from where* he acts, and *towards which* prayer and praise are directed. But the relationship between Creator and created being in general, and the relationship between God and human beings in particular, is different from the relationship between heaven and earth. The characteristics of the analogy which Barth advances – above-below, earlier-later, more-less – do certainly apply to the relationship between God and human beings in a certain sense. But they do not fit the general relationship of their particular 'dwellings' – heaven and earth. And in actual fact these general characteristics do not really tally with the relationship between God and human beings either. If we look at salvation history as a whole, and consider the becoming-human of the Son of God, and the participation of human beings in the divine nature, we see that the relationship between God and human beings is much richer than those simple marks of sovereignty and obedience would suggest. The love of God is quite evidently directed towards the earth, and the world in which human beings exist. The object of love cannot have a 'below' or a 'later', let alone a 'less'. Barth sees the analogy between heaven and earth on the one hand, and between God and human beings on the other, as based on the sovereignty of God, who rules from above downwards. His hierarchical doctrine of creation is an expression of his doctrine about the sovereign rule of the One God.[11] As a result, the characteristics of heaven and earth which he puts forward in his analogy turn up again in his doctrine about the relation between soul and body, and also in what he has to say about the relation between man and woman.[12] If we wish to relate heaven and earth to God in a trinitarian sense, not in a monarchical one like this, we should have to say that *heaven* is the chosen dwelling place of *the Father*, but that the chosen dwelling of *the Son* is the earth, on which he became a human being, died and rose again, and where he will come in order to fill it with his glory. But then the chosen place of *the Holy Spirit* must be seen in the coming direct bond between heaven and earth in the new creation, as whose energy the Holy Spirit already manifests himself now, in the present. That is why we cannot talk about a 'contrast' in the relationship between heaven and earth; we can only speak of a complementation. We cannot think of the one as over against or superior to the other; we can only talk about the fellowship and community of God's created beings.[13]

Is God's creation necessarily a dual world? If we assume that the work of creation was something completed once and for all, then the twofold division into heaven and earth seems merely fortuitous – a division that came about because the biblical traditions evidently love to think in dualities. But if we proceed from the idea of continuous creation, it immediately becomes clear that the unremittingly creative presence of God in creation makes of that creation this double world of heaven and earth. A world which has been created by God, and which continues to be created every moment, is bound to be a world *open to God*. It does not revolve within itself, either in absolute or in relative completeness and self-sufficiency. It exists in the presence of the Creator and lives from the continual inflow of his creative Spirit. The creating God makes the world an *ec-static* reality. It has its foundation, not in itself, but outside itself – in him. It has its unity, not in itself, but outside itself – in him. In this sense it is an 'open system'. We call the determined side of this system 'earth', the undetermined side 'heaven'.

The word 'heaven' is the term for the side of creation that is open to God. That is why there can be heavens in the plural. But the earth can never be anything else but singular. For the earth, 'the heavens' mean the kingdom of God's creative potentialities. 'The heavenly beings', the angels, are God's potencies in the realm of his potentialities. That is why we can call heaven the relative transcendence of the earth, and earth the relative immanence of heaven. If 'things visible' means the finite world, then 'things invisible' means the relatively infinite world. Men and women are God's finite and mortal creatures. Angels are God's finite but immortal creatures. That is why God's heaven can also be called a finite but immortal creation, while the earth can be seen as a finite and transitory creation. Then when we say that God 'dwells' in heaven, acts 'from heaven', and that his will is to be done 'on earth as it is in heaven', these symbolic expressions become comprehensible.

We can make the reverse-check and imagine a world without heaven. It would be a world which is not open 'upwards', or open for God; it would be a world without this qualitative transcendence. A world like this would be a closed system, resting and revolving within itself. A world without transcendence is a world in which nothing new can ever happen. It is the world of the eternal return of the same thing. And if a world without heaven is still supposed to be thought of as a world which nevertheless transcends itself, then it must be an indefinitely endless universe. The qualitative infinity of heaven is in this case replaced by the quantitatively indefinite endlessness of the universe's extension. If we relate this to time, the openness of the world which is symbolized by a heaven different in quality would have to be replaced by the openness to the future in which the world continually transcends itself. This too would mean the transformation of qualitative infinity into quantitative endlessness. The idea of the double world of heaven and earth cannot, therefore, be replaced at will by ideas such as 'the endless universe' or 'the cosmos'.

Finally, for theology 'heaven and earth' are not the petrified duality of a finished and completed universal condition. They are the two sides of the divine creative activity, the divine love and the divine glorification. It is therefore essential, theologically, to understand heaven and earth *in God*, which means in *the movement* of God. So in the movement of the Father's creative activity we call heaven *coelum naturae*; in the movement of the Son's incarnation and ascension we call it *coelum gratiae*, and in the movement of transfiguration through the Holy Spirit we call it *coelum gloriae*.[14] As created spaces, heaven and earth are caught up into this trinitarian history of God; and it is only in this history that they will become comprehensible in all the fullness of their relationships.

§2 THE HEAVEN OF NATURE

In early Protestant orthodoxy, *coelum naturae* was the term used to describe the heaven of the air and the aether, a notion which grew up out of the Christian fusion of biblical tradition with Aristotelian cosmology.[15] The term is consistent with the language of the first creation account, in which heaven is 'the firmament' above the earth and the region of the stars. It does not accord with the symbolic way of talking about heaven as God's dwelling place. If this symbolic phrase is introduced into the first creation account, we are faced with the familiar questions: why are we not told anything about the creation of the angels? And why is earth so richly furnished, whereas heaven is comparatively bare? If 'heaven' in the first creation account is interpreted in its symbolic sense, then the Creator passed over it with great rapidity in order to pay particular attention to the earth. On the other hand, although the Old Testament certainly gives no explicit *account* of the creation of heaven in its symbolic significance as the dwelling of God, heaven in this sense is never equated with the eternity and illimitability of God himself; so it will be permissible to conclude that it was in fact created.

There is an ambivalence at this point. This has led on the one hand to the reduction of heaven's symbolic significance to its direct meaning – that is to say, heaven has been naturalized. On the other hand it has also meant that heaven's direct meaning has been reduced to its symbolic one: heaven, that is, has been divinized. Is heaven nothing more than a part of nature? Or is it nothing other than God's presence itself?

In order to get away from this ambiguity and avoid both these misconceptions, we shall here use the word heaven to mean *the openness to God of the world he has created.* Then the *heaven* of nature cannot mean the heaven of the air and the firmament, as they still do in Johann Gerhard; for the sky and the astral systems are *parts* of nature. Instead the symbol 'heaven' has to mean the transcendent openness of all material systems – that is, if the theological expression is to be used in a way that is meaningful at all, where nature is concerned.

God dwells in heaven, he acts from heaven, and his will is done on earth as it is in heaven. Here we are interpreting heaven as the kingdom of God's energies, his potentiality (*possibilitas*) and his efficacious power (*potentia*). Out of the kingdom of his creative potentialities God creates the reality of the world, the firmament – the heaven of the stars – and the earth. Here we are using 'world' to mean the side of creation symbolized by 'the earth'. Consequently there is little to be said about the inner structure of heaven. God first of all creates for himself the possibility of the world's reality. He then goes forth from the kingdom of his positive potentiality, creating, forming and acting, and enters into the kingdom of actuality. This creative movement is expressed through the direction 'from heaven'. Consequently earth means the reality of the world which is knowable because it is real, and definable because it is definitive; whereas heaven means God's potentiality *for* the earth, which is unknowable and indefinable but defining.

If we interpret heaven as the kingdom of God's creative potentialities, this does not mean declaring that heaven is the potentiality of the earth. It is true that the kingdom of God's potentialities also contains potential worlds and earthly potentialities; but God's potentialities are not congruent with, or absorbed by, the realities and potentialities of the earth. God's potentialities are determined by the creative God himself, whose creative energies know no end. This means that when we consider the reality of the world, these divine potentialities cannot simply be thought of as what-is-not-yet-existent.

The kingdom of God's creative potentialities has ontological priority before the kingdom of the world's reality and the potentialities inherent in the world. In comparison with transient reality it is non-transient; but in comparison with God himself it is finite. That is why God's potentialities are not exhausted through their realization. The kingdom of God's potentialities contains potentialities in both the passive and the active sense of the word: *out of* his potentialities God creates reality, and he creates this *in* his potency or power. Heaven is the word that describes, not merely the kingdom of potentialities, but also the kingdom of God's potencies: the potentiality and the potency of the earth's being. That is why the angels are also termed ἀρχαί, ἐξουσίαι and κυριότητες (Col. 1.16).

But are these divine potentialities and potencies not part of God's eternal, uncreated Being? Does this interpretation not, after all, identify heaven with God?

The potentialities and potencies of God which are described by the symbol 'heaven' are not the potentialities and potencies of his eternal essence *per se*. They are the potentialities and potencies of the God who has designated himself to be the Creator of a world different from himself, which none the less communicates with him. Just as 'the time of creation' springs from the creative resolve of God, and just as 'the space of creation' comes into being through the contraction of the divine omnipresence which fills all things, so the divine potentialities and potencies described in the term 'heaven' are qualified through God's designation of himself to be Creator; and they are unfolded and disclosed by the Creator in the time and in the space of creation. In this respect heaven is the first world, the world which God created so that from there he might form the earth, encompass it, and finally redeem it.

Heaven is, as it were, the preparing and making available of the potentialities and potencies of the world's creation, redemption and glorification. That is why this heaven is called God's dwelling. The God who is present in heaven has so direct a relationship to his potentialities and potencies that these acquire almost no form of their own which could be defined; for – as has rightly been said of the angels – they are totally absorbed in the contemplation of God and in his service. That is why the intimate relations to God of the potentialities and potencies 'in heaven' take on significance for conditions in the reality of the world, and for the conditions of worldly possibilities: they are exemplary, and they provide a reason for hope – his will be done on earth 'as it is in heaven'.

If we look closely at the character of the speculative and fantastic embroidery that adorns Jewish and Christian ideas about heaven, we see that, however unreal these adornments may be, heaven is always the space of the possible, which invites us to utopian fantasy. In all these conceptions about heaven, heavenly conditions have lost the heaviness of earth: lightness, nimbleness, hovering, dancing, singing and playing all belong to these pictures of the heavenly life. These associations of 'the heavenly world' also point to the kingdom of potentialities, in which it is not only for God that all things are possible, but where created beings too participate in the creative wealth of potentiality of the Creator and lover of life.

If we apprehend 'the heaven of nature' theologically as the kingdom of *the Creator's* potentialities, then the (created) potentialities of his creatures are to be found in this kingdom as well. That is the essential reason why the Greek Fathers of the church took over the Platonic doctrine of Ideas, appropriating them for Christian theology.[16] The archetypes for all created realities are also prepared in the kingdom of the Creator's potentialities. The Ideas of created beings are not the eternal Ideas of the Deity; they are the Ideas of God *the Creator*. They are created Ideas. They are conceptions of the love of God and variations of the creative communication of his boundless goodness. If, like Plato and the Fathers of the church, we start from the assumption that the Ideas have a stronger and more intense degree of existence than sense phenomena, it is then quite understandable that they should be 'in heaven', and that they should be closer to the eternal Being of God than their realizations and correspondences on earth. But it then also becomes obvious that the realization of these Ideas on earth are closer to the concern of God's love, and therefore to his joy as Creator, than the archetypes or Ideas themselves. According to the biblical traditions, God's especial concern is men and women, not the angels.

As the kingdom of the potentialities and potencies of God *the Creator*, heaven is also the kingdom of the forms which God realizes on earth 'from heaven'. The embodiment and quintessence of all the forms which the Creator desires to create, and will create, is the kingdom, in which his name will be hallowed and his will done, and in which all created beings partake of his glory. That is why – now, in time, here on earth and by human beings – this kingdom is called 'the kingdom of heaven'. But then it is to be 'the new heaven *and the new earth*', united through the indwelling of the triune God in heaven *and* earth.

In interpreting heaven we have used the concept of potentiality with different qualifications. We must now try to distinguish these different strata of potentiality or possibility more precisely.

1. All perceivable processes display connections between reality and potentiality: potential realities become realized potentialities.

2. These processes are encompassed and made possible by potentialities which we have called *creative* potentialities. Since these are potencies, they are not fully congruent with, or absorbed by, the making-possible of the potentialities which are to be realized; for the potencies surpass these in quality. It is the kingdom of these creative potencies, or their field of force, to which we give the name of heaven.

3. It is of course true that these potencies are only creative in relation to the discernible processes; in relation to the Creator God they are *created* potencies. But if he dwells in them, they are his direct environment, and ceaselessly receive their being from the creative well-spring of God the Spirit.

4. God the Creator is the source of creative potentialities, and of the potencies for the creation and completion of the processes we have described. By determining that he will be the Creator of his world, God decides out of the whole wealth of his potentialities in favour of the potentialities which are creative, and against those that are destructive; he decides for the process of creation and against its omission, says the doctrine of decrees. But if this resolve is an essential resolve, and not an arbitrary decree, then the whole wealth of potentiality of the divine Being flows into this fount of creative potentialities. There is no 'dark side' to God – no side where he could also be conceived of as the destroyer of his creation and of his own being as Creator. If God is himself supreme goodness and truth, then the wealth of his potentialities is determined by his essential nature. 'All things are possible with God' does not mean his undetermined omnipotence; it means the determined power of his goodness.

5. These qualitative distinctions between possibilities then also enable us to interpret the phenomena of evil. Evil is the perversion of good, the annihilation of what exists, the negation of the affirmation of life. On the level of the life processes, perversions of this

kind continually occur – perversions of constructive potentialities into destructive ones. On the human level they make themselves evident as processes of separation – sin; and isolation – death. There are apparently also perversions of the same kind in the sphere of the potencies which are intended to make the life processes possible. These then hinder and destroy those life processes. Because these are potencies which do not belong to the human sphere but which yet have a destructive effect on that sphere, we talk about demonic or satanic forces. They make the life processes impossible instead of possible. It is these dimensions of evil, transcending human beings and the earth, that are meant by the symbols of 'the fall of the angels' and 'the rule of Satan'. Deliverance from evil therefore also means the restoration of the good in earthly potentialities for living *and* in the heavenly potencies which make these potentialities possible. The very powers which have been perverted into what is destructive will themselves be redeemed; for their power is created power, and is as such good. It is only their power of destruction that was evil.

§3 THE HEAVEN OF JESUS CHRIST

It is typical of most works on Christian dogmatics to treat heaven only when they arrive at eschatology.[17] This shows their messianic orientation: 'heaven' is the place of the blessed and the reality of their heavenly bliss. It is the symbol of fulfilled hope. But according to Christian understanding, the beginning of heavenly bliss is already present – and is also already experienced – in the grace of Christ and in the church of Christ; and this means that heaven has already been thrown open here. Johann Gerhard called the church which God gathers here on earth the *coelum gratiae.* It is 'the church militant' – the struggling church. Consequently he called the condition of the church triumphant with God and all angels, the *coelum gloriae.* 'The heaven of grace' is present here and now in the church; 'the heaven of glory' will be possessed by the blessed hereafter.[18] This division of heaven in terms of salvation history was apparently a general one.[19]

The Catholic theologian Michael Schmaus makes a somewhat different distinction. He defines 'heaven in its fullest form' as fellowship with the God who manifests himself directly, and fellowship among the men and women who have arrived at their final goal. He distinguishes between a 'pre-heaven' for believers in Christ after their death and before their resurrection, and 'the complete heaven' which will come into being with Christ's parousia.[20]

Here we shall take up Johann Gerhard's distinction, but our differentiation between the *coelum gratiae* and the *coelum gloriae* will be a christological one, not ecclesiological.

The *coelum gratiae* opens and is perceived in the movement of God towards the liberation and redemption of the world. The one side of this divine movement is the becoming human of the Son; the other side in his ascension into heaven. Here we shall look at this movement of God's only in the context of the relationship between heaven and earth.

The *coelum gloriae* opens and is perceived in the coming of the glory of the triune God. With the advent of God's glory, heaven and earth will be created anew. So final blessedness will be experienced 'in heaven as it is on earth'.

It is in the theological differentiation between the present 'heaven of grace' and the future 'heaven of glory' that we can find the points of approach for modern projects of 'heaven on earth' which are utopian and critical of religion. Surely, these projects tell us, heaven is really the future of the earth, and the utopia of the life which ultimately achieves success? But is there any way of talking about the heaven of glory except in terms of the visionary future of 'a new earth'?

Of course the essential thing about the incarnation of the Son is that it is an event by which God binds himself to humanity. But in the New Testament traditions, and in patristic theologies, this event was not simply viewed anthropologically. It was seen in cosmological dimensions too. It is true that modern christologies have confined themselves to the anthropological significance of God's becoming human, and have neglected its meaning for the interpretation of the cosmos. But it is not merely a decorative appendage to the Christmas story when, in Luke 2. 9–15, the heaven opens and angels in the glory of God appear, to proclaim from heaven the gospel about the birth of the Saviour. Nor is it merely poetic licence when an old German Christmas carol calls upon the earth to 'break into leaf'. It is true that everything the angels say refers to the divine Child in the manger; but we must not overlook the cosmic phenomena which accompany the event of his birth.

Ever since the story of the Fall, the symbol of 'the closed heaven' has been an emblem of the divine judgment and the exile into which human beings have been cast out. 'The closed heaven' is a sign that God hides his face. 'The darkened heaven' is ultimately a portent of the last, apocalyptic judgment. Against this background, 'the opened heaven' means that the era of grace is beginning, that God is turning his face towards men and women in kindness, that the alienation from true life has been overcome, and that 'the gateway' to the paradise of an achieved and harmonious life has now been opened.

But 'the open heaven' also means that the earth will be fruitful once more. Isaiah 45.8 already interprets this in a transferred sense, when the writer talks about righteousness 'raining down' from heaven and salvation 'springing forth' from the opened earth. But behind this transferred meaning stands the literal one: when heaven opens, earth will be fruitful and life will be born. In this sense the gospel is the message of the opened, and now open, heaven (Matt. 3.16; Acts 7.55f.; Eph. 1.20f.), for Jesus 'saw Satan fall like lightning from heaven' (Luke 10.18). But in this sense the gospel is also the message about peace with nature and the fruitful earth.

In Ephesians and Colossians the cosmic significance of Christ is theologically developed with particular emphasis: 'All things' are to be united in Christ, 'things in heaven and things on earth . . .' (Eph. 1.10). Since v. 11 is particularly concerned with human beings, in this verse we are supposed to think of the cosmos: in Christ the space of heaven and the region of the earth are to be united. The result of their union will be a new communication between them, and the outcome of this communication will be new life. 'In him all things were created that are in heaven and that are on earth, visible and invisible' (Col. 1.16). That is why everything will be reconciled through him, 'whether on earth or in heaven, so that he may make peace through the blood of his cross, through himself' (Col. 1.20). Here too it is only the next verse which talks about human beings, so the peace which Jesus has made through himself on the cross also includes heaven and earth as such.

In the movement of God, his becoming human and his self-surrender on the cross, heaven too opens itself for the earth, and earth for heaven. Heaven and earth are clasped and gathered into a whole, and in the all-embracing peace of Christ arrive at their open communication with one another.

In the New Testament the raising of Christ from the dead is always bound up with his enthronement as Lord of the divine rule.

The acknowledgment of Christ as Lord and the acknowledgment of the God who raised him from the dead belong indissolubly together (Rom. 10.9). As the lordship of the One who is risen, the lordship of Christ reaches out beyond the circle of his people, and was seen from the very beginning in cosmic dimensions: he 'must take possession of heaven' (Acts 3.21). He sits 'at the right hand of God' and rules over 'all things' (Eph. 1.20f.; Col. 3.1). To him is given 'all power in heaven and on earth' (Matt. 28.18). The risen One rules, not only over the church, but over heaven and earth as well. The Creator has given him the lordship over his world. That is why he fills heaven and earth with the glory of his resurrection life and will renew the universe. Through his sovereignty, the visible and the invisible things of creation will be brought into such community that what is invisible, with its potentialities and potencies, will cease to terrify human beings and the earth, but will minister to them (cf. Rom. 8.38f.; Eph. 4.8; Col. 1.16). Heaven and earth will be fruitful once more. For the movement of God in the raising of Christ and his ascension into heaven sets the whole universe on the move towards the coming kingdom of glory.

We have interpreted heaven as the kingdom of God's energies, potentialities and potencies. So when 'heaven opens', this means that God's energies and potentialities appear in the visible world, in order to open the life systems which are closed in on themselves and to guide them into their new, richer future. What was impossible before will then become possible. Energies will awaken which before were constricted. A future will be opened which was hitherto closed and inaccessible. Over against the reality of the visible world awaken the possibilities of change for that world, and its transformation into the kingdom of God. It is of course true that it is first of all through faith, within themselves and in their own spheres of living, that men and women perceive these changes in heaven and earth through the incarnation and resurrection of Christ. But that does not mean that the changes are confined to these things. No limits are set to the reality of the world of heaven and earth which has been changed and set free through the movement of God in Christ. The boundlessness of the new world which comes into being under the lordship of Christ finds expression in the cosmological dimensions we have described. And these dimensions also make plain the messianic neediness of the old heaven and the old earth.

But is heaven then really, after all, no more than 'a symbolic term for God'?[21] Isn't Christ's ascension really a way of expressing the truth that Christ is where God is? In face of the homogeneous cosmologies of modern times, which no longer recognize a dual world, this interpretation would seem to be the obvious one. This divinization of heaven certainly makes spatial conceptions, and speculations about worlds beyond this one, superfluous. 'It is not that God is where heaven is, but that heaven is where God is.'[22] If heaven means 'the nearness of God', then heaven does not define where God is; it is God who defines where heaven is. The notion of heaven is then excised from the world picture and related solely to God. This of course means surrendering the dual creation for the sake of the illusion of a unified, homogeneous world of unlimited transparency and unrestricted disposability by men and women.[23] But if heaven is pushed out of the doctrine of creation, it becomes difficult to go on interpreting the earth as God's creation at all.

The divinization of heaven which seems so modern in fact goes back to early Protestant orthodoxy. In the dispute between the Lutherans and the Calvinists about the presence of Christ in the Lord's Supper, the concept of heaven came up for discussion too. If Christ is risen and has ascended 'into heaven', is he then *certo loco* in heaven, and only by virtue of the Holy Spirit also present on earth in the Lord's Supper? Or is his ascension into heaven identical with his 'sitting at the right hand of God'? And does his sitting at the right hand of God mean that he participates in God's universal real presence in the world, and his sovereignty over it? Theologians who followed Calvin thought of Christ as now spatially limited in heaven, their concern being to safeguard the specific, bodily nature of the risen Christ, and his promised parousia in glory ('from whence he shall come . . .'). Lutheran theologians, on the other hand, like Luther himself, saw the exalted Christ, participating in all the attributes of the Godhead, now already in real presence on earth. Here we shall leave on one side these earlier disputes about the bodily nature of the risen Christ and the parousia of the exalted One which is still to come, and shall consider only the idea of heaven that corresponds to these concepts.

Luther – already deviating from Zwingli – identified heaven with the presence of God, so that he could say that the earthly Christ was simultaneously in heaven: 'for what is in God and in his presence, that is in heaven.'[24] Later on, he substantiated his view of the real presence of the body of Christ with Christ's Being at the right hand of God. 'The right hand of God' means God's essential omnipresence. From this Luther concluded 'that Christ is in heaven at the same time that his body be in the Lord's Supper'.[25] From that time on, Lutheran theologians increasingly ceased to view heaven as a cosmic place, or to see it as the invisible region of creation, and instead made it the equivalent of God's omnipotence, omnipresence and glory. But this is only possible if we cease to make any distinction between the ascension and the sitting at the right hand of God. For then to say that Christ sits at the right hand of God means that he participates completely, in his human nature, in the attributes of the divine nature. Christ's ascension is then merely a symbolic way of expressing his deification. The body of Christ is omnipresent, 'in heaven as on earth'. But then 'the right hand of God' can no longer be localized 'in heaven', as the Apostles' Creed suggests we should think of it. It is nothing other than the omnipotence and omnipresence of God in heaven as on earth.[26] Neither heaven nor God's omnipresence can then still be thought of in spatial terms. But this means that 'In the strict sense, heaven is nothing but God'.[27]

Johann Gerhard consequently described the *coelum gloriae*, not as a created place, but as the uncreated, eternal, invisible, unlimited and almighty majesty of God.[28] He allowed the true heaven to be completely congruent with God himself, because only God himself is eternal life and eternal salvation. By annihilating the world, this train of thought makes God himself ultimately the world of human beings. This is not the place to point out the consequences for eschatology of a salvation thought of in such world-less terms.

As far as the idea of 'heaven and earth' is concerned, it means that heaven is split up into the uncreated omnipresence of God on the one hand, and the earthly sphere of air and aether on the other. 'The heaven of nature' loses its transcendence over against the earth if God's heaven (*coelum spirituale*) no longer transcends it in creation, but is equated with God himself. This conclusion has been extolled as the surmounting of the mediaeval world picture.[29] But for an understanding of the world as creation, this partition of heaven has been a hindrance; for heaven was elevated into the transcendence of the uncreated majesty of God, while the world was brought into total immanence. The symbol of heaven signifies the inner, relative transcendence of creation; and this was now pushed aside.

When modern 'criticism of heaven' led on to atheism, the

Lutheran divinization of heaven was one of the preconditions that made this possible. For if God and heaven are identified, when heaven falls, God falls with it.

§4 THE MODERN 'CRITICISM OF HEAVEN'

Ludwig Feuerbach had studied Lutheran theology before – by way of Hegel's philosophy – he became a critic of religion and a 'sensualist' – or a naturalist – philosopher. The Lutheran identification of heaven and God is the premise of his criticism, which would like to bring heaven down to earth: 'But in truth there is no distinction between the absolute life which is conceived as God, and the absolute life which is conceived as heaven, save that in heaven we have stretched into length and breadth what in God is concentrated in one.'[30] The notion that God is heaven concentrated, and that heaven is God expanded, is only possible if the difference in creation between heaven and earth is abolished, and if God and heaven are the same in quality.

Feuerbach's second argument for the identity of God and heaven is the eschatological idea of 'heaven' as fulfilled hope:

> Here it is not as it ought to be; this world passes away:– but God is existence as it ought to be. God fulfils my wishes; this is only a popular personification of the position: God is the fulfiller, *i.e.*, the reality, the fulfilment of my wishes. But heaven is the existence adequate to my wishes, my longing; thus, there is no distinction between God and heaven.[31]

Quite apart from the logical error whereby in this statement Feuerbach turns God, 'the fulfiller' of my wishes, into God 'the fulfilment' of my wishes, he had in this respect also reason enough to appeal to Lutheran theology; for the identification of the heaven of glory with the uncreated, eternal God himself leads to the result that in eschatology too no difference between God and heaven is permitted any longer; and the fulfiller of hope is equated with hope's fulfilment. The fulfiller no longer transcends the fulfilment of the desires which he himself awakens. So God is turned into the fulfilment of the wish projections of human beings.

But when one thing is equated with another, this is always the result of a movement: whereas Johann Gerhard had identified heaven with God, Feuerbach makes God the same thing as heaven.

The identification of heaven with God is for him not deserving of any actual proof; it needs to be no more than pointed out, because it is obvious:

> As man conceives his heaven, so he conceives his God; the content of his idea of heaven is the content of his idea of God, only that what in God is a mere sketch, a concept, is in heaven depicted and developed in the colours and forms of the senses. Heaven is therefore the key to the deepest mysteries of religion . . . For this reason, religions are as various as are the kingdoms of heaven, and there are as many kingdoms of heaven as there are characteristic differences among men. The Christians themselves have very heterogeneous conceptions of heaven.[32]

For Feuerbach this counts as proof that God is heaven, and he thinks that it must be readily intelligible to everyone that 'heaven is the true God of men'. What is undoubtedly true about his proposition is that the kingdom where wishes and dreams are fulfilled is the kingdom of possibilities; and that is why it seems to vary so much in content: to each his own. The eschatologically promised 'heaven of glory' has always drawn to itself the visions of hope and the wistful dreams of men and women. As long as this future was bound up with God it was full of 'everything possible'. The variability in the definitions of what constitutes heaven is objectively due to heaven's general character as possibility; while subjectively it is founded on the hopes and desires awakened by the divine promises.

But if God himself is turned into the fulfilment of human hopes and desires, heaven is lost. In hope's fulfilment God and human beings become one: God is then human being, and the human being is God; and this deified condition no longer includes any transcendence, because it no longer includes any qualitative differences between God and human beings, heaven and earth, potentiality and reality. Feuerbach did not really 'reduce' theology to anthropology. What he did was to identify theology and anthropology, maintaining that what the two are talking about is the same Being. Consequently his criticism of religion ends in anthropotheism, and in the deification of life: 'Life is God, the enjoyment of life is the enjoyment of God, true joy in life is true religion.'

Feuerbach's criticism of religion is religious, not irreligious. It serves to establish 'the religion of this world', the religion of the earth; and it elevates politics into the new religion. It is here that his prophetic solemnity has its roots:

> In place of the Deity in whom merely the fathomless and luxurious desires of men are fulfilled, we must hence put the human race, or nature; in the place of religion, education; in place of the world beyond the grave in heaven, the world beyond the grave on earth, *the historical future*, the future of mankind.[33]

The transformation of the heaven of the world beyond, into the beyond of the historical future also became the foundation for the criticism of religion which Karl Marx went on to develop.

For Feuerbach, the duality of heaven and earth is merely a reflection of the dichotomy of the human being at odds with himself. When the human being comes to himself, he also abolishes the duality of heaven and earth, potentiality and reality, being and existence. The critical reduction of heaven to earth brings human beings to themselves, and nature to her own identity. This means that heaven must become the historical future of human beings who arrive at their true selves.

But for Marx the human being is 'not an abstract being, crouching outside the world'. 'The human being is *the world of human beings*, the state, society. This state, this society, produce religion, which is a distorted awareness of the world, because they are an inverted world.'[34] That is why the religious heaven cannot be reduced to the individual people who are at one with themselves; it can be reduced only to the true, all-human society. But it is for this historical future that the workers are struggling to liberate themselves. Religion is hence 'the expression of the true wretchedness' and 'protest against that true wretchedness'. So 'criticism of heaven' cannot be turned into the blessing of the earth, as it is in Feuerbach. It has to be transformed into 'criticism of the earth'. Criticism of religion has to be criticism of society. It therefore ends for Marx in the revolutionary imperative 'to overthrow all conditions in which the human being is a debased, enslaved, neglected and contemptible being'.[35]

Marx takes up Feuerbach's criticism of heaven, but he gives it a more realistic form. He too replaces the indissoluble duality of heaven and earth by the dissoluble difference between humanity's present condition and its historical future. But this 'historical future' can only be realized in the revolutionary imperative. The 'exposed secret' of religion is not 'the human being'; it is the future, true human society, in its unity with nature. At the same time, the all-human society must be nothing less than 'heaven on earth', just as for Feuerbach the person who is at one with himself is the true God on earth. But this means that this perfect, all-human – which is to say Communist – society must be a society without heaven. A society without heaven is on the one hand a society without religion – at least without what was called religion in the history of inhumane societies. On the other hand it is also a society without possibilities and without alternatives – at least without those alternative possibilities the remembrance of which was hitherto preserved in the heaven of the religions. If this society without transcendence is to be a closed social system, it has to be a society which abolishes human beings altogether, in the sense in which they have always hitherto been interpreted.

Ernst Bloch recognized these consequences of the criticism of religion based on the philosophy of identity which is to be found in Feuerbach and Marx, and he tried to avoid them by recasting the Marxist criticism of religion. He once more posed the question about heaven: 'What about the hollow space that is left when the God hypostasis is eliminated?'[36] Whereas Feuerbach had in mind the mystical form of Christianity, Bloch tries to take over critically the heritage of Christianity in its messianic character. For him, the essence of religion is 'hope in totality'. 'Where there is hope, there is religion.'[37] In all its different forms, the religious heaven fobs people off, in their earthly misery, with cheap and meretricious consolation; and yet that heaven always contains humanity's images of hope as well. So even though he adopts Feuerbach's 'reductionist' method in his criticism of religion, Bloch applies this method differently: it is not anthropology that is the truth of religion; it is eschatology.[38] The religious duplication of the world in heaven and earth derives from the human being's fundamental discord: the conflict between 'his present appearance' – 'present' in the sense of availably existent – 'and his non-present being'.[39] This conflict does not merely govern human beings. It dominates the whole cosmos. Human beings do not yet have their true nature within themselves; it is still in front of them. And, in the same way, nature too is only as yet 'a huge container full of future'. Life 'outside' is no more finished and complete than the life within, which works on this 'outside'. Consequently both human beings and the world should be apprehended in the process of their history, in which their truth and identity is at stake. The religious images of heaven are in reality images of the future which, with growing urgency and force, delineate the human and the cosmic incognito, with the aim of discovering the heart of existence and the foundation of the world. For Bloch, 'the kingdom' becomes the central symbol and concept for the apocalypse of human beings and cosmos. According to his view of things, Christianity already turned 'the mysticism of heaven' into 'the mysticism of the Son of man', and 'the glory of God' into 'the glory of the redeemed church'. It was therefore quite consistent when Christianity ceased to see heaven as 'above us' but rather as 'ahead of us', and for it no longer to define God's dwelling-place in terms of space but in terms of time, no longer cosmologically as heaven, but eschatologically, as the kingdom.

For Bloch as for Feuerbach, all images of God and concepts of God are projections of human longing, stamped by the misery under which men and women groan. Enlightenment requires us to recognize these religious ideas as the dreams of humanity, and to repossess them in this sense. But 'is *the emptiness* into which the illusions of the divine were projected not at least present as this very emptiness? Indeed does not mere reflection and re-reflection, if they are to happen at all, actually demand something which – if it can be doubled to a seeming – is not seeming itself? Does it not in fact require a mirror?'[40] That was what Bloch meant by his question to Feuerbach: 'What about the hollow space?' The problem about the space of religious projection is not for him a 'seeming', an illusory, problem. It is true that he does not see this space as 'present', in the sense of factually and availably existent. Nor is it a reality in the sense of the Platonic theory of the two worlds. For Bloch it is 'something kept open for a reality possible in the future but not yet resolved upon'. It is '*the open region of what is before us*, the new thing towards which the sequences of human purposes tend and in some mediated form continue.'[41] This forecourt of the future ahead of reality contains the possibility of all or nothing, heaven and hell. The atheistic criticism of religion leaves this forecourt untouched, and throws it open for what it is. Without this 'utopianly real hollow space' there would be no 'utopia of the kingdom'. For Bloch, the gods are projections and chimaeras; but the space into which they were projected and imagined is the real future. '*Homo absconditus* thus retains a pre-ordered, abiding sphere in which, if he does not founder, he is able to will his most elemental, his profoundest modality in the world opened to him.'[42]

In this way Ernst Bloch rehabilitated heaven, contrary to Feuerbach and Marx. Heaven is certainly transferred from the spatial sphere 'above us' to the temporal sphere 'before us'. But this 'forecourt' is more than 'historical future', for it also contains what puts an end to historical future: all or nothing, final undoing or life in ultimate fruition. It contains the possibility of both historical and eschatological future, of both future and eternity.

At this point Bloch indeed remains ambiguous. *Das Prinzip Hoffnung* – 'The Principle of Hope' – closes with a vista stretching towards the homeland of identity, whereas his book *Naturrecht und menschliche Würde* ('Natural Law and Human Dignity') ends with the vista of an open and religious society in solidarity. The critical question which this ambiguity inevitably raises is this: if the heaven of the possibilities of the creative God is transformed into the forecourt of a possible future without God, when will these possibilities be exhausted. If the qualitative difference of creative potentialities compared with the world is turned into a merely quantitative difference between what is not-yet-real and what is already-real, the end of these potentialities is already predictable. If 'heaven' is transformed into 'the historical future', heaven's past can be foreseen, because it then loses the dimension of eternity. Really and truly, Bloch's 'principle of hope' lives from the very thing it would like to deny: the future can only take the place of heaven as long as it represents the kingdom of heaven, and as long as people can await and hope for the eschatological future in the future of history. A historical future without heaven cannot be the forecourt of hope and the motivation for any historical movement. A 'transcending without transcendence' such as Bloch proposed turns infinity into indefinite endlessness, and makes of the striving for fulfilment merely an 'on and on'.

The theological reduction of heaven to God meant that criticism of heaven led to atheism. Bloch's attempt to rehabilitate heaven without God shows how necessary this category is for the forecourt of the possible before the actual. But a heaven without God is incapable of making accessible to the earth a future in which men and women might seek for happiness, salvation, the disclosure of what is hidden, identity and essential being. Without God's creative potentialities for the world, worldly potentialities remain determined by presently existing reality and are totally congruent with that.

§5 GOD'S GLORY 'IN HEAVEN AS IT IS ON EARTH'

Present-day Christian theology has not paid enough attention to the way heaven is talked about; and the Protestant theology of modern times has positively neglected heaven altogether. Because no one knew how to cope with it, people resorted, as we have seen, to reductions of heaven to God, to the universe, or to the future. But this made it difficult to understand the earth as creation, and its future as the kingdom of God. Let us sum up these reductions, looking to see where they went wrong, so that we may arrive at a way of talking about heaven which is clearly distinct from these earlier attempts, and which is theologically and cosmologically responsible.

1. The first reduction of heaven to something quite different was made in the Christian church itself. As the realistic eschatology of the kingdom of God receded, heaven was increasingly – and to the same degree – declared to be the place of salvation for the soul. The prayer for the coming of the kingdom 'on earth as it is in heaven' was replaced by the longing 'to go to heaven' oneself. The kingdom of God's glory and the salvation of the whole creation was reduced to heaven; and heaven was reduced to the salvation of the soul.

This religious reduction led to the heedless neglect of the earth and to the surrender of its future. Anyone who confuses the kingdom of God with heaven transforms his hope into resignation.[43]

2. If heaven is reduced to God himself, it ceases to be a part of creation, and is as uncreated and eternal as God himself. It is then God's essential Being before he resolved to become the Creator. A heaven divinized in this way contains the potentiality for creation – and the potentiality for creation's destruction. The reduction of heaven to God himself therefore delivers the earth over to the apocalyptic 'annihilation of the world'.

3. If heaven and earth are no longer distinguished qualitatively, what results is the concept of a homogeneous and self-contained universe. The understanding of the world as a creation open to God can then no longer be maintained.

4. If God is reduced to heaven, the concept of God also falls victim to criticism of heaven. The world which has become identical

with itself no longer knows any transcendence. Heaven is replaced by the historical future. Once this is fulfilled, what comes into being is the closed system of a world identical with itself. But without heavenly potentialities the historical future can neither bring anything new, nor can it bring salvation. It becomes the future of the past.

We must therefore establish that God's creation is *necessarily* the double world of heaven and earth. A God-created world is also a world open to God. As a world open to God, creation is an ec-centric reality which has its unity and its centre in its Creator and not in itself. We call the side of creation which is open to God 'heaven'. From heaven and through heaven God acts on earth. Heaven represents the relative 'beyond' of the world, and the earth is the relative this-worldliness of heaven. In heaven creation has its relative transcendence. In the earth creation finds its relative immanence. The ec-centric world open to God possesses in itself the dialectical structure of transcendence and immanence. It is therefore wrong to confuse this relative transcendence of heaven with the absolute transcendence of God; for *God himself*, the Creator of heaven and earth, is rather the transcendence of the transcendence and immanence of the world. God himself, who desires to fill heaven and earth with his glory, is also the immanence of the transcendence and immanence of the world.

The dual world described in the words 'heaven and earth' is the goodly form of God's creation; it is not a conflicting and divided world. Consequently all attempts to dissolve this duality lead to the world's destruction. 'Heaven' is the word used to describe the sphere of God's creative potentialities and energies. They are creat*ed* potentialities but, as such, creat*ive* possibilities of God's. 'The earth' is the term we use for the sphere of created reality and the possibilities inherent in that reality. By distinguishing between the quality of the created potentialities of God towards the world, and the quality of the world's own potentialities, we are also distinguishing between the world's historical and its eschatological future. But the distinction also leads to an understanding of the continual communication between God's creative potentialities towards the world, and the worldly potentialities themselves; for the worldly potentialities are made possible by the divine ones.

The continual making-possibilities-possible keeps the world in existence and all its life systems alive; for it keeps the future open for all open systems, and opens that future anew. To put it in theological terms, creation lives from the continual inflow of the energies of the Spirit of God. To put it symbolically: because heaven is open, and as long as it is open, the world has a future.

God's presence is understood spatially as being located in heaven – that is, in the sphere of his creative potentialities; and spatially it moves from heaven to earth. Understood in terms of time, his heavenly presence is his eschatological presence: he is present in his kingdom, and this kingdom is the future of the earth, because it comes to earth and through its future transposes the earth into its history.

Here we must clearly distinguish between heaven and the kingdom of God. Heaven is now the place of God's presence, but it is not yet the arena for the kingdom of glory. The kingdom of glory means a presence of God that is again new, even compared with his heavenly presence. The kingdom of glory embraces not merely heaven but earth too, and presupposes the creation of 'a new heaven' and 'a new earth'. It is not only earth that requires a new creation, tormented as it is by suffering and pain and crying and death. Heaven requires a new creation too. This would be quite incomprehensible if heaven were already, now, the place of salvation and blessedness. We do not need to enter into any super-terrestrial speculations about the pains and the 'waxing old' of heaven: 'heaven itself weeps' over an earth of blood and tears. Heaven and earth are certainly distinguished through their creation, but they none the less exist in the fellowship of creation, and are in continual communication. What happens on earth touches heaven too. Cain's fratricide 'cries out to high heaven' and 'there is joy in heaven over one sinner who repents'. If, in accord with the general Christian conception, the soul goes to heaven after death, it is not already redeemed there. It waits in its own way for the redemption which will bring the new heaven and the new earth and, in that new earth, the resurrection of the body also.

The kingdom of glory is therefore waited for 'in heaven as on earth'. It is to *renew* heaven and earth. What can it bring heaven and earth? We shall do no more than touch on that here, pointing to eschatology. The kingdom of glory is the indwelling of the triune God in his whole creation. Heaven *and earth* will become God's dwelling, the surroundings that encompass him, and his milieu. For created beings, this means that – all together, each created being in its own way – they will participate in eternal life and in the eternal bliss of the God who is present among them. It means for them too that, one with another, they will enter into an unhindered communication towards every side, a communication which has been known from time immemorial as 'the sympathy of all things'. It does not mean that the difference between heaven and earth will be ended: the earth will not become heavenly, and the heavenly will not become earthly. But it does mean that both these spheres of creation will enter into unhindered and boundlessly fruitful communication with one another. We can no longer talk about a hierarchical descent from heaven to earth once heaven and earth both, each in its own way, become 'the dwelling' of the God who is present in both realms.

But there is, all the same, one change, which must already be mentioned at this point. Earthly created beings are evidently finite and mortal, whereas heavenly created beings are finite but immortal. As finite creations, heavenly beings *participate* through contemplation in God's eternity. What is true of the angels is true also of the heaven of the angels: as God's creation it is finite, but through its participation in the presence of God it is eternal. These differentiations may sound speculative; but they are important for an understanding of eternal life and the modality of existence in the resurrection. The resurrection creates an immortal life for the dead, a life finite and created, but not infinite and divine. Even in the kingdom of glory the world remains God's creation and will not become God himself. But through its *participation* in God's eschatological presence, a 'world without end' comes into being, a life that is 'eternal', and a joy in existence 'which does not pass away'. For 'all live to him' (Luke 20.38).

VIII

The Evolution of Creation

§1 THE HUMAN BEING – A CREATURE IN THE HISTORY OF CREATION

In this chapter we shall be considering the transition from the theology of nature to theological anthropology. But we shall not begin by describing the human being *per se*. We shall start by pointing to the great natural cohesions which provide the setting in which human beings come forward to perform their role. Modern philosophical and theological anthropology[1] liked to start from the question: what distinguishes human beings from animals? And what determines their special position in the cosmos? But we shall begin differently. We shall start with the question: what links human beings with animals and all other creatures? And what do they have in common?

Modern European anthropology uncritically took the modern anthropocentric world picture as its premise. According to this conception, the human being is the centre of the world, and the world was created for his sake and for his use. Modern sciences have put an end to this naive attitude.

Modern astronomy overthrew the Ptolemaic world picture, and left us with the question: in the face of the infinite spaces of the universe and the immeasurable clusters of the stars, what are human beings on this earth?

Modern biology traced the species 'man' back to the evolutionary series of 'types' which come into being and can also disappear again. And this left us with the question: is the human being a fluke of selection, or is he a meaningful, late product of evolution?

Modern psychoanalysis showed that beneath the human being's feeble self-awareness, which is the sustainer of reason and will, lie worlds belonging to the unconscious – worlds of unrecognized drives and involuntary suppressions. This raised the question: is the human soul its own master, or merely the puppet of unconscious forces?

In these 'three successive steps in four centuries', wrote Teilhard de Chardin, 'man . . . has seemed definitely to redissolve in the common ground of things'.[2]

In the middle ages, Christian anthropology accepted the Ptolemaic world picture, and declared earthly beings to be the centre of the world; and in doing this it lost sight of its roots in the biblical traditions. It became one-sided when, in modern times, it continually drew on the biblical traditions solely in order to legitimate the special position of human beings in the cosmos, not in order to illuminate the fellowship of human beings with creation. It became narrow-minded and ultimately barren when it felt obliged to defend modern anthropocentricism against Galileo, Darwin and Freud, in order to rescue human dignity and morality.

If we are to understand what it means to be human in the widest sense, we must start with the complexes and milieus in which human beings appear and from which they live; and that means beginning with the genesis of the cosmos, the evolution of life, and the history of the consciousness, not with the special position of human beings in that cosmos, with what religion maintains to be their likeness to God, or with their conscious subjectivity. We shall therefore talk theologically first of all about the human being as 'a creature in the fellowship of creation'; and before we interpret this being as *imago Dei*, we shall see him as *imago mundi* – as a microcosm in which all previous creatures are to be found again, a being that can only exist in community with all other created beings and which can only understand itself in that community: 'Though made of body and soul, man is one. Through his bodily composition he gathers to himself the elements of the material world. Thus they reach their crown through him, and through him can raise their voice in free praise of the Creator.'[3] Can we find reasons for this viewpoint in the biblical traditions? And what perspectives do they throw open to us?

Every glance at the creation accounts in the Old Testament makes it clear first of all that the human being is one creature among others. There is a fellowship of creation and the human being is a member of it. But this fellowship of creation is constituted in a particular order, so that exegetically we can quite properly talk about a *history of creation*. What is described at 'creation in the beginning' is the history of the stages or 'generations' (*toledoth*) through which the world came into being at its creation (Gen. 2.4a).[4] The account of creation is the account of a history in temporal sequence. It is not the account of a timeless, primordial condition, or a dramatic primaeval struggle. In this history of creation human beings appear on the stage last of all. In this sense heaven and earth, light and darkness, the earth, plants and animals, are all creations which prepare for the creation of human beings. Human beings are the last to be created. In so far they are the apex of created things. But they are not 'the crown of creation'. It is the sabbath with which God crowns the creation which he beholds as 'very good'. Moreover, as the last thing to be created the human being is also dependent on all the others. Without them his existence would not be possible. So while they are a preparation for him, he is dependent on them. How does this dependency find expression?

He is taken from the earth, the second creation account tells us (Gen. 2.7). The account already makes this clear from his name: Adam – the earthly or human creature – is formed from *'adama*, the motherly earth.[5] This earthly creature therefore remains bound up with the earth, and when he dies he returns to the earth again. Curiously enough we are not told that animals are 'earthly' in this way. It is true that the biblical creation accounts avoid the expression 'mother earth'; but the anthropological ideas which are bound up with the phrase are still evident.

The human being is 'a living soul', says the second creation account (Gen. 2.7 AV), meaning by this that the human being is an animated body, not that he is a soul that has taken on flesh, as Plato maintained. But this animated embodiment links human beings with animals, for the animals too are described as 'living souls' (Gen. 1.30).[6] Because the Hebrew word for soul (*nepeš*) also means 'breath', this is intended to indicate that human beings and animals (apart from fish) are breathing creatures which are all alike dependent on the air, and live from it.

The human being is dependent on food to sustain his life. Together with the beasts, he finds his living space on earth, and his food in its vegetation (Gen. 1.20, 30; 2.19).

So that they may reproduce themselves, human beings are given bi-sexuality and fertility. On this the Creator confers his blessing: 'Be fruitful and multiply' (Gen. 1.28). The animals are given exactly the same blessing: 'Be fruitful and multiply' (Gen. 1.22).

So human beings have in common with animals their living souls, their living space, their food, and the blessing of fertility. What, then, distinguishes human beings from other creatures? What is the specific character of their particular fellowship of creation?

The human being is distinguished from the earth by the divine charge 'to subdue' that earth, although according to Genesis 1.28 this means nothing but the injunction to eat vegetable food. Literally speaking, only the earth is mentioned – not the world, for example, or the sky, or the waters.

He is distinguished from the animals because he is supposed to give them their names, and they are to be called by the names he gives them (Gen. 2.19). This is not merely an act of rule: it brings animals into a community of language with human beings. But there is no mention at all in the creation accounts of enmity between human beings and beasts, or of a right to kill animals. Human beings are appointed as 'justices of the peace'.

Finally, unlike animals, the human being is evidently a social being who is dependent on the help of others: 'It is not good that the man should be alone. I will make him a helper' (Gen. 2.18). This is said only about human beings.

It is only when we become aware of the things which human beings have in common with other creatures, and the things that differentiate them, that we can understand what the human being's designation to be the image of God really means (Gen. 1.26). This designation certainly sets him uniquely apart from the rest of creation. Not even the angels are said to be in the image of God. But the designation is not identical with the natural differences between human beings and animals, and is in no way intended to interpret these differences. It affects the whole human being, both in his community with other created things and in his difference from them. As God's image, human beings are God's proxy in his creation, and represent him. As God's image, human beings are for God himself a counterpart, in whom he desires to see himself as if in a mirror. As God's image, finally, human beings are created for the sabbath, to reflect and praise the glory of God which enters into creation, and takes up its dwelling there.

According to the order of the history of creation, heaven and earth are at the beginning, and human beings come at the end, immediately before the sabbath. But in the history of redemption the order is different: here the new human being is at the beginning and the new creation of heaven and earth comes at the end. The *new* creation, which is identical with redemption, begins with the sending, self-surrender and raising of Jesus Christ: the Son of the Father is the visible image of the invisible God on earth. This new creation passes from him to believers, who are made equal to the first-born brother (Rom. 8.29): they become children of God in the Holy Spirit, and are already in Christ 'a new creation' (II Cor. 5.17). The longing of the waiting creation is directed towards the future revelation of the liberty of the children of God, for in that, and through that, non-human creation is also to be freed from the curse of transience (Rom. 8.19ff.). The longing of the whole creation will be fulfilled when 'the redemption of the body' comes about in the resurrection of the dead, and in the annihilation of death – in Christ's parousia, with which the divine glory will enter into creation, liberating it and transfiguring it. Finally, for this eschatological entry of the divine glory heaven and earth will be created anew (Rev. 21.1,5): they will become the dwelling place of God and the banqueting hall for the eternal sabbath. Without going further here into these perspectives of the history of redemption, we should notice that according to the biblical traditions the order of the history of redemption is evidently diametrically opposite to the order of the history of creation. We see too that – both in creation and in redemption – the human being is not isolated, nor is he seen in confrontation with the world. He is viewed as belonging within the enduring cohesion of the whole creation. Creation has its meaning for human beings, and human beings have their meaning for the community of creation. If we are to understand what human existence is, and what human beings are destined or called to be, we must see these human beings as belonging within the all-embracing coherences of God's history with the world, the history of creation and the history of redemption. And from this perspective we gain an insight into a strange double function on the part of human beings.

1. As God's last creation before the sabbath, the human being himself is the embodiment of all other creatures. The complex system 'human being' contains within itself all simpler systems in

the evolution of life, because it is out of these that the human being has been built up and has proceeded. In this sense they are present in him, just as he is dependent on them. He is *imago mundi*. As microcosm the human being represents the macrocosm. As 'image of the world' he stands before God as the representative of all other creatures. He lives, speaks and acts on their behalf. Understood as *imago mundi*, human beings are priestly creations and eucharistic beings. They intercede before God for the community of creation.

2. Understood as *imago Dei*, human beings are at the same time God's proxy in the community of creation. They represent his glory and his will. They intercede for God before the community of creation. In this sense they are God's representatives on earth.

3. If human beings stand before God on behalf of creation, and before creation on behalf of God, and if this is their priestly calling, then in a Christian doctrine of creation human beings must neither disappear into the community of creation, nor must they be detached from that community. Human beings are at once *imago mundi* and *imago Dei*. In this double role they stand before the sabbath of creation in terms of time. They prepare the feast of creation.

§2 EVOLUTION OR CREATION? FALSE CONFRONTATIONS – GENUINE PROBLEMS

Is it possible to link the concept of evolution with the concept of creation? And is there any point in doing so? Or are they in principle mutually exclusive concepts?

The modern scientific theory of evolution has come up against the resistance of the Christian churches ever since its beginnings. In 1907, in the encyclical *Pascendi dominici gregis*, Pius X condemned it as a modernist error: the teaching that life developed out of matter, the encyclical alleged, led to materialism, pantheism and atheism.[7] In 1950, in the encyclical *Humani generis*, Pius XII confirmed the irreconcilability of evolutionary theory with the Christian faith: the theory of evolution permitted artificial contraception and abortion; only belief in creation preserved faithfulness to nature and reverence for the developing human life. Pierre Teilhard de Chardin's cosmology is a creative synthesis which combines the theory of evolution with belief in God; but even today his writings are considered suspect because they 'offend against Catholic doctrine'.[8] On the Protestant side too the theory of evolution seemed at first to be irreconcilable with belief in creation. Here public dispute flared up on the appearance in 1859 of Charles Darwin's epoch-making *Origin of Species by means of Natural Selection, or the Preservation of Famous Races in the Struggle for Life.*[9] In the following year the famous debate took place in the British Association for the Advancement of Science between Samuel Wilberforce, the Bishop of Oxford, and T. H. Huxley – a debate in which the generally acknowledged victor was Huxley, not the theologian. However the actual theory about the evolution of organisms and species had in fact developed earlier. The philosopher Herbert Spencer made use of the theory before Darwin, and it was he who coined the phrase 'the survival of the fittest'. Darwin himself uses the word 'evolution' only hesitantly, preferring the expressions 'transformism' and 'the doctrine of descent'.[10] And although the much-quoted sentence with which he closed *The Origin of Species* – 'Light will also fall on Man and his history' – certainly seems to point in the direction of a social evolution, he himself probably had no idea of transferring the theory of descent and selection to the processes of society in the simplistic way we find illustrated in what is known as 'social Darwinism'.[11] The capitalist competitive struggle, European colonialism, white racism and patriarchalism – 'the white man's burden' – and, not least, the class struggle, were all interpreted in the light of social Darwinism as natural events of selection. But the new socialist forms of community were also interpreted in the same sense, in the light of the principle of selection, as representing higher stages in the evolution of human beings.

It was not merely this political ideologization of a scientific theory which first roused theological resistance. On the contrary, this was the very point at which resistance failed. The opposition was levelled against the world view itself. If the assumption of a divine creation is replaced by the assumption of a natural 'origin', the human being ceases to feel that he is in the hands of a God who cares for every individual; he sees himself as a cog in the mechanism of natural laws – the laws of a nature which seems to deal indifferently with its individual examples, when species adapt themselves to a changed environment, selecting in the adaptation process.[12] How can natural evolution be the meaning of the world, if the majority of all living things represent vain experiments on nature's part?

In 1925, in the state of Tennessee, fundamentalist circles in the United States procured the so-called 'monkey trial'. The court ruled that evolutionary theory must not be taught in schools contrary to the wishes of parents. Even today, the dispute between scientific 'evolutionists' and fundamentalist 'creationists' continues in the United States, though with the significant innovation that now the 'creationists' see themselves as believing scientists and carry on independent research in their own scientific institutes.

In German Protestant theology, Karl Beth, Adolf Titius and Karl Heim tried to achieve a productive synthesis between evolutionary theory and the doctrine of creation.[13] This attempt was of interest to both sides, but it ceased to be pursued once the ethical theology of liberalism, and also the new dialectical theology, accepted what Heinrich Ott calls 'the indifferentist solution', which meant the mutual 'non-interference' of theology and science. But this proposal brings no solution to the problems. It simply means excluding them from consideration. Consequently theology must start again from the early attempts at a synthesis, if it is to comprehend creation and God's activity in the world in a new way, in the framework of today's knowledge about nature and evolution, and if it is to make the world as creation – and it's history as God's activity – comprehensible to scientific reason also. If this is to be our purpose, we must first of all be critical, and must get rid of the bias and narrowness which have taken root in the Christian doctrine of creation in the wake of the polemic against the theory of evolution.

1. Like the other writings of the Old and New Testament, the biblical creation narratives originated in different historical eras. Each of them itself represents a successful synthesis between belief in creation and knowledge of nature. It is a biblicist misunderstanding of the biblical testimonies to think that they are laying down once and for all particular findings about nature, and render all further research superfluous. The history of the biblical traditions themselves shows that the stories of creation belong within a hermeneutical process of revision and innovation, as the result of new experiences. Since they are testimonies to the history of God with the world, they themselves actually direct their readers to new experiences of the world in this divine history. This means that they offer themselves for productive new interpretation and further development. So it is not merely possible to relate the biblical testimonies about creation and God's history with his creation, to new insights about nature, and new theories about the interpretation of these insights; it is actually necessary to make this connection,

and to reformulate the biblical testimonies in the light of these things. The openness for ever-new syntheses is rooted in the openness for the future which we find in the biblical testimonies themselves. But it is of course also true that this openness for the future turns every synthesis into a provisional draft, and permits no dogmatism.

2. In the dispute about that part of evolutionary theory which is concerned with the descent of man, the Christian doctrine of creation came to be narrowed down to creation in the beginning (*creatio originalis*); and this was further contracted still to the aspect of God's creative activity. The doctrine of the divine 'making',[14] the doctrine of continuous creation (*creatio continua*) and the doctrine of the new creation still to be consummated (*creatio nova*) all receded into the background and were forgotten. As a result, creation in the beginning was declared to be a finished and complete creation, capable of no history and in need of no evolution. The human being too, created to be 'the image of God', was viewed as a being created once and for all, and therefore finished and complete; he was not a being intended for evolution. Finally, the relation between God and his creation was restricted to a relation of causality, and the wealth of God's other relationships to the world, and the world to him, was disregarded. These ideas were put forward in an attempt to vindicate the doctrine of creation. But in fact they only succeeded in tying the picture of God's creation inexorably to the notions about the static comsos which were current coin in the Christian middle ages. The contradictions between the biblical belief in creation and the ancient world's veneration for the cosmos were overlooked; though these contradictions had in fact remained unresolved in the mediaeval synthesis.

3. But what finally, and most of all, disturbed the idealistic Christian view of the human being in the nineteenth century was the place given to him in the evolution of life. Is the human being an animal in an advanced stage of development, or is he 'the crown of creation'? Is he a link in the evolutionary chain, or is he the image of God? The theory of evolution shook the self-interpretation of Christians and the self-understanding of civic society alike – the self-understanding of the European who, in the name of God, had made himself the lord of nature. It rocked the whole modern, anthropocentric view of the world: the species human being is no more than one small link in an evolutionary sequence whose end cannot be foreseen. But if the human being is merely an interim

result, not the definitive end-total of previous cosmic history, then he cannot be the goal of creation; and creation cannot, either, have been on his account. The unduly violent reaction of the churches and the civic community to Darwin's evolutionary theory can be explained by the anthropocentric view of the world which it assailed. But can we call this viewpoint biblical, let alone Christian? Is it not merely the ideological self-justification of nineteenth- and twentieth-century man, in his conquest of the world, his exploitation of nature, and his self-deification?

On the other hand, we cannot disregard the fact that the theory of evolution was the perfect instrument for developing a materialist outlook. One philosophical root of the concept 'evolution' can already be found in pantheism of the Neoplatonic kind: the One develops into the Many (*explicatio*), the Many return to the One (*implicatio*), 'God' is the quintessence of the whole, and in his Being all things are enfolded (*complicatio*).[15] John Scotus Erigena, Nicholas of Cusa, Giordano Bruno and even, in our own century, Teilhard de Chardin, used the concept of development in this pantheistic framework. Friedrich Engels and Karl Marx at once welcomed the appearance of Darwin's *Origin of Species* in 1859 as offering 'the foundation in natural history for our own view'.[16] Ernst Haeckel used Darwin's theory as evidence for his 'monistic philosophy' (1899): 'Pantheism teaches that God and the world are one', he wrote. 'The idea of God is identical with that of nature or substance . . . Pantheism is *the world-system of the modern scientist*.'[17] Albert Einstein too answered the question about his belief in God by saying: 'I believe in Spinoza's God, who shows himself in the orderly harmony of what exists, not in a God who concerns himself with the destinies and actions of human beings.'[18] The terms used in evolutionary theory today, such as the 'self-organization', 'self-reproduction', 'self-ordering', 'self-planning', 'self-direction' and 'self-transcendence' of matter, are no more than elements of a theory; but they can of course easily be employed for a comprehensive world view, whether that view be materialistic, or religious and spiritualistic in kind. The world then exists *ex se*, not *ab alio*. Divine attributes are ascribed to it. The exponents of evolution do not always realize clearly enough that the ideological application of their theoretical concepts hinders their scientific work rather than promotes it.

Glaring examples of the ideologization of a concept drawn from evolutionary theory are Darwin's notion about 'the struggle for existence' and his evolutionary law of 'the survival of the fittest'. Darwin developed these ideas on the basis of the selection of species in the struggle with environmental conditions. It was Huxley who first transferred them to the competitive struggle in modern capitalist society, interpreting 'the struggle for existence' in Hobbes's sense, as 'the struggle of all against each'. This 'social Darwinism' was not Darwin's own intention at all. In contrast, as early as 1880 and 1896, the Russian zoologists Kessler and Peter Kropotkin demonstrated the evolutionary law of mutual help among animals and human beings: in the struggle for existence it is precisely those beings that live symbiotically which prove to be the strongest.[19] The isolation of the human being in the competitive struggle of modern society is therefore his weakness. Darwin also already observed and described phenomena of social organization among animals and particular animal species. It was only 'social Darwinism' which suppressed this, misusing Darwin's theory ideologically in order to justify early capitalism and the racist policies of imperialism: if this is the way things are among animals, the argument ran, then the suppression of the weak by the strong among human beings is 'quite natural'.

Whenever attempts are made to interpret uncomprehended conditions by way of transferences from one evolutionary stage to another, on the basis of analogy, the result is generally misinterpretation. This applies both to the anthropomorphism with which non-human conditions are interpreted on the basis of human analogies, and to bio-morphism, in which human conditions are supposed to be interpreted and regulated on the analogy of types of animal behaviour and forms of living. It is a criticism which can also be levelled against the fashionable description of natural processes on the analogy of automata and computers. For this is nothing but what I should like to call an ergo-morphism.

It is only possible and meaningful to link the concept of evolution with the concept of creation if both concepts are de-ideologized, and if we keep them strictly for the sectors to which they were intended to apply. On ideological levels, belief in creation and pantheism are mutually exclusive. On ideological levels, the integration of human beings into the evolutionary process and their religious elevation to God are mutually exclusive. But on these ideological levels neither concept says what it originally meant and was really intended to say.

If we are interpreting the Christian belief in creation in the context of the knowledge of nature disclosed through evolutionary theory, we should bear the following points in mind:

1. Strictly speaking, evolution has nothing to do with 'creation' itself. It is concerned with the 'making' and 'ordering' of creation. Creating and making, creating and separating, are biblically distinct concepts which must not be confused.[20] Creation is the term that describes the miracle of existence in general. The act of creation gathers into one single divine moment the whole of existence, even though this existence is in itself extended in time, and differentiated in its protean forms. Consequently there is in principle no contradiction between creation and evolution. The concepts belong on different levels. They are talking about different sides of the same reality.

2. Evolution describes the continued building up of matter and systems of life. This means that the theory of evolution has its place where theology talks about continuous creation (*creatio continua*). But how does God create and act in the ongoing history of creation? It is theologically wrong to transfer the forms of divine activity in the beginning to the forms of divine activity in history. Theologically we have to describe the forms through which God preserves, suffers, transforms and advances creation in their open-ended history – a history open to the future; though here the theological concept of openness to the future absorbs and transcends openness as the theory of a given system. In this respect our underlying theological premise must be that *creation is not yet finished, and has not as yet reached its end*. In common with other forms of life and matter, the human being is involved in the open process of time.[21] Today, the direct continuation of the evolution that led to the origin of the human species on earth lies in the hands of human beings themselves. They can either destroy this stage of evolution, or they can organize themselves into a higher form of common living than before, and advance evolution further.

3. The biblical – and especially the messianic – doctrine of creation fundamentally contradicts the picture of the static, closed cosmos, resting in its own equilibrium or revolving within itself. Its eschatological orientation towards a future consummation accords far more with the concept of a still incomplete *cosmic history*. But

this means departing from the anthropocentric picture of the world. The human being is certainly the living thing with the highest development known to us. But 'the crown of creation' is God's sabbath. It is for this that human beings are created – for the feast of creation, which praises the eternal, inexhaustible God, and in this hymn of praise experiences and expresses its own joy. The enduring meaning of human existence lies in its *participation* in this joyful paean of God's creation. This song of praise was sung *before* the appearance of human beings, is sung *outside* the sphere of human beings, and will be sung even *after* human beings have – perhaps – disappeared from this planet. To put it without the images of biblical language: the human being is not the meaning and purpose of the world. The human being is not the meaning and purpose of evolution. The cosmogenesis is not bound to the destiny of human beings. The very reverse is true: the destiny of human beings is bound to the cosmogenesis. Theologically speaking, the meaning and purpose of human beings is to be found in God himself, like the meaning and purpose of all things. In this sense, every single person, and indeed every single living thing in nature, has a meaning, whether they are of utility for evolution or not. The meaning of the individual is not to be found in the collective of the species, and the meaning of the species is not to be found in the existence of the individual. The meaning of them both is to be found in God. Consequently no reduction is possible. All that is open to us is conciliating balance and mediation. We have to overcome the old anthropocentric world picture by a new theocentric interpretation of the world of nature and human beings, and by an eschatological understanding of the history of this natural and human world. Unless we do this, we shall not be able to find an adequate theological perspective for evolutionary theory.

§3 EVOLUTIONARY PROCESSES IN NATURE

A whole series of different evolutionary processes can be found in nature, and this inevitably means a whole series of evolutionary theories as well: the evolution of matter, the evolution of life, the evolution of consciousness; hylogenesis, biogenesis, noogenesis. If wider cohesions in natural events are to be grasped, the different evolutionary theories have to be gathered together and built up into synthetic theories of evolution. What interests us here is not so much the synthesis between physics, chemistry and biology, as the possibility of a synthesis between scientific theories of evolution and theories of history developed in the humanities. The parallels are too obvious for this synthesis not to be attempted. From all the various concepts of history developed in the liberal arts, we shall here consider the hermeneutical theories. 'The hermeneutical circle' offers a wealth of models for the chance-selection-necessity process from which natural evolutions emerge, so that it is possible to see the evolution of matter and the evolution of life as simple hermeneutical processes. We might therefore call the synthetic theory of evolution which we are seeking, a hermeneutical theory of evolution. In this context we shall consider a few elements belonging to scientific theories of evolution.[22]

1. The Evolution of the Cosmos. For thousands of years, the stars, with their regular revolutions, were for men and women the quintessence of the cosmos reposing within itself, completely ordered and therefore stable. The circular course of the stars reflected the eternity of the gods. Their conformity to law revealed the reasonableness of the world. Their unshakeability guaranteed the stability of the world in the equilibrium of its forces. This picture of 'the cosmos' was superseded by the new discoveries brought about by radio astronomy, infra-red astronomy, x-ray astronomy and gravo-astronomy. With these new ways of acquiring knowledge, unguessed-at cosmic movements were discovered, in which stars and galaxies come into being, develop and are destroyed. Quasars, pusars, collapsed stars, novae and 'black holes' are not evidence of a stable universe. They reveal a highly unstable one.[23]

But what is even more important is the discovery of the movement in which the universe itself seems to be involved. Edwin Hubble's interpretation of the everywhere observable red shift of the light that comes to us from galaxies outside our own as the sign of a 'flight' or recession movement, makes the theory of the exploding and expanding universe probable. This theory states that there is no such thing as a stationary universe; the universe as a whole, and all the bodies in it, are involved in a unique movement, and in an *irreversible 'history'*. This leads to the assumption of an initial point at which the world broke away from an original concentrate, and then began to expand at the speed of light. The 'big bang' theory is certainly only a speculation about the origin of the universe; but the undoubted fact which it interprets is the present expansion of the world known to us. The galaxies are flying apart like splinters from a huge explosion. And here we have to consider the effects on our understanding of nature and natural laws.

In the light of this knowledge, Carl Friedrich von Weizsäcker has talked about 'the history of nature'.[24] He took over this phrase from Schelling, using it to surmount the dualism of science and historical studies which had been general in the nineteenth century. History in this sense was the name given to unique happenings and series of events which are characterized by an irreversible direction in time. If we apply the concept of history, in this definition of it, to nature, nature then ceases to be a term for regular, recurring and repeatable processes. Natural events then also become a unique, irreversible and non-repeatable process with a particular direction. 'The non-historicity of nature is an optical illusion', he writes. 'It is simply a question of the relative time involved.'[25] But if nature is involved in a unique history, then no natural course of events is ever exactly repeated. Every single one of them is really a unique process. But for unique events and unrepeatable processes there can be no natural laws in the cosmological interpretation of law hitherto used. For natural laws are determined through the recurrence or recurrability of the process. That is why, according to the earlier cosmological interpretation, natural laws have 'timeless validity'. They eliminate time and equalize the times, for they are supposedly applicable at all and every time. And this apparently still applies to 'laws' today.

This reasonableness of natural laws corresponds to the earlier notion of the stable cosmos, resting within itself, and of the universe as a great system of equilibrium. But if the universe is not a closed system, as classical physics assumed, but an open one – if the universe does not represent a great equilibrium at all, but if it is in that imbalance which the 'big bang' theory talks about – then the natural *laws* relate to the unique and irreversible *history* of nature. They are a deduction from this – a conceptualization. They are no more than approximations to reality. Their verification by way of recurrence and repetition is simply an abstraction from what is in actual fact unrepeatable historical reality. 'No one ever enters the same river twice', declared Heraclitus in a cryptic saying. The knowledge of the history of nature relativizes natural laws, because it nullifies the impression of the regularity of happening, which is the real basis on which natural laws rest.[26]

This suggests some important questions.

Did the natural laws, valid as approximations in the history of nature, also apply to the state of the world before 'the big bang'?

If they are approximations to the unique history of nature, are they then themselves also historical in kind, and involved in long-term changes? How can the laws of the history of nature be historically formulated?

Do we not have to abandon the deterministic ideal in the formulation of natural laws, since nature is not a closed system of equilibrium?

Is there any way of understanding the contingency of nature except within the framework of a contingent order?

Newton's mechanistic world picture was absorbed into the more comprehensive, dynamistic world picture of Maxwell and Einstein. And, in a corresponding way, the strict principle of causality can be absorbed into the principle of the contingent and flexible order of the contingent. This integration preserves the truth of the earlier perception, while surmounting its rigidity.[27]

2. *The Evolution of Life.* The laws of classical physics are deterministic laws. The premise under which they applied was that all processes in the world were processes in a closed system. The familiar fundamental principles of classical thermodynamics about the conservation of energy and entropy apply to processes in a system of equilibrium. The aim of arriving at knowledge of natural laws could be formulated in Leibniz's words: 'If we have precise knowledge of the present, we can predict the future.' The connection between cause and effect is therefore supposed to be identical with the historical connection between present and future. But for this to be true, the future must already be completely inherent in the present; otherwise extrapolation into the future is impossible. That was why Laplace ascribed to 'the Universal Mind' knowledge of all natural laws. So if we still cannot in actual fact predict the future – or only with the help of statistical laws or laws of probability – this is due, classical physics tells us, to our still defective knowledge of the present and its determinants.

But the quantum theory now tells us something different. It says that the limits of knowledge are due to the nature of reality itself. The laws of probability are in no way imperfect deterministic laws; on the contrary, they accord precisely with the partial indeterminacy of nature itself. Already determined behaviour can be predicted with certainty under given environmental conditions; but still-undetermined behaviour can only be predicted according to laws of probability. This means that the future is not completely inherent in the present. The future also includes randomness, because it can bring something new. Consequently, laws of probability are not imperfect deterministic laws. On the contrary, deterministic laws are in fact themselves laws of probability – probability to the point of certainty, as we say.

In complex systems of matter and life, time is experienced in a more complex way than the simple mechanics of cause and effect suggest. The complexity lies in the experience of the difference between past and future. The experience of the difference between past and future is not a pre-scientific notion; it is a primary scientific concept. Every complex system 'experiences' the difference between the tenses or times, and the irreversibility of time's direction, for it is in precisely this experience that the system exists. Complex systems, each in its own way, exist between a fixed past and a partially open future; and they organize and shape themselves between the times that are qualified in this sense. They mould their form in the difference of the tenses. 'The direction of time is a "primary" concept, a precondition for all forms of life . . . An amoeba which seeks nourishment could not do so if it did not know the difference between past and future.'[28] We can deduce from this, not merely that the universe and all part-systems in it exist in the experience of the difference between the times or tenses, and the irreversibility of time's direction; we can conclude too that all part-systems have 'their time', and that their growing community must consist in the *synchronization* of their experiences of time; for their history is a common formation in which they are all involved.

This observation leads inescapably to the metaphysical question: is the universe a determined system, or a partially undetermined one? Is it a 'closed' system or an 'open' one?

The processes which lead to the build-up of structures of matter, and to the construction of inorganic and organic life systems, are apparently irreversible processes. They take place, not in systems of equilibrium, but in systems of imbalance. Laws which determine the movements of parts of a closed system are symmetrical as regards past and future, and invariant towards the reversal of time. But the evolution of systems of matter and life shows the qualitative difference between past and future: the past, which determines the present, is fixed; but the future, which opens itself to the present, is not fixed – it is partially undetermined. This means that the present is partially determined and partially undetermined. It hovers between necessity and randomness, and unfolds its character in its selection of chances.

All structured matter shows a partially undermined range of possibility, which leaves its behaviour open.

> We have been forced step by step to forego a causal description of the behaviour of individual atoms in space and time, and to reckon with a free choice on the part of nature between various possibilities to which only probability considerations can be applied.[29]

The declarations of the law of causality are restricted purely to reality. They make no distinction between past and future, actuality and possibility.

But the declarations of the laws of probability quantify possibilities, and are statements which take into account statistically the difference between future and past, and therefore also the temporal direction in which possibilities are realized. This temporal direction is irreversible: actuality proceeds out of possibility, not possibility out of actuality; future becomes past, past does not become future.

The process of the evolution of systems of matter and life is not a unilinear chain of causality. It more nearly resembles a growing and spreading web of elementary particles and structures. These structures fan out, extending not merely in existing environments, but also in the range of possibilities offered by the future. Here each individual reality is the realization of only one among numerous possibilities. 'If we wanted to depict every possible protein structure, each of them in no more than a single example, we should have to do with a number which could not be fitted into the whole universe, however tightly they were packed together.'[30] Each individual reality is in actual fact a unique reality. 'No two eggs are alike.'

With every possibility that is realized, even more complex structures also come into being, and these in their turn again open up new ranges of possibility. This means that as possibilities are realized, possibilities as such do not diminish. They increase. The richer wealth of forms is bound up with a growing indeterminacy of behaviour, and this again involves increasing future possibilities. In the graduated build-up of matter and life, indeterminacy of behaviour grows, and with it the capacity for adaptation to changes in the environment, and for self-transformation or a new self-interpretation. But if with growing complexity the range of possibility grows, the degree of vulnerability and destructibility of course increases at the same time. So certain highly complex systems have a particularly rapid rate of decay.

If the systems of matter and life are described as open systems, this means, where time is concerned: 1. The future condition of systems changed through irreversible processes is different from the present condition which is the starting-point. 2. The concept of possibility expresses the fact that the system can go through various processes of change. 3. The indeterminacy of behaviour which is conditioned by this, and which is quantified through laws of probability, points to the fact that the system possesses a certain open range of anticipation. 4. Open systems are determined by the time structure of the qualitative difference between future and past. They realize possibilities, and through this realization again acquire new ones. 5. Finally, the openness of the system is always matched by its relative closedness; for without this, openness would lead to self-dissolution. Only relatively stable systems can afford openness for communication and for anticipation.

The structure of the evolution of life shows both continuity and qualitative leaps. Let us take as stages the following sequence:

elementary particle
– atom
– molecule
– macro-molecular cell
– multi-cellular organism
– living organism
– organism populations
– living thing
– animal
– transitional field from animal to human being
– human beings
– human populations
– community of humanity . . . .

If we look at this sequence, we see that *parts always give rise to a whole* – that is to say, to a new structure and a new organizational principle. These are 'leaps' from quantity in a particular area into a new quality. It can also be seen that, with the complexity of the structure, the capacity for communication grows. And with this capacity for communication, the capacity for adaptation and transformation increases in its turn. This, again, widens the range of anticipation. There is little to suggest that the growing webs of communication of the open life systems are in principle limited. And there is also little sign that the evolution of complex systems and new principles of organization is at an end.

This brings us to the final question in this connection: if the evolutionary process in systems of matter and life can only be understood if we assume that these are open systems, not closed ones, how is the universe as a whole to be interpreted – as a closed system, or an open one?

If we take a closed universe as our premise, evolution then means processes within sub-systems which communicate and which operate with possibilities that are in principle limited. The law of entropy remains valid for the universe as a whole, even if it does not apply in the individual open system.

But if, on the other hand, we understand the universe itself as involved in an irreversible history and in the course of evolution, then we are interpreting it as an open system. In this case an entropy may be demonstrable in individual systems and processes, but it does not apply to the whole. We must then, however, assume that the universe itself has a transcendent encompassing milieu, with which it is in communication, and a transcendent future into which it is evolving.

Here we are trying to comprehend the evolutionary cosmos itself as an irreversible, communicating system open to the future. The history of nature and the whole structure of evolution show a direction which differentiates between future and past. Evolution only becomes possible through the reproduction and growing communication of the open systems. Through their growing interdependence, richer and richer possibilities are opened up. The ever-widening warp and weft of open systems accumulates a growing surplus of possibilities. This surplus is not only the result of the interchange of presently existing energies. It also emerges from the expansion of anticipations into the scope of the transcendent future in any given case. If the symbol of 'the open system' is applicable to all systems of matter and life, must not the whole world then be regarded as an open system too? But in this case how are we to understand the encircling milieu of the universe itself? And what is meant by the making-possible of its possibilities and its evolution themselves?

1. If the individual systems out of which the universe is built up are open systems, it would seem obvious to interpret the universe analogously as 'an open system'.

2. If the evolution of open systems leads to complex open systems, and if we can see no end to this evolution, it would seem obvious to think of the universe itself as a 'self-transcending system'.

3. Understood as an open system, the universe is:

(*a*) a *participatory* system,[31] which is aligned towards, and dependent on, ever-richer and more diverse communication between the different open part-systems, whether their levels of organization are the same or different. Out of the accumulation of quantitative variety on the same levels emerge the possibilities of leaps into the new quality of higher levels of organization. It would seem that the universe contains within itself the trend towards the universal symbiosis of all systems of life and matter, by virtue of 'the sympathy of all things' for one another.

(*b*) As a system aligned towards growing communication, we must also view the world as an *anticipatory* system. As communication towards every side grows, so too does the scope for anticipation in the realms of possibility. The open system of the world is characterized by self-transcendence, both in individual cases and as a whole. It thrusts beyond itself because, by virtue of its imbalance, it cannot apparently 'tarry' in any given condition. This permanent self-transcendence points towards the forecourt of an inviting and guiding transcendence, and it is only in this forecourt that the self-transcendence is possible.

(*c*) In saying this we are interpreting the universe as the self-transcending totality of a diversity of communicating, individual open systems. All individual systems of matter and life, and all their complexes of communication as a whole, 'ex-ist' into a transcendence and subsist out of that transcendence.

If we call this transcendence of the world 'God', we can then tentatively say:

The world in its different parts and as a whole is a system open to God. God is its extra-worldly encompassing *milieu*, from which, and in which, it lives. God is its extra-worldly *forecourt*, into which it is evolving. God is the origin of the new possibilities out of which its realities are won.

We then have to understand God, for his part, as a Being open to the world. He encompasses the world with the possibilities of his Being, and interpenetrates it with the powers of his Spirit. Through the energies of his Spirit, he is present in the world and immanent in each individual system.

The recognizable trends to communication towards every side, and the thrusts towards permanent self-transcendence in all open systems, are signs of the presence of God's Spirit in the world, and reactions to that presence. This is what was already meant by the ancient doctrine of the *vestigia Dei*.[32]

It is therefore impossible to think of this world-transcendence of God unless we think simultaneously of his world-immanence; and it is equally impossible to conceive of God's evolutive immanence in the world without his world-transcendence. The two are mutually related. It is only if we perceive the this-worldliness of God that we can usefully talk about a divine presence beyond the world; and the reverse is equally true. Because the church's theology continually withdrew more and more into the 'other-worldliness' of God, in its dispute with evolutionary theory, old and new evolutionary theorists, understandably enough, seized on pantheism as a way of describing the divine this-worldliness which they perceived.

Theologically, the world is comprehended as an open, participatory and anticipatory system once we grasp the history of creation as an interplay between God's transcendence in relation to the world, and his immanence in that world. But of course any such theological statements based on scientific hypotheses can only be working sketches; they can never be dogmas.

§4 CONTINUOUS CREATION

If we are trying to find a new interpretation of the Christian doctrine of creation in the light of the knowledge of nature made accessible to us by evolutionary theories, we must distinguish more clearly than did the traditional doctrine of creation between creation in the beginning, continuous creation, and the consummation of creation in the kingdom of glory. This distinction has to be made if we are to be able to survey the process of creation as a whole. In what follows we shall try to think theologically in the context of creation as 'an open system'.[33]

1. According to the texts of the creation narrative, creation in the beginning is evidently creation without any preconditions or presuppositions. The later phrase about the *creatio ex nihilo* is a way of expressing the miracle of the world's existence in general, and the initial contingency of being itself. The existence of the world, and then the existence of all the stages of evolution in its history, are 'chance', even if, seen theologically, they are not pure chance (what German calls 'blind chance') but an intentional fortuitousness – free creations of God for the purpose of the self-communication of his goodness, with his glorification as their end and goal. In the theological concept of God's creation, chance and the purposefulness of stages of evolution are neither contradictions nor contrasts.[34]

Creation in the beginning is simultaneously the creation of time. Because time is only manifested in change, and because it is only in change that it can be perceived, the initial creation has to be understood as *creatio mutabilis*. It is not closed within itself; it is open for its history, which can bring both prediction and salvation, annihilation and consummation. If God made creation to be the kingdom of his glory, then it was he who gave it movement and set it in motion, at the same time lending it an irreversible direction. He accompanies it in this movement by opening up new possibilities, and entices it in this direction through the fellowship of his creative Spirit. Because of this openness for its own history, we have to view even creation in the beginning as an 'open system', which has neither its foundation, nor its goal, nor its equilibrium, within itself, but which is from the very outset ec-centrically designed, and aligned in the direction of the future. By saying that creation in the beginning is an open system, we are also saying that this beginning establishes the conditions that make possible its history of perdition and deliverance, as well as its consummation.

The goal of this history of creation is not a return to the paradisal primordial condition. Its goal is the revelation of the glory of God. It is true that this end 'corresponds' to the beginning in the sense that it represents the fulfilment of the real promise implanted in creation itself; but the new creation of heaven and earth in the kingdom of glory surpasses everything that can be told about creation in the beginning.

The notion of a perfect, self-sufficient equilibrium in the resting, stable cosmos contradicts the biblical – and even more the messianic – view of a creation aligned towards future glory.[35] The idea of the future as a *restitutio in integrum* and a return to the original paradisal condition of creation (*status integritatis*) can neither be called biblical nor Christian.[36] A simple comparison between the first chapter of the Bible and the last is enough to refute this traditional doctrine.

2. Seen theologically, evolutionary theories have a bearing on the order of creation and on the continuous creation which follows that creation-in-the-beginning. They in no way contradict the doctrine of *creatio ex nihilo*. But they do compel theology to take up once again the neglected doctrines of the *creatio continua*, the *concursus Dei generalis* and the *providentia Dei*, and to interpret these anew. Here we shall take as our basic assumption a 'tripartite' concept of creation: *creatio originalis – creatio continua – creatio nova*.

(*a*) We have already seen that it is essential to distinguish between God's initial creation and his creative activity in history. The initial creation is without preconditions, whereas the precondition of historical creation is creation in the beginning. In the same way we have to distinguish between initial contingency and the contingency of events in the processes of open systems. Yet for a long time theological tradition limited God's creative work to the original bringing into being of creation; his creative activity in history was seen as his preserving and accompanying work. But this picture of creation and preservation is not a biblical one. *Bara'*, the unique word for the divine creation, is used much more frequently in the Bible for God's creation of liberation and salvation in history than for the initial creation of the world. The New Testament talks about 'the new creation in Christ', and about 'the life-giving Spirit' and the eschatological promise 'Behold I make all things new'. So it is theologically inadequate if we restrict the divine creative activity to the beginning, and in a historical context talk only about 'preservation', and eschatologically only about 'redemption'. This was the traditional theological way of talking. But it reflects the systematic compulsions exerted by the cosmology of the ancient world, rather than the scarlet thread running through the biblical perspectives.

(*b*) The presupposition of God's creative activity in history is his creation at the beginning. Creation in history is a creating on what has already been created. It can mean God's activity in preserving creation from the powers of annihilation. The doctrine about the *creatio continua* then means the continuous sustaining of the creation which was once brought into being. We might say that every moment the Creator reiterates his primal Yes, and repeats both his creative and his ordering activity.[37] God does not create anything new, but creates unremittingly what he once created by sustaining and preserving it. According to this view, the *creatio continua* does not produce any new contingencies; it preserves the contingency of the creation once created, by unceasingly repeating it. This means that we perceive *creatio continua*, not from any new contingent events, but from the continuity of the remaining-the-same.

However, in prophetic theology, the creative acts of God in history are discerned in the unexpected 'new thing' of liberation and salvation (Isa. 43.18f.). Here God's historical activity is directed, not towards the preservation of what was once created, but towards the anticipation of the salvation in which creation will be consummated. It is not merely *creatio continua*. It is at the same time *creatio nova*. And as *creatio nova* it is also *creatio anticipativa*. God's creative activity in history anticipates the consummation in time. The creation of liberty, righteousness and salvation in human history initiates the fulfilment of that promise which creation at the beginning represents in its very self. The revelation of the rule of God in history initiates the consummation of creation as the kingdom of God. It is true that these new creating and fulfilling acts of God are initially perceived only in human history. But they have their effects, and even their parallels, in the history of nature: 'And thou renewest the face of the ground' (Ps. 104.30).

A detailed doctrine of the *creatio continua* must see God's historical activity under both aspects: the *preservation* of the world he has created, and the *preparation* of its completion and perfecting. The historical activity of God stands between initial creation and the new creation. Theological tradition has laid a one-sided stress on the preservation of the world: *conservatio mundi*. In the new theologies of evolution and process, a one-sided stress is laid on the world's development. But if we discover the *creatio continua* between the *creatio originalis* and the *nova creatio*, we shall perceive the unremitting creative activity of God as an activity that both preserves *and* innovates. God's preserving activity manifests hope, and his innovating activity, his faithfulness. But at heart every preserving activity is innovatory, and every innovating activity is preserving.[38] God's historical activity is then eschatologically orientated: it preserves the initial creation by anticipating the consummation and by preparing the way for that consummation. The historical activity of God has cosmic dimensions: it brings the whole cosmos into a new condition.

The open system of creation is aligned towards God's creative activity in history, in which both the trend of creation and its future find their realization.

(*c*) God's creative activity at the beginning, which was without any preconditions, is presented in the traditions about creation as an effortless creativity: 'And God said "Let there be light", and there was light.' But God's historical creation of liberty, righteousness and salvation is described differently in prophetic theology; there it is described as God's burden and weariness (Isa. 43.24).[39] The Creator suffers the contradiction of the beings he has created. He lays the sins, misdeeds, pains and sicknesses of his creatures on the new Servant of God: 'Through his wounds we are healed' (Isa. 53.5). The creation of salvation proceeds out of the suffering of contradiction. The creation of righteousness proceeds out of the suffering of injustice. So God's creations in history contain at once passion and action. Even the traditional doctrine which teaches that God sustains the world in spite of its sin, already saw this as God's patience, and understood it as an expression of his long-suffering.[40] The inexhaustible creative power of God in history always makes itself known first of all in the inexhaustibility of the power of his suffering. This is not a sign of his weakness; it is the revelation of his strength. The beatitude 'Blessed are the meek, for they shall inherit the earth' (Matt. 5.5) applies to God first of all.

Even when we look at created things, we can make the generalization that the more a life system is capable of bearing strain, the stronger and more capable of survival it shows itself to be. It absorbs hostile impulses and assimilates them productively, without destroying the enemy or itself. In so doing, it itself becomes richer and more flexible. For the more an open life system is able to suffer, the more it is able to learn.

We therefore have to see God's inexhaustible patience and his active capacity for suffering as the root of his creative activity in history. He even maintains communication with all the life systems that have broken off their communication with him, becoming petrified as closed systems and condemning themselves to death. By enduring this breach of communication, God keeps their future open for the beings he has created; and, with that future, he also keeps open the possibilities for conversion, or a new direction, which it offers. God's activity in history consists essentially in opening up systems which are closed in on themselves; and he does this by way of suffering communication. Through his inexhaustible capacity for suffering and readiness for suffering, God then also creates quite specific chances for liberation from isolation, and quite specific chances for the evolution of the various open life systems. Because it is a fundamentally suffering and enduring creating, the activity of God in history is also a silent and a secret one. It is not through supernatural interventions that God guides creation to its goal, and drives forward evolution; it is through his passion, and the opening of possibilities out of his suffering. Seen in terms of world history, the transforming power of suffering is the basis for the liberating and consummating acts of God. Teilhard de Chardin was also thinking of this when he wrote:

> Is there any need to recall that, far from being incompatible with the existence of a First Cause, transformist views, as here expounded, show us, on the contrary, the noblest and most reassuring way of imagining its influx? The Christian transformist does not conceive of God's creative action as an intrusion of His works into a world of pre-existing beings, but as a *bringing to birth*, in the heart of things, of the successive stages of His work. It is none the less essential, none the less universal, nor in any way less inward on that account.[41]

If we try to conceive of the nature of 'the accompanying activity of God' (*concursus Dei generalis et specialis*) in the history of the world and the life history of each individual creature in it, we can think of a whole series of relationships: God acts *in* and *through* the activity of his creatures; God acts *with* and *out of* the activity of his creatures; created beings act *out of* the divine potencies and *into* a divine environment; the activity of created beings is made possible *by* the divine patience; the presence of God in the world is the space free *for* the liberty of created beings; and so on. We do not have to expect the accompanying activity of God to take the form merely of supernatural interventions and spectacular disruptions. Any such expectation would actually distort our perception of that accompanying activity. But the pointer to God's still and unobtrusive accompaniment of history by no means excludes experiences of 'signs and wonders'. The discernment of these is only possible at all in the light of the unremitting experience of God's accompanying activity.

Through his Spirit God himself is present in his creation. The whole creation is a fabric woven and shot through by the efficacies of the Spirit. Through his Spirit God is also present in the very structures of matter. Creation contains neither spirit-less matter nor non-material spirit; there is only *informed* matter. But the different kinds of information which determine the systems of life and matter must be given the name 'spirit'. In human beings they arrive at consciousness in a creaturely way. In this sense the whole cosmos must be described as corresponding to God – as in accord with him: because it is effected through God the Spirit, and exists in God the Spirit, it also moves and evolves in the energies and powers of the divine Spirit.

Why, in fact, does pantheism seem so plausible a philosophy to many evolutionary theorists, whether it be pantheism of matter, nature or life? The reason is not merely a striving for emancipation, in rebellion against the church. The reasons are factual, substantial ones. When eyes were turned towards the initial contingency of the world, theism always presented itself as the obvious philosophy; for theism distinguishes between God and the world. But when we are thinking about the evolution of the cosmos and of life from the contingency of events, dynamic pantheism seems much more plausible: the matter that organizes itself also transcends itself and produces its own evolution. So in this sense it is self-creative. This phenomenon *can* certainly be interpreted with the help of Spinoza's holistic theory. *Natura est natura naturans*. Consequently, *deus sive natura*. But the trinitarian doctrine of creation suggests a pneumatological interpretation. The God who is present in the world and in every part of it, is the creative Spirit. It is not merely the spirit of God that is present in the evolving world; it is rather God the Spirit, with his uncreated and creative energies.[42]

3. *The Future of Creation*. We have termed creation in the beginning an open system, and have interpreted the creative activity of God in history as the opening up in time of closed systems. The question that inevitably follows is whether we have to conceive of

the consummation of the process of creation as the final conclusion and completion of the open and the opened systems. Is the kingdom of glory the world system that has finally arrived at its conclusion? In this case the new creation would be the end of time, and would be in itself timeless. The open system 'human being' would then be merely a system that is unfinished, and the open systems of nature would be only systems-that-are-not-yet-closed. History would be the condition of a cosmos that is not yet fully and utterly determined. The completion would then be the end of human liberty and the end of all the possibilities made possible by being-that-is-not-yet.[43] Time would be taken up and absorbed into eternity, and potentiality into actuality. But completion cannot be thought of theologically like this. If the process of creation is to be completed through God's indwelling, then the new creation is indwelt by the unbounded fullness of the divine life, and glorified creation is wholly free in its participation in the unbounded existence of God. So the indwelling of the unbounded fullness of God's eternal life means the openness *par excellence* of all life systems, and hence also their eternal livingness, not their finite petrification. The openness of all life systems for the inexhaustible fullness of the divine life also leads to their perfected communication among themselves; for God's indwelling drives out the forces of the negative, and therefore also banishes fear and the struggle for existence from creation. So 'the kingdom of God' is also the kingdom of the universal 'sympathy of all things'.

It is also even permissible to assume that in the kingdom of glory there will be time and history, future and possibility, and these to an unimpeded degree, and in a way that is no longer ambivalent. Instead of timeless eternity it would therefore be better to talk about 'eternal time'; and instead of 'the end of history' we should talk about the end of pre-history and the beginning of the 'eternal history' of God, human beings and nature. This of course means thinking of change without transience, time without the past, and life without death. But this is difficult in the history of life and death, becoming and passing away, because all our concepts are moulded by these experiences of transitoriness. Yet finitude is not necessarily bound up with mortality. There can also be finite creatures which are immortal. According to Luke 20.36, men and women who have been raised from the dead will be new human beings and 'like the angels'. But the angels are at once finite and immortal. Paul tells us that believers are already transformed in the Spirit, 'changed from one degree of glory to another' (II Cor. 3.18); so we may assume that there will be a process of transformation of this kind in 'the kingdom of glory' as well.

The way in which the system of nature is built up also points in this direction, like the human experience of history. The structures of matter already display scope for undetermined behaviour. In proceeding from atomic structures to more complex systems, we discover greater openness to time and a growing wealth of possibility. With the evolution of complex systems, indeterminacy of behaviour grows, because the possibilities increase. The human person and human social systems are the most complex systems known to us. They display the greatest degree of indeterminancy in their behaviour, and the most extensive degree of openness to time and the future. But every realization of possibility by open systems creates openness for yet more new possibilities. It is by no means a question of merely realizing possibility and transferring future to past. And this means that it is impossible to conceive of the kingdom of glory, which completes the process of creation through the indwelling of God, as a system that has finally been brought to completion and is therefore itself now closed. We have to see this kingdom as the openness of all finite life systems for the fullness of life. Of course this also means no longer thinking of the Being of God as merely the highest reality for all realized possibilities. We have then to conceive of his Being as the transcendent making-possible of all possible realities.

IX

God's Image in Creation: Human Beings

From ancient times, the fundamental concept of theological anthropology has been *imago Dei*: human beings have been created to be God's image on earth.[1] And yet the biblical traditions do not offer any justification for the central place given to this concept.[2] We find it only in the Priestly Writing (Gen. 1. 26,27; Gen. 5.1; Gen. 9.6), although the idea underlies Psalm 8.5, and Wisdom 2.23 and Ecclesiasticus 17.3 are familiar with it. In the New Testament it is used as if it were a traditional concept (James 3.9; I Cor. 11.7), but it is not developed any further. These findings in the history of the tradition make it understandable enough that theological anthropology should always have considered the human being's likeness to God only in the context of the doctrine of creation. The term was used to describe the ideal picture of human beings in their primal condition, the image that – obscured or destroyed through the Fall – is restored through God's grace. With this one-sided viewpoint, theological anthropology strayed very close to the origin myth, and came under its spell; and in so doing it overlooked the messianic alignment and trend of human history which is the foundation actually required of it by the New Testament.

In this chapter we shall try to understand human beings as the image of God, looking at this idea historically in three different ways:

(1) as the original designation of human beings: *imago Dei*;

(2) as the messianic calling of human beings: *imago Christi*;

(3) as the eschatological glorification of human beings: *gloria Dei est homo*.[3]

Hermeneutically this means that, although we shall begin with a theological exposition of the Old Testament's creation accounts, we shall illuminate this interpretation from the messianic gospel of Christ, and shall therefore relate the original designation of human beings to their final glorification in the kingdom of God. In this way we shall perceive the character of what comes first in the light of what comes last, and shall understand the beginning in the perspective of the completion. This theological exposition – or, to be more precise, this messianically orientated exposition – differs both from historical exegesis and from theological exegesis in the light of the Torah. But of course it presupposes both of these, and rejects neither of them; it integrates them.

Having discussed the idea of human likeness to God in the threefold history of God with human beings, we shall then go on to consider problems of Christian anthropology in the framework of systematic theology. One traditional problem, which has also given rise to controversy between denominations, is the question how the human being as he now is can be understood as at once the image of God and a sinner; and here we shall offer a solution which differs from the answer given by the Reformers, but which can be biblically justified. Anthropology and theology are always mutually related; so in surmounting Western monotheism in the concept of God, we have also to overcome the individualism that corresponds to it in anthropology. Human beings are *imago trinitatis* and only correspond to the triune God when they are united with one another.

§1 THE ORIGINAL DESIGNATION OF HUMAN BEINGS: *IMAGO DEI*

The text which provides the basis for the concept of likeness to God already presents us with difficulties when we come to translate it. Here we shall take the following translation as our starting point:

> And God (Elohim) said:
> Let us make human beings as our image, as our very form. They shall rule over the fish in the sea and over the birds of the air and over the cattle and all beasts on earth and over every creeping thing that creeps upon the earth.
> And God (Elohim) created the human being as his image: as man and as woman he created them . . .
>
> (Gen. 1. 26,27).

The whole textual complex, vv. 26–30, is built up in the following way: introduction, resolve, creation of human beings, blessing and commission, provision.[4]

In order to understand the passage theologically we may pick out the following points:

(*a*) The creation of human beings is the final work of creation. It begins with a solemn introduction, in which a special resolve on God's part is announced. When light is created, we read: 'He said . . . and there was' (Gen. 1.3). When the animals are created, we read 'He said . . . he created' (Gen. 1.20f.). But when human beings are created, the passage reads: 'Let us make . . . So God created.' Human beings come into being, not through God's creative word but out of his special resolve. The word which precedes the resolve is addressed by God to himself. It is a self-exhortation. In a resolve, the author of the resolve acts on himself first of all. He resolves 'for himself' before he acts on anyone or anything else. In the self-exhortation we have here, God designates himself to be the Creator of his image before he creates that image. 'God resolves for himself.' Inherent in this resolve is God's *contraction* to this single possibility, and already inherent in this contraction is also a first self-humiliation on God's part. This is apparent from the fact that God 'implants' his image and his glory in his earthly creation, the human being, which means that he himself is drawn into the history of these creatures of his.[5]

The plural in Genesis 1.26 has always been seen as a puzzle, and has evoked many different interpretations. Is Elohim speaking to an assembly of gods? Is Elohim talking to a goddess? Is it a 'plural of majesty' – 'the royal we'?[6]

None of these interpretations explains God's address to himself in this passage. We have to understand this particular address as 'a plural of deliberation' – as 'a communing with his own heart'. But a self-exhortation in a conversation with oneself presupposes that the author of the self-exhortation has a relation to himself. And a relationship to one's own self in its turn presupposes a self-differeniation and the possibility of self-identification. The subject is then a singular in the plural, or a plural in a singular. These shifts between singular and plural at this particular point are important: 'Let *us* make human beings – *an* image that is like *us*.'[7] That is to say, the image of God (singular) is supposed to correspond to the 'internal' plural of God, and yet be a *single* image. In the next verse the singular and plural are distributed in the opposite way: God (singular) created the human being (singular), as man and woman (plural) he created them (plural). Here the human plural is supposed to correspond to the divine singular. Whereas the self-resolving God is a plural in the singular, his image on earth – the human being – is apparently supposed to be a singular in the plural. The one God, who is differentiated in himself and is at one with himself, then finds his correspondence in a community of human beings, female and male, who unite with one another and are one.

The interplay of singular and plural here is evidently deliberate; and the theology of the patristic church saw it as revelation of the Trinity. Of course, historically speaking and in the light of the Torah, no doctrine of the Trinity is to be found in the text. And yet this passage is one of the roots of the later understanding of God as the triune God, an understanding arrived at in the light of the messianic gospel of Christ.

(*b*) God created human beings '*to be* his image'. But the traditional translations say '*according to* his image' – on the pattern of his image. In saying this they are presupposing an 'archetype' in God, a pattern on which human beings are modelled and of which they are the copy, the sensible counterpart. This is based on the Platonic 'archetype-representation' thinking of patristic theology. But it also has the christology of the New Testament behind it. Christ is 'the image of God' through whom everything is created (Col. 1.15f.; Heb. 1.3). Consequently, as the Son of God, he is also the 'first-born' to whom believers 'are to become like in form' (Rom. 8.29). The *imago Christi* is an *imago Dei* mediated through Christ. Christians therefore liked to translate the Genesis passage we are considering as 'according to his image'. But the christological bearing of the phrase can also be read into the translation '*to be* his image', if this is taken to mean that the human being has been created 'in the direction of' the image of God which Christ is – that this is the whole trend of his designation – so that the creation of human beings is open for the incarnation. Then the christology is understood as the fulfilment of the anthropology, and the anthropology becomes the preparation for the christology.

The designation of human beings is described in two different words: *ṣelem* and *demuth* – in Greek, εἰκών and ὁμοίωσις, in Latin *imago* and *similitudo*. The first of these terms is used for the concrete representation, the second is used for the similarity. The first

first expresses more the outward representation, the second rather the reflexive inward relationship. Both terms have probably been borrowed from Egyptian royal theology. The Pharaoh is the reigning copy of God on earth, his representative, his deputy, his reflection and his mode of appearance in the world. Psalm 8 also presents the human being who has been created to be the image of God as a royal personage. According to the 'representation' thinking of the ancient East, the Pharaoh was actually present in the statues which he had set up in all the provinces of his empire. In the same way, the human being is understood as 'the emblem of God's sovereignty' set up on earth. If it is correct to see the terminology about the image of God as derived from royal theology, then this derivation itself contains revolutionary political potential: it is not a prince who is the image, representative, deputy and reflection of God; it is the human being – men and women in like degree, all human beings and every human being. Whether or not, historically speaking, we can say that the Priestly Writing already contains a 'democratization' of royal theology, this passage has certainly had a 'democratizing' effect throughout the whole of Jewish and Christian political history.[8] As far as the subsequent charge to rule over the earth is concerned, there is no distinction at all between human beings; there is only equality.

As his image, human beings represent God on earth; as his similitude, they reflect him. It would be one-sided if we were to see the likeness to God as consisting solely in the divine commission to rule. As the concept of similarity stresses, the image is also inherently a divine 'mode of appearance'. It is 'a reflection of his glory', as Psalm 8 emphasizes, and as was so important for Paul. God is present in human beings. 'He appears wherever the human being appears.'[9] The human being is God's indirect manifestation on earth. To be an image of something always means letting that something appear, and revealing it.

What constitutes the human being's likeness to God? The answers which theological tradition has given to this question may be briefly summed up as follows.

1. According to the analogy of substance, the soul (which is the human being's reasonable and volitional nature) is the seat of human likeness to God, for it is immortal, and similar to the divine nature.[10]

2. According to the analogy of form, it is the human being's upright walk, and his upward glance.[11]

3. According to the analogy of proportionality, the likeness is to be found in man's lordship over the earth, since this corresponds to God's general lordship over the world.[12]

4. According to analogy of relation, finally, it consists in the community of man and wife, which corresponds to the fellowship of God within the Trinity.

We find the starting point for all these answers in 'the phenomenon human being'. They all begin with characteristics which distinguish the human being from animals, and interpret whatever is specifically human about men and women in religious terms as their likeness to God. Likeness to God then means the human being's general relationship to God, which distinguishes him from animals.

But this point of departure is based on a false inference. The human being's likeness to God is a theological term before it becomes an anthropological one. It first of all says something about the God who creates his image for himself, and who enters into a particular relationship with that image, before it says anything about the human being who is created in this form. Likeness to God means God's relationship to human beings first of all, and only then, and as a consequence of that, the human being's relationship to God. God puts himself in a particular relationship to human beings – a relationship in which human beings become his image and his glory on earth. The nature of human beings springs from their relationship to God. It is this relationship which gives human nature its definition – not some characteristic or other which sets human beings apart from other living things. The God who creates for himself his image on earth finds his correspondence in that image. So human likeness to God consists in the fact that human beings, for their part, correspond to God. The God who allows his glory to light up his image on earth and to shine forth from that image, is reflected in human beings as in a mirror. Theological tradition has always understood God's image as a mirror-reflection of God himself. The God who allows himself to be represented on earth by his image also appears in that image; and the image becomes an indirect revelation of his divine Being in earthly form. So as God's image and appearance on earth, human beings are involved in three fundamental relationships: they rule over other earthly creatures as God's *representatives* and in his name; they are God's *counterpart* on earth, the counterpart to whom he wants to talk, and who is intended to respond to him; and they are the *appearance* of God's splendour, and his glory on earth.

Only the human being is *imago Dei*. Neither animals nor angels, neither the forces of nature nor the powers of fate, may be either feared or worshipped as God's image or his appearance or his revelation. The Old Testament prohibition of images also protects the dignity of human beings as God's one and only image.

If we start from God's relationship to human beings, then what makes the human being God's image is not his possession of any particular characteristic or other – something which distinguishes him above other creatures; it is *his whole existence*. The whole person, not merely his soul; the true human community, not only the individual; humanity as it is bound up with nature, not simply human beings in their confrontation with nature – it is these which are the image of God and his glory. This does away with the question about particular phenomena constituting the image of God.

And yet, according to the biblical traditions, there is apparently one point at which God's relationship to human beings is manifested and can be recognized: the human face. It is the human face which becomes the mirror of God: 'But now we all *with unveiled face* reflect the glory of the Lord' (II Cor. 3.18). It is 'the light of the knowledge of the glory of God *in the face of Jesus Christ*' (II Cor. 4.6). 'Now we see through a mirror in a word hard to interpret' (Luther's version), '*but then face to face*' (I Cor. 13.12). After Moses had looked upon the glory of God on the mountain, 'his face shone' so unendurably for the people that he had to cover it with a veil (Exod. 34. 33–35). When Jesus was 'transfigured' on the mountain 'his face shone like the sun' (Matt. 17.2). And we are told (Rev. 1.16) about the coming Judge of the world that 'his face was like the sun shining in full strength'. 'The face of God' is a commonly used symbol for God's turning to men and women in kindness, for his attentive mindfulness and his purposefully directed presence. It is true that the word πρόσωπον can also mean the whole person. But the whole person is known first of all in his committed attention, and his committed attention first of all in his open eyes and his attentive face. The play of emotions is reflected in the face, and a person's 'heart' is best expressed in his face; and the same is true of the glory of God, when it is perceived in the face of Christ and when it is reflected a thousandfold in the faces of the men and women who behold and recognize it. Whatever else may be called 'the seat' of the divine likeness, whether it be the soul or the upright posture, domination or community, it is expressed in concentrated form in the person's face. That is why the human being's original designation to be God's image already implies the eschatological promise of perceiving God 'face to face'. We might sum this up in a physiognomic doctrine of human likeness to God.

(*c*) The next anthropological point where likeness to God can be seen is the sexual differentiation and community of human beings. To be *imago Dei* means designation to a common, shared humanity. According to Genesis 1.26, Adam, human being, is a singular who corresponds to a divine plural. According to Genesis 1.27, men and women are a plural that corresponds to a divine singular. This grammatical shift between singular and plural is intentional and important. From the very point of creation, to be human means sexual differentiation and sexual relation. Genesis 1.27 can also be translated 'male and female he created them'; so we may also remember the difference between *animus* and *anima* which C. G. Jung has shown occurs in varying form in everyone, whether man or woman. The links between singular and plural are apparently also intended to avoid the suggestion that being human is the generic term for which man and woman are simply sub-divisions, or that man and woman are two different creatures. The shift from singular to plural is meant to bring out the fact that to be human means being sexually differentiated *and* sharing a common humanity; both are equally primary. Why is the sexual difference especially stressed at the creation of human beings? When the bi-sexual animals are created, we read only that God made 'everything according to his kind'. That is apparently sufficient for the blessing of fertility. But at the creation of human beings, bisexuality itself is particularly mentioned. The blessing of fertility is something given in addition to this creation (Gen. 1.28). So if the sexual relationship is not tied to fertility, and if it is not, either, presupposed as a matter of course (as it is in the case of the animal species), then it is here that the real likeness to God and the uniquely human quality must lie.[13] Sexual difference and community belong to the very image of God itself; they are not merely related to human fertility. So this community already corresponds to God, because in this community God finds his own correspondence. It represents God on earth, and God 'appears' on earth in his male-female image. Likeness to God cannot be lived in isolation. It can be lived only in human community. This means that from the very outset human beings are social beings. They are aligned towards human society and are essentially in need of help (Gen. 2.18). They are gregarious beings and only develop their personalities in fellowship with other people. Consequently they can only relate to themselves if, and to the extent in which, other people relate to them. The isolated individual and the solitary subject are deficient modes of being human, because they fall short of likeness to God.[14] Nor does the person take priority over the community.[15] On the contrary, person and community are two sides of one and the same life process.

But if we presuppose that likeness to God means God's relationship to human beings first of all, and that after that it also means human relationships, it will be justifiable for us to ask a further question: what is the nature of the God who in his image appears in male and female form? Do we have to think of the Creator of this human nature and condition in bisexual terms, as god and goddess at the same time?[16] Do we have to conceive of the Creator transsexually, as indifferent towards his masculine and feminine image on earth? The God who can allow his glory to appear at one and the same time in male and female form cannot, at all events, be a merely masculine God. This God is not 'a man', even if he is principally addressed and proclaimed in the Old and New Testaments in male metaphors – Lord, Father, Saviour, Judge, and so forth. But the God who creates his image as male and female is not a neuter either. So the metaphysical metaphors which philosophical theology uses for the Deity – Being, Essence, Ground, etc. – are not a particularly helpful way of surmounting masculinity in talk about God.[17] The third and best way of understanding him is the later doctrine of the Trinity, which discovers in God difference and unity, and also the unity of difference and unity, so that it talks about the God who is in his very self community and a wealth of different relationships. In human likeness to God, the analogy is to be found in the differentiation in relationship, and the wealth of relationship in the differentiation. It is this which, in the triune God, constitutes the eternal life of the Father, the Son and the Spirit, and among human beings determines the temporal life of women and men, parents and children. This socially open companionship between people is the form of life which corresponds to God. The trinitarian concept of community is able to overcome, not merely the ego-solitariness of the narcissist, but also the egoism of the couple –

man and wife.[18] Consequently the trinitarian concept of perichoresis, which is a community concept, is better than the assumption of a duality in God, as a model for the bisexual image of God on earth. Of course no developed trinitarian doctrine underlies the creation account in the Priestly Writing; but it is open for such a doctrine.

(*d*) The creation of God's image on earth is followed in v. 28 by the commission to rule over the animals, and in vv. 28 and 29 by the charge to 'subdue the earth'. These commissions are not identical with the likeness to God; they are a specific addition to it. This means that the likeness to God is not, either, to be found essentially in these commissions to rule. The two different charges evidently complement one another, and the second limits the first. To 'subdue the earth' refers to the nourishment of human beings which, according to vv. 29 and 30, is evidently supposed to be exclusively vegetarian.[19] The beasts are also to eat only vegetarian food. This means that the right to kill animals is excluded from the lordship of human beings over them. If human beings and animals alike eat vegetarian food, then the 'lordship' of human beings over animals can mean no more than that human beings have the function of a 'justice of the peace'. Human lordship on earth is the lordship exercised by a tenant on God's behalf. It means stewardship over the earth, for God. Only human beings know God's will, and only they can consciously praise and magnify him. Does the Creator need a representative and steward on earth? Apparently he does, for he transfers to human beings the preservation and continuation of the earthly side of creation, which assumed its first, initial form with the sabbath. Human beings become the authors of the further history of the earth. The prophetic visions of the messianic kingdom of peace (Isa. 11.6ff.) give sublime and ultimate form to this initial peaceful order between animals, human beings and the plants of the earth. But the beginning teaches that human lordship over the animals has to be distinguished from human subjection of the earth for the purposes of nourishment, and distinguished more clearly than is the case in the traditional theological doctrine of the *dominium terrae*; for this doctrine throws the two together and intermixes them, with disastrous consequences for the world.

The specific designation to rule follows from the essential being of men and women as God's image on earth. This sequence is not reversible. Peoples, races and nations which set themselves up to be masters of the world by no means become God's image in the process, or his representative, or 'God present on earth'. They become at most a monster. It is only as God's image that human beings exercise divinely legitimated rule; and in the context of creation that means: only as whole human beings, only as equal human beings, and only in the community of human beings – not at the price of dividing the human person into spirit and body – not at the price of dividing human beings into ruler and ruled – not at the price of dividing mankind into different classes.

At the end of this chapter we shall draw the systematic conclusions from these theological perceptions about the original destiny of human beings which we have derived from the first creation account.

§2 THE MESSIANIC CALLING OF HUMAN BEINGS: *IMAGO CHRISTI*

The true likeness to God is to be found, not at the beginning of God's history with mankind, but at its end; and as goal it is present in that beginning and during every moment of that history. In the New Testament it is Paul, more than anyone else, who uses the concept of likeness to God; and he applies it in order to present Jesus, the raised and transfigured Messiah, as God's true image.[20] Christ is the image and glory of the invisible God on earth. In his fellowship, people become what they are intended to be. Their glorification is promised them with their justification and in the process of their sanctification.

(*a*) According to II Corinthians 4.4, 'the glory of Christ' which appears in the apostolic gospel is explained by calling Christ 'the likeness of God'. In saying this Paul, in true rabbinic fashion, is combining Genesis 1.26 and Psalm 8: the image of God and his glory on earth belong together; they are one and the same. If Christ has been raised and transfigured into the divine glory, he is the true image of God on earth. In making this statement Paul is not looking either at the earthly Jesus or at the incarnate Son of God; he has in his mind's eye *the risen Christ* who has appeared in the glory of God to the Easter witnesses, and last of all to Paul himself. The gospel therefore proclaims the appearance of the glory of God in the face of Christ (II Cor. 4.6), giving this as reason for the sure and certain hope of the beginning of the new creation.

In taking up this messianic resurrection theology of Paul's, according to which Christ is 'the first-born from the dead', the author of the Epistle to the Colossians has projected it back to creation. He calls Christ 'the image of the invisible God, the first-born of all creation; for in him all things were created'. This archetypal christology is probably derived from Jewish Wisdom literature. As the image of the invisible God, Christ is the mediator in creation, the reconciler of the world, and the Lord of the divine rule: God appears in his perfect image, God rules through his image, God reconciles and redeems through his image on earth. Since it is through Christ that the new, true creation begins, Christ must already be the mystery of creation in the beginning. The earlier is understood in the light of the later, and the beginning is comprehended in the light of the consummation.

(*b*) Anthropologically too, Paul proceeds from the unity of God's image and his glory. According to Romans 1.23, sin consists in the fact that human beings have transformed 'the glory of . . . God' into a human or animal image, as they did in the worship of the golden calf (Ps. 106.20). Here 'glory' means the power 'to know and understand God as God',[21] which is an intrinsic part of being God's image. If the human being deifies created things instead of God, he becomes like them, both in his nature and in his behaviour. If he deifies beasts he becomes 'bestial' and inhuman. According to Romans 1.23, sinners have perverted the glory of God; according to Romans 3.23 they have lost it. This ambiguity led to the doctrinal dispute about whether sin has caused a perversion of the likeness to God or its loss.

The restoration or new creation of the likeness to God comes about in the fellowship of believers with Christ: since he is the messianic *imago Dei*, believers become *imago Christi*, and through this enter upon the path which will make them *gloria Dei* on earth. According to Romans 8.29, they will become 'conformed to the image of the Son' and, through their discipleship, grow into the messianic form of Jesus. Certainly, it is God alone who, according to Paul, causes believers to be conformed to the image of his Son; and he does this, as v. 30 says, through predestination, calling, justification and glorification. With his justification, the sinner receives through grace the righteousness which he lost through sin: he once again becomes God's image on earth. But the glorification is a future glorification, for it consists in 'the redemption of the body' (Rom. 8.23) – that is to say, the transformation of the human being's 'lowly body' so that it becomes like the 'glorious' or transfigured body of the risen Christ (Phil. 3.21). Justification is therefore the beginning of glorification here and now, in the present; glorification is the future completion of justification. Both come about through God's free gracious election (Rom. 11.5: ἐκλογὴ χάριτος; *electio gratiae*) – the Creator's relation to human beings which proves itself in faithfulness. Between the experienced justification of the sinner and the hoped-for glorification of the person justified lies the path of sanctification, which has to do with 'putting on the new human being, created after the likeness of God' (Eph. 4.24; cf. also Col. 3.10). So likeness to God is both gift and charge, indicative and imperative. It is charge and hope, imperative and promise. Sanctification has justification as its presupposition, and glorification as its hope and its future. In the messianic light of the gospel, the human being's likeness to God appears as a historical process with an eschatological termination; it is not a static condition. *Being* human means *becoming* human in this process. Here too, the image of God is the whole person, the embodied person, the person in his community with other people, because in the messianic fellowship of Jesus, people become whole, embodied and social human beings, whom death no longer divides into soul and body, and whom death no longer divides from God and from one another. They already live, here and now, in the process of resurrection, and in this process experience themselves as accepted and promised, wholly, bodily and socially. In history, the messianic becoming-human of the human being remains incomplete and uncompletable.[22] It is only the eschatological annihilation of death, the redemption of the body on a new earth and under a new heaven, which will consummate the 'becoming' process of human beings, thereby fulfilling their creaturely destiny.

In the messianic light of the gospel, the appointment to rule over animals and the earth also appears as the 'ruling with Christ' of believers. For it is to Christ, the true and visible image of the invisible God on earth, that 'all authority is given in heaven and on earth' (Matt. 28.18). His liberating and healing rule also embraces the fulfilment of the *dominium terrae* – the promise given to human beings at creation. Under the conditions of history and in the circumstances of sin and death, the sovereignty of the crucified and risen Messiah Jesus is the only true *dominium terrae*. It is to 'the Lamb' that rule over the world belongs. It would be wrong to seek for the *dominium terrae*, not in the lordship of Christ, but in other principalities and powers – in the power of the state or the power of science and technology. The perspective of eschatological glorification, and the focus this gives to the messianic justification and sanctification and to the creaturely designation of human beings, permits no separation of powers. It is whole, integral and all-embracing, because it is redemptive.

§3 THE ESCHATOLOGICAL GLORIFICATION OF HUMAN BEINGS: *GLORIA DEI*

Just as creation is creation for the sabbath, so human beings are created as the image of God for the divine glory. They themselves are God's glory in the world – *Gloria Dei est homo*, as Irenaeus said. In glorifying God, the creatures created to be the image of God themselves arrive at the fulfilment of what they are intended to be. Another writer, Amandus Polanus, brought out this second point when he said that *gloria hominis est Deus*.[23] We have already mentioned the pointers given in the biblical traditions to the eschatological glorification of God and human beings: human beings are the last to be created before the sabbath, and are created for that. They are priestly by nature, and stand before God on behalf of the earth, and before the earth on behalf of God. As God's earthly image, they reflect the Creator's glory. They are not merely commissioned by God; they are also the mode of his appearance in his creation. The messianic calling of human beings to be 'conformed' – like in form – to Jesus the Messiah brings them into the eschatological history of the new creation: from calling to justification, from justification to sanctification, from sanctification to glorification. Just as the coming glory of God lights up the face of the raised Messiah, so believers, filled with the Spirit, even here, and even now, also reflect the glory of God 'with unveiled face'. A strong eschatological drive pervades the messianic present. What is *here* only perceived in fragmentary form, through a mirror 'in a saying hard to interpret', will *then* be seen 'face to face' (I Cor. 13.12). Even for those who are 'God's children now' it still 'does not yet appear what we shall be. But we know that when he appears we shall be like him, for we shall see him as he is' (I John 3.2).

If we sum up these biblical hints systematically, we can say that as God's image human beings conform to the presence of the Creator in his creation, and as God's children they conform to the presence of God's grace; but when the glory of God itself enters creation, they will become like God, and transfigured into his appearance. The *imago per conformitatem gratiae* points beyond itself to the *imago per similitudinem gloriae*.[24]

The eschatological becoming-one-with-God of human beings (*theosis*) is inherent in the concept of 'seeing', for the seeing face to face and the seeing him as he is transforms the seer into the One seen and allows him to participate in the divine life and beauty. Participation in the divine nature and conformity to God, flowering into perfect resemblance, are the marks of the promised glorification of human beings. The God-likeness that belongs to creation in the beginning becomes God-sonship and daughterhood in the messianic fellowship with the Son, and out of the two springs the transfiguration of human beings in the glory of the new creation.

The image of God always corresponds precisely to the presence of God in the world, for it represents that presence. Consequently it is never fixed, once and for all, but is transformed, in correspondence with the history of God's presence in the world. What human beings are, is not thoroughly determined. It will only be known out of this divine history.

§4 AT ONCE GOD'S IMAGE AND A SINNER

Has the human being's likeness to God been lost through sin, as Paul suggests in Romans 3.23? Or has it been perverted, as he seems to think in Romans 1.23? Or is it merely clouded and obscured, as later theological tradition has taught? If the likeness to God is 'lost' through sin, then humanity as such is lost at the same time; for it is in order to be the image of God that human beings are created. So is the sinner no longer a human being? But then what happens to his responsibility, which is the reason why he is culpable, and is called to account for his sins? On the other hand, if sin merely clouds and obscures a person's likeness to God, how can a human being 'be' a sinner, and acknowledge himself as such? For in this case he remains essentially, and at the core of his being, good. He has simply made mistakes, and has merely committed this or that particular sin. So how can he be condemned in the divine judgment? This is the dilemma: that according to the biblical traditions we have to talk about human beings as God's image and as sinners at the same time.

A whole series of solutions have been propounded in the history of theology, but they can really be reduced to three different answers.

(*a*) A first answer is offered by the traditional two-stage anthropology.[25] The two definitions of God's image as *ṣelem* and *demuth*, *eikon* and *homoiosis*, *imago* and *similitudo*, already point to this possibility, in the process of their translation into other languages: *imago* expresses the ontic participation (methexis), *similitudo* the moral correspondence (mimesis). *Imago* has to do with the nature of human beings in their consciousness, reason and will. *Similitudo* means the human virtue of fearing God and obeying him. If a person becomes a sinner, he becomes disobedient and contends against God. This happens in the sphere of the *similitudo*, not in the realm of the *imago*. So in sin it is the *similitudo Dei* which is lost; the *imago Dei* can never be forfeited. We find this explanation in Irenaeus and John of Damascus, and the solution dominates patristic theology, largely speaking. It finds a certain degree of support in Paul himself, for in Romans 3.23 he talks only about the loss of the δόξα τοῦ θεοῦ, not about the loss of the εἰκών. The more differentiated two-stage anthropology of Thomas Aquinas also adheres to this pattern of thinking. Sin results in the loss of the human being's supernatural equipment of grace, and in the total derangement of his nature. It clouds his reason and impairs his will; but it does not destroy them.[26]

It was in the same tradition when Emil Brunner tried to express the simultaneity of being-human and being-a-sinner by making a distinction between a 'formal' *imago Dei* and a 'material' *imago Dei*; for Brunner maintains that the formal *imago Dei* is retained by the sinner, since he remains a responsible being endowed with reason; whereas the material *imago Dei* is lost when 'man lives in revolt' against God through sin.[27] What Brunner says certainly differs from scholastic tradition inasmuch as he talks about reason and responsibility in actual relations, but not in habitual substances: the human being's 'essential nature' is his 'relationship' to God.[28] In this relationship the human being always remains a human being. The word 'sinner' is intended to mean that this special and unrepealable relationship is now qualified in a negative sense. But although Brunner interprets 'formal' and 'material' in a relational sense, not a substantial one, the assertions of the mediaeval two-stage pattern of thinking are in fact retained, transposed into the modern pattern of two relations; and statements of this kind are only able to resolve the dilemma by saying that the human being is partially, or in one respect, a sinner, and partially, or in another respect, God's image. He cannot be entirely a sinner and entirely God's image at one and the same time. The underlying anthropology makes this impossible, for it premises that human beings possess various strata of being or relations, which are affected by their sin to a greater or lesser degree.

(*b*) The second answer was tried out in Reformed theology. Instead of starting from an ideal creation anthropology, it begins with *the event of justification*. Human beings are entirely and wholly sinners and are incapable of contributing to their justification before God through any 'works' or achievements of their own. They become righteous solely by faith through grace for Christ's sake. The Protestant doctrine of sin is part of the doctrine of justification, and has nothing to do with a pessimistic view of sin or with a denial of creation.[29] But does this doctrine necessarily presuppose that the sinner has 'lost' his likeness to God, as the Reformers said? The problem was talked out in exemplary fashion in the dispute between Flacius Illyricus and Victorinus Strigel.[30] We shall look briefly at the two different positions, though only from a systematic point of view.

Flacius was the author of the notorious thesis that sin is the actual substance of the human being who has not been born again. Strigel's counter-position was that sin is an accident of the human being created by God ('accident' in the Aristotelian sense of something non-essential, as distinct from substance). Flacius had already developed his anthropology in his theology of history. There are three fundamental human situations, he maintained: as creature, the human being is the image of God; as a sinner, he is the image of Satan; when justified, he is the image of Christ. Human beings are never *per se*. They are always delivered over to other powers, by whom they are determined: in creation by God – in sin by Satan – in grace by Christ. These kingdoms determine the human being in history, and he simply reflects them with his whole being. Consequently sin is not a blemish in the human being who is *per se* good, nor is it a loss of original righteousness. The person who has become the slave of sin has become the image of Satan. Sin has become his 'substance'. The *forma diaboli* replaces the *forma divina*. Anyone who is justified by Christ in faith is freed from the power of sin. He comes under the lordship of Christ. Just as he was once a slave of sin, so he now becomes the servant of righteousness. His 'substance' is then the divine righteousness. This anthropology, derived from a theology of history, is the basis of Flacius's thesis, which can therefore be precisely formulated as: sin is the *substantia hominis in theologia*. Its subjective basis is the confession before God that 'I *am* a sinner.'

Strigel, on the other hand, starting from the educational theory of his teacher Melanchthon, maintained that the conversion and regeneration of human beings take place in a human way, i.e., through reason and will. Faith is arrived at, not through supernatural coercion but through conscious conviction. The Holy Spirit acts on the sinner by human means. Sin has completely eclipsed human reason and paralysed the human will, but it has not extinguished them. It is therefore wrong to term sin *substantia hominis*; it is merely *accidentia*. If it were to be termed substance, it would have an existence of its own; and this would be in contradiction to the concept of sin. Satan would then be a creator of substances, which would mean denying creation and its Creator God.

Flacius saw Christ and Satan locked in the End-time struggle for rule over the world, and human beings as caught up in this struggle. Strigel was thinking of human beings *per se*, in the process of their religious and moral regeneration. Both used Aristotelian terminology; and this provoked the misunderstandings which the formulations of the Lutheran *Concordiae* laboriously tried to eliminate.[31] An important insight which should be remembered is that sin is not something evil about the human being who has been created good; it is an evil and godless *power* to which human beings have come to be subjected through their own fault. They are 'slaves of sin' (Rom. 6.17). Flacius rightly brought out this point. And yet God, in his faithfulness, is still the Creator and sustainer of human beings. Consequently human beings remain 'in substance' God's image on earth. Neither in the Old Testament nor in the New is there any evidence that after the Fall the human being ceased to be the image of God and therefore a human being (cf. Gen. 5.2,3; 9.6).

(*c*) The only way out of the impasse is to abandon the anthropology of substance, and to understand the human being in the relations given by the history of God, and in that light. In this case the *imago Dei* is neither the indestructible substance of the human being, nor can it be destroyed by human sin. We have defined it as God's relationship to human beings. God puts himself in a particular relationship to the human being – the relationship in which that human being is his image. Human sin may certainly pervert human beings' relationship to God, but not God's relationship to human beings. That relationship was resolved upon by God, and was created by him, and can therefore never be abrogated or withdrawn except by God himself. Consequently the sinner is subjectively speaking wholly and entirely a sinner and godless. But he remains at the same time wholly and entirely God's image, and does not lose this designation as long as God adheres to it and remains faithful to him. The presence of God makes the human being undeprivably and inescapably God's image. Even the person who is God-*less* does not succeed in losing God objectively, if God on his side remains that person's counterpart. Even the human being who is totally *in*human remains a human being and cannot escape his responsibility. By virtue of the relationship in which God puts himself to men and women, the handicapped person is also God's image in the fullest sense of the word; the image is in no way a diminished one.[32] The dignity of human beings is unforfeitable, irrelinquishable and indestructible, thanks to the abiding presence of God. Since the Fall, and under the conditions of sin's domination, this human designation to be God's image on earth must certainly be viewed as grace – the grace of the God who holds fast to his relationship to human beings in spite of their opposition. The graciousness of this faithfulness of God's to his refractory image is a pointer to the messianic calling of human beings through Christ, and finds expression in that calling. The completion of the *imago Dei* is therefore to be found at the end of God's history with human beings.

But within God's relationship to human beings there is also the human being's relationship to God – the reflecting, responsive existence which is inherent in his nature as image. Is this forfeited through sin, and is the human being's relationship to God lost at the same time? What is evil only emerges in the light of what is good; and in the same way sin can merely pervert something which God has created, but cannot destroy it. Sin is the perversion of the human being's relationship to God, not its loss. The relationship to God is turned into idolatry, faith in God becomes superstition, love of God becomes love of self, fear and hatred. Even love that has foundered so disastrously is love, even superstition is belief, even the service of idols is a relationship to God. 'The faith of the heart makes both God and idol', said Luther in his Large Catechism, commenting on the first commandment; and he called mammon the most detestable idol on earth: 'Whereon thy heart is set and whereon it relies – that is in truth thy God.' So the human being's relationship to God goes on existing. If it is centred on other created beings, or on works, or on its own self, the result is the idolatry which destroys the finite beauty of created things, because it demands more of them than they can give. Because neither created things nor one's own self can give what one expects of God, superstition evokes fear, and love hate, and hope disappointment. What Kierkegaard called 'sickness unto death' begins. To emphasize the mirror character of human beings in their likeness to God means, as Flacius rightly stressed, that the human being never ceases to be an *imago*; but from being *imago Dei* he turns into an *imago satanae* or an *imago mammonis*. In his attitude and his practical living, the person always reflects what he most of all fears and what he most of all loves.

But if hate is really love-gone-wrong, if superstition is distorted faith, and if sin is a perverted relationship to God, then – odd though it may sound – it is not only human beings who must be redeemed from sin; the energies of sin themselves have to be redeemed too: hate must be changed into love, superstition into faith and despair into hope. Although it is always only sinners who are justified, never their sins, yet it is not only sinners who are redeemed. In this sense sins themselves are also redeemed and put right.

§5 SOCIAL LIKENESS TO GOD

In the course of its history, Christian theology has taken two different analogies as a way of understanding human likeness to God in God's own presence. One of these parallels is the psychological analogy of the soul that dominates the body; the other is the social analogy of the community of women and men, parents and children. Ever since Augustine, the first of these has led in the West to the development of the 'psychological' doctrine of the Trinity, while in the East the second suggested the beginnings of a social doctrine of the Trinity. The first shows a tendency towards monotheism in the concept of God, and a trend towards individualism in anthropology; whereas the second finds in the triune God the archetype of true human community.

The doctrine of human beings as the image of God which is developed by Gregory of Nazianzus and Augustine brings out an initial difference between the theology of the Eastern church and Latin theology. We shall look first at this early conflict, before going on to a critical discussion of the psychological doctrine of likeness to God which we find developed in Augustine and Thomas Aquinas. We shall then come back in our own way to the early beginnings of a social doctrine of the likness to God, as a way of overcoming the one-sidedness of Western anthropology.

In order to explain the Trinity, Gregory of Nazianzus took as example the original 'nuclear' family, Adam, Eve and Seth.[33] It is not the human individual, all by him- or herself, that corresponds to the triune God – it is not even the first couple, Adam and Eve; it is the family, as the nuclear cell of every human society. Just as the three divine hypostases form a unity, by virtue of their common Being, so these three human persons also share the same flesh and blood, and form a single family. In the primal human community of husband, wife and child, the Trinity sees itself reflected and appears on earth.

Augustine considered this social analogy and rejected it.[34] He did so, not merely because he shrank from adopting the (gnostic) notion of a divine family in heaven, but because he interpreted Genesis 1.26f. differently. If people were created on the pattern of a single Person of the Trinity in each given case, then the passage could not read: 'Let us make human beings . . .' The expression created 'after *our* likeness' means according to the image of the Trinity, which 'is the One God'. So Augustine understands the divine plural at this point as a singular, to which only a singular can correspond among human beings. According to Augustine, we must not think, either, that the Father created human beings according to the image of the (eternal) Son. If this were the case, the verse would have to read: 'Let us make human beings after *your* likeness.' But it reads 'after *our* likeness, because in this way 'man is the image of the one true God. For the Trinity is itself the one true God'.[35] The human being corresponds to the single Being of the triune God, not to the threefold nature of God's inner essence. The Trinity does not contain 'three Gods'; it is 'the One God'. Finally, Augustine argues that, according to the social doctrine of likeness to God a man would surely only be God's image from the moment when he found a wife and she had a child; whereas the son Seth is not mentioned at all in the creation narrative. Like Paul, Augustine settles the problem of sexual differentiation in God's image (Gen. 1.27) in the man's favour: the man is 'the image and glory of God', whereas the woman is only 'the glory of the man' (I Cor. 11.7). The man is 'the head of the woman', just as Christ is the head of the man, and God is the head of Christ (I Cor. 11.3). Augustine concludes from this that although the woman is God's image inasmuch as she possesses the same human nature as the man, she is not in herself and independently God's image, since she was created to be the man's helper. She is his image only under her 'head', the man. Augustine therefore maintains that every individual person is in him- or herself the image of the One God, because likeness to God is stamped on every individual soul, which becomes the body's 'form', or determining principle (Aristotle's entelechy); and that it is only in the domination of the man over the woman that this likeness to God acquires social relevance.

Augustine reduces the *imago Dei* to the human soul: God's image is engraved in the soul as if it were a seal. And the soul governs the body from the very outset: *anima forma corporis*, said Aristotle. It is precisely this which constitutes the analogy in the likeness to God: just as God dominates the world, so the soul dominates the body. God's image is therefore God's emblem of sovereignty, and the token that he is liege lord of the earth. For Augustine, the *imago* doctrine belongs to the theological doctrine of sovereignty.

He goes on to develop the details of this anthropology of sovereignty in vividly pictorial form. The soul is the best part of the human being, for it is superior to the body. It animates and dominates the body, using it as its instrument. The soul influences or acts on the body, but the body does not influence or act on the soul, for the soul is the part of the human being that is related to God. It resembles the divine nature, and corresponds to it. Unlike the soul, the body is similar to other earthly creatures and corresponds to them. The soul mediates between heaven and earth, the invisible and the visible. 'Nothing is mightier than that creature which we call the reasonable spirit', declares Augustine. 'When thou art in the spirit, thou art in the centre: when thou lookest down, there is the body; when thou lookest up, there is God.'[36] God himself is spirit. So only the invisible soul – which is the reasonable spirit – can be the image of God.

'Essentially one is the divinity of the holy Trinity, and the image after which man was made.'[37] The human being therefore discovers in himself a copy of the essential divine Being, not a copy of the three divine Persons. Does this invalidate the doctrine of the Trinity? And is the One, the God who rules the world, made the archetype, first of the soul which dominates its body, and then of the man who dominates the woman? Augustine is able to differentiate the unity of God and the unity of the soul in a trinitarian sense: 'Man was made in God's image in that we are, and know that we are, and love that being and knowing.'[38] In its inwardly subjective differentiation into spirit – knowledge – love the soul corresponds to the one God who is in himself differentiated in a threefold sense. The inner threefold character of the soul is the image of the threefold God on earth. Augustine does not interpret the soul as substance, like Aristotle. He sees it as subject. The spiritual subject exists through self-awareness, self-knowledge and self-love, and is in this way the perfect image of the divine Trinity. In its subjective identity the soul corresponds to the essential unity of God and of the one divine sovereignty. In its inner subjective differentiation it corresponds to God's inner threefold Being. Here Augustine finds no difficulty in making a division corresponding to the three divine Persons: being corresponds to the Father, knowledge to the Son, love to the Spirit; or, as Aquinas says: 'An image of the divine Trinity is to be found in the soul . . . in so far as we exhibit in the mind a word proceeding from an utterer, and love from both.'[39] The word proceeds from the spirit, the love proceeds from the word and the will. This corresponds to the proceeding of the Son from the Father, and the proceeding of the Spirit from the Father and the Son.

Thomas also sees the likeness to God as belonging to the *natura intellectualis* of human beings, for by virtue of this 'intellectual nature' the human being can imitate God and come to resemble him:

> Since man is said to be after God's image in virtue of his intelligent nature, it follows that he is most completely after God's image in that point in which such a nature can most completely imitate God. Now it does this in so far as it imitates God's understanding and loving of *himself*.[40]

So the intellectual or spiritual nature of human beings corresponds to the nature of God. It is not an image of any one of the three divine Persons, or of the divine community of Persons. God created human beings according to the image of the whole Triunity. Whereas a 'trace resemblance' (*similitudo vestigii*) is to be found in all God's creatures (since the cause always communicates itself to the effect in some sense), in the intellectual nature of the human being there is an image-likeness of God (*similitudo Dei per modum imaginis*).

> As far as the divine nature is concerned, rational creatures seem to achieve some sort of portraiture in kind, in that they imitate God not only in his being and in his living, but also in his understanding.[41]

It follows from this that the likeness to God is imprinted merely on the reasonable soul. The body, on the other hand, displays only traces of God. In the created body God proves himself Creator, but in the soul, which resembles him in kind, he shows himself according to his inner nature.

> In the case of the uncreated Trinity . . . the persons are distinguished in terms of the procession of a word from its utterer and of love from both . . . Now since the rational creature also exhibits a word procession as regards the intelligence and a love procession as regards the will, it can be said to contain an image of the uncreated Trinity by a sort of portraiture in kind.[42]

In the intellectual nature of human beings the difference of the sexes is not relevant. 'There is neither male nor female', says Thomas at this point, quoting Paul (Gal. 3.28). The intellectual (or spiritual) nature is sexless, because the body does not determine it; on the contrary, it determines the body. Of course the body shows certain traces of the 'God-like' soul. Thomas, like Augustine, finds these in the human being's upright posture: 'The body of man, alone among earthly animals, is not slung belly downwards on all fours, but has a posture more suited to the contemplation of the heavens.'[43]

Let us sum up what Augustine and Thomas have to say:

1. God's image is the sexless soul, which dominates the body.

2. This soul does not correspond to a single Person of the Trinity, or to the fellowship of Persons in the Trinity. It corresponds to the One divine Being and the One divine sovereignty.

3. The analogy is not related initially to God's inner being, but to his outward relationship to the world. God's relationship to the world as its ruler corresponds to the soul's relationship to the body. Just as God possesses the world, so the soul possesses its body.

4. The individual human being in his spiritual subjectivity corresponds to the absolute subject, God. So it is to the spiritual subjec-

tivity alone that the dignity of likeness to God is ascribed. Human relationships, mediated through body and soul, are secondary to this. Every individual soul must be esteemed as an *imago*, whereas the conditions of the body and the social relationships mediated through the senses can be deemed no more than *vestigia Dei*. This theological decision in Western anthropology has had far-reaching and tragic consequences.

5. And yet we find in both Augustine's and Thomas's concept of the *imago Trinitatis* in the spiritual subjectivity of the human being, a preference for one Person of the divine Trinity: the subject of reason and will corresponds to the Father; the 'procession' of the word from the reason corresponds to the Son; while the procession of love from the word and the will corresponds to the Holy Spirit. Augustine and Thomas assume that the Trinity has a monarchical structure: the Father is the origin of the godhead of the Son and the Spirit. Consequently they both assume that the spiritual nature of the human being also has a monarchical structure: the subject is the origin of the word, as effect of the understanding, and of love, as an effect of will. They seem to see the Trinity as a single subject with two 'processions', and to interpret the human soul correspondingly, as also a subject of reason and will. This means that as the image of God the human being corresponds to God the Father.

The critical questions which we have to put to the psychological doctrine of likeness to God emerge from the aspects of the creature 'human being' which this doctrine suppresses; for it forces us to ask: what about the dignity of the body? And what about the dignity of the woman?[44]

1. If the body does not belong to the *imago Dei*, how can the body become 'a temple of the Holy Spirit', as Paul after all maintains that it is (I Cor. 6.13ff.)? The statement only makes sense if the human being, soul and body, is a single whole.

In considering this question, we may look at a discussion which was pursued in the Reformation period.[45] Andreas Osiander answered the enquiry about the body by saying that the body is also part of the image of God, because the whole human being (*totus homo*) is created to be that image. Calvin initially denied this thesis, following mediaeval tradition in its Augustinian form and maintaining that the *imago Dei* is essentially spiritual in kind (*spiritualis*), because God is spirit. Only the soul, as the human being's spiritual nature, can be the seat of the *imago Dei*. Only the invisible, spiritual soul is the image of the invisible, spiritual God. So the body does not belong to the image. But Calvin then – following biblical tradition – distinguished between the *imago Dei* in creation and the *imago Dei* in redemption: it is true that human beings are created to be the image of 'the invisible God', but they are redeemed according to the image of the incarnate God. The believer in Christ becomes the image of Christ, God become human, the Word made flesh; so his body too becomes the temple of the Holy Spirit. In the process of his redemption and perfecting, the human being becomes God's image 'in body as in soul' (*tam in corpore quam in anima*).

We may add to this that the biblical creation narrative knows nothing about a primacy of the soul. It declares that the whole human being, body, soul and spirit, is the image of God on earth. There can be no question of any subjection of the body by a dominating soul among those who wait for 'the resurrection of the body', and 'a new earth' in the world to come. Body and soul therefore already form a community of mutual influence (perichoresis) here and now, under the guidance of the life-giving Spirit.

2. But if the human being is God's image in his whole existence – which means in his bodily nature too – then he is also God's image in the sexual differentiation between masculinity and femininity. If God created his image on earth 'as man and as woman', then this primal difference is not a subsidiary, physical difference. It is a central, personal one. It is not the sexless soul, in abstraction from the body, which is counted worthy to correspond to God and to resemble him; it is the human community of persons.

This inevitably brings us back to the concept of the social image of God developed by the Greek Fathers of the church. Even Augustine and Thomas could not evade it. It is true that they were able to reduce the *imago* to the sexless soul of every human being; but they had to subordinate the woman to the man, just as they subordinated the body to the soul. As we have seen, for this purpose they used Pauline cephalic theology (I Cor. 11). Aquinas actually went further still when he maintained: 'Man is the beginning and end of woman, just as God is the beginning and end of all creation.'[46] The soul (of the man) which dominates the body, and the man who dominates the woman, correspond, and in actual fact constitute the human being's likeness to God. *Imago Dei* is then on the one hand a pure analogy of domination, and on the other, as we have seen, a patriarchal analogy to God the Father.

But if we instead interpret the whole human being as *imago*, we then have to understand the fundamental human community as *imago* as well. Of course the image of Adam and Eve and Seth is open to misunderstanding. It does not mean a religious family ideology. Family status cannot be of decisive importance for likeness to God, either for men or women; nor is the Christian doctrine of the Trinity suited to provide a religious legitimation for a family ideology. But the logical conclusion of this criticism is not necessarily individualism; for the anthropological triangle determines the existence of every human being: everyone is a man *or* a woman, *and* the child of his or her parents. The relation between man and wife signifies the inextinguishable sociality of human beings, while the relation between parents and children denotes the equally unalterable generativity of human beings. The first is the simultaneous community of the sexes in space; the second the community of the generations in time. If the whole human being is designated the image of God, then true human community – the community of the sexes and the community of the generations – has the same designation.

In their various communities, human beings are to be understood, not merely as the image of God's rule over creation, but also as the image of his inward nature. The inner fellowship of the Father, the Son and the Holy Spirit is represented in the fundamental human communities, and is manifested in them through creation and redemption. The so-called 'sovereignty' of the triune God then proves to be his sustaining fellowship with his creation and his people. This becomes evident in the messianic fellowship of human beings with Jesus, the Son: 'That they may all be one, even as thou, Father, art in me, and I in thee, that they also may be in us', runs Jesus' high priestly prayer (John 17.21). Here the social analogy applies to the divine fellowship which is formed through the mutual indwelling of the Father in the Son, and of the Son in the Father through the Spirit. Here it does not mean the Fatherhood or the Sonship; it means the community within the Trinity. It is the *relations* in the Trinity which are the levels represented on earth through the *imago Trinitatis*, not the levels of the trinitarian *constitution*. *Just as* the three Persons of the Trinity are 'one' in a wholly unique way, *so, similarly*, human beings are *imago Trinitatis* in their personal fellowship with one another. It is not that one person is supposed to represent the Father, and another the Son, and a third the Holy Spirit. In the framework of the social likeness to God, what Augustine and Thomas (on the Platonic model) called the *natura intellectualis* of every individual soul is secondary compared with the communicative speech which the persons share, which brings about their fellowship and quickens it, and in which the Spirit is present among them.

In considering what the *imago* means in its divine destination, or from God's side, Augustine and Thomas proceeded from the unity of the Trinity in the divine being, and from the divine sovereignty 'outwards'. In this way they raised to divine dignity the human subject of reason, will and domination. The Orthodox theologians who followed Gregory of Nazianzus proceeded differently. They started from the essential fellowship of the Trinity (perichoresis) and found the *imago Dei* in the primal human community. We have taken up these ideas as a basis for a pronouncedly social doctrine of human likeness to God in a theology of the open Trinity.[47] Instead of starting from a closed and self-contained Trinity which manifests itself outwardly without differentiation, we have taken as our premise an open Trinity which manifests itself outwardly in differentiated form. And this means that, in closing, we have to go one step further.

According to Augustine, human beings are the image of 'the whole Trinity', since in the unity of the Tri-unity the Trinity itself is 'whole'. But how does the Trinity 'open' itself, in order to establish its image on earth, and through whom? Created as God's image, human beings are not merely restored from their sins to this divine image through the messianic fellowship with the Son; they are also gathered into the open Trinity. They become 'conformed to the image of the Son' (Rom. 8.29). This does not merely presuppose that the eternal Son of God becomes human and is one like themselves; it also means that as a result human beings become like the Son and, through the Holy Spirit, are gathered into his eternal fellowship with the Father. So, contrary to Augustine's view, human beings are in fact fashioned according to a single Person of the Trinity: the person of the Son. Only the Son becomes human, and embodies the image for which human beings are created. Christ is the only-begotten Son and, as the image of God the Father, is at the same time the first-born among many brothers and sisters. So as *imago Christi* human beings are gathered into his relationship of sonship, and in the brotherhood of Christ the Father of Jesus Christ becomes their Father also. This is to say that through the Son the divine Trinity throws itself open for human beings. The Son becomes human and the foundational image of God on earth. Through the Son, human beings as God's image on earth therefore acquire access to the Father. As God's image, human beings are the image of the whole Trinity in that they are 'conformed' to the image of the Son: the Father creates, redeems and perfects human beings through the Spirit in the image of the Son.

X

'Embodiment is the end of all God's works'

This thesis of Friedrich Oetinger's interprets embodiment as the movement and goal of all God's works.[1] It is a postulate which sets human reality in the history and surrounding field of God's creation, reconciliation and redemption. That is its advantage compared with other analyses, which talk about the human being's 'body and soul', or about his 'body, mind and soul'. In dichotomic or trichotomic conceptions, the soul has always already been abstracted from the body, or the body has been split off from the soul through the operation of the mind. In these patterns we can no longer perceive the total human person who is the object of these differentiations and separations, and in whom they take place. But when definitions are arrived at by way of separation instead of through particular forms of relation, acts of domination are involved which hinder an understanding of the whole, instead of promoting it.

From its earliest beginnings, the history of Western anthropology shows a tendency to make the soul paramount over the body, which is thus something from which the person can detach himself, something to be disciplined, and made the instrument of the soul.[2] This tendency is an essential element in the history of freedom in the Western world. The liberty of self-control grows in proportion to a person's detachment from his own body. 'The wise soul' is superior to 'the foolish body'. 'The commanding self' subjects 'the submissive body'. The technological production of artificial organs makes parts of the body interchangeable, replaceable, and to some extent superfluous. The whole trend towards a 'spiritualizing' of the soul and a 'materialization' of the body also unconsciously dominates the whole of Western anthropological theory. No historical view of the human being is value-neutral. Unless the total trend in which the theories are embedded is consciously taken into account, it is to that trend that the theories will contribute. Christian views of the human being and the anthropologies of Christian theology are seldom an exception: the theology of the patristic church was pervaded by the Platonic idea of the liberation of the soul from the body; mediaeval theology was determined by the Aristotelian view that the body is formed by the soul; and modern European anthropology is dominated by the will to give the conscious mind power over the instrument of the body, in accord with the expositions of Descartes and Lamettrie.

Here we shall deliberately choose an alternative approach to this general trend. If 'embodiment' is the end of all God's works, then the human body cannot be viewed as a lower form of life, or as a means to an end – and certainly not as something that has to be overcome. For if embodiment is the end of God's works, it must correspondingly be the supreme goal of the human being too, and the end of all *his* works.

According to the biblical traditions, embodiment is the end of God's works in creation. The earth is the object and the scene of the Creator's fertile and inventive love. It was bodily, sensuous human beings whom he created to be his image, and his first commandment was 'Be fruitful and multiply . . .' (Gen. 1.28). It is not the spirituality of men and women, and not what distinguishes them from animals, which makes them God's image on earth. They are his image in their whole and particular bodily existence. It contradicts belief in creation if we define the human being's essential quality, and what corresponds to God in him, by subtracting the animal and then regarding what is left as something on its own. The movement in which the world was created proceeds from the resolve to the word, from the word to the act, and from the act to created reality. In this movement the human being becomes aware of himself as God's creature and image. Embodiment is his goal. All the paths of his spirit and all the words of his speech end in the lived form and configuration of his body.

According to the biblical traditions, embodiment is also the end of God's work of reconciliation: 'The Word became flesh . . .' By becoming flesh, the reconciling God assumes the sinful, sick and mortal flesh of human beings and heals it in community with himself. God's eternal Logos becomes a human body, a child in the manger, a saviour of the sick, a tortured human body on Golgotha. It is in this bodily form of Christ's that God brings about the reconciliation of the world (Rom. 8.3). In his taking flesh, exploited, sick and shattered human bodies experience their healing and their indestructible dignity. The Christ dying in physical torment on the cross identifies himself with the sick, the tormented, and those who die in torment. That is why they are able to find in him the healing which is fellowship with God, the wellspring of eternal life.

Finally, embodiment is also the end of the redemption of the world, the redemption which will make it the kingdom of glory and peace. 'The new earth' completes redemption (Rev. 21), and the new 'transfigured' embodiment is the fulfilment of the yearning of the Spirit (Rom. 8). That is why the patristic church ran counter to the general Platonic trend of its cultural environment which I have already mentioned, and introduced into the Apostles' Creed: I believe in 'a resurrection of the body and a life everlasting'. Redemption begins with the gift of the Spirit and ends with the transfiguration of the body. It begins with the new righteousness 'of the heart' and ends in the new, just and righteous world. It begins in faith and ends in the new, sensory experience of God which is called 'seeing'.

These works of God in creation, reconciliation and redemption also surround and mould the living character of created, reconciled and redeemed men and women. We shall therefore theologically understand being human as being part of this history of God with the world. What is human is not revealed in isolation from the history of God and the encirclement of his Spirit; it is manifested through integration, and through differentiated correspondences to these things. We arrive at the theological perception of the truth of the human being in the arc that reaches from his physical creation to the resurrection of the body. The general observation that follows from this is that we should not, either, always try to grasp the internal relationships of human society and the inner differences of individuals purely analytically, by way of more and more demarcations and exclusions. We should understand them in the field constituted by organism and environment as inward or outward relationships, always seeing them in the context of human totality. In definitions which are arrived at by way of exclusions and divisions, violence is made the principle.[3] In particular forms of relationship and differentiated correspondences, the total structure, Gestalt or configuration becomes the principle. The subject of this present chapter is the bodily Gestalt in the radius of its life.

§1 THE PRIMACY OF THE SOUL

Tendencies to spiritualize the human subject and to instrumentalize the human body are so general and so profoundly embedded in the major enterprise we know as Western civilization that it is difficult for us to free ourselves of them. We can no doubt find their beginnings in the myths of prehistoric times. These myths describe the conquest of death and sexuality.[4] It was through the awareness of individual death that the first differentiating experiences of soul and body emerged. The body became the very personification of mortality, transience and frailty. These experiences led to a yearning for the soul to be delivered from the body. This longing was originally religious in kind; but in the world of modern technological possibilities it was translated into a programme for overcoming disease, for prolonging human life, and for constructing a more perfect human organism by way of the introduction of machines into the human body and the attachment of the brain to computers. Hand in hand with the notion of overcoming or abolishing the mortality of the body went the hope and programme for overcoming or abolishing the sexual reproduction of human beings. From time immemorial this kind of reproduction has been viewed as a sign of earthly imperfection; for procreation, conception, pregnancy and birth put people at the mercy of a capricious nature. Redeemed human beings will be like the angels and 'neither marry nor be given in marriage, for they cannot die any more' (Luke 20.35f.). Modern experiments in extra-uterine insemination and genetic cloning point in the direction of controlled human reproduction by technological – i.e., non-sexual – methods.[5] This tendency in the history of civilization to eliminate the body can be lamented, as the root of all evil; or it may be seen as the fulfilment of the ancient dream of the remaking of an imperfect creation. Unless a new point of departure can be found, the conflict between soul and body is going to end fatally for human beings. In this chapter we shall be looking critically at some important stages in the ancient history of 'the primacy of the soul', considering it from its 'lower' side, so to speak – that is to say, in the light of the history of the subjected body. And we shall do this by asking about the structure of the lived life in each given case.

1. *Plato and the Death of the Body*

In Greek, the word *soma* developed initially from the fact that the person experiences his body as something alien to himself.[6] In Homer the word is used exclusively for the *dead* body. What lies inanimate and lifeless is *soma*, the body. From the fifth century onwards other lifeless things were called 'body' as well. Along another line of linguistic development, *soma* came to mean 'self' and stood for the reflexive pronoun. We find *soma* used in this way in Euripides – but in Paul too. What appears when the person confronts himself – makes himself the object of his own observation – is *soma*, his self, his body. But where does he quite certainly experience this reflexive self-differentiation? And where is he inescapably faced with his bodily nature? He experiences it in the awareness of his own death, for in the face of death he becomes inexorably conscious of the mortality of his body.

Plato describes this in the context of the immortality of the soul. Death is 'the separation of the soul from the body'.[7] If the body is the part of the human being that has to die, then the person perceives death through his physical senses. But he is unable through his physical senses to perceive the part of the human being which transcends death – the soul. He can only perceive the soul in direct self-awareness:

> When the soul [contemplates things] it does so through bodily senses – that is with the assistance of the body. But when it makes enquiry all by itself, it goes off to what is pure and everlasting and deathless and invariable, and as though akin to it remains with that kind of being.[8]

In life, this direct divine self-awareness of the soul is always bound up with the *meditatio mortis* of the body:

> The facts are rather these: let us suppose that it escapes purely, dragging nothing of the body with it, as having (wilfully anyhow) had no dealings with the body during its lifetime, but having shunned it and kept itself to itself, making that its constant aim and practice – which simply means, in fact, pursuing philosophy

> in the correct manner, and in very truth practising death; or wouldn't you call this 'a practice of death'? Then in this state it goes away to the place which is like itself, invisible, to that which is divine . . .[9]

The soul's direct awareness of immortality is therefore simply the reverse side of the continual spiritual anticipation of death, of the final separation of the soul from the body. This separation already takes place in life, if the soul does not expend its energies but 'keeps itself to itself', flees the body with its needs and its pains, and confronts it in a properly sovereign manner. Death divides what is mortal in the human being from what is immortal, the body from the soul. Because it is the immortal which corresponds to the divine and resembles it, not what is mortal, true human life is to be found, not in the body, but in the soul. If the human being identifies himself with his soul, not with his body, he will discover that he is himself immortal and immune against death.

This anthropological theory about 'the immortality of the soul' is not a doctrine about an eternal life after death. What it is talking about is a human identity beyond life and death. For what cannot die with the body has never lived in the life of the body either. The soul is immortal because it has never lived in a bodily sense. What has never lived can never die. So it is not the lived life of the human being which is immortal and beyond the bounds and jurisdiction of death; it is his unlived life. The unlived life is surrounded by 'the protective zone of the not-yet-living'.[10] The soul can acquire for itself this protective zone of not-lived bodily and sensory life if it has become conscious of the body's mortality in the *meditatio mortis*. It must then 'escape purely', 'keep itself to itself' and 'have no dealings with the body'. It must draw back from the life of the body, which leads to death.

The Platonic *meditatio mortis* stresses the primacy of the soul. The attitude to life based on this primacy was further developed in Stoic philosophy: serenity and sovereign indifference in happiness and suffering, in health and sickness, in life and death. The power of imperturbability (*ataraxia*) is to be found in the impassivity of the soul (*apatheia*). But what the Platonic *meditatio mortis* also stresses is the baseness of the body. It withdraws vital interest from bodily life, which it degrades to an insignificant casket for the soul. It de-animates the body, as it were, reducing it to a remnant of earth which is merely an embarrassing burden. If the death of the body is the feast of freedom for the soul (which is what Plato shows it to be in the death of Socrates), then the death of the body can only be something to be desired. This detachment, degradation and de-animation of the body means that the notion of 'the immortality of the soul' can hardly be reconciled with the biblical belief in creation, even though the church's theology took over the idea at an early stage and has continued to maintain it to some extent, down to the present day.

2. *Descartes and the Mechanistic Body*

In Plato, the anthropological dualism of body and soul belonged within the framework of the ontological dualism of non-transient Being and transient existing things. As microcosm, the human being mirrors the conditions of the macrocosm and participates in these conditions. That is why Plato talked about the soul as being a higher, immortal substance. In Descartes we enter another world, although the basic pattern of thinking is preserved. Following the Christian tradition in its Augustinian form, Descartes no longer understands the soul as a higher substance: he sees it as the true subject, both in the human body and in the world of things.[11] He translates the old body-soul dualism into the modern subject-object dichotomy.

If the human subject is assured of itself through reflection, and not through sensory perception, the human body with its sensory perceptions enters the sphere of objective things, the essential characteristic of which, compared with the cognitive subject, is simply corporeal extension.

> Although I perhaps (or indeed certainly, as I shall later expound) have a body which is closely associated with me, yet – since I on the one hand have a clear and plain idea of myself (in so far as I am merely a thinking, and not an extended, thing) and on the other hand have a clear idea of the body (in so far as it is merely an extended and not a thinking thing) – so much is certain: I am in very truth different from my body and can exist without it.[12]

As a non-thinking thing, merely characterized by extension, the body has to be viewed like a machine – that is to say, like a clock (which in Descartes' time was the most complicated and most admired of all machines):

> And just as a clock, put together out of wheels and weights, observes all the laws of nature no less precisely if it has been badly made (so that it does not register the hours correctly) than if it meets the wish of the maker in every respect, the same is true of the human body, if I view it as a kind of machine, which is so arranged and put together out of bones, nerves, muscles, veins, blood and skin that even if no mind were to exist in it, it would still have exactly the same movements which now take place in it, not through the lordship of the will and hence not through the mind.[13]

What links the thinking but non-extended soul with the extended but non-thinking body is for Descartes 'an assembly (*complexio*) of everything which God has assigned to me'.

> Nature further teaches me through a sensation of pain, hunger, thirst, and so forth, that I am not merely aware of my body as the mariner is aware of his vessel, but that I am intimately linked with it, and as it were mingled with it, so that together we form a certain unity.[14]

Because Descartes conceives the thinking mind as being without extension, he can think of the 'assembly' which represents the whole person as being present in all the extended organs of the body. At the same time he ascribes to the brain and (in the brain) to the pineal gland – 'which is said to be the seat of common sense' – a mediating function between mind and body.[15] The relation of the non-extended, thinking mind or subject to its non-thinking, extended body or object is described by Descartes as a one-sided relationship of domination and ownership: *I am* the thinking subject and *I have* my body. The 'I' stands over against its body, which it commands and utilizes as its property.

But if soul and body are defined by way of mutual exclusion – thinking as against non-thinking, extended as against non-extended – it becomes impossible to conceive how there can be a link between soul and body.[16] How can a non-extended soul exert any influence on an extended body? How can a non-thinking thing operate on a thinking thing? Can a soul which is defined as non-spatial dwell in a particular spatial body at all? If extension is made the sole objective hallmark of the body, then all other sense perceptions – smell, colour, taste, sound – are quite evidently secondary; they are subjective impressions of objects. But then how are we to judge the sense perceptions of our own bodies? If human subjectivity is localized in non-extended cognition, then the human body has to be assigned to the objective world of machines and automata. Its connection with a specific, thinking 'I' is purely fortuitous and, for the 'I' itself, non-essential. The cognitive 'I' 'can exist without it', said Descartes, no doubt thinking of eternity. This means that it can co-exist on earth with parts of the body which are in principle interchangeable. This objectification of the body is the practical result of identifying the human being as a thinking self. It is only possible to arrive at this kind of spiritualization of human existence at the cost of banishing the body into what is considered to be 'non-spirituality'.

3. *Karl Barth and 'the Ministering Body of a Ruling Soul'*

Karl Barth did not put the anthropological question about the difference between soul and body in the context of death, like Plato; nor, like Descartes, did he see it in the light of the cognitive subject's certainty of itself. He viewed it in the theological context of reflection about the human being Jesus Christ and the experience of God's Spirit.[17] And yet, in spite of that, his answers too were in line with the general trend of Western civilization – spiritualization on the one hand, instrumentalization on the other. So what he says only slightly modifies the answers given by Plato and Descartes. The key statement in his chapter on 'The Human Being as Soul and Body' is this:

> Through the Spirit of God the human being is the subject, form and life of a substantive organism, the soul of his body, both wholly and simultaneously: in ineffaceable difference, inseparable unity, and indestructible order.[18]

This crucial statement identifies the human being as 'the soul of his body.' That is a literal translation of the Aristotelian-Thomist definition *anima forma corporis*. By using it, Barth preserves the Platonic primacy of the soul and takes over the Cartesian view that the relationship of the soul to the body is a relationship of ownership. Soul and body form an ordered unity. The order of this unity is superordination and subordination. The soul 'rules', the body 'serves'.[19] The soul 'precedes', the body 'follows'.[20] The soul is 'higher', the body is 'lower'.[21] The soul is 'the first', the body is 'the second'.[22] The soul 'dominates', the body is 'dominated'.[23]

This 'indestructible order' is laid down by the divine Spirit[24], for according to Barth the Spirit is nothing other than the subjective reality of God's sovereignty. The Spirit is 'the principle which makes the human being into a subject'.[25] That is why the relationship of the Spirit-dominated soul to the body corresponds to God's relationship of domination towards the world. In its lordship over its body, the soul participates directly in God's lordship over his world. That is why Barth calls this order, in which the soul dominates the body, 'indestructible'. The body, for its part, through its ministering subordination to the dominating soul, acquires a mediated correspondence to the lordship of God and so to its own truth. 'The human being is the ruling soul of his body, or he is not a human being.'[26] Barth then goes on to describe what this means for the human being's body:

> The same sphere which from the standpoint of the soul is the domain in which the human being must rule is from the standpoint of the body the domain in which he may be subject to himself and serve. As body he does not dispose of himself, but stands at his own disposal; he does not use himself, but is used by himself. As body he does not go beyond himself, for it is not as body but as soul that he has a direct relationship to the Spirit and therefore to God. As body, then, he cannot precede himself, but only follow.[27]

Here Barth draws on Platonic concepts to express the hierarchical relationship between soul and body; but he can then also describe the same hierarchical structure in terms deriving from the Cartesian philosophy of subjectivity:

> He (the human being) is identical with his body, in so far as he is its soul. He thinks and wills and therefore fulfils the human act of living; and in so doing he treats his sphere, i.e., his body, as his own domain, and controls and uses it, striding ahead of it in precedence. . . . His soul is his freedom over his body and therefore over himself. As he acts in this freedom, as in thinking and willing he is his own lord and director, he is spiritual soul. For in order to be active in this way, he is given Spirit by God and through the Spirit he is awakened to be a living being.[28]

Here Barth, like Aquinas before him, defines 'the human act of living' exclusively as thinking and willing.[29] He defines being a person as being ruler in the domain of his own body. To control himself, to command himself, to use himself, to 'pull himself together', and to decide for himself: this is what is truly human, because it is in this that the human being corresponds to God. The secular model for the rule of the dominating soul over the continually subservient body is apparently 'the monarchy of God's grace'; for Barth never mentions a right to resistance on the part of the misused body, nor does he concede to the feelings any right to a say in the decisions of the reasonable soul. He does not even suggest that a harmony between the body and its dominating soul is something to be desired.[30] The liberty of the soul is defined unilaterally, as the right to rule, and it is given an individual connotation, so that everyone is 'his own master and sovereign', thereby having 'a direct relationship to the Spirit, and therefore to God'.[31]

The human being is the image of God his Lord in that he belongs to himself, controls himself and disposes over himself. Through his self-control he corresponds to his divine master, for it is as a being who can be subservient to himself that he is claimed by God. The rule of the soul over its body is an expression of the rule of God, and the self-control of the human being is its parable. But logically speaking this simply means that it is the human being who controls himself, and who disposes over himself because he belongs to himself, who is the image and likeness of his divine Lord.[32] The man's relationship to the woman is then also supposed to correspond to this subordination of the body to the rule of the soul without there being any reciprocity:

> But the human being as preceding soul of his obedient body, is also the parable of what Scripture, talking about the relationship between man and woman, describes as the resemblance to God in this human existence, which is only perfect in this duality; since in this perfection too, the dominating and the ministering, as the work of the single person, are different and yet completely interlocking.[33]

Here Barth's theology is a theological doctrine of sovereignty: the order of the ruling Father and the obedient Son within the Trinity corresponds to the extra-trinitarian order of God's rule over the world. The relationship of heaven to earth in cosmology,[34] the relationship of the soul to the body in psychology,* the relationship of man and woman in anthropology, all correspond to the same order – to mention only the correspondences in the doctrine of creation. In his account of these analogous structures of domination, Barth is following the ancient metaphysicians, especially Aristotle, who even then treated heaven and earth, soul and body, man and woman, according to the same pattern. The metaphysicians did this in order to preserve the harmonious correspondences of the Logos in the cosmos. But more modern developments in cosmology, psychology and anthropology have long since left these ancient relationships of correspondence behind. Nor is it advisable to revert to them. The progression of terms on the 'top' level – heaven – soul – man – already prompts ironic comment enough. But the progression on the 'lower' level – earth – body – woman – is open to more radical criticism still. A world with an 'order' of this kind can hardly be called a peaceful one.

§2 SOUL AND BODY

In the history of civilizations, ideas about 'the self' have undergone a remarkable transmigration. As long as the living character of the human being was seen in the inhaling and exhaling of air, the self was localized in the diaphragm. The person is alive in the rhythm of his breathing, and his life ends when 'he breathes his last'. Later on, people viewed the living character of the human being in his powerful emotions, in the trust of the heart and in 'cordial' love. So the centre of life was localized in the human heart. When the heart stops beating the person is dead. But then the human being came to be viewed as the subject of reason and will; and the self migrated once again, in the world of the imagination, and came to be lodged in the human brain, generally behind the eyes. Today 'brain death' counts as real symbol for the death of the human being. As the self moved upwards in this way, the person is centred no longer in the middle of his body but in the head. It is now no longer the respiratory

* The translation of the words 'Seele' and 'Geist' presents difficulty, because in both cases what is a single concept in German is differentiated in English, according to the context: 'Seele' can be soul, mind or psyche; 'Geist' can be spirit or mind. 'Geist' has occasionally been translated here as 'mind', where this seemed to be imperatively required. But in general I have adhered to the translations 'soul' and 'spirit' throughout, in order to preserve the wholeness and fluidity of the German. (Translator)

organ which is considered to represent the person; it is the brain. And this means that it is no longer the breathing community of the human being and his natural environment which is declared to be 'the human act of living'; it is now the acts of cognition and will through which the human being dominates the world and his own body. The result is 'the primacy of the mind' on the one hand, and, on the other, the corresponding de-sensualization of 'scientific and technological civilization'.

1. *Thinking with the Body in the Old Testament*

The biblical anthropologies of the Old and New Testaments date from early periods of civilization and in part from other cultural areas. If, together with the biblical message itself, we bring them face to face with our own period and area of culture, what emerges from the difference is not merely the recognition that these are notions that are dead and gone. We see that they also possess an inherent critical potential for surmounting the one-sidedness of our own civilization.

The fundamental anthropological differentation between soul and body is foreign to the Old Testament tradition, because the ontological distinction between immortal Being and the mortal individual existence is foreign to them as well.[35] In these traditions, the person experiences himself differently; he sees himself rather as belonging within a particular divine history. Its narrower circumference is traced by the history of call, liberation, covenant and promise. Its wider horizon is the history of the world's creation and redemption. In this divine history, the human being always appears *as a whole.*

Soul and body are not analysed as a person's component parts. When, according to the Yahwist's creation narrative, God breathed his breath into the lump of earth, we are told that 'man became a living soul' (Gen. 2.7 AV). He does not *have* a soul. He *is* a living soul. When the person dies he can lament: 'I am encompassed by death, I am flesh.' He does not possess his flesh. He *is* flesh.[36] Body, mind and soul are never used as parallel anthropological terms and cited as mutually complementary. Apparently the person is always affected as a whole, though he assumes a different specific form in different relationships. Nor does he find in his God any opportunity for withdrawing to an immortal, spiritual substance, so as to surmount the happiness and pains, life and death of his body. He can only appear before God as a whole. The *Sh^ema'* Israel makes this plain: 'You shall love the Lord your God with all your heart, and with all your soul, and with all your might' (Deut. 6.5). Hebrew thinking does not enquire into the essence and individual components of a thing. The Hebrew asks about its becoming and its effects. Consequently the human being perceives himself, not through reflection and introspection, but in the experiences of the history of the covenant and the promises of his God. This outward theological orientation brings the human being to expression only in the context of surrounding and overriding instances of the divine efficacy. The human being has really no substance in himself; he is a history. That is why the anthropology of the Old Testament does not deal so much in definitions as in narratives. These do not establish what the person is by way of definitions. They present him in the relationships in which he lives.

This general principle is reflected in the striking fact that the mental or emotional impulses are localized in different parts of the body. The person thinks with his body. The brain and the bodily organs instruct one another. The 'inner parts' (*qereb*) of the human being are represented by the inner organs. The kidneys are often the seat of the conscience (Ps. 16.7). God proves a person's heart and kidneys (Ps. 7.9 and frequently elsewhere). The liver can be called the organ of profound grief (Lam. 2.11). His bile makes a person 'bitter'. The person's life is his breath and also his blood. The heart can be called the organ of the will and the desires. Here feelings, ideas, intentions and decisions are linked with a whole series of representative bodily organs. This surely indicates that in this anthropology soul and body, the core of the inner life, and the outward mental horizon are seen as existing in reciprocal relation and mutual interpenetration. Here a reduction of the 'human act of living' to thinking and willing, and its localization in the soul or the brain, are unknown. There is no 'primacy of soul'. An inner hierarchy, according to which the soul is to be thought of as 'higher' and the body as 'lower', the soul as dominating and the body as subservient, is alien to this way of thinking.

The concept of a relationship of community, partnership and mutual influence is closer to biblical anthropology: 'I have made a covenant with my eyes', says Job (31.1). Because Israel experienced its God *in the covenant*, it liked to express its correspondences to that God in relationships of covenant as well. The unity of soul and body, what is inward and what is outward, the centre and the periphery of the human being is to be comprehended in the forms of covenant, community, reciprocity, a mutual encircling, regard, agreement, harmony and friendship.

2. *The Perichoretic Pattern of Body and Soul*

Unlike Karl Barth, we have started from the assumption that the unity of the triune God is not to be found initially in his subjectivity and the sovereignty of his rule; it is already to be discovered in the unique, perfect, perichoretic fellowship of the Father, the Son and the Holy Spirit.[37] Following Johannine theology, we are taking as archetype of all the relationships in creation and redemption that correspond to God, the reciprocal perichoresis of the Father and the Son and the Spirit (John 17.21). We are not therefore assuming that there is 'in God himself an above and a below, a prius and a posterius, a superiority and a subordination post-order'; and neither do we see the divine unity in the fact that 'in himself God is as the one who is obeyed One and as the one who obeys Another.'[38] We are assuming a unity of divine love within the Trinity, in which this command-obedience structure of divine rule is certainly one possibility, but not the essentially determining element.

This means that we have not, either, understood the relationship of the triune God to the creation of his love as a one-sided relationship of domination. In contemplating the wealth of this eternal love, we have seen it as a complex relationship of fellowship; and in this complexity and plurality as therefore also reciprocal. 'Creation in the Spirit of God' is an understanding which does not merely set creation over against God. It also simultaneously takes creation into God, though without divinizing it. In the creative and life-giving powers of the Spirit, God *pervades* his creation. In his sabbath rest he allows his creatures to exert an influence on him. From the aspect of the Spirit in creation, the relationship of God and the world must also be viewed as a perichoretic relationship.[39]

Finally, we have understood human likeness to God in this same context of the divine perichoresis; that is to say, as a relationship of fellowship, of mutual need and mutual interpenetration. The true human community is designed to be the *imago Trinitatis*. We shall therefore view the relationship between soul and body, the conscious and the unconscious, the voluntary and the involuntary, or however this fundamental anthropological differentiation may be defined, as a *perichoretic* relationship of mutual interpenetration and differentiated unity; but we shall not introduce one-sided structures of domination into it. We are neither starting from the assumption of a primacy of the soul, nor assuming a primacy of the body. We are looking at the *Gestalt* – the configuration or total pattern – of the lived life. This presupposes theologically that the presence of God in the Spirit is not localized solely in the consciousness or in the soul, or in the subjectivity of reason and will; but that its place is the whole human organism – that historical Gestalt which people, body and soul, develop in their environment.

A person's Gestalt emerges in the field formed by the human being and his environment.[40] This field has a number of distinguishable dimensions: nature, in the form of the human being's genetic structure, and in the form of the region of the world in which he is born; the society and culture in which he grows up; the history which moulds his origins and conditions his future; and the sphere of transcendence, which is represented by religion and the system of accepted values. The influences of all these different types of environment and the way in which he comes to terms with them form his Gestalt. In acquiring Gestalt, the person acquires both individuality and sociality; for the Gestalt binds him and his environment into a living unity, and at the same time distinguishes him from that environment as this particular living thing. Gestalt is the form of exchange with the various environments in which a person is identifiable, and with which he can identify himself. As the natural conditions show, it is to some extent fixed, and is historically open to considerable modification. Different kinds of occupation, age and life history show how contacts with the environments vary, and how open, therefore, the frontiers of the specific human Gestalt are.

The human being's Gestalt does not develop merely in the outward structures I have mentioned. It develops too in the corresponding inward structures which are called body and soul, the conscious and the unconscious, the centre and the periphery. It is also in relationship to himself that the human being forms his Gestalt, and that his Gestalt is formed. It comes into being on the borderline of the anthropological differentiation, and is always moulded by both sides of this differentiation, even if only the one side is conscious and willed. Consequently, in the lived Gestalt of a human being, body and soul, the conscious and the unconscious, what is voluntary and what is involuntary, interpenetrate. The Gestalt that is then arrived at is marked by both differentiation and unity, because it gives form to the exchange and the mutual interpenetration. In considering the human being's lived Gestalt, it is not possible to start from a one-sided domination by the soul over a subservient body. If we do define the anthropological differentiation in a person's relation to himself as 'soul and body', then the body 'informs' its soul just as strongly as the soul informs its body. The body talks continually to the soul, just as the unconscious continually influences what is conscious, and just as the involuntary is always present in all voluntary acts. If we assume a one-sided relationship of domination by the soul over its body, we thereby suppress the responding language of the body, and make the body mute. It reacts by petrifying and dying – a parallel to 'the silent death of nature' in the ecological crisis.

In the lived Gestalt, body and soul arrive intermittently at a tenable consensus, even if in human history the Gestalt always remains a broken, fragmentary unity. Body and soul, the inward and the outward life, have made a covenant. They have arrived at a certain equilibrium. If we are to see this equilibrium from both sides, we must start from the assumption that in its soul the human body arrives at awareness of itself; while the psychic consciousness, with its experiences and workings, for its part influences the human body. Here it is impossible to assign any fundamental primacies. In every case the common task of body and soul is to develop the Gestalt. Through its perceptions and its workings the psychic consciousness influences the body. It talks to the body. But the body has its own language too, through which it talks to the awareness of the soul. The body has its own remembrances, which are often different from the conscious recollections of the soul. The body has its own involuntary reactions, which often deviate from the person's conscious reactions and express something different. The body language of a human Gestalt is at least as complex and as effectual as its conscious and verbal language. The difference between verbal language and body language shows that a person's lived Gestalt is generally equivocal. This does not merely apply to the human Gestalt of particular people. It is equally true of the Gestalt of human organizations. The body language of the church, for example, does not always agree with the church's verbal proclamation, either because body language is not considered to be important, or because no consensus has been arrived at in the Gestalt.

A difficult question is the centring of the human person in the fields 'human being – environment' and 'body – soul'. Can we start from a self-evident, fixed structure of subjectivity, according to which the human being who is in the possession of reason and will is always 'master in his own house'? If we say that the human being is 'the ruling soul of his body, or he is not a human being', is he really and truly this, or only by definition? If it is only by virtue of the definition, then this is the definition of an ideal of what the person should be – an ideal on which the real person must often enough run aground. But if we instead see the human person in his living Gestalt, it is more realistic to expect that the centrations will shift and change. It is then fruitful, too, to see both the centrations and the decentrations as convergencies into a particular and determining self, and as the dissolution of these convergencies.

Centrations emerge on the basis of particular concerns, and represent these. If a certain concern dies away, the centration slackens, and the structure of reason and will which was built up to satisfy the concern disintegrates again. This does not mean that this inner personal centration can be described as merely secondary, let alone capricious. Human life is always concerned life, involved life, accepted and loved life. Consequently there is no human life without centrations. But these centrations are not rigid. They are not the same everywhere, at all times and with everyone. Moreover they are probably as a rule caught up into a certain rhythm of growth and dissolution; for what they represent is not an abstract person but a life history, which is to say a person in a quite specific sense. But just because the inner centrations represent the life history of specific persons, it is too little if we see them as merely developing and passing away in processes of 'self-realization', 'committing themselves spontaneously to satisfying contact processes, permitting their free development, and then letting them go again once satiation has been reached'.[41]

Just because the human being is a flexible being, and his centrations waver and change, he has to see to it that he is *dependable*, for other people and for himself. The human being is the being who can make promises. He can and will be, for himself and other people

– not, indeed, calculable (to use the language of today's political controllers); but he must try to make his constitutional equivocalness unequivocal. He does this in promising and in keeping the promise, in faithfulness. In his promise, a person commits himself, acquires a particular Gestalt, and makes himself someone who can be appealed to. Through faithfulness the person acquires his identity in time, because he remembers, and permits himself to be reminded, and recollects the promise he has given. It is in the historical link between promise and fulfilment of the promise that a person acquires his continuity. And it is only through this continuity that he finds his lived identity. If he remains true to his promise, he remains true to himself. If he breaks his promise, he is untrue to himself. If he keeps his promise, he wins trust. If he breaks it, he really loses his own identity, and no longer knows who he is. This identity of the person in his life-history is denoted through *his name*. Living together socially consists of a dense web of promises and fulfilments, compacts and dependabilities, and cannot exist without these structures of trust. The order within the human being himself can also be viewed as a web of conscious 'compacts' between his organs, and their generally unconscious harmonization. If the person is at one with himself – and that means at one with the needs and powers of his body – he forms an identity for himself and is worthy of trust. If he is not at one with himself, he is not identical with himself, and destroys his social dependability. The process whereby a person becomes a configuration or Gestalt is both inwardly and outwardly to be seen as a process of dependability and faithfulness. This view is not an infringement of the human being's liberty, for promise and trust are the specific forms which his liberty takes. They presuppose liberty, and unremittingly respect it.

3. *Spirit and Gestalt*

Through his Spirit, God the Creator calls his creatures into life, and in his Spirit he preserves and quickens them. This cosmic understanding of the Spirit also includes the anthropological understanding of the Spirit in the human being. But the anthropological understanding of the Spirit in human beings is dependent on the cosmic horizon. The modern understanding of spirit in the human being became narrow and one-sided when it lost sight of the spirit in nature and made spirit, or mind, the power which differentiates the human being from the nature that surrounds him and gives him a more elevated status. The modern understanding of the spirit in the human being became equally narrow and one-sided when it surrendered the view of the spirit in the body, and saw spirit only as 'mind': the capacity for reflection through which the human being can stand over against himself and differentiate himself from his body. If the spirit in the human being is once more to be integrated in the surrounding field of nature, and in his own embodiment, we must go back to the full and comprehensive concept of the cosmic Spirit.

We have called 'spirit' the forms of organization and communication of all open systems of matter and life.[42] It follows from this that the human being's consciousness is reflective spirit – a becoming aware of the organization of his body and his soul, and an awareness, too, of the vitally necessary forms of communication of the human organism in society and nature. Human embodiment is embodiment that is pervaded, quickened and formed by the creative Spirit: the human being is a *spirit-body*. The human being's soul – his feelings, ideas, intentions, and so forth – is a soul that is pervaded, quickened and formed by the creative Spirit: the human being is *spirit-soul*. The Gestalt of the human being, in which body and soul have become united, is a Gestalt formed by the creative Spirit: the human being is a *spirit-Gestalt*. But the Spirit whose efficacy forms body, soul and their living Gestalt is not merely the creative Spirit: he is at the same time the cosmic Spirit: for body, soul and their Gestalt can only exist in exchange with other living beings in nature and in human society.

This all applies to the human being, as well as to other living things, when we are considering the Spirit of creation, preservation and development. Theologically this Spirit must be called the Spirit of God and the presence of God in the creature he has made. But according to biblical usage, this is not the Holy Spirit. The Holy Spirit is the name given to the Spirit of redemption and sanctification – that is to say, to the presence of the redeeming and newly creating God. It is the Spirit of Christ and the Spirit of God, who allows Christ, the new human being, to be formed – to become Gestalt – in believers and in the fellowship of love (Phil. 2.6). 'The Holy Spirit' does not supersede the Spirit of creation but transforms it. The Holy Spirit therefore lays hold of the whole human being, embracing his feelings and his body as well as his soul and reason. He forms the whole Gestalt of the person anew by making believers 'con-form', or 'like in Gestalt' to Christ, the first-born among many brethren (Rom. 8.29). He embraces the whole 'lowly body' in order that it may 'be like (the) glorious body' of the risen Christ, who has overcome death (Phil. 3.21). It would be too narrow and one-sided if we were to try to relate the direct operation of the Holy Spirit only to the reasonable soul of the human being, and connect it with his embodiment only to the extent in which the soul ruled by the Spirit in its turn dominates its body. Where the Holy Spirit begins to 'leaven' the children of God (Rom. 8.14), he becomes the new fermenting power of their whole life. It is then not merely the verbal language of their reason which witnesses to his presence; it is their unconscious body language as well. It is not only their intentional and willed actions which show his liberating power, but also their unconscious actions and reactions. 'The redemption of the body' from death begins already here and now, in the liberation of the bodily nature which has been suppressed out of fear, with its stifled needs and powers. The *testimonium Spiritus Sancti internum* also enables the human being to give himself up to the instinct, the impulse and the guidance of the Holy Spirit: the Spirit is present and at work in the feelings and in the unconscious as well.

Paul emphatically stressed the bodily character of the Christ who is present in the Spirit. Remembering the persecutions which he has suffered as Christ's apostle, he says: 'We always carry *in the body* the death of Jesus, so that the life of Jesus may also be manifested *in our bodies*' (II Cor. 4.10). And to the Greek congregation in Corinth he propounded the totally un-Greek thesis: 'The body (belongs to) the Lord *and the Lord to the body* . . . Your body is a temple of the Holy Spirit' (I Cor. 6.13,19).

The bodily form which Christ takes and the bodily indwelling of the Holy Spirit are not 'the work' of the reason and will of the human subject. They are 'experienced' in the surrender of the whole person to God. They are also perceived more readily by other people than by the person involved, because it is not this person himself who 'testifies'; it is God who makes him a witness for others.

4. *Spirit as Anticipation*

All living things which we can describe as 'open systems' exist in the direction of their future. Their future is the scope of their open possibilities, a scope limited by their past and their environment. This means that their impulses, perceptions, ways of behaving and actions have an anticipatory character. This structure is most fully developed in the human being. When we talk about a person's spirit, we do not mean his reflective subjectivity, or his fixed, 'static' identity. We mean the anticipatory structure of his whole physical, mental and spiritual existence. People always live in a certain direction – the direction of something lying ahead of them. Consequently they continually cross the borders of their own present, projecting themselves towards the open possibilities of their future, and changing in the course of their historical existence. Of course the human being can be viewed as the subject of reason and will. Of course he can make himself the object of his cognition and his will. But this subjectivity and objectivity are secondary forms of reflection in the totality of his lived life. This totality shows itself in his alignment towards *the project* of his life. As a totality, a whole, concentrated in himself and yet at the same time open, the human being lives in the project of his future. 'This wholeness is the Spirit as the directional character of the human being.'[43]

It is in his movement, his intentions and his hope that the human being's spirit shows itself to be the spirit that animates his life. In the living alignment of his existence, the different sides of his organism harmonize – the physical, the mental and the spiritual. The human being always realizes himself in the light of his direction. He *is* in that he *becomes*. We can understand him if we understand the purpose of his life, his project. It is the *intentio vitalis* which gives his life meaning. If this is persistently disappointed, the person concerned, losing his orientation, will become ill. Without direction and without a future, the human being becomes 'distraught'; his senses break down and the unity of his being disintegrates. What people seek for, and their aim, is always reflected in the structure of their lives. The *history* of their lives takes its impress from what they *expect* of life. If this expectation is thwarted, their affirmation of life is affected too. If their essential hope in life is disappointed, inner rifts develop which often enough find expression in physical illness.

This 'directionality' of life is also shown in the structure of human thinking. All acts of human thought which have a reference to truth have an anticipatory form. And if we call these acts of thinking that are related to truth 'reason', we are then also saying that the essence of human reason is a kind of productive imaginative power.[44] Possibilities are explored and tried out in search images and provisional projects, in anticipations and proleptic realizations of future conditions. What is to be and what is not to be is then selected according to the wishes and fears of the underlying *intentio vitalis*.

These anticipations do not merely take place in the limited individual sphere. They occur much more strongly still in the realm of social communication. Here joint projects are recollected, devised and realized. Individual projects and directions in which to live are related to the corresponding social ones, and are conditioned by these. As long as people can distinguish past and future, and can recognize in the temporal dimension of the future the open scope of the possibilities ahead of them, we shall be able to interpret the anticipatory structure of their organism and their social organizations as 'spirit'. We can then also describe what happens when the spirit disappears and 'dis-spirited' conditions come into being: petrifications result which can lead to individual and collective death.

5. *Spirit as Communication*

Since we have termed the *anticipatory* structure of the human constitution 'spirit', we shall have to interpret its complementary structure of *communication* as spirit too. Human life is dependent on natural and social communication and only exists in such communication. Life is relationship. Life is exchange. 'It is only in exchange with what we are not, that we live; the prime example is the air which we breathe.'[45] This exchange creates community and is only possible in community. Human life is necessarily life in community. It is communication in communion. Human life is what happens *between* individuals. If we isolate individual human life from natural and social life, we kill it. That is why mutual participation is part of human life's very definition. We are failing to grasp these complexes properly if we start from the individual awareness of the spirit and consider that natural and social relationships are merely secondary. As against this individualistic misunderstanding of the spirit, we have to go to the other extreme, and maintain that spirit is whatever happens *between* people to promote and foster life.[46]

Friedrich Hölderlin already perceived this with particular clarity at the time when German Idealism was in its beginnings:

> Neither from himself alone nor solely from the objects that surround him can man experience that there is more to the world than mechanical process, and that the world contains a Spirit, a God. But it is indeed open to him to discern this in a more living relationship, elevated above the requirements of necessity – the relationship which he shares with that which surrounds him. And in this sense every man would have his own God, inasmuch as everyone has his own sphere, in which he acts and which he experiences; and it is only to the extent that several persons have a sphere in common in which they act and suffer as human beings – that is, elevated above the requirements of necessity – that they in the same measure share a common deity; and if there is a sphere in which all live simultaneously, and in which they feel bound to one another in a more than necessary relationship, there, but only in this measure, do they share a common deity.[47]

God the Spirit is 'the common deity' who binds human beings into higher life with one another and, in this common sphere, makes of them again particular individuals. For though the Spirit in the person is certainly 'the common spirit' animating the shared life, he also gives each separate person his own Gestalt and the right to his own unique individuality. The social character of the human being and his individuation are not antitheses. They are merely the two sides of the differentiating life process which we call spirit.

The 'common sphere' in which the 'common deity', the Spirit, is experienced has nothing to do with a mystical or collective self-dissolution of the human person. It consists of agreements and concurrences in which people become persons for the first time. It is not the reduction to the lowest common denominator which creates truly human community; it is the construction of complex forms of organization which allow and give people the degree of personal liberty and the opportunity to shape their lives to which they are entitled. To recognize this is important in the context of the structure of anticipation which I have described; for forms of communication must not be allowed to narrow down the scope of anticipation. A human society is imaginative and inventive in the people who belong to it. The reduction of individual people to examples and 'representatives' of society certainly guarantees the stable reproduction of that society; but by restricting its future it also restricts the society's potentialities for change; so in the long run the society itself will be destroyed. 'The species is conservative. The individual is the place where changes happen.'[48] In the life projects and life histories of individual people, a society experiments with its future. It develops its collective future project out of the fullness of experience drawn from the projects of individuals. So every 'spirited' and 'in-spirited' human society will develop into a democracy that is both anticipatory and participatory.[49] The future literally belongs to social forms of this kind.

6. *Spirit as the Affirmation of Life*

The humanity of human life apparently depends directly on the interest in life which we call love. Only a loved life is a life that can be experienced as human, as every child knows. Only a loving life, a life acepted and affirmed in love, can be lived as human, as every adult knows. The human being does not just live out his life passively from day to day. He is alive as human being to the degree in which he accepts his life, affirms it and animates it through his love. In this passionate affirmation the human being opens himself, with all his senses, for the happiness of life, and experiences the joy of living. But the more unreservedly and passionately he loves life, the more intensely he also experiences the pains of life. Love will make him capable of happiness and at the same time capable of suffering. This is also true of life and death: the more living the experience of life, the more deadly the experience of death. Only a loving life exposes itself to the wounds of disappointment, contradiction, sickness and death. So human beings experience their mortality, not from mere naked life as such, but only in life that is loved and loving. This is the insoluble paradox of human life: the more a person loves, the more intensely he experiences both life and death. It is the Spirit as love who differentiates happiness and pain, life and death so acutely. But if a person keeps back this love of life, or kills it, he will become insensitive to happiness and pain. Life and death will become a matter of indifference to him. He then becomes immortal – but he has never lived either; while in every act that affirms life, people become both alive and mortal.

As we have seen, the Platonic doctrine of the immortality of the soul draws a protective circle round the soul to shield it from death.

But it is only 'the protective circle of the Not-Yet-Living', for it is not the life lived in the body but the life unlived in the body that becomes unassailable by bodily death. In the parable of the grain of wheat, the New Testament describes the relationship between life and death very differently: 'Unless a grain of wheat falls into the earth and dies, it remains alone; but if it dies, it bears much fruit' (John 12.24). Luke says the same thing about the soul: 'Whoever shall seek to save his soul shall lose it; and whoever shall lose his soul shall preserve it' (17.33). And Paul declares: 'What is sown is perishable, what is raised is imperishable. It is sown in dishonour, it is raised in glory. It is sown in weakness, it is raised in power. It is sown a physical body, it is raised a spiritual body' (I Cor. 15.42–44).[50] The first thing to notice about this image is the infertility of the life that is not lived, and which is therefore not mortal either. If the grain of wheat does not fall into the ground – that is, unless it is given up and dies – it remains 'alone'. It remains unfruitful. What this intends to say is that there is *a death before life*. It is the life that is held back – not lived, not committed life. The 'remaining alone' is the death that is meaningless because it is hopeless. If life is lived in embodiment and if it is committed in its earthly context, it becomes vulnerable and mortal. But because it is spent, it brings fruit. The death which this life experiences is a fruitful and therefore a meaningful death.

The secret of human life is easy to understand: anyone who wants to keep his life, and therefore holds on to it and keeps it back, will lose it; he already loses it by becoming incapable of living. But anyone who lives his life and commits it and surrenders it, will gain that life; he already gains it by becoming alive. Keeping his life means withdrawing his soul from the body, withdrawing his interest from life in the body, 'keeping himself to himself' and, out of the sheer remembrance that he has to die, not daring to live at all. Anyone who holds himself back like this does not become immortal. He remains dead. Surrendering one's life means going out of oneself, exposing oneself, committing oneself and loving. In this affirmation life becomes alive in the truly human sense. Anyone who lives like this will be mortal, but he dies meaningfully. Life that is never lived cannot die. But life that is truly and fully affirmed can die. Dying belongs to the lived life and is part of it.

If we talk about the Spirit of life in this affirmation of happiness and pain, life and death, we are saying that in this life there is already a life that is in fact immortal, eternal. It is not the life that is kept back and unlived. On the contrary, it is the life that is lived wholly and without reserve. In the Old Testament the Spirit is understood as the divine energy of life, the creative Spirit of life. In the New Testament the Spirit is described as the power of the resurrection. This life-giving Spirit is experienced in this life in unconditioned and unconditional love. This means that unconditioned and unconditional love is also certain of the resurrection of the dead. In the Spirit of the resurrection, eternal life is experienced here and now, in the midst of the life that leads to death: it is experienced as unconditional love. There is an eternal life before death.

A life lived in the divine power of the resurrection does not die. It is transformed through death into eternal life after death. For the eternal life of God revealed in the death and the resurrection of Christ is manifest here in the surrender of love, and there in the resurrection of the dead. Human life and human death participate in the divine life and are raised into it (Rom. 14.7–9). Wherever the divine Spirit of the resurrection becomes alive in us and we perceive him, duration without transience already begins, and eternity is experienced in the present moment. Human life is then so intensely alive that death disappears. This experience of eternal life in the Spirit of the resurrection is reflected in the experience of human life in the spirit of affirmation, which leads into the joys of life and into the pains of death. In the hope of being raised from the dead the human being can here live wholly and die wholly. In expectation of the transfiguration of the body, he can be wholly present in our bodily existence. The life of the Spirit, says Hegel rightly, 'is not one that shuns death and keeps clear of destruction. It endures its death and in death maintains its being'.[51]

§3 LIFE IN HEALTH AND SICKNESS

I cannot end this chapter on human embodiment without a critical comment on the view of health and sickness which is current at the present day. The understanding of what counts as 'healthy' at a particular time in a particular society changes considerably in the history of civilization. It reflects the system of received values in the society in question, and serves the adaptation of the human body to the demands of that society. But this does not mean that these ideas of 'health' are necessarily healthy in themselves. They can also alienate the human body and make it sick. Conversely, the reactions of human bodies to the standards of 'health' imposed on them are often enough healthy at the very points where they count as 'sick'. This means that we cannot measure 'health' merely against the system of values of the particular society in question. We also have to note the agreement and the contradictions between the bodily Gestalt of human beings and their social environment. 'Health' must be defined in several different dimensions if the concept of health is to be conducive to the life of human beings. It must find its definition in the flux of the history between person and society, society and nature, past and future, immanence and transcendence.

Sigmund Freud and many others defined health as the capacity for work and for enjoyment. If a person's capacity for work is diminished, and his capacity for pleasure impaired, he counts as ill. Once both these capacities have been restored he can he dismissed from medical treatment as 'healthy'. This simplistic but very generally employed definition of health is precisely in line with industrial society, whose central values are aligned towards production and consumption. Pre-industrial societies once had other ideas of health, and non-European societies still have. This emerges particularly clearly with the spread of Western medicine in African societies.[52]

The World Health Organization has propounded an expanded, modern definition of 'health': 'Health is a state of complete physical, mental and social well-being, not merely the absence of sickness and handicaps.' This is a maximum definition. It presents health as an ideal which – at least where 'social well-being' is concerned – can be achieved not merely by individuals but also by the society in which these individuals live. Measured against this ideal, only a few people – and even these few only seldom – will be able to call themselves 'healthy'. Measured against this ideal, there are no healthy societies which can guarantee their members the state of general well-being. On the basis of this ideal of 'health', the claims made by individuals on the health system and the medical care of a society are growing to the point where they simply cannot be fulfilled. The result is an excessive estimate of medicine, and permanently excessive demands on doctors.

'Health' as an ideal of the undisturbed functioning of the physical organs, an existence free of conflict, and a state of general well-being, is a utopia, and not a particularly humane utopia at that. It is the utopia of a life without suffering, happiness without pain, and a community without conflicts. Fundamentally speaking it is the ancient utopia of the immortal, eternal life; for only a life of that kind could logically be thought of as a 'state' of well-being like this.

If this condition is called health, then to be a person in the fullest sense of the word is to be healthy. In this case, every impairment of the state of general well-being must be viewed as an impairment of the state of being human. And then everyone must have a claim to the appropriate medical care. 'Health' becomes a human right to which everyone is entitled. It is quite true that health is a fundamental human right. It is part of the right to live, and is correctly advanced against the use of torture in the context of the claim to freedom from mental and physical harm. But the 'state' of general well-being does not take in the strength to be human itself; it merely ties that strength down to an unattainable condition. If we wanted to adhere to this definition of health, therapy for the body would have to be expanded by psychotherapy and social therapy. Not least, a political therapy would have to be developed in order to make this state of well-being possible. The proposals for expanding clinical medicine do in fact tend in this direction.[53] But they evoke contradiction, with the reminder that this would inevitably lead to the complete deprivation of a person's rights over his own health. If someone makes over to the medical system of his society his rights to his own health, he is really reverting to the state of serfdom – for which the German word *Leibeigenschaft* (property rights over a person's 'body') is a precise definition. So must not a counter-movement be initiated, to rescue the humanity of the people concerned? Must there not be a personalization of the health which has been socially expropriated, so that human beings can be called 'healthy' in a human sense? In view of the spread of iatrogenic illnesses, a personalization of health, and a stronger personal responsibility on the part of the individual person, would be more conducive to his 'well-being'. But this suggestion leads to different definitions of health.[54]

Health can be viewed as an objectively ascertainable *state* of the human being's physical, mental and social well-being (Health A).

But health can also be viewed as a subjectively ascertainable *attitude* on the part of the person concerned to his fluctuating condition. This is the direction in which more modern definitions of health tend: 'Health is the term for the process of adaptation . . .

the capacity to adapt to a changing milieu, to become older, to recover one's health, to suffer, to await death in peace.' Health is then 'the ability to cope with pain, sickness and death autonomously'.[55] To put it more simply: 'Health is not the absence of malfunctionings. Health is the strength to live with them.'[56] In this case, health is not, either, a state of general well-being; it is 'the strength to be human' (Health B).[57]

If we take up these personally related definitions of health, then a person can have healthy attitudes (B) to his health (A) and his illnesses; and he can have morbid attitudes to his states of health and sickness. The strength to be human is displayed in the person's capacity for happiness *and* suffering, in his acceptance of life's joy *and* the grief of death.

If health as a state of general well-being is declared to be the supreme value in a human life and in a society, this really implies a morbid attitude to health. Being human is equated with being healthy. This leads to the suppression of illness in the individual life, and means that the sick are pushed out of the life of society and kept out of the public eye. To turn the idea of health into an idol in this way is to rob the human being of the true strength of his humanity. Every serious illness which he has to suffer plunges him into a catastrophe, robs him of his confidence in life, and destroys his sense of his own value.

But if we understand health as the strength to be human, then we make being human more important than the state of being healthy. Health is not the meaning of human life. On the contrary, a person has to prove the meaning he has found in his own life in conditions of health *and* sickness. Only what can stand up to both health *and* sickness, and ultimately to living *and* dying, can count as a valid definition of what it means to be human.

Severe illnesses often lead to crises in personal life, crises which are really crises of significance. The sick person no longer understands what his life is about. The illness withdraws the basis of confidence on which his life has hitherto depended, and on which he has relied. He reacts with aggression towards other people, and rage towards himself. When he senses that he can no longer base his confidence on his health, and can no longer make his sense of his own value depend on his own performance and his pleasures, then he either breaks down, or he finds the strength for a greater confidence and a deeper respect for himself. A crisis triggered off by a severe illness offers the chance to free the confidence of the heart from the foundations that are threatened and have been withdrawn, and to base it on firm ground. The self-righteousness which is brought into play through the vanity of good works and pride in one's own achievements, is innocuous compared with the self-righteousness which is built up through trust in one's own health and the anxious cult of that health.

The modern cult of health produces precisely what it wants to overcome: fear of illness. Instead of overcoming illness and infirmity, it projects a state of well-being which excludes the sick, the handicapped, and the old who are close to death. In turning away from these people, the healthy condemn them to social death. What is supposed to minister to the healthy life becomes death for the people who are excluded from it. The definition of health put forward by the World Health Organization is open to such misunderstanding because it talks only about illness and infirmity, but not about death. But without the remembrance of dying, every definition of health is illusory.

If we start from health as the strength to be human, we must not merely bring this strength to bear on the illusory notions of the modern cult of health; we must discover it still more in sickness and in dying. Here it is helpful if we do not view illness in a single dimension, as a malfunctioning of particular organs, but if we look at the sick person himself. Of course certain illnesses are also due to the malfunctioning of particular organs, and have to be treated as such. But severe and long-lasting illnesses affect the whole person. They affect him in at least four dimensions.

1. *In his relationship to himself:* the sick person experiences himself in a new way. He is no longer at one with himself. He has to find himself anew.

2. *In his social relationships:* to be ill generally means a disturbance of social relationships, loss of human attention, the experience of isolation, etc. The sick person has to learn his new role first of all, just as the people closest to him have to adjust to him in a new way.

3. *In his life history:* sickness and infirmity evoke a conflict between the person's project in life and his experience of life. Often enough,

being ill means burying hopes. The sick person then undergoes experiences of parting and a foretaste of death.

4. *In the relationship to the transcendent sphere:* suffering calls in question the sense, and also the nonsense, of the sick person's life. Severe suffering often makes human life seem meaningless. But severe suffering also often reveals the nonsense of normal life. In this respect illnesses and lasting suffering can lead to crises of basic trust.

Illness, that is to say, is experienced as a malfunctioning of the organs of the body, as a shaking of personal confidence, as loss of social contacts, as a crisis of life itself, and as loss of significance. This means that the healing of a sick person cannot be viewed in a single dimension. It must take into account the four human dimensions of the sick person which we have described, and in all these strengthen and renew the capacity to be a human person. What we have described here as 'the strength to be a human person' is nothing other than *love*, which is what we in the previous section called the Spirit as the affirmation of life.

It is difficult to define human life in such a way that certain essential sides of it are not denied and excluded, but so that human life can develop in every direction in all its fullness. The definitions which we can offer in closing are minimum definitions:

Human life is accepted, affirmed and loved life.

The strength to be a human person lies in the acceptance, the affirmation and the love of frail and mortal life.

Seen in the light of this strength for living, dying is not an end, and death is not 'the separation of the soul from the body', or the ultimate 'lack of relationship'. It is a transition to a different kind of being, and a metamorphosis into a different Gestalt.

The human being in his embodiment is not created to end in death; he is made for transformation through and beyond death. Hope for the resurrection of the body and a life everlasting in redemption corresponds to the bodily creation of the human being by God, and perfects that. The hope of resurrection is belief in creation that gazes forward to what is ahead.[58]

XI

The Sabbath: The Feast of Creation

The goal and completion of every Jewish and every Christian doctrine of creation must be the doctrine of the sabbath; for on the sabbath and through the sabbath God 'completed' his creation, and on the sabbath and through it, men and women perceive as God's creation the reality in which they live and which they themselves are. The sabbath opens creation for its true future. On the sabbath the redemption of the world is celebrated in anticipation. The sabbath is itself the presence of eternity in time, and a foretaste of the world to come. The observance of the sabbath became the identifying mark of Jews in exile; and in the same way, the doctrine of the sabbath of creation becomes the identifying mark of the biblical doctrine of creation, distinguishing it from the interpretation of the world as nature. It is the sabbath which manifests the world's identity as creation, sanctifies it and blesses it.[1]

Curiously enough, in the Christian traditions, and especially the traditions of the Western church, creation is generally only presented as 'the six days' work'. The 'completion' of creation through 'the seventh day' is much neglected, or even overlooked altogether. It would seem as if Christian theology considered that both the sabbath commandment to Israel and the sabbath of creation were repealed and discarded when Jesus set aside the sabbath commandment by healing the sick on that day. As a result, God is viewed as the one who in his essential being is solely 'the creative God', as Paul Tillich says; and it follows from this that men and women too can only see themselves as this God's image if they become 'creative human beings'. The God who 'rests' on the sabbath, the blessing and rejoicing God, the God who delights in his creation, and in his exultation sanctifies it, recedes behind this different concept. So for men and women too, the meaning of their lives is identified with work and busy activity; and rest, the feast, and their joy in existence are pushed away, relegated to insignificance because they are non-utilitarian.

But according to the biblical traditions creation and the sabbath belong together. It is impossible to understand the world properly as creation without a proper discernment of the sabbath. In the sabbath stillness men and women no longer intervene in the environment through their labour. They let it be entirely God's creation.[2] They recognize that as God's property creation is inviolable; and they sanctify the day through their joy in existence as God's creatures within the fellowship of creation.

The peace of the sabbath is peace with God first of all. But this divine peace encompasses not merely the soul but the body too; not merely individuals but family and people; not only human beings but animals as well; not living things alone, but also, as the creation story tells us, the whole creation of heaven and earth. That is why the sabbath peace is also the beginning of that peace with nature which many people are seeking today, in the face of the growing destruction of the environment. But there will never be peace with nature without the experience and celebration of God's sabbath.

If we look at the biblical traditions that have to do with the belief in creation, we discover that the sabbath is not a day of rest following six working days. On the contrary: the whole work of creation was performed *for the sake of the sabbath*. The sabbath is 'the feast of creation', as Franz Rosenzweig says.[3] It was for the sake of this feast-day of the eternal God that heaven and earth were created, with everything that exists in them and lives. So although the creation story tells us that each day was followed by a night, God's sabbath knows no night but becomes the 'feast without end'.[4]

The feast of creation is the feast of completion or consummation – the consummation of creation which is realized through this feast. Because this consummation of creation in the sabbath also represents creation's redemption – the redemption enabling it to participate in God's manifested, eternal presence – it will also be permissible for us to understand the sabbath as the feast of redemption. But if, as the feast of creation, it is also already the feast of creation's redemption, it is understandable that the whole of creation should have been brought into being for the sake of that redemption. 'The sabbath is the feast of creation', writes Franz Rosenzweig, 'but a creation which took place for the sake of the redemption. It is manifested at the end of creation, and manifested as creation's meaning and destination.'[5]

We shall now look at the individual elements of the sabbath as the Jewish understanding of God's revelation comprehends them, and shall then use these as a point of departure from which to work out the messianic elements of the sabbath which emerge from the Christian understanding of God's revelation. For it is from this, ultimately, that the long-neglected problem about the connection between Sunday and the sabbath arises.

§1 THE COMPLETION OF CREATION

According to the creation narrative in the Priestly Writing, the creation of the world ended on the sixth day: 'And God saw everything that he had made, and behold, it was very good' (Gen. 1.31). And yet: 'On the seventh day God *finished* his work which he had done' (Gen. 2.2). What did he add to his 'very good' creation on the sabbath? What did the finished creation still lack? In what does the completion of creation consist? It consists in *God's rest.* It is a completion through rest.[6] Out of God's rest spring the blessing and sanctification of the seventh day. The work of creation is completed through the Creator's rest, his creative activity is completed through his blessing, and his work through his sanctification of the sabbath. Exodus 31.17 adds after God's rest that 'he drew a breath of relief'. That is a very strange way of 'completing' a work.

Let us first of all try to understand the metaphors used. What is called 'God's rest' is a rest '*from* all his work which he had done' (Gen. 2.3). The Creator stands aside from his creative activity and confronts his works. In doing this he also comes to himself again, as it were, and is wholly concentrated in himself, after he had gone out of himself in his creative activity and was wholly with his creation. In his creative activity he was free *for* his works, which are in accordance with himself; in his sabbath rest he becomes free *from* his works again, and returns to himself. Is this a return to the eternal being before the creation of the world and human beings?[7] It is certainly a cessation from creating, and hence a quiescence in himself; but it is not a return to the world-less, eternal glory which precedes creation and out of which God creatively acts. The God who rests on the sabbath is the Creator who rests from his creation. After creation he comes to himself again – only not without his creation but with it. So his rest becomes at the same time the rest of his creation; and his good pleasure in his creation becomes the joy of created things themselves.

God rests 'from his works' on the sabbath, but in doing so he at the same time rests *in face* of his works. This means that he has not merely created and made creation; he also lets his creation exist before his face and co-exist with himself: a finite, temporal world co-exists with the infinite, eternal God. So the world is not merely created *by* God; it also exists *before* God and lives *with* God. By coming to his rest, God lets his creation be what it is on its own account. In his present rest all created beings come to themselves and unfold their own proper quality. In his rest they all acquire their essential liberty. By 'resting' from his creative and formative activity, he allows the beings he has created, each in its own way, to act on him. He receives the form and quality their lives take, and accepts the effects these lives have. By standing aside from his creative influence, he makes himself wholly receptive for the happiness, the suffering and the praise of his creatures. In the works of creation, created beings, through their existence and their modality, 'experience' the power and wisdom of God. But on the sabbath the resting God begins to 'experience' the beings he has created. The God who rests in face of his creation does not dominate the world on this day: he 'feels' the world; he allows himself to be affected, to be touched by each of his creatures. He adopts the community of creation as his own milieu. In his rest he is close to the movement of them all. This closeness of his in the sabbath does not neutralize the tensions in creation, nor does it do away with the possible opposition of created things to the Creator and to themselves; but it thrusts towards their transformation to correspondence and to identity. With God's sabbath of creation, his history with the world begins, and the world's history with God.

Finally, God does not merely 'rest from' his works, or rest only in face of his works. He also rests *in* his works. He allows them to exist in his presence. And he is present in their existence. The resting God is wholly present as the one who he is in himself; but he is present with and in his creation. If he finds rest in face of the works of his creation, then he also finds the rest *in* the works of his creation.

Otherwise his infinite Being would have to drive him beyond his finite creation and, in the face of his limited creation, make him eternally restless. The sabbath of God's creation already contains in itself the redemptive mystery of God's indwelling in his creation, although – and just because – he is wholly concentrated in himself and rests in himself. The works of creation display in God's acts the Creator's continual transcendence over his creation. But the sabbath of creation points to the Creator's immanence in his creation.[8] In the sabbath God joins his eternal presence to his temporal creation and, by virtue of his rest, is there, with that creation and in it. He rests wholly in himself and is, as himself, in his creation wholly there. The sabbath is the day when God is present. That is why sabbath is also one of the divine names.

So what does creation lack before the sabbath? What does the sabbath add to creation? We can sum this up by saying that the completion of activity is rest, and the completion of doing is simple existence. Creation is God's work, but the sabbath is God's present existence. His works express God's will, but the sabbath manifests his Being. In his works God goes out of himself; in the sabbath of creation he comes to himself. So the mystery of the sabbath is a profounder mystery than the mystery of the work of creation. God is present in the sabbath stillness, just as for Elijah on Horeb, the mount of God, God was in 'the voice of a hovering silence' (Buber's translation). The works of creation show God exoterically and indirectly, as it were, as the Creator. But the sabbath, in its peace and its silence, manifests the eternal God at once esoterically and directly as the God who rests in his glory. Creation can be seen as God's revelation of his works; but it is only the sabbath that is the revelation of God's self. That is why the works of creation flow into the sabbath of creation. That is why the sabbath of creation is already the beginning of the kingdom of glory – the hope and the future of all created being. Because the sabbath of creation is *God's* sabbath, and because in his rest his eternal glory becomes present, every human sabbath becomes 'a dream of completion', as Franz Rosenzweig says.[9] And when men and women rest from their human works, this becomes a fore-token of the eternal feast of the divine glory. The sabbath is not a day of creation; it is 'the Lord's day'.

§2 THE BLESSING OF CREATION

God blessed the sabbath because on it he rested from all his work which he had done in creation (Gen. 2.3). According to the creation account in the Priestly Writing, blessing is always something extra – something added to creation.[10] Both after the creation of the great beasts of the sea (Gen. 1.22) and after the creation of human beings (Gen. 1.28), God confers blessing, and he links this blessing of animals and human beings with the command to be fruitful. The creation of living things is God's act alone, but their fertility and increase issue from their own power. According to the language of the biblical writer, this is not 'procreation' – a 'creating forth' or continuation of the divine creation. It is an independent power of reproduction belonging to these created beings themselves. The Creator gives this his blessing. That is to say, he affirms the potency of these creatures of his and accepts their independent power of increase. He allows it to succeed and seals it with the approval of his presence.

But what is blessed on the sabbath is not any living thing, but a time: the seventh day. This is remarkable, for a time is not an object, nor is it a counterpart of God. A time is invisible. It is impossible to picture it. A time is also transitory, according to our human view of things; we cannot hold on to it. What does it mean, when God blesses a time – the seventh day – and how are we to understand this 'blessed' time?

The blessing of the sabbath differs from the blessing of created beings, because God blesses it, not through his activity but through his repose. This means that we too must not expect that through his blessing the potency of anything created will be increased, and that its activity will be crowned with success. Blessing that is grounded in the tranquillity of the sabbath, and blessing given on that account, is something incomparable and unique. Here the Creator does not impart to his creatures a degree of independent power; here the resting God imparts to the day of his rest the power to allow all his creatures to find rest. He gives this day its particular quality through his complete, though reposing, presence. The sabbath rest (*menuha*) is not a created grace; it is the uncreated grace of God's presence for the whole creation. Because it is the seventh day for his whole creation and all his creatures, through his reposing presence he imparts the sabbath blessing to everything he has made.

In his rest all created beings find their own rest. In the presence of his existence is the blessing of their existence. Everything that is made has been called by the Creator from non-being into being. Everything that exists is menaced by non-being, for it can again be made a nothingness. That is why everything that *is*, is restless and on the search for a place where this menace cannot reach it – for a 'resting place'. It is not merely the human heart which is 'restless until it finds rest in Thee', as Augustine said. The whole creation is filled with this same unrest, and transcends itself in the search for the rest in which it can abide.

The resting place it looks for is not the world beyond, or heaven, or God himself, as the gnostics and the mystics have always maintained. It is God's sabbath. In the resting, and hence direct, unmediated presence of God, all created beings find their dwelling. In the resting presence of God all creatures find their sustaining foundation. The sabbath preserves created things from obliteration, and fills their restless existence with the happiness of the presence of the eternal God. On the sabbath all creatures find their own place in the God who is wholly present. The world is created 'out of nothing', and it is created 'for the sabbath'; so on the sabbath it exists 'in' God's presence. This is the sabbath blessing. It does not spring from God's activity; it springs from his rest. It does not come from God's acts; it comes from his present Being. Consequently God does not confer the sabbath blessing on some activity or other pursued by the beings he has created. It is a blessing given to their whole existence. Because created beings can be wholly present in the reposing presence of his existence, the sabbath blessing wakens the joy in existence of all creatures, unhindered and unclouded. This also makes the repose of the sabbath the prefiguration of redemption, which the Epistle to the Hebrews calls 'entering God's rest': 'There remains a sabbath rest for the people of God; for whoever enters God's rest also ceases from his labours as God did from his' (Heb. 4.9–10). The Book of Revelation (14.13) also talks about 'the blessed dead' who 'rest from their labours, for their works follow them'.

God does not bless one of his creatures. He blesses a day. By blessing the seventh day, he makes it a blessing for all created beings that experience that day. This means that the sabbath blessing is universal, whereas the blessing given to one or the other creature remains particular and special to them.

God created everything in twos, says a wise old Jewish saying: day and night, heaven and earth, light and darkness, man and woman, and other things as well. Only the sabbath is solitary. It is an 'uneven' day. Where is its partner? According to this idea, the sabbath of creation is an 'uneven' day because it is related to the whole 'six days' work'. It is the day belonging to all these days of creation. The blessing of this seventh day makes it the blessing of all the days of creation.

The sabbath of human time is related to Israel, said Jewish wisdom, interpreting the sabbath's uneven and special existence. The sabbath is 'Israel's sister' and Israel is 'her brother'. The sabbath is Israel's 'bride': 'Come, O bride, come Queen Sabbath'. But when it celebrates its sabbaths in history, Israel is celebrating the mystery of the sabbath of creation, as the prayers for the sabbath eve make clear. Through the feast of 'the seventh day', Israel experiences and diffuses the blessing of the whole creation through the reposing presence of God, which gives enduring being to all things. That is why Israel's sabbath has cosmic dimensions and gives Israel a special place in creation, just as it provides the ground for Israel's special existence.

§3 THE SANCTIFICATION OF CREATION

God 'hallowed' the sabbath because 'on it he rested from all his work which he had done in creation' (Gen. 2.3). Here for the first time in the biblical traditions we find the word 'hallow'. To hallow or sanctify means, roughly speaking, choosing or electing, separating off for oneself, declaring something to be one's own property and inviolable.[11] Significantly enough, the word is not applied either to a creature or to a space in creation; it is kept for a time, the seventh day. Again, one might say that the sanctification of any creature or space would be particular, whereas the sanctification of the sabbath benefits all created things on the seventh day; that is to say, it is universal.

But the sanctification of this time is singular in another way too. If what is sanctified is a time, and not a special domain, a mountain or a place, the result is a curious view of the world; for the world is then viewed predominantly in terms of time, in events and sequences of events, in generations and histories, not in spaces and regions. Is Judaism the religion of time, as Abraham Heschel maintained?[12] Is the sabbath the Jewish cathedral, Judaism's holy mountain? Spaces, precincts and domains are distributed according to power and possession, but time is the same for everyone, because it is there for everyone. In the temple, heaven and earth touch, according to the archaic view. According to the Jewish view, in the sabbath eternity and time touch. When the sabbath is sanctified, a time is sanctified which is there for the whole creation. When the sabbath is celebrated, it is celebrated for all created being. The primary orientation towards time, which is grounded in the sanctification of the sabbath, seems breathtaking to peoples whose cultures are aligned to holy places and divine precincts.

Other religions represent the divine in images – Israel in time; the sabbath is the presence of God without pictures or figuration. Other relations delineate the cosmogony in cultic dramas. Israel knows no imitation of creation; it knows only participation in God's sabbath rest through the sanctification of the sabbath. The sabbath quiet is diametrically opposite to all the notions and cultic imitations of struggles between the gods out of which the world emerges. 'Whereas the closed space full of forms is the sphere of Greek truth, Israel's is the open, formless flow of time. There we have the circle of the cosmos, returning to itself again – here the line of creation, striving towards infinity; there the world of seeing and beholding – here the world of hearing and perceiving; there image and parable – here decision and act. . . . In space there is presence and remembrance; in time there is danger and hope.' That is Margarete Susman's apposite description of this singular 'religion of time'.[13]

All the Jewish feasts take up the phenomena celebrated in the nature festivals – seedtime and harvest, the summer and the winter solstice. But they pour into them the remembrance of the events of the salvation history to which Israel owes her existence and her calling. Old Testament theology has often stressed this remarkable proceeding, which came about in the transition from nomadic to settled life in the land of promise.[14] But we do not find the sabbath only in salvation history (the interpretation of the manna story (Exod. 16) is certainly a later interpolation). The sabbath belongs to the fundamental structure of creation itself. That is why the sabbath is Israel's most sacred time – holier than all the other feasts.

The Deuteronomistic version (Deut. 5.15) gives the Exodus tradition as reason for keeping the sabbath: 'You shall remember that you were a servant in the land of Egypt, and the Lord your God brought you out thence with a mighty hand and an outstretched arm; therefore the Lord your God commanded you to keep the sabbath day.' But the version in the Priestly Document (Exod. 20.11) gives the story of creation itself as foundation: '. . . and rested on the seventh day; therefore the Lord blessed the sabbath day and hallowed it.' The difference and the parallels in the reasons given for the sabbath and the sabbath commandment draw into a single perspective the exodus experience and belief in creation, making it clear that the God of the exodus is the Creator of the world, and that God the Creator is also the God of the exodus.

The sabbath is not related to the moon either. The seven-day week is certainly known elsewhere, but the sabbath is defined simply by the creation story, not by any natural cycle. The sabbath is Israel's holiest time, because it is the first thing that God sanctified: holy is God and holy is his Name, sanctified is the sabbath, sanctified is the people, and sanctified is the land of Israel. The sanctification is in that order. The sabbath comes before people and land.

The sabbath commandment given to Israel (Exod. 20.8–11) is the longest of the ten commandments, and it is therefore considered to be the most important.[15] God sanctified the sabbath because on that day he rested from creation; so his people are to sanctify it too. Everyone is to sanctify it, parents and children, masters and servants, human beings and animals, Israel's own people and strangers. The sabbath is an order of peace for everyone. It is impossible to celebrate and enjoy it at the cost of other people. The feast can only be celebrated and enjoyed together with all the others. If human beings are to 'have dominion' over the animals (Gen 1.26), here animals are to enjoy the sabbath too. Later on, the sabbath year is extended to the earth as well: it is to remain free from human cultivation for a year (Lev. 25.11). People sanctify the sabbath by abstaining from every kind of productive work, and by recognizing the whole of reality as God's creation – the creation from which, in face of which, and within which he himself rested. The human beings who rest on the sabbath day, and who in their rest are wholly present, are God's image. Just as the sabbath is sanctified by God's resting presence, so men and women also sanctify the sabbath through their recollection of their existence, and their grateful expression of that existence.

Existence precedes activity. So activity ends in simply being present. The reposeful existence which has found enduring being in the presence of God excels efficaciousness. The celebration of the sabbath leads to an intensified capacity for perceiving the loveliness of everything – food, clothing, the body and the soul – because existence itself is glorious. Questions about the possibility of 'producing' something, or about utility, are forgotten in the face of the beauty of all created things, which have their meaning simply in their very selves.

Sanctifying the sabbath means being entirely free from the striving for happiness and from the will for performance and achievement. It means being wholly present in the presence of God. The sabbath is sanctified through God alone – through grace alone – through trust alone. The peace of the sabbath can be viewed as the Jewish 'doctrine of justification'. Anyone who looks at Israel on the sabbath cannot reproach her with a 'righteousness of works'. And on the other hand, Christian faith in justification must be understood analogously as 'the sabbath rest' of Christians.

When the Reformed catechisms of the sixteenth and seventeenth centuries define 'the chief end' of human beings as 'to glorify God and to enjoy him forever', this applies pre-eminently to the sabbath. But because it applies explicitly to the sabbath, it interpenetrates the whole of everyday life and all the labours of the world.

The sabbath commandment given to men and women divides up human time. It brings interruption, interval and rhythm into human temporal experience. But of course all the other 'festal' divisions of time do this too. What is special about the sabbath commandment is, on the one hand, *the remembrance* of God's eternal sabbath of creation, from which the command to sanctify the sabbath springs; and, on the other, *the promise* of the eternal sabbath of the messianic era. This means that though, formally speaking, the sabbath belongs to the cycle of human time, its nature allows it to break through the cyclical rebirth of natural time by prefiguring the messianic time. The sabbath is part of the cycle of the week, and yet, by virtue of the promise which, in the mode of anticipation, it already fulfils, it is the sign of the coming freedom from time's cyclical course. The sabbath stands in time, but it is more than time, for it both veils and discloses an eternal surplus of meaning.

By stopping interference with nature for one day, time is elimin-

> ated; where there is no change, no work, no human interference, there is no time. Instead of a Sabbath on which man bows down to the Lord of time, the biblical Sabbath symbolizes man's victory over time. Time is suspended; Saturn is dethroned on his very day, Saturn's day. Death is suspended and life rules on the Sabbath day.[16]

On the sabbath day recollection of God's creation sabbath and the promise of the messianic era lead beyond the day itself, and on that day burst apart the law of time. This makes the human sabbath the rhythm of eternity in time, and the presence in history of the future world of glory.

Israel has given the nations two archetypal images of liberation: the exodus and the sabbath. The exodus from slavery into the land of liberty is the symbol of external freedom; it is efficacious, operative. The sabbath is the symbol of inner liberty; it is rest and quietude. The exodus is the elemental experience of God's history. The sabbath is the elemental experience of God's creation. The exodus is the elemental experience of the God who acts. The sabbath is the elemental experience of the God who is, and is present. No political, social and economic exodus from oppression, degradation and exploitation really leads to the liberty of a humane world without the sabbath, without the relinquishment of all works, without the serenity that finds rest in the presence of God. But the reverse is also true: men and women never find the peace of the sabbath in God's presence unless they find liberation from dependency and repression, inhumanity and godlessness. So exodus and sabbath are indivisible. They are the necessary complements of one another. They wither and do not lead to freedom if they are once divided, and if we attempt to make only one of them the foundation for the experience of liberty.

§4 THE FEAST OF REDEMPTION

We have to understand the sabbath as the consummation of creation – the completion given through the reposeful presence of the Creator in what he has created. This divine presence is the first revelation of God in his creation. It is not a revelation through creative activity; it is a revelation through rest. It is not an indirect and mediated revelation; it is a revelation direct and unmediated. If we combine the two – the sabbath as the completion of creation and the sabbath as the revelation of God's reposing existence in his creation – then these two elements point beyond the sabbath itself to a future in which God's creation and his revelation will be one. That is redemption.[17] We therefore have to understand redemption as both 'the eternal sabbath' and 'the new creation'. When 'the whole earth is full of his glory' (Isa. 6.3), when God is 'all in all' (I Cor. 15.28 AV) and when God 'dwells' in his whole creation (Rev. 21.3), then creation and revelation are truly one. God is then manifest in the whole creation, and the whole creation is the manifestation and mirror of his glory: that is the redeemed world.

It is true that both the sabbath of God's creation and Israel's sabbath commandment initially have a retrospective significance; for the sabbath follows six days' labour and crowns the completed work. On the sabbath we can really say, 'All's well that ends well'. The Jewish sabbath is also tuned to the note of the completion of work, and thanks for the Creator's gifts and for the goodness of his creation. The celebration of the Jewish sabbath communicates the wisdom of existence and age. The famous image with which Hegel describes the nature of philosophy can very well be applied to the sabbath: 'As the thought of the world, it does not appear until reality has completed its formative process, and made itself ready . . . The owl of Minerva takes its flight only when the shades of night are gathering.'[18]

Yet in this retrospective, completing and tranquillizing character, the sabbath at the same time conceals an unheard-of promise for the future. For the sabbath, which is for the whole creation, opens that creation for the coming kingdom of God. It is not by chance that it is the sabbath that has so often kindled the messianic and eschatological hopes of Israel and Christians, or that it is the sabbath that has given these hopes their bearings. In the messianic and eschatological hope Israel's sabbath was futurized and universalized. 'The eternal sabbath' was the burning-glass which drew to itself all God's revelations in history; it became the quintessence of all historical redemptions. In 'the eternal sabbath' people saw the redemption of the whole cosmos in the manifest presence of God. This progression of ideas is clearly perceptible in the development of the sabbath even in the Old Testament.

According to Exodus 20.8–11, the sabbath day is to be 'hallowed' through cessation from any kind of work, after six days' labour.

The sabbath rest is to benefit the whole house, strangers too. On the seventh day creation is 'restored' and celebrated every week.

The weekly sabbath corresponds to the sabbath year. According to Leviticus 25.1–7, after Israel's settlement of the promised land, that land was to 'keep a sabbath to the Lord'. After it had been worked for six years, it was to find rest in the seventh, 'in which you shall not sow your field or prune your vineyard'. But whatever the land bore of itself during its sabbath year was to be eaten by all alike – parents and children, masters and servants, Israelites and strangers, human beings and animals. This 'sabbath year of the land' makes it clear that the sabbath is not merely a feast for human beings. It is the feast of the whole creation. In the seventh year *the land* celebrates.

This sabbath year then corresponds to the Year of Jubilee. According to Leviticus 25.8–55, after seven sabbath years, on the Day of Atonement, the trumpets were to sound throughout the land, to proclaim the fiftieth year as 'God's year of release'. It was to be sanctified through the restitution of the original righteousness of God's covenant among his people: 'Then each of you shall return to his property and each of you shall return to his family.' The saie of what had originally been provided by God was to be cancelled, and debts were to be wiped out. Slavery for debt had to be annulled, and the liberty of every member of God's people had to be restored – but the liberty of every stranger as well. In this Year of Jubilee too the sabbath of the land was to be celebrated: 'You shall neither sow nor reap . . . but eat what it yields out of the field.' The special thing about this Year of Jubilee seems to be that God's laws and edicts were to be imposed on the people, and were then to be passed on by the people to creation, to strangers, animals and land.

Whether Israel was ever in its history in a position to celebrate a sabbath year undisturbed, let alone a Year of Jubilee, is historically uncertain. That may be an external reason for the prophetic vision of the messianic sabbath. Isaiah 61.1–11 expects that the arrival of the one messianic prophet will bring with it the proclamation of the End-time Year of Jubilee: 'to bring good tidings to the afflicted, to bind up the broken-hearted, to proclaim liberty to the captives, and the opening of the prison to those who are bound; to proclaim the year of the Lord's favour, and the day of vengeance of our God.' When this prophetic Messiah comes, the messianic era will dawn, and this is pictured in the image of the sabbath. Looking back to the

Year of Jubilee, the image tells us that the messianic era will bring the liberation of the oppressed, and God's justice and righteousness in everything. Looking back to the sabbath year, it means that the messianic era will allow the land to be free, and everything that lives to have the nourishment it is properly due. Looking back to the sabbath day, finally, it means that rest and peace will spread out in the presence of God.

It is only this messianic sabbath that will be 'a sabbath without end' (Jub. 2.19–24). The new covenant is everlasting; and this sabbath will be everlasting too. In this sense the messianic sabbath of the world is the End-time correspondence of the original sabbath of God's creation. Every sabbath in time has an end. Every feast day becomes another working day. That is why Franz Rosenzweig calls the weekly sabbath 'the dream of completion, but only a dream'.[19] Sabbath day, sabbath year and Year of Jubilee point in time beyond the time of history, out into the messianic time. It is only the sabbath at the end of history that will be 'a feast without end'. It is only this sabbath that will fulfil God's creation sabbath and the sabbath feasts of Israel's history in the world. If the historical sabbath is 'the dream of completion', this messianic, eternal sabbath is surely 'the completion' of Israel's dream.

The apocalyptic speculation about the seven ages of world history, finally, also points towards this. Following Daniel 9.24–27, the Babylonian Talmud (Sanhedrin 97a) already talked about a 'universal sabbath' in the final age of the world's history. The Slavonic Book of Enoch (33.1ff.) took this notion further. The school of Elijah even taught that 'there are three epochs: two thousand years of chaos, two thousand years of Torah, two thousand years of the Messiah, and after that the end – the world which is only sabbath, the peace of eternal life.' This messianic alignment of history towards the sabbath of the End-time had an enduring influence on the Christian theology of history in the middle ages and, by way of Joachim of Fiore, put a lasting impress on historical messianism in modern European thinking.

§5 JESUS AND THE SABBATH

In New Testament theologies and in dogmatic christologies, Jesus' attitude to the sabbath commandment and to the rabbinic sabbath halakah is always treated under the heading: 'Jesus and the Old

Testament Law'.[20] The texts chosen for the exposition are generally Jesus' disputations about the sabbath which the synoptic Gospels have passed down to us – passages where Jesus' curious attitude to the sabbath is justified. 'Jesus breached the sabbath through his demonstrative conduct.'[21] 'Jesus rejects the Rabbinic sabbath Halakah.'[22] Jesus healed on the sabbath and he allowed his disciples to pluck ears of corn on the sabbath. The explanations given in the Gospels are, first: 'The sabbath was made for man, not man for the sabbath' (Mark 2.27); and, second: 'The Son of man is lord of the sabbath' (Mark 2.28).

Rabbinic interpretation was also well aware that the sabbath 'was made for man'. When life is in danger, people are dispensed from the obligation to keep the sabbath. (This was so during the struggles of the Maccabean period, for example.) But when Jesus healed the sick on the sabbath, it was not a question of saving life. Is Jesus simply putting the commandment of love before the sabbath commandment, as Mark 3.4 suggests? Is 'the commandment to love as the law of life under the reign of God' the foundation for Jesus' criticism of 'the divine law of the old aeon', as Jeremias says?[23] Does the discipleship of Jesus, as 'total demand', free people from the individual commandment and abolish the sabbath altogether, as Leonhard Goppelt thinks?[24]

It is quite right to see Jesus' attitude to the sabbath commandment in the context of his messianic mission. But it is misleading if we read into his attitude the freedom from the sabbath commandment which Gentile Christians later enjoyed (though the commandment was still observed by Jewish Christians). It is surprising that Jesus' attitude to the sabbath commandment should be explained in the context of the commandment of love, or of discipleship, not in the light of his proclamation of the messianic sabbath. For what Jesus preaches is not a higher ethic. His proclamation is the proclamation of the imminent kingdom of God, whose unparalleled closeness he authenticates through the signs of the messianic age: 'The blind receive their sight, and the lame walk, the deaf hear, and the dead are raised up, and the poor have the kingdom promised to them' (Matt. 10.7,8; 5.6). According to Luke 4.18ff., Jesus' public ministry began with his proclamation of the messianic sabbath in Nazareth. He himself puts into force the promise of Isaiah 61.1–4: 'Today this Scripture has been fulfilled in your hearing.'[25] If it is true that Jesus' proclamation of the kingdom of God puts the messianic sabbath into effect, then freedom towards the sabbath and the sabbath year is the entirely logical consequence of the End-time fulfilment. Jesus never 'transgressed' the sabbath commandment, and he certainly never made it 'a matter of indifference'.[26] Nor did he 'abolish' it, as if people are confronted with the alternative: Jesus or Judaism.[27] The liberty towards the law which Jesus disseminated is nothing other than the liberty of the messianic era which was promised by the prophets and expected by Israel. The sabbath commandment itself points to this very freedom, like the commandment about the sabbath year and the Year of Jubilee. The messianic age fulfils these commandments of the covenant in a way that is not yet possible in the historical era. That is why the messianic age makes a dead letter of the ethical and cultic constrictions and minutiae of the sabbath interpretation, which are understandable enough in history.

Jesus preached no Gentile Christian freedom from the sabbath. What he proclaimed was the messianic fulfilment of the Israelite 'dream of completion'. He did not profane the law and the cult. He did not abolish the sabbath in favour of good works and good working days. On the contrary, he raised working days into the messianic festivity of life, of which Israel's sabbath is a unique foretaste. Jesus' proclamation of the imminent kingdom makes the whole of life a sabbath feast.

§6 SUNDAY: THE FEAST OF THE BEGINNING

The roots of the Christian feast-day reach back to the earliest days of Christianity. But at that time the day had as yet no name of its own. It was understood, according to the Jewish way of counting, as 'the first day of the week' (Acts 20.7; I Cor. 16.2; Mark 16.2; John 20.1,19). The new Greek term 'the Lord's day' (Rev. 1.10; Did. 14.1; Ignatius, *Magn.* 9.1) probably originated in Syria. It was in the second century that the curious phrase 'the eighth day' (Barn. 15) was used for the first time.[28] The name Sunday derives from the Roman planetary week used in the later period of the ancient world, and meant the second day, dedicated to the cult of the sun. Under the influence of the Mithras cult, this also came to be considered 'the first day' of the week.[29]

It is generally accepted today that the original significance of the Christian feast-day is to be found in the celebration of Christ's resurrection. But H. Riesenfeld and W. Rordorf have shown that it was not until the second century that the remembrance of Christ's resurrection on this day was given as reason for the Sunday celebration. The beginnings of the Christian feast-day are obscure. But it does not go back to the Jewish sabbath and cannot be interpreted either as the Christian sabbath or as the Christian way of observing the fourth commandment. Nor can we assume that the Christian church simply took over the pagan Sunday and provided it with a different content. This would in any case only have been conceivable as a late adaptation in the Roman empire.

None the less, the beginnings must be found among Jewish Christians. We may assume with Riesenfeld that Jewish Christians continued to observe the law, including the sabbath commandment, even after their conversion. We may also assume that, after celebrating the sabbath of their own people, they gathered together in their own homes as a special Christian community.[30] This evening, Rordorf thinks, had a particular significance for the meals shared by the disciples with the risen Lord in the Spirit. In the Pauline congregations as well, the breaking of bread took place on this evening. The next morning Christians met together for the celebration of baptism and, according to Rordorf, the phrase 'the eighth day' points to this as well. Whatever opinions may be about this historical reconstruction, it assumes that there was a close connection between the celebration of the Jewish sabbath and the Christian feast day, without the one feast's supplanting the other.

The separation of the Christian feast from Israel's sabbath also has a considerable history, which can only be reconstructed with difficulty. An important part in this history was probably played by Stephen and 'the Seven' – the so-called Hellenists. Their prophecy that the temple would be destroyed, and their demand for freedom from the law (Acts 6 and 7, especially 6.14) first brought the conflict about the law into the early church. After the council of the apostles (Acts 15, cf. also Gal. 4.8–10; Col. 2.16ff.), if Gentiles wished to become Christians, they did not have to become Jews first of all. As Christians, they were not subject to the law and did not have to be circumcised, so they did not have to keep the sabbath either. Their position with regard to the law distinguished Jewish Christians from Gentile ones. Even Paul treats them differently. But Jewish messianic freedom towards the law now came to be increasingly influenced and overlaid by Gentile Christian freedom from the law. And as a result the Christian feast-day parted company from Israel's sabbath, becoming an independent Christian feast-day, as more and more Gentile Christian congregations came into existence and celebrated it.

Historically speaking, the increasing independence of the Christian feast-day, and its subsequent replacement of Israel's sabbath, must no doubt be interpreted as the visible sign of Christianity's abandonment of Judaism or, to be more precise, as the sign of the end of the determining influence of Jewish Christians on the Christian faith.[31] The Bar Kochba rebellion of 132 to 135, the destruction of Jerusalem by the Emperor Hadrian, and his prohibition of the observance of Jewish laws in the Roman empire were the events of decisive importance in this process. Now the celebration of Sunday became the identifying mark of Christians, and at the same time the sign differentiating them from the Jews. This meant that they were not subjected to the *fiscus judaicus* and did not have to suffer the anti-Jewish repressions of the state. In the Christian community in Rome, the sabbath was even degraded into an anti-Jewish fast-day. The declarations of many popes and theologians belonging to this period prove that it was now that the resurrection of Christ was introduced into the complex of arguments justifying the independent Christian Sunday. The transference of the Jewish sabbath commandment into a command to hallow the Christian Sunday is found for the first time in the state legislation of the Christian emperors. March 3, 312 may be viewed as the 'birthday' of Sunday as a state day of rest: 'The Emperor Constantine to A. Helpidius. All judges, townspeople and all occupations (*artium officia cunctarum*) should rest on the most honourable day of the sun.'[32]

However, as far as the theological legitimation is concerned, it is important to run counter to this historical development of the Christian Sunday and to preserve the link between the Christian feast-day and Israel's sabbath; for otherwise the Christian feast-day is threatened with paganization. The Christian Sunday neither abolishes Israel's sabbath, nor supplants it; and there should be no attempt to replace the one by the other. To transfer the sabbath commandment to the Christian Sunday is wrong, both historically and theologically. The Christian feast-day must rather be seen as the messianic extension of Israel's sabbath. 'The dream of completion' still awaits the completion of the dream.

If the reason for the Christian feast-day is that it is the day of Christ's resurrection, and hence 'the Lord's day', then this very reasoning makes it clear that the day anticipates, not merely the sabbath rest of the End-time, but also the beginning of 'the new creation'. According to the Christian view, the new creation begins with the raising of Christ from the dead, for the new creation is the world of the resurrection of the dead. Just as Israel's sabbath turns our gaze back to God's works in creation and to our own human week-day work, the Christian feast of the resurrection looks forward into the future of a new creation. Just as Israel's sabbath confers a share in God's repose, so the Christian feast of the resurrection confers a share in the power of the new creation of the world. Just as Israel's sabbath is pre-eminently a day of remembrance and thanksgiving, so the Christian feast of the resurrection is pre-eminently a day of a new beginning, and of hope. That is why Franz Rosenzweig can say, if with a certain exaggeration: 'The Christian is the eternal beginner; completion is not his line: all's well that begins well.'[33] It is not for nothing that the church looks upon the day of the Christian feast of the resurrection as 'the first day' of the week. Every week is set within the vision of the new creation, and is begun in the hope of resurrection and eternal life. After all, although the sabbath of creation was the seventh day for God, for the human beings who were created on the sixth day, it was the first day they experienced.

If we may be permitted to distribute the weight of the 'completing' and the 'beginning' in this way between the seventh day and the first, then the day of creation's completion is open for the day of the new creation, and the first day of the new creation has as its precondition the day when the original creation was completed. When the early church called the day of the Christian feast of the resurrection 'the eighth day', its counting of the days themselves was at fault; but through this designation it pointed the Christian Sunday towards the sabbath of Israel, and laid before Israel the vista of the day of the new creation.

The division between Christianity and Judaism brought with it the depreciation and extinction of the Jewish Christianity to which, as all the New Testament writings make plain, the world-wide Christian faith owes its very existence. This separation turned the day of the Christian feast of the resurrection into 'Sunday', and so essentially paganized it. If we want to rid ourselves of this paganization, we must again seek the link between the Christian

'Lord's day' and Israel's sabbath. We have to find a Christian way of sanctifying the sabbath.

It would be a useful practical step in this direction if the *eve* of Sunday were allowed to flow into a sabbath stillness. The Saturday evening devotions which are held in many congregations, and which many Christians like to attend, always unconsciously and involuntarily contain something of the rest and happiness of Israel's sabbath. After the week's work one comes to rest in God's presence, sensing on this evening something of the divine 'completion' of creation. Worship on Sunday morning can then be set wholly in the liberty of Christ's resurrection for the new creation. This worship should spread the messianic hope which renews life. Sunday will again become the authentic Christian feast of the resurrection if we succeed in celebrating a Christian sabbath the evening before.

The day of 'the new creation' presupposes the ecological 'day of rest' of the original creation, if that new creation is to complete the first and not to destroy it.

The ecological day of rest should be a day without pollution of the environment – a day when we leave our cars at home, so that nature too can celebrate its sabbath.

Christianity celebrates the messianic feasts of Christ's salvation history. It does not know the feast of creation. Judaism celebrates the feasts of its salvation history; but before all else it celebrates the sabbath of creation. In the ecological crisis of the modern world it is necessary and timely for Christianity too to call to mind the sabbath of creation.

APPENDIX:

Symbols of the World

Symbols take the form of pictures, parables and metaphors. If we want to find our bearings in some sector of life which we cannot fully grasp, we have recourse to images of particular experiences which have impressed us, and transfer them. But, essentially speaking, the whole of life is tacitly present in every individual experience of life, and the world itself is latent in every experienced impression of a particular object. Consequently our attempt to use symbols as a way of finding our bearings in the all-embracing whole is not really a transference at all. It merely brings to the fore that dimension of the relative wholeness of life which is inherent in any individual experience – the individual, personal dimension of the particular world of the experience itself. Every experience that happens to us brings with it a context of meaning without which we cannot take in the experience at all. This wider horizon literally 'dis-closes' itself, in its first, daybreak colours, in the individual experience. But it is not wholly absorbed by that experience. It is the transcending element in the individual experience. Symbols represent this inherent tension, present in every experience, between the determined and the undetermined – the tension between particularity and totality, present and future. It is this tension that is the ground of the symbol's surplus of meaning. Through the movement of their 'meaning more', symbols do not establish facts; they release experiences. Symbols do not define; they 'give us something to think about', and invite us to new discoveries. Symbols should be understood as the initiatives for processes of perception and interpretation.[1] Symbols cannot be 'made'. They can only be discovered and dis-closed, for they are present in all languages and all traditions of awareness. There are fundamental patterns which lend bearings to human life, and to which language reverts again and again, because they provide an order for the unconscious. We call images which put a fundamental impress on the soul or psyche, 'archetypes'.[2] Every archetype has its own world of symbols and its own wealth of images and its own possible methods of transferred speech. An archetype is a predisposition of the soul which produces and orders concepts, absorbs experiences and gives them expression.

With this definition in mind, in this chapter we shall look at some archetypal symbols for the world, and shall compare them with one another. The sequence in which we shall consider them is not intended to suggest any evolution in cultural history. My purpose is rather to compare the biblical symbol of the world as God's creation with other symbols of the world, and to relate them critically to one another.[3] We shall be comparing the symbols in the light of the messianic viewpoint, not purely in the context of religious history. My intention is to indicate the points at which the Christian world of symbols has absorbed these other symbols of the world, and to show how they have been transformed in the process.

§1 THE GREAT WORLD MOTHER

The earliest testimonies of human culture and religion are evidently matrifocal in their definition.[4] The divine, and the mystery of life were worshipped in the Great Mother. The earliest cultic figures from the palaeolithic age are mother figures. The early civilizations which the immigrating Indo-Germanic tribes in Greece, Persia and North India took as foundation for their own forms of living were apparently cultures determined by matriarchal religions. In historical times, the World Mother, the Queen of Heaven and Mother Earth were worshipped under many names throughout the whole Mediterranean area. The creation narratives in the Old Testament are polemics against the Canaanite matriarchal cults, aiming to supersede them through the patriarchal Yahweh faith.[5] What archetypal symbols of the world do the early mother cults embody?

Behind the symbol of the World Mother is the notion of the world as a great human being, and the human being as a little world: the world is a macranthropos, the human being is a microcosm. All human life comes from the mother and its nurtured by her. That is why the world as a whole has the form of mother. All living things are born of, and nurtured by, the World Mother. She is the cosmic archetypal human being. The pre-Aryan, Indian Jains saw the universe as a colossal human being: the World Mother.[6] The organism of this cosmic human being was populated by living things without number. The region of its head formed the heavenly regions, earth was situated in the trunk, the living space of human beings was the centre, while hell was to be found in the lower abdominal areas. The astral heaven which vaults the earth was the cranium. The entry to hell was the *anus mundi*. According to their behaviour, good or bad, human beings rose to the heavenly regions or descended to the infernal ones. It is true that according to the actual teaching of the Jains, the cosmic human being was androgynous; while their ascetics considered it to be male. But archeologically the figure of the World Mother is clearly evident in this cosmic being. She also reflected the earliest experience of every human child: the experience of shelter in the mother's womb. That is the origin of the symbol for the mother which we find everywhere: mother = body = container = space. The human being feels at home in the world as the embryo feels at home in the womb. The world surrounds him like the womb, protecting and nurturing him. The symbol of the World Mother is not yet sexually polarized. All forms of life are virgin births or, to put it more precisely, the birth of living things has no causal connection with sexual acts. We find remnants of this symbol of the world as the Great Mother in figures of speech like 'the navel of the world', 'the heart of everything', 'the bosom of the earth' and 'the anus mundi'.

The symbol of the cosmic archetypal human being was also taken up by Christianity, and transformed. The direct connecting link was probably Stoic cosmology, which saw the world as the visible body of the invisible deity, and the deity as the invisible soul of the visible world. It is not in the 'creation' symbols connected with the world's origin that the idea of the cosmic human being can be discovered; but we can find it in Christian redemptory ideas about the purpose of the world. The christology of the Epistles to the Ephesians and the Colossians transfers the image of Christ, the head of the church, and the church as the body of Christ to the redemption of the universe.[7] In the ἀνακεφαλείωσις τῶν πάντων Christ will become head of the universe, and the universe will become his body. 'But he offers the united creation to God, interceding for it before the

Father, in the totality of his own Person. Summing up the universe in himself, he shows the unity of that universe to be the unity of a single, unique human being, the cosmic Adam.'[8] The relationship between Christ and the church is also compared with the relationship between man and wife (Eph. 5). As the body of Christ, the church was therefore also later understood as 'the mother of the faithful'. If in his redeeming work Christ becomes 'the head of the universe, then the church is here the beginning and the sacrament of that universe, and is in a sacramental sense already the mother of the universe here and now; and Mary, the virgin 'Mother of God', becomes its symbol.

Here the head-body symbolism is still expressed in male-female metaphors. But when the universe redeemed through the *anakephalaiosis* is termed 'the cosmic Adam', the reference is to the archetypal being who is still as yet undifferentiated in a male and female sense. In this Christian concept the original symbol of the World Mother as the cosmic human being has certainly been clearly de-matriarchalized; for the head-body symbolism is essentially patriarchal. But the idea of Christ, the cosmic human being who will redeem the world, again goes beyond the sexual differentiation, and resolves it.

The interpretation of the world which emerges right down the line, from the symbol of the World Mother to the symbol of the redeeming cosmic human being, Christ, is the panentheistic understanding of the world as the sheltering and nurturing divine environment for everything living: 'In him we live and move and have our being' (Acts 17.28).

Scientifically, this ancient symbol of the world led to the Gaia hypothesis which I have already described: all higher forms of life on earth develop in multi-layered system-environments. Like other living things on earth, human beings belong to the ecosystems that surround and embrace them – the biosphere, the atmosphere, and the multi-layered ecosystem of this planet earth. James Lovelock and Lynn Margulis have suggested, as interpretation of these cosmic connections and conditions of human life, that the planets themselves have to be viewed as a single living organism, *in* which people live, and whose parts and members they are.[9] With this thesis they have called into play elements of truth in the ancient symbol of the world as 'Gaia', the World Mother, Mother Earth.

§2 MOTHER EARTH

The idea of Mother Earth also belongs to the symbol of the Great Mother; and this somewhat more limited notion can be found in many places.[10] Mother Earth is often viewed as 'the universal mother', but she is sometimes also set over against 'the Father of Heaven'. When the single world becomes the double world of heaven and earth, and when heaven and earth are described in male and female metaphors, this probably expresses the transition from a matrifocal culture to a patriarchate.

The worship of the Universal Mother Earth was reflected in many rituals, down to our own time. Newly born children were laid on the earth and picked up from it again. Midwives were called 'earth mothers'. When death came, the dying were taken out of bed and laid on the earth. The human being was supposed to die on the earth from which he had come. The place of the dead was 'under the earth'. The burial of the dead (in*ter*ment) signifies that they are returning to the womb of the earth. Burial in the flexed or foetal position points to the retransformation to the embryo in the mother's womb. Birth from Mother Earth and the return to her in death belong to the religious concept of birth and reincarnation. 'The earth is the mother of all human beings who proceed from her, and who return to her in order to be born again to a new life from this same womb.'[11] The cycle of 'die and come into being' runs its course on the receiving and re-engendering Universal Mother Earth. Plato's philosophical doctrine of the transmigration of souls also probably reflects the cult of Mother Earth.

Mother Earth cults were disseminated over the whole earth. Gaia, the Universal Mother Earth (παμμάτηρ γή), 'the mother of all' (μάτηρ πάντων) was worshipped in Olympia, Delphi, Dodona, Athens and in many other places, before these cultic sites were taken over by the religion of Apollo and Zeus.[12] In Asia Minor she was called Ishtar, Astarte or Diana; in Egypt we find her in the form of the supreme goddess Isis. Even in Rome, worship of the telluric Mother held its ground under male supremacy; and Roman tomb inscriptions provide evidence that the cult of the Earth Mother was still in existence. The omphalos idea, which can be found in the Mediterranean area, in Mesopotamia and also in India, seems to make a centralistic assumption: out of one comes all. Everything that lives has been born from a single womb and grows out of the navel, like the embryo. This is also the meaning of the lotus flower symbol.

Once Mother Earth is set over against a heavenly Father, the connection between the begetting of life and its birth is recognized and emphasized. Mother Earth is ascribed a conceiving and engendering role. In European, Indian and American cults alike, this polarity can also be expressed as 'the sun my father – the earth my mother.'[13] But the reverse is possible too: in the worship of the heavenly goddess Nut in Egypt we find: 'heaven my mother – the earth my father.' In the fertility cults of Mother Earth, this polarity was depicted in sacred copulation.

The connection between the human being and the earth is present in the biblical traditions as well. Adam is 'taken from the earth'. He is the archetypal 'earth-born being' before he is formed into man and woman (Gen. 2.7).[14] But now the earth is no longer the human being's 'mother'. It is merely the raw material for the Creator's work. The patriarchalist monotheism of the Yahweh religion shattered the matriarchal pantheism of the earth through a male concept of creation. The idea of birth, death and rebirth as a single process was a concept that was retained; but the author of the process was changed. That is why, down to the present day, the Christian burial service includes the words: 'Earth to earth, ashes to ashes, dust to dust, in sure and certain hope of the Resurrection to eternal life'; or, in the German service: 'From earth hast thou been taken, to earth shalt thou return; from this earth shall Christ raise thee at the Last Day.' The symbol of the grain of wheat which Paul and John use also has as its premise the ancient cult of the earth: 'It is sown in corruption; it is raised in incorruption' (I Cor. 15.35ff.). When the Eastern church pictures the birth of Christ as taking place in a grotto, it is intending to say that the Redeemer was born in the womb of the earth. But otherwise the symbols connected with Mother Earth are consistently transferred to Mother Church. Out of the motherly womb of the church, outside which there is no salvation, believers are born again to new life, in a parthenogenesis – 'in a virgin way'.[15] The font was given the shape of a womb, and was understood in this sense.[16] 'We cannot have God as Father without having the church as mother', said Cyprian in some famous words: 'Out of her womb we are born, with her milk we are fed, through her spirit we are animated.'[17] But are these still matrifocal female symbols or are they, even at this stage, the mother images of a patriarchate?

§3 THE FEAST OF HEAVEN AND EARTH

'One has to be very coarse in order not to feel the presence of Christians and Christian values as an oppression beneath which all genuine festive feelings go to the devil . . . The feast is paganism *par excellence*', said Nietzsche.[18] He was right in so far as 'paganism' really was, and still is, essentially a festal religion, an interruption of everyday life, ec-stasy out of the transitory world, and the game of the great alternative to common life.[19] But does Christianity have to destroy this religious festivity of life?

Sacred places and sacred times are among the *outward* features of the religious feast.[20] In the temple, the place where the gods are present is hallowed. In the temple the world is open 'upwards'. That is why every temple stands at the centre of the world. In the temple feast human beings become co-dwellers with the gods. In the festal seasons time is sanctified. All time is used up, and passes away. But the festal time interrupts passing time and regenerates it. Every festal time is a return to the origin of time, and hence to the time of origin. In the sacred times of the feast, men and women become not merely co-dwellers with the gods, but also their con-temporaries.

The repetition and presentation of the primal happening of the world, the cosmogony, belongs to the *inward* character of the pagan festal religion. In the feast the renewal of life is celebrated. Time is renewed, space is sanctified, human beings are born again out of the origin of life. In the feast eternity is experienced in the form of the eternal present: 'Time without a goal' (in Nietzsche's phrase) and joy without end. The feast is of its very essence ecstatic. The cultic myth in any given case tells of the origin of life and actualizes the cosmogony in the sacred story. The cultic ritual imitates the primal happening of the world. 'We must do what the Gods did in the beginning.'[21]

'The feast of heaven and earth' presents the original birth of life from the marriage of heaven and earth, sun and earth. The fertility of the earth proceeds from the hierogamy. If the earth is mother and heaven father, then all life proceeds from the fertilization of the earth through light and rain. What are called fertility cults actualize and invoke the procreative potency of the heavens and the fecundity of the earth. What the rigorous adherents of the Yahweh faith in the Old Testament condemned and hunted down as 'temple prostitution' were the rituals of the Canaanite festal religions of the fruitful Great Mother. They have little to do with what was later termed prostitution by Christian morality. If the feast celebrates and reiterates the fertility of life, then human fertility for its part also participates in this original primal mystery of life: 'I am Heaven, thou art Earth', says the bridegroom to the bride in the Upanishads.[22] Every human union participates in the hierogamy of the heavenly god and the earthly goddess, and imitates it. And every human union acquires a cosmic significance if the human beings involved experience in their own union their unity with the universe. In the biblical traditions this 'feast of heaven and earth' is gathered up and transformed into the sabbath.[23]

The Christian feast is at heart the feast of the resurrection.[24] Consequently this eschatological feast of the new creation of the world absorbs the various elements of the pagan feast of heaven and earth, as well as the elements of Israel's sabbath feast; but it aligns them towards the messianic hope. The kingdom of God will be celebrated as the joy of the marriage feast (Matt. 22.2ff.; 25.1ff.); the coming Christ will be received as a bridegroom; the church goes to meet him 'as a bride adorned for her husband'; expectant faith is the wedding garment; the Lord's Supper becomes the messianic banquet of joy; and eternal life in the kingdom of God is like a marriage feast without end.

So the biblical traditions take up 'the pagan feast' and give it a messianic form which points towards the eschatological future; but they do not destroy it.

§4 THE WORLD AS DANCE

The world as dance, and dance as symbol of the world is the mystery of many African and Asiatic rituals. It reaches one of its finest forms in the dance of Shiva Nataraja, who is worshipped in South Indian Hinduism as the Lord of the Dancers, the creator and destroyer of worlds.[25] His dance is magic, and leads the dancer into the ecstasy in which he receives divine energies and himself becomes one with the divine. The dance transforms the dancer into the god he depicts. In the dance of Shiva Nataraja, the dancer becomes the cosmic dancer. He concentrates in himself the energies of the divine and utters them again out of himself in the rhythms of the dance. His whirling movements manifest the forces of the world's creation, preservation, destruction and dissolution. Shiva's right hand holds high the drum for the beating of the rhythm. Its sound also signifies the aether out of which all the other elements of the world are unfolded. His upper left hand bears a tongue of flame, the element of world destruction. The balance of the two upper hands illustrates the counterpoise between the world's creation and its destruction, in which the cosmic dance moves. 'Ceaselessness of production against an insatiate appetite of extermination, Sound against Flame.'[26] The lower right hand is raised in a gesture of protection and blessing. The lower left hand points down to the raised left foot, which signifies release. With one right foot Shiva stands on the prostrate body of the demon – the symbol of the blindness of human beings towards true life, and their ignorance. A ring of light and flame encompasses the dancing god. It shows the rhythm which streams out from the cosmic dancer – the dance of nature as it is moved by God. The dance of the whirling limbs is thrown into relief through the immobile, majestically tranquil and sovereign countenance of the dancing god. The eternity reflected here makes time dance. The quiescent countenance brings the limbs into passionate movement.

The cosmic dance of Shiva presents five divine activities: creation; preservation; destruction; the giving of rest; and release and salvation. 'Creation arises from the drum: protection proceeds from the hand of hope: from fire proceeds destruction: the foot held aloft gives release.'[27] According to this concept, Shiva is present wherever life is truly living because it is life lived in rhythm: in the pulse beat of the blood, in the breathing of the lungs, in the succession of day and night, in the ebb and flow of the tides, in the vibrations of sounds and waves.

> The dancing foot, the sound of tinkling bells,
> The songs that are sung and the varying steps, ...
> Find out these within yourself, then shall your fetters fall away.[28]

A three-fold significance is ascribed to the dance of Shiva. 1. Its rhythmical play is the source of all movements in the cosmos. 2. The purpose of his dance is to release souls from the deceitfulness of illusion. 3. The place of the dance is the centre of the universe – in the heart of every human being. Shiva dances the world out of delight, out of joy in the dance itself, out of the overflow of his energies and the wantonness of his perfection. 'He is the dancer, he is the dance, and what the dance dances, is he himself.'[29]

The special thing about this dance metaphor is the link between space and time forged by rhythm. In the rhythmic vibrances and movements of the dance steps, space is measured in terms of time, and time in terms of space. In the movements of the dance, the antithesis is united and the unity divided. Union and disunion alternate and are one in their alternation. In the rhythm of the dance the antitheses are reconciled. So in the dancing, pulsating energies of the world, heaven and earth, eternity and time, life and death are one. And the One is again divided into eternity and time, into heaven and earth, into life and death. The symbol of the world as cosmic dance reminds us that the mystery of structures of matter, like the mystery of life systems, is rhythm, the ordered pulse of time. Modern bioenergetic ideas belong to this tradition.

The Christian traditions of the patristic church took over the image of the world as dance from the ancient cosmologies, and liked to associate them with eschatological notions about 'the play of the heavenly dance'. 'All play has somewhere deep within it an element of the dance; it is a kind of dance round the truth.'[30] In the rhythm of the dance, the human being presents himself whole and entire. Out of his enslaved body comes released embodiment. Freed from the weight of earthly life, he sways in the heavenly round. But this is only possible if the human being can present himself for what he is before the divine itself. To divulge the ineffable mysteries is called in Greek ἐξορχεῖσθαι 'dancing them away'.[31] On earth and in transitory time this is only possible in the cult. It is only in the eternal, blissful contemplation of God that the hiddenness disappears, that the human being issues from his mystery and becomes wholly manifest before God, and in his dance begins on his own account to manifest God himself. The Logos, who is from the beginning with God, and is in eternity his delight, is 'the sacred leader of the heavenly round' of the redeemed. These are Neoplatonic ideas and images. Plotinus called the dancer 'a mirror of life'. He developed his cosmology in the image of the great theatre of the world: the genesis and fashioning of the cosmos out of the One is said to be like a drama in which the antitheses are reconciled and the different elements are brought into symmetrical and rhythmical proportions. The sacral dance is the bodily imitation of the vibrations which the divine communicates to the cosmos, and living participation in these vibrations. The eternal harmony of what is divine and cosmic finds its correspondences in the harmony of human beings with nature and of the body with the soul in dance. The stars, as the Pythagoreans said, are the choric dances of the cosmos, and the soul which finds in the stars the seat of its bliss will in eternity dance in the rounds of the constellations.

Gregory of Nyssa was drawing on images like this when he described the primal condition and the state of redemption in dance metaphors:

> Once there was a time when the whole of rational creation formed a single dancing chorus looking upwards to the one leader of this dance . . . And the harmony of that motion which was imparted to them by reason of his law found its way into their dancing . . . And this victory will come and thou shalt be found in the dancing ranks of the angelic spirits.[32]

Hippolytus' Easter hymn belongs to the same world of images:

> O thou leader of the mystic round-dance! O thou leader of the spiritual marriage feast! O thou leader of the divine Pasch and new feast of all things! O cosmic festal gathering! O joy of the universe, honour, ecstasy, exquisite delight by which dark death is destroyed . . . and the people that were in the depths arise from the dead and announce to all the hosts of heaven: 'The thronging choir from earth is coming home.'[33]

In San Marco in Florence Fra Angelico painted the dance of the angels with the redeemed in paradise on the way to the ecstasy of the beatific vision. The well-known Shaker song 'The Lord of the Dance' goes back to these ancient and patristic metaphors about the world as dance, and the Logos as the leader of the dance which moves the world. The eternal perichoresis of the Trinity might also be described as an eternal round danced by the triune God, a dance out of which the rhythms of created beings who interpenetrate one another correspondingly rise like an echo.

But it is noticeable that, compared with the Shiva Nataraja, the creative dance out of which the world comes into being possesses no destructive power. It is noticeable too that in the Christian traditions 'the world as dance' is turned into the image of redemption and future glory. The cyclical element in the Indian concept is broken through, because now an irreversible finality is introduced. This gives the symbol a new meaning. The 'cosmic rounds' of birth and death become the messianic dance of eternal life.

§5 THE GREAT THEATRE OF THE WORLD

The drama metaphor is also an old one. In this image the world, life and history are interpreted as the theatre of the gods.[34] Plato said that the human being was 'a puppet in the hand of God, and in truth this is the best thing about him'. The world is the stage on which human beings, directed by God, play their predetermined roles, whether they know it or not – in pain or joy, 'life's tragedy and its comedy alike'.[35] In the societies of the ancient world, the theatre was the forum of public life. So the theatre was the place where important events were 'put on' – not merely games and triumphs, but executions as well. That is why Paul called the martyrdom of the apostles 'a spectacle' for the world (I Cor. 4.9). Clement of Alexandria tells how the Christian martyrs 'receive the victor's laurels in the theatre of the world'. Ever since then, the *theatrum mundi* metaphor has been common coin in European tradition. From Calderon to Hugo von Hofmannsthal, the great theatre of the world was an established dramatic phrase. And the expression is also continually used to interpret the world itself. We find this in *As You Like It*: 'All the world's a stage . . .' Men, women and children, young and old – all play their parts, but without as yet knowing who they are. When the play ends they all become alike in death.

Theatrum mundi can mean that human beings are actors and learn their different roles; that the goddess Fortuna, or some other divinity, is the producer, and that heaven is the audience which looks on.

But *theatrum mundi* can also mean that the universe is the theatre, the cosmos is the stage, living things are the actors, and human beings the audience.

Finally, *theatrum mundi* can mean that the world is what Calvin called *theatrum gloriae Dei*. God is putting on the play of his glory and the men and women who look on are participants as well as audience. Then world history with all its actors is what Luther describes as 'God's mummery'. Like the 'guisers' of carnival and the folk plays, God is at work, hidden under many masks. The human beings who provide the cast are nothing but the countless roles which God himself plays.[36] What does the metaphor of the world as a theatre mean for human beings' understanding of the world and themselves?

Human beings have *to fashion* the world in which they live. But in the work through which they shape this world of theirs, they at the same time always portray themselves. The things with which a person surrounds himself do not have a merely utility value for him. They have value as a portrayal of what he is. In everything a human being produces, he also unveils and decodes himself, interprets himself, exposes himself to view. Every relationship to the world in a social sense implies a relationship to the self; and the reverse is equally true. So every human life, both personal and social, is life that is interpreted and acted out. But who is the audience before whom people try to portray themselves? Does anybody watch them? Do they watch themselves?

The 'authority' which encourages and provokes human beings to present themselves as what they are, evidently always transcends the particular sphere of a person's life and his environment; for the sphere in which he lives and the world surrounding him are, after all, part of the performance. Without the transcending dimension the play would stop being a play, and the portrait of life it gives would no longer be a reflective portrayal.

In another sense, human beings evidently also feel that in their own subjectivity they have been assigned only minor roles in a great play which they themselves do not as yet understand. In this performance it is not the auditorium which transcends the stage; it is the producer who transcends his actors. In terms of the world this means: God is the actor and producer of the world drama. Human beings are his chief actors. But they do not yet know their lines, or how the play ends. If the world is the stage of the divine drama, and if history is the play itself, then this world theatre has no audience. Every onlooker becomes one of the players. But is the human being then an actor, or 'a living toy', as Plotinus said? If 'all the world's a stage', is the human being acting out his own life, or is the divine life playing a game of love with him? Or is it impossible to distinguish here either?

Let us try to arrive at a theological interpretation. God is acting his play on the stage of the world, the play of his inexhaustible, inventive love. In the history of the world he is acting the drama of his grace, which he intends shall one day be fully manifested in the liberty of all his creatures. If it is really God who is interpreting himself on the world stage, then the subject of his play is his self-revelation. In all his creatures and through all the roles he plays he wants to portray himself as he is. Men and women are his image, his reflection, his roles and his masks, and also his *dramatis personae* in this great world theatre. His appearance in human form is the unveiling of his hiddenness in his revelation of what he is. When he enters the stage, the hidden meaning of the whole, and the hidden sense of every individual human role, becomes plain. When he enters the stage, the purpose and end of the great world drama can also be foreseen: when the kingdom of glory appears, nature too will be gathered into the liberty of eternal life.[37]

§6 PLAY AS SYMBOL OF THE WORLD

The metaphors of the world as theatre, or as dance and the music of the spheres, can be summed up in the symbol of play. This symbol is as old as human civilization itself, and proves its fruitfulness down to the present day in the most widely differing sectors.[38] Here we shall look only at the interpretation of the world which is inherent in this symbol.

'Lifetime is a child at play, moving pieces in a game. Kingship belongs to the child', said Heraclitus.[39] The genesis of the world and the order of everything in that world have the character of play. In play, gods and human beings give themselves up to the world in its wholeness. In play, the world displays its beauty. As play, the world hovers over the abysss. That is why the kingdom of the world belongs to the child. In modern philosophical interpretation this means:

> The world is unfathomable. We are open to the world, and this openness of human existence is haunted by an awareness of the unfathomableness of the overriding whole. And it is only because of this that we can play at all.[40]

It is only in play that human beings can endure the fundamental contingency of the world and adapt to that contingency. In play human beings display and maintain their own liberty. In play they weigh up the chances of a fortuitous world and the forces of their own freedom. The kingdom of freedom is the kingdom of play.

In the Old Testament traditions play is also used as a symbol for the world. God has created everything through his daughter Wisdom. Wisdom was there before anything was created at all. She is from eternity. When God created heaven and earth, the author of the Book of Proverbs makes Wisdom says: 'Then I was daily his delight, rejoicing before him always, rejoicing in his inhabited world, and there was delight over me among the sons of men' (Prov. 8.30f.). According to this tradition, the creation of the world has the character of play, which gives God delight and human beings joy. This means that the world does not exist of necessity. It exists because God created it out of liberty. He created it freely but not arbitrarily. So the world is not a matter of chance. He created what gave him pleasure, and what gives him pleasure is what accords with his inmost nature. That is why God's creation is a good creation.

This unity of free creation and the pleasure that corresponds to God's own nature is best described through the category of play:

> When, therefore, we speak of God the Creator 'playing', there lies concealed in that phrase the metaphysical truth that the creation of the world and of human beings, though a divinely meaningful act, was by no means a necessary one so far as God himself was concerned.[41]

Meaningful but not necessary: this is what characterizes play compared with purposeful and utilitarian work. The creative God plays with his potentialities and creates out of nothing what is his good pleasure, because it corresponds to himself. The deeply felt contingency of the world in general, and the continually experienced contingency of events in the world, lose their terrors for the human being if he sees them as part of the great game which is being played with the world in its evolution, and with himself in the history of his own life.[42] It may often seem to him a cruel game, unless he can put his trust in a providence.

Play is a symbol of the world which is also used for the world's redemption. Mystical theologians especially have used categories of play in ideas about the divine 'play of grace'. The Redeemer plays a wonderful game of love with the beloved soul, in order to redeem her in liberty. The game of redemption perfects a unique feature of the creative play of human beings with the world; for human play with the world is always at the same time the world's play with human beings. In art, human beings create and receive at the same time. Impression and expression alternate. If this is true of games in life, it is truer still of the game of life itself:

> The more profoundly the analysis of existence proceeds, the more evident it becomes . . . that the human being still also has the chance to be, not the player, but the game that is played and the one sheltered in his playing. Then a mysterious transformation takes place. The human being discovers that the encompassing, loving ground of his existence is playing a marvellous game with him. As the poet Charles Péguy has shown us, the game is called 'Qui perd gagne' – the loser wins.[43]

This is a wise old insight belonging to Spanish mysticism.[44] In the game of grace, 'the last shall be first and the first last'.

Play as the symbol of the world includes the creative role of 'chance'; for it understands chance as the event of something new – something underivable and undeducible from anything that already exists – something to which a living being adapts itself playfully and which he copes with through the free play of his energies. The fortuitous event is not something irritating, because it is incalculable according to known laws. On the contrary, the 'necessity' imposed by the regularities of law is merely an open grid of adaptations and assumptions which have grown up out of the experiences of the past, as a way of grasping and perceiving future possibilities. The different forms of play embrace both necessity and chance, law and liberty, actuality and possibility, past and future, as a way of building up still more complex systems of life.

§7 THE WORLD AS WORK AND AS MACHINE

Let us now look, finally, at the symbol of the world as God's work. According to the monotheistic forms of the biblical traditions, the world is neither itself divine, nor is it a divine emanation. As God's creation, it is 'the work of his hands'. It is not born of God, nor is it begotten. It is 'made'. The monotheistic form of the creation narrative which has been passed down to us emphasizes the difference between God and the world, and stresses the transcendence of the Creator over his creation. For this, the patriarchal image of the creation of the man, and 'the work of his hands', was helpful. It is true that the Hebrew verb *bara'* is used solely and exclusively for God's creative activity, to which no human act can correspond. But in the biblical traditions 'a work' is the expression used both for the result of the divine activity and for the result of human labour. This is particularly apparent when the metaphor of handicraft – the artefact – is used: the heavens 'the works of thy fingers', 'the work of thy hands (Pss. 8.3,6; 19.1; 103.22). Like heaven and earth, human beings too are 'the work of thy hand' (Isa. 64.8). The human being, God's image and reflection on earth, is not born of God; he is 'made'. Even for the reconciliation, sanctification and redemption of the world, the similes chosen are similes of labour and work (the works of Christ: Matt. 11.2; John 5.36; 7.21; the works of the Holy Spirit: John 14.12).

In German the word for 'real' – 'wirklich' – means being actively operative, taking place through act, consisting in doing.[45] Out of this, German mysticism formed the word 'Wirklichkeit' – reality. But the word 'Wirklichkeit' originally meant 'activity through work'. The English words act – actual – actuality are related in a similar way. Accordingly the world has to be understood as God's 'reality'. It is the process and the result of his working activity. The analogy of handiwork and the artefact is obvious. As a result, God is himself conceived of as agent and pure act (*actus purus*). The pictorial world of this symbol covers the *efficacious* world – the world of work and the world of works. It is pre-eminently a man's world. A child is conceived and grows in the mother's womb, and the mother *bears* it. But the man works on something external, *creating* a world which exists outside himself. He is aware of a distance between himself and 'the work of his hands'. His work has not proceeded from his essential being, and will never be the same as himself, however much it may be in accord with him. In spite of all dissimilarities, 'the world as God's work' reflects the view of the world taken by 'man the worker'. Where this view of the world prevails, belief in creation drives out the universal myths of the World Mother, Mother Earth and the feast of heaven and earth. The symbol of the world as God's work strips the world of gods and demons, and makes it profane – the world of the man addressed in the Fourth Commandment, the man who corresponds to his Creator in the six days of his work.

During the age of the Enlightenment, the symbol of the world as God's work became the matrix for the modern symbols of the world: the world as machine, the world as workshop and the world as experiment.[46] The metaphors used here correspond to the latest stage of human technology at any given time, the aim being to reconstruct and refashion nature into the world of human beings, turning it into the clock, the machine or the computer.

Christian Wolff made the notion of the world machine (*machina mundi*) the foundation of his enlightened theology of nature, after the old organic world picture which had been developed out of the assumption of an *anima mundi*, or World Soul, had been pushed aside by Newton, Descartes, Gassendi and others in favour of the new mechanistic world view, built upon the assumption of the wise, divine Lord of the world. In 1719 Wolff brought out his book *Vernünftige Gedanken von Gott, der Welt und der Seele des Menschen* ('Reasonable Thoughts about God, the World and the Human Soul'), in which he writes:

> Every reasonable being acts according to particular intentions. God is the most reasonable of all beings. He must therefore act according to particular intentions . . . A machine is an assembled work whose movements are accounted for by the nature of the assembly. The world is accordingly a machine . . . Consequently the world and all things in it are God's instruments by means of which, since they are machines, he executes his intentions. From which it becomes evident that they become a work of God's wisdom through the very fact that they are indeed machines. Accordingly the man who explains everything in the world through the dictates of reason (as one is accustomed to do in the case of machines) is the man who leads us to the divine Wisdom.[47]

When the machine is taken as model for the world, the underlying premise is an unbroken chain of causality which determines every event in the world. The laws of nature are eternal laws which regulate all happening. If it were possible at any moment in the world to know all its laws, we could reconstruct the past and foretell the future with complete certainty. Consequently chance events are merely subjective impressions based on laws which are not yet comprehended. In reality there is no such thing as chance. It should therefore be our concern to find a formula for the world which is able to explain all events in a uniform way. The formula would be in accordance with 'the central order of all things', which is the underlying assumption of the theory.

> Even when we try to probe into the subjective realm, we cannot ignore the central order or look upon the forms peopling this

realm as mere phantoms or accidents. [For] in the final analysis, the central order, or the 'one' as it used to be called and with which we commune in the language of religion, must win out.[48]

These remarks of Heisenberg's on the philosophy of science show that the deistic model of a world mechanism which first came into vogue at the Enlightenment still continues to exert an influence even today.

As a foundation for his philosophy of hope Ernst Bloch took the idea of the world as experiment.[49] The *experimentum mundi* can be distinguished from the world machine through the openness to the future which it postulates and through the unfinished nature of the cosmos which it assumes. The world is not a 'closed system', either as a whole or in its individual parts. It is an 'open system' whose future is not yet determined. The world process which is open in a forward direction represents a unique experiment – an *experimentum possibilis salutis* certainly, but also an experiment which can undoubtedly fail. 'The world is full of a disposition towards something, a tendency towards something, a latency of something; and the Something of this intention is the fulfilment of what is here and now being intended; it is a world more in accordance with what we are, without unworthy pain, anxiety, self-alienation, nothingness.'[50] For in the human being the world experiment has reached its highest, its decisive, and hence its critical phase. The human being can complete it; he can also foil it. The world experiment is pregnant with future; and in the mediation between human beings and the world this future will be realized or thwarted.

For Christian Wolff the present glory of a cosmos determined through and through and towards every side was a mirror of God's wisdom. But for Ernst Bloch this shifts into the future that has not yet been found. The world is now merely an experiment; but it is intended then to be 'a home of identity' for human beings and nature. The world is 'not yet' finished, but it is intended that it should be finished one day in this still undiscovered future.

Yet as long as 'the open system' of the world is viewed only as an experiment through which the ideal 'closed system' may be found, this model of the world still belongs to the same level as the world machine of the Enlightenment. It is only if the open system of the world ceased to be understood as something negative – as a 'not yet' completed world system – and were comprehended in a positive sense as the 'living' world system, that true progress would be achieved.

We are bound to establish that the conceptual sphere of this symbol of the world has also been taken from the male world of work. The world becomes the experimental field of human beings.

Here we can clearly discern the developmental stages of modern technology. The world as God's work corresponds to human handicrafts. The subject is unremittingly active on his own account. This is a theistic conception. The world as machine corresponds to an early industrial enterprise: the subject resigns his own physical activity to the machine. That is a deistic concept. The world as experiment corresponds to the world of modern laboratories, in which discoveries and inventions are made which are then transferred to cybernetically controlled, automated mass production. The human subject resigns to computers all mental activities that can be regulated, and concentrates on activities that are creative.

But is it enough if the human being who is trying to find his bearings in a world he cannot survey, reaches out in general for symbols and images derived merely from the sector which he dominates and controls, and which speak to him himself in his capacity as worker, inventer and experimenter?

> At the end of a long spiritual and cultural history, this view of the world as an 'entente secrète' – the metaphysics of harmonizing and conflicting life forces – has been destroyed. It has been destroyed by monotheism on the one hand and, on the other, by the scientific and technological mechanism for which monotheism itself first cleared the path when it de-demonized and de-divinized nature. God and the machine have survived the archaic world, and now confront one another quite alone.[51]

Should this be the goal of the development, then – since it means the destruction of nature – it also means the end of human beings.

§8 SYMBOLS COMPARED IN THE MESSIANIC LIGHT

In comparing the symbols of the world which I have described, our aim will be to move from images and the visions of the imagination to concepts. Our purpose is to arrive at a mutual complementation of the ideas inherent in the different symbols of the world, so that we can evolve an understanding of the human being in his world which is richer than any single world symbol is capable of achieving. Finally – as I have already indicated through my account of the Christian reception of the different symbols – we shall ask what form a Christian integration of these symbols of the world could take. Here Christian integration does not mean an appropriation by the church. It means the interpretation of religious history in the messianic light.[52] This interpretation also suggests the possibility that the creation traditions of the Old Testament might also be relativized and integrated into a new total picture. Christian belief in creation is messianic belief in creation. Messianic belief in creation is a perception of the world and human beings in the messianic light of their redeeming future.[53]

Let us first of all compare the content and the conceptual background of the symbols of the world I have put forward. The symbol of the World Mother expresses a particular feeling about life – the feeling of being at home in the world as the child is at home in the womb. The world encompasses the human being as a home, and nurtures him from every side. In the world he is sheltered and in safe keeping. There is as yet no separation from the origin of everything living, and hence no fear of life either. Everything is one. The redemptive image of the macranthropos also contains this dream of unity without division; for beneath his head the macranthropos comprehends heaven and earth, so that the universe becomes his body and functions as his body. The conceptual world which corresponds to this is the world of pantheism, which tries to think the all-embracing immanence of God, and seeks to abolish every distinction between transcendence and immanence.

The symbol of Mother Earth takes the path of sexually determined polarity (although this is not the absolutely necessary corollary of the concept). The human being experiences himself as being on the mother, no longer in her. He exists *on* the earth, beneath a superterrestrial heaven. The dualism of Father Heaven and Mother Earth liberates him from the all-embracing shelter of the universal Mother, and exposes him to the differentiations and divisions of individuation. It is true that Mother Earth remains the home out of which life comes and to which life returns. But heaven keeps the 'die and come into being' in continual movement. Here the corresponding conceptual world is worked out in the difference between transcendence and immanence. But because in the duality of heaven and earth, man and woman, soul and body, the One is merely drawn apart, the difference cannot be conceived of dualistically. It is at heart *the dialectical movement of the One*. So on the level of this symbol it is possible to develop the conceptual world of dialectically moved pantheism.

The feast, the dance, the theatre, music and play are all symbols of the world which comprehend the inter-space, the 'inter-time' and the inter-play in this primal differentiation. They do not present the unity of what has been differentiated by way of regression into an original All-One. They explore the possibilities of a new con-junction. The feast con-joins, and the new life proceeds out of that festal conjunction. Dance unites what has been divided, by means of rhythm. Music unites through time ordered into metre and cadences. Play, finally, confers the freedom to shape conjunctions within the wealth of potentiality, because it can avail itself of chance. In rhythm, in melody, in the theatre and in play, the world is determined by an immanent transcendence or by a transcendent immanence.

It is only the symbol of the world as work and as machine that makes God so transcendent that the immanence cannot be an equal counterpart for him, because it no longer partakes of his nature. The monotheism of the transcendent God and the mechanization of the world put an end to all ideas about God's immanence. This development was the beginning of the segregation of the divine from the world of human beings. Deism made God the far-off God. Atheism was the inevitable result; for the world machine must be able to function all by itself, even without God.

Secondly we have to compare the human concerns and hopes which are linked with those symbols of the world. It is evident that the transformation of symbols used for the world always simultaneously reflects human struggles for domination. Symbols of the world are like pictures of the world: they are not merely *im*pressions of the external world applicable in any given case; they are also valid *ex*pressions of the given human society. Consequently the history of these symbols shows the transition from the matriarchate of early cultures to the patriarchate of historical civilizations. The symbols of the World Mother and of Mother Earth gave the woman her divinity and her closeness to the mystery of the world: the divine mystery of the world speaks through the woman. Mother cults were therefore served by priestesses – in Delphi, for example, before the priests of Apollo came. But the symbols of the Great Mother also determined matrilinear succession from mother to daughter, and thereby legitimated female possession and rule. Male possession and man's seizure of power is bound up with the emergence of patriarchal symbols for the world. Male gods speak through male priests, and before the gods the man becomes the head of the woman and her possessor. The patriarchal symbols of the world determine patrilinear descent from father to eldest son. In order that the rights of fatherhood and sonship may be secured there has to be a patriarchal family order. The monotheism of the modern world is certainly the provisional final point in this development of the patriarchate.

Patriarchy certainly succeeded in expelling matrifocal culture from the symbolism of the world's origin and from the power systems of life. But at the same time this process was the germ of messianism – probably because of the influence of repressed matriarchal traditions. And this messianism was consistently the messianism of the child: 'Unless you turn and become like children you will never enter the kingdom of heaven' (Matt. 18.3). The messianic visions of the future break the power of archaic symbols of origin and set men and women free.

In the messianic images and eschatological symbols of the Bible we no longer find patriarchalism; but there is no return to matriarchy either. The kingdom is the kingdom of the child. This is probably a symbolic way of expressing a human situation before sexual differentiation. If in the kingdom of God people 'neither marry nor are given in marriage' (Luke 20.34ff.), there cannot be matriarchy either, let alone patriarchy. The very images used for the fellowship of Jesus, the 'child' of God, are no longer images of fatherhood and motherhood; they are images of brotherhood, sisterhood and friendship.

In Christianity, the messianic endowment with the Spirit which abolishes the religious dominance of man or woman is symbolized by the baptism of men and women, which takes the place of Israel's purely male circumcision. Baptism is the symbol of the eschatological endowment with the Spirit and the sign that believers are sealed for the messianic kingdom; and this creates the fundamental principle that men and women have equal rights. This is finally shown by the new eschatological law of inheritance. Every believer, man and woman, acquires in messianic fellowship with Christ the same eschatological right to inherit the kingdom. They become heirs of eternal life and fellow heirs with Christ (Rom. 8.17;

Gal. 3.29; 4.7; Eph. 1.14; 2.8; Heb. 6.17). The eschatological law of inheritance replaces matrilinear and patrilinear succession and transference of power. But this means that right through the history of religion, with its shifting struggles between patriarchate and matriarchate, a scarlet thread of messianism can be discerned, which puts an end to patriarchy.

For this reason too we should seek to replace the modern mechanistic world picture; for it is a view of the world that is one-sidedly patriarchal. The transition to an ecological world view is more fully in accord, not merely with the reality of the natural environments of the world of human beings, but also with the natural character of this human world itself – the world of women and men. This means that this ecological world view is bound up with new egalitarian forms of society, in which patriarchal rule is ended and co-operative communities are built up. The centrations of the mechanistic world picture give way to concurrences in the network of reciprocal relationships. On this path from the mechanistic domination of the world to an ecological world community, the earlier matrifocal symbols of the world are pregnant with promise for the future, because they once again 'give us something to think about'.

NOTES

I God in Creation

1. Cf. Jonathan Edwards, 'The End for which God Created the World' (1765), *Works*, vol. 1, Edinburgh 1974, pp. 92–121.

2. E. Bloch, *Das Prinzip Hoffnung*, Frankfurt 1959, p. 1408: 'The wish at the heart of religion is still that the human being should feel at home in *the mystery* of existence . . .' This messianically religious idea also determines the goal of Ernst Bloch's own philosophy of hope. Cf. ibid., p. 1628: 'Once he (the human being) understands what he is and comprehends what he has, without self-emptying and alienation, in real democracy, something comes into being in the world which glimmers forth to everyone in childhood, and where no one as yet ever was: home.'

3. E. Benz, 'Der Mensch und die Sympathie aller Dinge am Ende der Zeiten (nach Jakob Boehme und seiner Schule)', *Eranos Jahrbuch* 1955, 24, Zürich 1956, pp. 133–97.

4. Berakoth 57b.

5. H. Gese, *Zur biblische Theologie*, Munich 1977, p. 79: 'The point of the sabbath is not primarily that human beings should rest from their labours. The main purpose is the non-intervention of human beings in the environment – the *restitutio in integrum* of creation . . . In principle, what is at stake is the inviolability of creation, which at least on every seventh day is to be preserved from man, as a sign and symbol.' An astonishing parallel to the Jewish doctrine of the sabbath can be found in Taoist wisdom. Lao-Tse, *Tao-Tê-King*. ch. 16: 'Stillness means rediscovering roots.' Ch. 45: 'Pure stillness gives back to the world its proper measure.' (Cf. *The Texts of Taoism*, Sacred Books of the East 39, London 1891, pp. 59, 88.)

6. K. Rahner, *Theological Investigations* I, ET London and Baltimore 1961, pp. 163ff.; IV, 1966, p. 117. Also the comment by K. P. Fischer, *Der Mensch als Geheimnis, Die Anthropologie Karl Rahners*, Freiburg 1974, pp. 293ff.

7. Basil, *On the Holy Spirit*, ch. 38 (PG 32, 136B).

8. J. Calvin, *Institutes of the Christian Religion* I, 13.14: 'For it is the Spirit who, everywhere diffused, sustains all things, causes them to grow, and quickens them in heaven and in earth. Because he is circumscribed by no limits, he is excepted from the category of creatures; but in transfusing into all things his energy, and breathing into them essence, life, and

movement, he is indeed plainly divine.' (ET, Library of Christian Classics XX, London and Philadelphia 1961, p. 138.) W. Krusche, *Das Wirken des Heiligen Geistes nach Calvin*, Göttingen 1957, esp. ch. II: 'Der Heilige Geist und der Kosmos', 15ff. On M. Luther cf. R. Prenter, *Spiritus Creator*, Göttingen 1954. There are also beginnings in this direction in Barth. Cf. *CD* I/1, 2nd rev. ed. 1975, p. 450: 'In both the Old Testament and the New the Spirit of God, the Holy Spirit, is very generally God Himself to the degree that in an incomprehensibly real way, without on this account being any the less God, He can be present to the creature, and in virtue of this presence of His effect the relation of the creature to Himself, and in virtue of this relation to Himself grant the creature life. The creature needs the Creator to be able to live. It thus needs the relation to Him. But it cannot create this relation. God creates it by His own presence in the creature and therefore as a relation of Himself to Himself. The Spirit of God is God in His freedom to be present to the creature, and therefore to create this relation, and therefore to be the life of the creature.'

9. Cf. here F. Capra, *The Tao of Physics*, London 1975, Berkeley 1976, p. 302: 'In the new world view, the universe is seen as a dynamic web of interrelated events. None of the properties of any part of this web is fundamental; they all follow from the properties of the other parts, and the overall consistency of their mutual interrelations determines the structure of the entire web.'

10. Capra gives an excellent survey in *The Turning Point: Science, Society and the Rising Culture*, New York 1982. Cf. also G. Freudenthal's historical investigation, *Atom und Individuum im Zeitalter Newtons*, Frankfurt 1983, and the earlier work by E. J. Dijksterhuis, *Die Mechanisierung des Weltbildes*, Berlin 1956; F. W. Matson, *The Broken Image; Man, Science and Society*, New York 1964.

11. F. Oetinger, *Inquisitio in sensum communem et rationem*, Tübingen 1753, p. 150.

12. F. Rosenzweig, *Der Stern der Erlösung*, Heidelberg 1954, Pt. III, Book 3, p. 192. Cf. also A. M. Goldberg, *Untersuchungen über die Vorstellung von der Schekhinah in der frühen rabbinischen Literatur*, Berlin 1969; G. Scholem, *Von der mystischen Gestalt der Gottheit*, Frankfurt 1973, esp. IV: 'Scheckhinah; das passiv-weibliche Moment in der Gottheit', pp. 135–92.

13. Cf. I. D. Zizioulas, 'Wahrheit und Gemeinschaft', *KuD* 26, 1980, pp. 2–49.

14. K. Barth, *CD* IV/1, pp. 200f. (slightly altered): 'We have not only not to deny but actually to affirm and understand as essential to the being of God the offensive fact that there is in God Himself an above and a below, a *prius* and a *posterius*, a superiority and a subordination. His divine unity consists in the fact that in Himself He is as the one who is obeyed One and as the one who obeys Another.' Barth develops this further in the pages that follow.

15. William Blake, The Book of Thel II, *Poetry and Prose* (The Nonesuch Library), ed. G. Keynes, London and New York 1939, p. 164.

16. Here I am using the biological terminology of E. Jantsch in *Die Selbstorganisation des Universums*, Munich 1979.

II In the Ecological Crisis

1. Cf. here *The Global 2000 Report to the President. Edited by the Council on Environmental Quality*, Washington 1980; *Global Future – Es ist Zeit zu handeln*, Freiburg 1981; A. Peccei, *One hundred pages for the future. Reflections of the President of the Club of Rome*, New York and Frankfurt, 1981; also the Club of Rome's earlier study, *The Limits to Growth*, New York 1972. One of the most important forecasts: whereas the population of the earth today is about 4.5 billion, in the year 2,000 it will be 6.35 billion, and in 2030 10 billion.

2. The forecast of the HABITAT Conference 1978, Vancouver, talked about more than 2,500 mass cities of 8 to 12 million inhabitants in the year 2000. On the development of the city into the megalopolis cf. L. Mumford, *The City in History*, London and New York 1961; H. Lefèbvre, *La révolution urbaine*, Paris 1970.

3. Report of the Central Committee to the 8th Party Conference of the East German United Socialist Party (SED), East Berlin 1971, 38: 'The chief task of the Five Year Plan is the further increase of the material and cultural level of the people, on the basis of a rapid development of socialist production, increased efficiency, further scientific and technological progress, and the growth of the productivity of labour.' For a critical view of this agglomerate of dogmas of progress without any consideration of the cost, cf. H. Falcke, 'Verantwortung der Christen in einer sozialistischen Gesellschaft für Umwelt und Zukunft des Menschen', *Die Zeichen der Zeit*, 1979, pp. 243–63.

4. E. von Weizsäcker (ed.), *Humanökologie und Umweltschutz. Studien zur Friedensforschung* 8, Stuttgart 1972; Cf. also A. Auer, *Umweltethik. Ein theologischer Beitrag zur ökologischen Diskussion*, Düsseldorf 1984.

5. H. B. Friedgood especially has drawn attention to this: cf. 'Unmenschliche Menschlichkeit' in *Humanökologie und Umweltschutz*, pp. 23f.

6. The connection between the capacity to learn and the readiness to suffer has long been a familiar fact. In Greek there is assonance between μάθειν and πάθειν.

7. I. G. Barbour, *Issues in Science and Religion*, London and New York 1966; E. C. Rust, *Science and Faith. Towards a Theological Understanding of Nature*, New York 1967; H. Nebelsick, *Theology and Science in Mutual Modification*, New York 1981; A. R. Peacocke, *Creation in the World of Science*, Oxford 1979.

8. Cf. here H. Marcuse's analysis and criticism, *One-Dimensional Man*, London and New York 1964; J. Habermas, *Knowledge and Human Interests*, 2nd rev. ed., ET London 1978; M. Horkheimer, *Zur Kritik der*

instrumentellen Vernunft, ed. A. Schmidt, Frankfurt 1967 (Pt. I is a translation into German of *The Eclipse of Reason*, 1947).

9. R. L. Shinn (ed.), *Faith and Science in an Unjust World. Reports of the WCC's Conference on Faith, Science and the Future*, Geneva 1980; P. Abrecht (ed.), *Faith, Science and the Future*, Philadelphia 1978. 'Life, liberty and the pursuit of happiness' are among the inalienable basic rights of human beings, according to the American Declaration of Independence of 1776. Cf. here H. M. Jones, *The Pursuit of Happiness*, New York 1966.

10. E.g., C. Amery, *Das Ende der Vorsehung. Die gnadenlose Folgen des Christentums*, Hamburg 1972. For comment cf. U. Krolzik, *Umweltkrise-Folge des Christentums?* 2nd ed., Stuttgart 1980; G. Liedke, *Im Bauch des Fisches. Ökologische Theologie*, Stuttgart 1979; P. Schmitz (ed.) *Macht euch die Erde untertan? Schöpfungsglaube und Umweltkrise*, Würzburg 1981; E. Drewermann, *Der tödliche Fortschritt. Von der Zerstörung der Erde und des Menschen im Erbe des Christentums*, 2nd ed., Regensburg 1981. Cf. also G. Altner et al., *Manifest zur Versöhnung mit der Natur*, Neukirchen 1984.

11. H. Blumenberg, *Die Legitimität der Neuzeit*, Frankfurt 1966; H. E. Richter's psycholanalysis of cultural history, *Der Gotteskomplex*, Frankfurt 1979, follows Blumenberg. English and American research is summed up in L. White, 'The Religious Roots of our Ecological Crisis', *Science* 155, 1967, pp. 1203–7, and W. Leiss, *The Domination of Nature*, New York 1972.

12. Quoted in Leiss, op. cit., pp. 48ff. What 'the Lordship of man over nature' meant for Bacon is shown by the slavery image he uses: 'I am come in very truth leading to you Nature with all her children to bind her to your service and make her your slave' (op. cit., p. 55). According to this image, 'Mother Nature' with her children is subjected to the man, not to the human being. For critical comment see R. Ruether, *New Woman, New Earth. Sexist Ideologies and Human Liberation*, New York 1975, pp. 186ff.

13. R. Descartes, *Discours de la Méthode* (1692), *Oeuvres Philosophiques* I, ed. F. Alquié, Paris 1963, p. 634. Cf. G. Liedke, 'Von der Ausbeutung zur Kooperation' in E. von Weizsäcker (ed.), *Humanökologie und Unweltschutz*, pp. 36–65, esp. *These 12*.

14. C. F. von Weizsäcker, *Der Garten des Menschlichen. Beiträge zur geschichtlichen Anthropologie*, Munich 1977, pp. 253ff.

15. M. Heidegger, 'Die Zeit des Weltbildes' in *Holzwege*, Frankfurt 1957, pp. 69ff., esp. pp. 80ff.; G. Rohrmoser, *Subjektivität und Verdinglichung. Theologie und Gesellschaft im Denken des jungen Hegel*, Frankfurt 1961.

16. F. Baader, *Über den Zwiespalt des religiösen Glaubens und Wissens*, 2nd ed., Darmstadt 1958, p. 49.

17. A. Mitscherlich, *Thesen zur Stadt der Zukunft*, Frankfurt 1971, p. 139.

18. A. Schmidt involuntarily makes this clear; cf. *Der Begriff der Natur in der Lehre von Marx*, Frankfurt 1962, 1971.

19. Cf. criticism of the dependence theories by F. H. Cardoso, T. dos Santos, A. G. Frank, A. Pinto and others. The liberation theology of G. Gutierrez, H. Assmann, J. C. Scanone, J. L. Segundo, E. Dussel and others is based on their analyses.

20. Amery, op. cit., pp. 15ff.

21. O. H. Steck, *World and Environment* (1978), ET Nashville 1980, presented the first ecological interpretation of the Old Testament belief in creation.

22. F. Gogarten, *Der Mensch zwischen Gott und Welt*, Heidelberg 1956, p. 319. For criticism of Gogarten's apologetic theology cf. R. Weth, *Gott in Jesus*, Munich 1968; M. Welker, *Der Vorgang Autonomie*, Neukirchen 1975, pp. 129ff.

23. The most thorough-going criticism comes from K. Löwith, *Gesammelte Abhandlungen. Zur Kritik der geschichtlichen Existenz*, Stuttgart 1960; *Zur Kritik der christlichen Überlieferung*, Stuttgart 1966.

24. In spite of my contention that apocalyptic is 'the beginning of an eschatological cosmology or an eschatological ontology' (p. 137), there is an open frontier here even for the *Theology of Hope*, ET London and New York 1967.

25. This is the postulate of Karl Marx which also dominates the Marxist view of nature: 'We know only a single science, the science of history' (*The German Ideology*, ET, Collected Works 5, London, New York and Moscow 1976, p. 28 n.). Strangely enough W. Pannenberg has taken this up. Cf. 'Redemptive Event and History', in *Revelation as History*, ET New York and London 1969, pp. 15–80; 'Hermeneutic and Universal History', *Basic Questions in Theology* I, ET London and Philadelphia 1970, pp. 96–136.

26. C.F. von Weizsäcker, *The History of Nature*, ET Chicago 1949, London 1951, the title of which was vigorously disputed by theologians such as R. Bultmann.

27. Habermas, *Knowledge and Human Interest*.

28. Cf. I. D. Zizioulas, 'Wahrheit und Gemeinschaft in der Sicht der griechischen Kirchenväter', *KuD* 26, 1980, pp. 2–49.

29. On meditative knowing see von Weizsäcker, Der *Garten des Menschlichen*, esp. ch. IV. Cf. also T. Merton, *Contemplation in a World of Action*, New York 1965; J. Moltmann, *Experiences of God*, ET London and Philadelphia 1980.

30. Barbour, *Issues in Science and Religion*, gives a detailed account of the history.

31. Thomas Aquinas gave this concept its classic form; cf. *Summa Theologica* I, q 44–119.

32. The Conference of the World Council of Churches in Boston in 1979 demonstrated this change of awareness. Cf. n. 9.

33. For the historical aspect cf. H. Blumenberg, *Die kopernikanische Wende*, Suhrkamp ed. 138, Frankfurt 1965, pp. 92ff.

34. W. Elert, *Morphologie des Luthertums*, I, Munich 1931, pp. 363ff.; E. Hirsch, *Geschichte der neueren evangelischen Theologie*, Gütersloh 1949, pp. 115f. Later Cardinal Bellarmin took a similar view where Galileo was concerned, Cf. Barbour, op. cit., p. 33.

35. J. Hübner, *Die Theologie Keplers zwischen Orthodoxie und Naturwissenschaft*, Tübingen 1975.

36. F. Schleiermacher, 'Sendschreiben an Dr. Lücke' as introduction to *Der Christliche Glaube nach den Grundsätzen der evangelischen Kirche*, as quoted in the ed. *Bibliothek theologischer Klassiker*, vol. 13, 1889, p. 36 (not in ET).

37. Gogarten, *Das Mensch zwischen Gott und Welt.*

38. R. Bultmann, 'The Understanding of Man and the World in the New Testament and in the Greek World', *Essays Philosophical and Theological*, ET London and New York 1955, p. 88: 'From Christianity there comes no protest against secular science, because the eschatological understanding of the world is not a method of explaining it, and because "taking out of the world" can be implemented not by an explanation of the world but only in the decision of the "moment".' Bultmann also employs the apologetic catchword 'emancipation'.

39. E. Brunner, *Dogmatics* II; *The Christian Doctrine of Creation and Redemption*, ET London and Philadelphia 1952, pp. 7ff.

40. G. Ebeling, *Dogmatik des christlichen Glaubens*, I, Tübingen 1979, p. 302.

41. Barth, *CD* III/1, Preface.

42. P. Althaus, *Die christliche Wahrheit*, 6th ed. Gütersloh 1962, §28, *Schöpfung*, pp. 301ff.

43. Brunner, *op. cit.*, p. 7.

44. A. M. K. Müller, *Die präparierte Zeit*, Stuttgart 1972.

45. A. N. Whitehead, *Science and the Modern World*, New York 1925, pp. 13f.; T. F. Torrance, *Christian Theology and Scientific Culture*, Belfast 1980.

46. The complete verse is as follows:

Schau doch aber unsre Ketten,
da wir mit der Kreatur
seufzen, ringen,
schreien, beten
um *Erlösung von Natur*,
von dem Dienst der Eitelkeiten,
der uns noch so hart bedrückt,
ob auch schon der Geist zuzeiten
sich auf etwas Bessres schickt.

47. On the following passage cf. W. Schmidt-Kowarzik, 'Die Dialektik von gesellschaftlicher Arbeit und Natur', *Wiener Jahrbuch für Philosophie*,

X, 1977, pp. 143–76; and E. Rudolph, 'Entfremdung der Natur', in C. Eisenbart (ed.), *Humanökologie und Frieden*, Stuttgart 1979, pp. 319–41. I share Rudolph's criticism but am not taking up here his suggestion for compensating the work-orientated relationship to nature by an aesthetic one. Cf. also K. M. Meyer-Abich, *Wege zum Frieden mit der Natur. Praktische Naturphilosophie für die Umweltpolitik*, Munich 1984.

48. Heidegger, 'Die Zeit des Weltbildes' in *Holzwege*, pp. 69ff.

49. K. Marx, 'Economic and Philosophical Manuscripts', *Early Writings* (Pelican Marx Library), Harmondsworth 1975, pp. 349f.

50. This was shown by K. Bockmühl, *Leiblichkeit und Gesellschaft. Studien zur Religionskritik und Anthropologie im Frühwerk von Ludwig Feuerbach und Karl Marx*, Göttingen 1961, esp. pp. 234ff.

51. Marx, op. cit., p. 348.

52. Bloch, *Das Prinzip Hoffnung*, ch. 37: 'Wille und Natur, die technischen Utopien', pp. 729ff., esp. pp. 802ff.; 'Mitproduktivität eines möglichen Natursubjekts oder konkrete Allianztechnik.'

53. Ibid., p. 786. By the 'That' factor in existence Bloch means: '. . . the intensive factor of realization which brings and keeps the world in motion . . . the "That" is every moment as if still unresolved: the riddle of why anything is at all, is asked by the immediately existing thing itself, as its own riddle' (*Prinzip Hoffnung*, p. 358).

54. Ibid., p. 787.

55. Ibid., p. 807.

56. Ibid., p. 814.

57. R. Schulz, 'Blochs Philosophie der Hoffnung im Lichte des historischen Materialismus' in *Ernst Blochs Revision des Marxismus*, Berlin 1957, p. 65: 'Our young people should study science and technology, and not speculate spiritualistically whether and when we human beings will hear stones and apples talk, and they will understand us as human beings.'

58. A. Schmidt, *Der Begriff der Natur in der Lehre vom Marx*, p. 159. So too Rudolph, op. cit., pp. 334f.

59. Schmidt, op. cit., p. 211.

60. Ibid., p. 163.

61. This shows the parallels and the connection between the founder of the environmental theory, Uexküll, and the founder of psychosomatic medicine, V. von Weizsäcker: see J. von Uexküll, *Umwelt und Innenwelt der Tiere*, 2nd ed., Berlin 1921; *Theoretical Biology*, ET London and New York 1926; and V. von Weizsäcker, *Der Gestaltkreis. Theorie der Einheit von Wahrnehmen und Bewegen*, 4th ed., Stuttgart 1950. For the theological evaluation, cf. M. von Rad, *Anthropologie als Thema von psychosomatischer Medizin und Theologie*, Stuttgart 1974.

62. On these ideas of V. von Weizsäcker and L. von Krehl, cf. J. Moltmann, 'The Humanity of Living and Dying', in *The Experiment Hope*, ET London 1974, Philadelphia 1975, pp. 158ff.

63. B. Staehelin, *Haben und Sein*, Zürich 1979; E. Fromm, *To Have and To Be*, ET New York 1976.

64. M. Weber, *The Protestant Ethic and the Spirit of Capitalism*, ET London and New York 1930.

65. D. S. Landes, *Revolution in Time. Clocks and the Making of the Modern World*, Cambridge, Mass., 1983.

66. This applies particularly to 'the theology of nature' which is developed from A. N. Whitehead's process thinking: J. Cobb, *God and the World*, Philadelphia 1969; *Is it too late? A Theology of Creation*, New York 1971; C. Birch, *Faith, Science and the Future*, Geneva 1978.

67. E. von Weizsäcker, *Offene Systeme I. Beiträge zur Zeitstruktur von Information, Entropie und Evolution*, Stuttgart 1974; K. Maurin, K. Michalski and E. Rudolph, *Offene Systeme II. Logik und Zeit*, Stuttgart 1981.

68. G. Altner, 'Der Tod – Preis des Lebens – evolutionsbiologische und zeitphilosophische Aspekte', *EvTh* 41, 1981, pp. 19–29.

69. Cf. Julian Huxley's definition of the human being as 'evolution become conscious of itself' – a definition which Teilhard de Chardin took up; cf. *The Phenomenon of Man*, ET London and New York 1959, p. 243. Cf. also T. Runyon, 'Conflicting Models for God' in D. Kirkpatrick (ed.), *The Living God*, New York 1971, p. 42: Man is the place where the process transcends itself and becomes aware of itself.'

70. See ch. VIII §1 below.

71. M. Scheler, *Die Stellung des Menschen im Kosmos*, Munich 1949, p. 44; cf. ET, *Man's Place in Nature*, Boston 1961, pp. 42f.

72. H. Plessner, *Die Stufen des Organischen und der Mensch*, 3rd. ed., Berlin 1975, pp. 127ff.

III The Knowledge of Creation

1. I have described the connections in 'Creation as an Open System' in *The Future of Creation*, ET London and Philadelphia 1979, pp. 115–30, and *The Trinity and the Kingdom of God*, ET London 1981 (= *The Trinity and the Kingdom*, New York 1981), pp. 99ff. Here I am confining myself to a development of systematic aspects.

2. Cf. also Barbour, *Issues in Science and Religion*, p. 5: 'The view we will propose is not a new "natural theology", but rather a "theology of nature", an attempt to view the natural order in the framework of theological ideas derived primarily from the interpretation of historical revelation and religious experience.' Cf. also A. Ganoczy, *Theologie der Natur*, Theol. Meditationen 60, Zürich 1982.

3. G. von Rad, *Old Testament Theology* I, ET London and New York 1962, reissued London 1975, pp. 136ff. (citation, p. 138).

4. Thomas Aquinas, *Summa Theologica* I q 65–74. Also Barth, *CD* III/I, 'The Work of Creation'.

5. This is also Brunner's comment on Barth's doctrine of creation (see his *Dogmatics* II, p. 7 n.l.). He himself would like to make John 1, not

Genesis 1, the point of orientation for the Christian doctrine of creation. Because the Old Testament's testimony to creation is as provisional in the light of the New as its testimony about the Messiah, 'our belief in the Creator (should not be) bound up with the *narrative* of the Old Testament' (ibid.). Our messianic interpretation of the creation narratives in the Priestly Writing and the Yahwist does not 'degrade' these to something 'provisional' which Christianity has superseded. It absorbs them into the conditions of the messianic hope.

6. We are here adopting the formulas Barth uses in his *Doctrine of Creation* (*CD* III/I), §41, 'Creation and Covenant', modifying them in the direction of the federal theological tradition from which he has taken them: creation and covenant serve the coming kingdom.

7. The eschatological alignment of history towards the new creation was overlooked by K. Löwith in his criticism of historical and Christian existence. Cf. his *Gesammelte Abhandlungen zur Kritik der geschichtlichen Existenz*, Stuttgart 1960, and *Vorträge und Abhandlungen zur Kritik der christlichen Überlieferung*, Stuttgart 1966.

8. M. Pohlenz, *Die Stoa*, I, 3rd ed., Göttingen 1964, p. 198.

9. In the following passage I am following the summary account by H. Schmid, *Die Dogmatik der Evangelisch-Lutherischen Kirche*, 7th ed., Gütersloh 1983, §15, pp. 67ff., 'Cognitio Dei naturalis et supernaturalis', and H. Heppe and E. Bizer, *Die Dogmatik der Evangelisch-Reformierten Kirche*, Neukirchen 1958, 'Locus I: De theologia naturali et revelata.' For comment cf. C. Link, *Die Welt als Gleichnis, Studien zum Problem der natürlichen Theologie*, Munich 1976.

10. This function is especially stressed in the more recent hermeneutical theology of Bultmann, Fuchs and Ebeling.

11. In the whole history of the church, natural theology has never been set up as a rival to revealed theology. No theologian ever used natural theology as a self-justification of the human being before God. It was always stated that natural theology conferred wisdom but not salvation. It was Barth who saw this alternative for the first time and said 'no' to natural theology. What he was really criticizing was not a 'natural theology' but the 'political theology' of the 'German Christians' (the pro-Nazi section of the German church during the Third Reich). In his late work, the concern of natural theology therefore appears in the traditional way as the 'theology of lights' (*CD* IV/3, pp. 113ff.).

12. Through the energies of the Holy Spirit, natural circumstances are seized and employed on behalf of the kingdom of God and the new creation (I Cor. 7). Cf. E. Käsemann, 'Ministry and Community in the New Testament', in *Essays on New Testament Themes*, London and Naperville, Ill., 1964, pp. 63ff., esp. pp. 75f. For Calvin too the subjects of *theologia naturalis* belonged to pneumatology. Cf. W. Krusche, *Das Wirken des Heiligen Geistes nach Calvin*, Göttingen 1957, pp. 13ff. I first maintained the pneumatological interpretation of natural theology in 1966 in 'Gottes-

offenbarung und Wahrheitsfrage' in *Parrhesia. K. Barth zum 80, Geburtstag*, Zürich 1966, pp. 149–72.

13. Cf. H. J. Iwand, *Glauben und Wissen. Nachgelassene Werke*, I, Munich 1962, pp. 287ff., esp. pp. 290f.: 'The reversal required of theology today is to assign revelation to our era, but natural theology to the era that is to come.' With this thesis Iwand was merely picking up the basic ideas of the German Enlightenment. Cf. G. Söhngen, art. 'Natürliche Theologie', *Lexikon für Theologie und Kirche* VII, pp. 811–16, esp. p. 815: 'There was now a radical change: whereas hitherto natural theology had its place in the forecourt, as it were, as a preliminary to the real doctrine and study of God, and prepared for that, now everything supernatural and superrational is placed in the outskirts, before natural theology. As what is merely positively or historically given or conditioned, it becomes the preparatory vehicle of the moral beliefs of reason. This reasonable faith therefore becomes the key for spelling out religion in natural terms and for seeing (natural) religion in and above the (positive) religions.'

14. D. Bonhoeffer, *Ethics*, ET London and New York, 2nd ed. 1971, pp. 120ff.: 'The Natural'.

15. Barth, *CD* IV/3, pp. 113–54. Here he was picking up ideas which he had already developed for the section on culture in 'Church and Culture' (1926) in *Theology and Church*, ET London and New York 1962, esp. pp. 342ff., and for the political sphere in 'The Christian Community and the Civil Community', ET in *Against the Stream: Shorter Post-War Writings 1946–52*, London and New York 1954, pp. 30ff.

16. *CD* IV/3, p. 113.

17. Ibid., pp. 114f.

18. Ibid., pp. 136f. Cf. also below: 'Appendix: Symbols of the World', section 5: The Great Theatre of the World.

19. Ibid., p. 138. Cf. also III/3, pp. 48ff.

20. Ibid., p. 140.

21. *CD* III/3, p. 48: 'The created cosmos, including man . . . is this theatre of the great acts of God in grace and salvation. With a view to this he is God's servant, instrument and material. But the theatre obviously cannot be the subject of the work enacted on it. It can only make it externally possible.' Barbour rightly asks (*Issues in Science and Religion*, p. 424): 'But does not nature participate in a more direct way – is it not, in fact, part of the drama?'

22. IV/3, p. 151.

23. Link, *Die Welt als Gleichnis*, pp. 292ff., sees this clearly and expounds it as implicit criticism of Barth.

24. John Milton, *Paradise Lost* V, lines 574–6.

25. Cf. P. Ricoeur, 'The Hermeneutics of Symbols and Philosophical Reflection' in *The Conflict of Interpretations* ET Evanston, 1974, pp. 287–334. Ricoeur starts from the 'surplus of meaning' in the symbol, and finds that it expresses the self-differentiation and self-transcendence of

experienced reality. Symbols do not pin things down. They set free. In messianic symbols, realities are manifested as *vestigia regni Dei.*

26. Bloch, *Das Prinzip Hoffnung*, pp. 1410f.: 'The idea of the kingdom . . . in its anticipations contains an absolute in which contradictions other than the social ones are to cease, in which the understanding of all previous interconnections changes also. '

27. E. Cardenal, *Love*, ET London 1974, p. 24.

28. G. Scholem, 'Zum Verständnis der messianischen Idee im Judentum' in *Judaica* I, Frankfurt 1963, pp. 72f. Similarly Bloch, *Das Prinzip Hoffnung*, pp. 1408ff. For comment cf. J. Moltmann, 'Philosophie in der Schwebe des Messianismus' in *Im Gespräch mit Ernst Bloch*, Munich 1976, pp. 73–89.

29. Cf. H. Schwantes, *Schöpfung der Endzeit*, Stuttgart 1962, which is a valuable exception here; P. Stuhlmacher, 'Erwägungen zum ontologischen Charakter der Theologie bei Paulus,' *EvTh* 27, 1967, pp. 1–35.

30. On the following passage cf. E. Käsemann, *Commentary on Romans*, London and Grand Rapids, Mich., 1980.

31. Käsemann, 'Ministry and Community in the New Testament' in *Essays on New Testament Themes*, pp. 63ff.

32. E. Käsemann, 'The Cry for Liberty in the Worship of the Church' in *Perspectives on Paul*, ET London and Philadelphia 1971, pp. 122ff.; P. von der Osten-Sacken, *Römer 8 als Beispiel paulinischer Soteriologie*, Göttingen 1975; H. R. Balz, *Heilsvertrauen und Welterfahrung. Strukturen paulinischer Eschatologie nach Röm. 8 18–39*, Göttingen 1971; W. Bindemann, *Die Hoffnung der Schöpfung. Römer 8, 19–27 und die Frage einer Theologie der Befreiung von Mensch und Natur*, Neukirchen 1983.

33. This experience of nature is brought out very well in a poem by Annette von Droste-Hülshoff, 'Die ächzende Kreatur' ('sighing creation') (1846):

> Und dennoch gibt es eine Last,
> Die keiner fühlt und jeder trägt,
> So dunkel wie die Sünde fast
> Und auch im gleichen Schoss gehegt;
> Er trägt sie wie den Druck der Luft,
> Vom kranken Leibe nur empfunden,
> Bewusstlos, wie den Fels die Kluft,
> Wie schwarze Lad' den Todeswunden.
>
> Das ist die Schuld des Mordes an
> Der Erde Lieblichkeit und Huld,
> An des Getieres dumpfem Bann
> Ist es die tiefe, schwere Schuld,
> Und an dem Grimm, der es beseelt,
> Und an der List, die es befleckt,
> Und an dem Schmerze, der es quält,
> Und an dem Moder, der es deckt.

(And yet there is a heavy weight
Which no one feels, and each one bears,
Almost as dark as sin itself
And fostered in the self-same womb.
He bears this weight as sickness knows
The weight of air, by health unfelt,
Unwitting, as cleft bears the rock,
As coffin holds the mortal wounds.

It is the guilt of murder done
On nature's dear delights and grace.
It is the deep and heavy guilt
For brooding curse on rav'ning beasts;
Guilt for the rage that quickens them,
Guilt for the guile that sullies them,
Guilt for the pain that tortures them,
Guilt for the mould that covers them.)

W. Benjamin also understood nature in the light of this significance. Cf. his *Ursprung des deutschen Trauerspiels*, Frankfurt 1969. It is in its very sadness that the messianic character of nature is to be found.

34. Käsemann, 'The Cry for Liberty', op. cit., p. 135.

35. P. Evdokimov, 'Nature', *SJT* 18, 1965, pp. 1–22, esp. pp. 14ff.; K. Ware, *The Orthodox Way*, Oxford 1979, pp. 54ff., 68ff.; cf. also G. Wainwright, *Doxology. The Praise of God in Worship, Doctrine and Life*, London and New York 1980; H. H. Guthrie, *Theology as Thanksgiving. From Israel's Psalms to the Church's Eucharist*, New York 1981; T. Runyon, 'The World as the Original Sacrament', *Worship*, vol. 54, No. 6, Nov. 1980, pp. 495ff.

IV God the Creator

1. In the exegesis I am here following F. Delitzsch, *Commentar über die Genesis*, 3rd. ed. Leipzig 1860, and B. Jacob, *Das erste Buch der Thora Genesis*, Berlin 1934. These two commentators were also followed by G. von Rad and K. Barth, a fact which explains what would otherwise be some remarkable parallels between the two. Cf. also H. Graf Reventlow, *Hauptprobleme der alttestamentlichen Theologie im 20. Jahrhundert*, Darmstadt 1982. Recent literature is dealt with by C. Westermann in his great commentary on Genesis: ET of vol. 1 (*Genesis 1–11*), London and Minneapolis 1984.

2. Jacob, op. cit., p. 20. The expression in the English Apostles' Creed, 'Maker of heaven and earth', blurs this difference.

3. G. Scholem presents the Jewish tradition in 'Schöpfung aus Nichts und Selbstverschränkung Gottes', *Eranos Jahrbuch* 1956, 25, pp. 87–119; G. May, *Schöpfung aus dem Nichts. Die Entstehung der Lehre von der Creatio ex nihilo*, Berlin 1978, shows that as Christian doctrine this took

on final form in the dispute of the church Fathers with gnostic theology. It has been an integral part of the Christian doctrine of creation ever since Irenaeus. Cf. here E. Wölfel, *Welt als Schöpfung. Zu den Fundamentalsätzen der christlichen Schöpfungslehre heute*, Theologische Existenz heute 212, Munich 1981, pp. 27ff.; G. Hendry, 'Nothing', *Theology Today* XXXIX, No. 3, Oct. 1982, pp. 274–90, takes up my idea about the self-contraction in God (p. 288).

4. Plato, *Timaeus*, 28a.

5. E. Bloch, *Philosophische Grundfragen. Zur Ontologie des Noch-Nicht Seins*, Frankfurt 1961, pp. 42ff., interprets the 'not' as productive not-having: ' "Nothing" is not able to endure itself.' He distinguishes it quite clearly from the hard, meaningless Nothingness, from which nothing can grow. But according to Bloch what is at stake in the leavening, fermenting 'Not' is 'all or nothing'. It is 'not-yet' decided. In this way Bloch turns the protological concept of Nothing into an eschatological one, putting the productive not-yet-being in the protological position.

6. Cf. here, Moltmann, *The Trinity and the Kingdom of God*, pp. 52ff. A. O. Lovejoy, *The Great Chain of Being*, 1936, 14th impression, Cambridge, Mass., 1978, pp. 67ff., describes the history of the Christian absorption of the Neo-platonic doctrine of emanation in the early middle ages. It goes back to Plato's classic thesis *in Timaeus*, 29e: 'Let us state the cause wherefore he who constructed it *did* construct Becoming and the universe. He was Good, and in one that is good no envy of anything else ever arises. Being devoid of envy, then, he desired that everything should be as far as possible like himself.'

7. *Inferno* I, 39f.

8. Moltmann, *The Trinity and the Kingdom of God*, pp. 111ff.; so also K. Ware, *The Orthodox Way*, p. 56.

9. D. Bonhoeffer, *Creation and Fall*, ET London and New York 1959, pp. 19ff.

10. A. N. Whitehead, *Process and Reality*, corrected ed. by D. R. Griffin and D. W. Sherburne, New York 1979, esp. p. 348; J. B. Cobb and D. R. Griffin, *Process Theology*, Philadelphia 1976, Belfast 1977, esp. pp. 65ff. For critical comment cf. M. Welker, *Universalität Gottes und Relativität der Welt*, Neukirchen 1981, esp. pp. 206ff.

11. Cobb and Griffin, op. cit., p. 65. But Thomas Aquinas does not find eternal creation inconceivable either. Cf. A. Antweiler, *Die Anfanglosigkeit der Welt nach Thomas von Aquin*, Trier 1961.

12. F. Schleiermacher, *The Christian Faith* §39, §40, ET Edinburgh and New York 1928, pp. 148–52. For comment cf. F. Beisser, *Schleiermachers Lehre von Gott, dargestellt nach seinen Reden und seiner Glaubenslehre*, Göttingen 1970, p. 115: 'According to Schleiermacher, God's relation to the world is fundamentally that of *preserver*. The concept of creation is practically reduced to the concept of preservation.' Cf. also, with a wealth of evidence, M. Trowitzsch, *Zeit zur Ewigkeit. Beiträge zum Zeitver-*

ständnis in der "Glaubenslehre" Schleiermachers, Munich 1976, esp. pp. 69ff.

13. The reduction of the doctrine of creation is in accordance with Schleiermacher's reduction of Christ's cross and resurrection to Jesus' consciousness of God, and the raising of the dead to the immortality of the soul.

14. Moltmann, *The Trinity and the Kingdom of God*, p. 99.

15. Heppe and Bizer, *Die Dogmatik der evangelisch-reformierten Kirche*, Locus VII: De decretis Dei, pp. 107ff.

16. Ibid., p. 107.

17. Ibid., p. 109: 'Deus 1) decrevit *gloriam suam* foris, idque multifariam, neque propter suum, sed propter *creaturae bonum* patefacere . . . 2) decrevit *creare mundum* . . . .'

18. I have put forward this criticism in *The Trinity and the Kingdom of God*, pp. 52ff.

19. Barth, *CD* II/2, p. 166; similarly IV/2, pp. 345f., II/2, p. 10, and frequently.

20. On this problem cf. M. Welker, 'Das theologische Prinzip des Verhaltens zu Zeiterscheinungen. Erörterung eines Problems im Blick auf die theologische Hegelrezeption und Gen 3,22a', *EvTh* 36, 1976, pp. 2/25ff.

21. For critical comment on my criticism of Barth, cf. H. Urs von Balthasar, 'Zu einer christlichen Theologie der Hoffnung', *Münchener Theologische Zeitschrift* 32, 1981, pp. 101f.; he shrinks back from the adoption of the doctrine of emanation.

22. P. Tillich, *Systematic Theology* I, ET Chicago 1951, London 1953, pp. 252ff.

23. Ibid.

24. I am here developing further ideas which I have already put forward in *The Trinity and the Kingdom of God*, pp. 109ff.

25. Scholem, 'Schöpfung aus Nichts und Selbstverschränkung Gottes', op. cit., pp. 115ff. The *zimsum* idea also plays a leading part in the Yiddish novels of Isaak Bashevis Singer, especially in *The Slave*, ET New York 1962, London 1963. He uses it in the form of the biblical metaphor: 'God hides his face.'

26. Scholem, op. cit., p. 117.

27. Ibid., p. 118.

28. Brunner, *Dogmatics* II, p. 19: 'This, however, means that God does not wish to occupy the whole of Space Himself, but that He wills to make room for other forms of existence. In doing so He limits Himself. . . . The κένωσις, which reaches its paradoxical climax in the Cross of Christ, begins with the creation of the world.' Cf. here Hendry, 'Nothing', in *Theology Today*, XXXIX, 1982, pp. 286ff.

29. Cf. in contrast Barth, *CD* III/3, §50: 'God and Nothingness', pp. 289–368. In his doctrine of creation Barth does not go beyond the Platonic definition of nothingness. However, in his doctrine of election (CD

II/2) he develops insights into the annihilating nothingness drawn from the theology of the cross which lend theological depth to the Platonic Non-Being. For Barth's interpretation, cf. W. Krötke, *Sünde und Nichtiges bei Karl Barth*, 2nd ed., Neukirchen 1983.

30. *Paradiso* I.1–2.

31. Cf. here J. Moltmann, 'Justification and New Creation' in *The Future of Creation*, pp. 149ff. Grace is really already to be found in the divine *preservation* of the creature who closes himself against God. Theological tradition has already given expression to this through the distinction between πάρεσις and ἄφεσις ἁμαρτίων. But if there is grace even in the preservation of the world, then there must also be grace in the creation of the world, from the very beginning.

32. This is the main problem in Bloch, *Philosophische Grundfragen* I, esp. pp. 60ff. For criticism cf. Moltmann, *Theologie der Hoffnung*, 3rd ed., Munich 1965, Anhang: ' "Das Prinzip Hoffnung" und die "Theologie der Hoffnung" ', pp. 313ff., esp. pp. 326ff. (appendix not in ET).

33. W. Benjamin, *Illuminationen*, Frankfurt 1961, pp. 270f.

34. K. Stock, *Annihilatio mundi. Johann Gerhards Eschatologie der Welt*, Munich 1971.

35. I am here taking up and developing ideas already put forward in *The Trinity and the Kingdom of God*, pp. 102ff., though without entering again into the form of creation within the Trinity, as I did there on pp. 105ff.

36. F. Mussner, 'Schöpfung in Christus', *Mysterium Salutis II,* Zurich and Cologne 1975, pp. 460ff.

37. Calvin, quoted in Krusche, *Das Wirken des Heiligen Geistes nach Calvin*, p. 15.

38. Quoted in K.–D. Buchholtz, *Isaac Newton als Theologe*, Witten 1965, p. 68.

39. Calvin, *Institutes* I, 13. 14, concluded from this that 'not only is the beauty of the world as we now see it sustained by the power of the Spirit, but that the Spirit, before all these adornments had their being, already preserved the unordered material'.

40. Cf. H. Wheeler Robinson, *The Christian Experience of the Holy Spirit*, London and New York 1928; Rust, *Science and Faith*, pp. 182ff.; A. Heron, *The Holy Spirit in the Bible, in the History of Christian Thought and in Recent Theology*, London and Philadelphia 1983, esp. pp. 137ff.; Y. Congar, *I Believe in the Holy Spirit* II: 'He is Lord and Giver of Life', ET London and New York 1983, pp. 218ff.

41. F. D. E. Schleiermacher, *On Religion: Speeches to its Cultured Despisers*, ET 1893, reissued New York 1958, II, 'The Nature of Religion': Religion is contemplation of the Universe: 'The Universe is ceaselessly active and at every moment is revealing itself to us. Every form it has produced, everything to which, from the fulness of its life, it has given a separate existence, every occurrence scattered from its fertile bosom is an operation of the Universe upon us. Now religion is to take up into our lives

and to submit to be swayed by them, each of these influences and their consequent emotions, not by themselves but as a part of the Whole, . . . as an exhibition of the Infinite in our life' (pp. 48f.). F. Oetinger's theology of life also starts from the *spiritus rector*, which enlivens and moves everything, and which manifests itself in all created things. Cf. *Theologia ex idea vitae deducta*, 1765, and E. Zinn, *Die Theologie des Friedrich Christoph Oetinger*, Gütersloh 1932.

42. R. Bultmann, *Theology of the New Testament* I, ET New York 1951, London 1952, p. 209. Cf. also A. Come, *Human Spirit and Holy Spirit*, Philadelphia 1959.

43. Käsemann, 'The Cry for Liberty in the Worship of the Church' in *Perspectives on Paul*, pp. 122ff., esp. pp. 134ff. It may be added that according to Rev. 22.17 it is not only the church which eschatologically cried 'Come!' It is the Spirit too. Cf. also W. Bindemann, *Die Hoffnung der Schöpfung. Römer 8, 18–27 und die Frage einer Theologie der Befreiung von Mensch und Natur*, Neukirchen 1983, pp. 118ff.

44. H. Wheeler Robinson, *The Christian Experience of the Holy Spirit*, pp. 87ff.; Rust, *Science and Faith*, pp. 195ff. V. Lossky, *In the Image and Likeness of God*, New York 1974, London 1975, p. 92, also talks about a *kenosis* of the person of the Holy Spirit in the economy of salvation which makes it difficult to grasp his hypostatic existence.

45. K. Stock, 'Creatio nova – creatio ex nihilo', *EvTh* 36, 1976, pp. 202ff., 215. He has taken up my ideas about the immanence of the Spirit of God in the world and developed them further: the Spirit is 'just as much the power of the approaching future of God and his kingdom of freedom as it is also, as the movement of matter . . . "the drive, the vital spirit, the tension . . . the torment of matter" (*Perspektiven der Theologie*, Munich 1968, pp. 209f.). The quotation is taken from Karl Marx, *Die Heilige Familie*, ch. VI.3 (d); cf. ET, *The Holy Family*. Collected Works 4, London, New York and Moscow 1975, p. 128. In this passage Marx is referring to Jakob Böhme's materialistic doctrine of the Spirit, a doctrine which also put its stamp on Friedrich Oetinger's organic view of nature.

46. Rust, *Science and Faith*, p. 198, rightly says: 'That cross is borne in the immanence of the Creator Spirit and finds its culmination in the Incarnation and Cross on Calvary's hill.' From this he draws the correct conclusion: 'Any doctrine of creation and providence has a cross at its heart.'

47. H. Heine, *Die romantische Schule* (1835), Stuttgart 1979, pp. 46f. Cf. ET, *The Romantic School*, New York 1882, pp. 57f.

48. On Capra, *The Turning Point*, pp. 93ff; also *The Tao of Physics*, p. 302.

49. A critical comment on E. Jantsch, *Die Selbstorganisation des Universums. Vom Urknall zum menschlichen Geist*, Munich 1982, pp. 411ff., and especially his statement: 'God is not the Creator but he is the Spirit of the universe' (p. 412).

V *The Time of Creation*

1. Augustine, *Confessions*, XI, 14, trans. R. S. Pine-Coffin (Penguin), Harmondsworth 1961.

2. M. Eliade, *The Myth of the Eternal Return*, ET New York and London 1954; S. G. F. Brandon, *History, Time and Deity*, Manchester and New York 1965. On the history of the concept of time cf. S. Toulmin and J. Goodfield, *The Discovery of Time*, London and New York 1965.

3. Eliade, op. cit., p. 56.

4. E. Hornung, *Geschichte als Fest*, Darmstadt 1970, demonstrates this on the basis of the rituals of the Egyptian and pre-Columbus Mexican religions. With respect to the modern experience of history, cf. T. Darby, *The Feast. Meditations on Politics and Time*, Toronto 1982.

5. A. Gehlen, *Urmensch und Spätkultur*, Bonn 1956; R. Seidenberg, *Post-Historic Man*, Chapel Hill 1950; and in his own way also C. Lévi-Strauss, *The Savage Mind*, ET London and Chicago 1966.

6. Plato, *Timaeus*, 37d, trans. F. M. Cornford, London and New York 1937, reissued 1956: 'Now the nature of that Living Being was eternal, and this character it was impossible to confer in full completeness on the generated thing. But he took thought to make, as it were, a moving likeness of eternity; and, at the same time that he ordered the Heaven, he made, of eternity that abides in unity, an everlasting likeness moving according to number – that to which we have given the name Time.' Cf. G. Picht, *Die Erfahrung der Geschichte*, Frankfurt 1958, pp. 42f.

7. Aristotle, *Physics*, 223 b 29. Cf. G. Picht, 'Die Zeit und die Modalitäten' In *Hier und Jetzt: Philosophieren nach Auschwitz und und Hiroshima* Stuttgart 1980, I, pp. 362–374, esp. pp. 363f.

8. Plato, *Timaeus*, 27d.

9. Parmenides, Fragment 2 (ET based on F. M. Cornford, *Plato and Parmenides: Parmenides' Way of Truth and Plato's Parmenides* trans. with commentary, London and New York 1939, pp. 30f.).

10. Ibid., Fragment 8, lines 1–6, 19–21.

11. Picht, op. cit., pp. 365ff.

12. I. Kant, *Critique of Pure Reason*, trans, J. M. D. Meiklejohn, Everyman, London and New York 1934, reprinted 1979, pp. 143f. (altered). 'For change does not affect time itself, but only the phenomena in time.'

13. Ibid., pp. 120f.

14. Cf. here U. Duchrow, 'Der sogenannte psychologische Zeitbegriff Augustins im Verhältnis zur physikalischen und geschichtlichen Zeit', *ZThK* 63, 1966, pp. 267ff., and T. Pierce, 'Spatio-temporal Relations in Divine Interactions', *SJT* 35, 1982, pp. 1–11; J. Quinn, *The Doctrine of Time in St Thomas*, Washington 1960.

15. *Confessions* XI, 12.

16. *De civ. Dei* XI, 6.

17. *Confessions* XI, 13.

18. Ibid.

19. Ibid., XI, 30. Cf. also XI, 10, where Augustine sees the coming into being of a resolve of will in God as a contradiction of the eternity of its becoming: 'But if God's will that there should be a creation was there from all eternity, why is it that what he has created is not also eternal?'

20. Ibid., XI, 14.

21. Ibid., XI, 12; also XI, 14.

22. Ibid., XI, 20.

23. Ibid., XI, 18; 28.

24. K. Barth, *CD* III/1, 70.

25. Ibid., III/1, p. 71.

26. G. von Rad, *Old Testament Theology* II, ET Edinburgh and New York 1965, reissued London 1975, p. 100. S. de Vries, *Yesterday, Today and Tomorrow: Time and History in the Old Testament*, Grand Rapids 1975, may be held to be the best study on the subject.

27. Von Rad., op. cit., p. 106.

28. On the concept of narrative in narrative theology, see the summing up by J. B. Metz, *Glaube in Geschichte und Gesellschaft*, Mainz 1977, pp. 181ff.

29. Von Rad, op. cit., p. 113. Cf. also p. 112.

30. Ibid., p. 118.

31. I have discussed this in more detail in *Theology of Hope*, ch. IV: 'Eschatology and History', pp. 230ff.

32. L. Landgrebe, 'Das philosophische Problem des Endes der Geschichte' in *Phänomenologie und Geschichte*, Gütersloh 1967, pp. 182–201; J. Moltmann, 'Das Ende der Geschichte' in *Geschichte – Element der Zukunft. Vorträge an den Hochschultagen der Evangelischen Studentengemeinde Tübingen 1965* von R. Wittram, H.-G. Gadamer, J. Moltmann.

33. Cf. here Ricoeur, 'Freedom in the Light of Hope', in *The Conflict of Interpretations*, pp. 402–24.

34. G. W. F. Hegel, *Vorlesungen über die Philosophie der Weltgeschichte*, *Werke* XI, p. 557. Cf. ET, *Lectures on the Philosophy of History*, London 1857, p. 466.

35. A. Vilmar, quoted in R. Strunk, *Politische Ekklesiologie im Zeitalter der Revolution*, Mainz, Munich 1971, p. 236.

36. On the concept of "project", cf. R. Garaudy, *Le projet espérance*, Paris 1976.

37. P. Miller, 'Temporal Concepts: A schematic analysis' in *Process Studies* 9/1, 1979, pp. 22–29, 26.

38. Augustine, *Confessions* XI, esp. 20.

39. G. Picht, *Hier und Jetzt: Philosophieren nach Auschwitz und Hiroshima*, Stuttgart 1980, I, pp. 362–74; 'Die Zeit und die Modalitäten'.

40. A. M. K. Müller, *Die präparierte Zeit*, Stuttgart 1972.

41. A. N. Prior, *Past, Present and Future*, Oxford and New York 1967.

42. N. Luhmann, 'Weltzeit und Systemgeschichte' in *Soziologische Aufklärung* 2, Opladen 1975, pp. 103–133.

43. R. Koselleck, 'Geschichte, Geschichten und formale Zeitstrukturen' in R. Koselleck and W. D. Stempel, *Geschichte – Ereignis und Erzählung*, Munich 1973; D. M. Lowe, 'Intentionality and the Method of History' in M. Natanson (ed.), *Phenomenology and the Social Sciences*, Toronto 1979, pp. 103–130.

44. E. Jantsch, *Die Selbstorganisation des Universums*, Munich 1982, esp. pp. 315ff.

45. M. Heidegger, *Being and Time*, ET London and New York 1962, §74: 'The Basic Constitution of Historicality', pp. 434ff.; cit. from p. 378.

46. R. Wittram, *Zukunft in der Geschichte*, Göttingen 1966; R. Koselleck, *Vergangene Zukunft. Zur Semantik geschichtlicher Zeiten*, Frankfurt 1979. I myself am taking up, and modifying, ideas expressed by W. Benjamin, 'Geschichtsphilosophische Thesen' in *Illuminationen*, pp. 268–280.

47. D. F. Strauss, *Die christliche Glaubenslehre* I, 1840, p. 71.

48. Scheler, *Die Stellung des Menschen im Kosmos*, p. 31; cf. ET, *Man's Place in Nature*, p. 27.

49. W. Dilthey, *Gesammelte Schriften* VIII, Leipzig and Berlin 1931, p. 225.

50. "The future in the past" is something to which Bloch pointed emphatically; cf. *Das Prinzip Hoffnung*, p. 7: 'The rigid divisons between future and past then collapse of themselves, future which has never become future becomes visible in the past; revenged and inherited, mediated and fulfilled past in the future.' Cf. also D. M. Lowe, *History of Bourgeois Perception*, Chicago 1982, esp. ch. 2, 'Temporality', pp. 35ff. Lowe draws on E. Husserl's analysis of the sense of time. In the appendix on 'History and the Past' (pp. 174f.), he points to 'Prospectivity within retrospection' as the indispensable reflection of the historical sense: 'How is it possible to represent a past without losing sight of its unique prospective reality? This I believe is the crucial problem in historical method. History ought to be the present representation of the prospective reality of a past, within the historian's retrospection.'

51. Luhmann, op. cit., p. 252, following K. Löwith, *Zur Kritik der christlichen Überlieferung*, Stuttgart 1966, p. 155.

52. For a more detailed exposition cf. J. Moltmann, 'The Future as a New Paradigm of Transcendence' in *The Future of Creation*, pp. 1–17. Cf. also E. Brunner, *Das Ewige als Zukunft und Gegenwart*, Munich 1965; G. Sauter, *Zukunft und Verheissung*, Zürich 1965, p. 154.

53. J. Moltmann, title essay in *Hope and Planning*, ET London and New York 1971, pp. 178–99.

54. Extrapolation cannot be the principle of Christian eschatology. This critical comment must be made in response to Rahner, 'The Hermeneutics of Eschatological Assertions', *Theological Investigations* IV, pp. 323–46, and H. Berkhof, *Gegronde verwachting*, Leyden 1967. Cf. Heidegger,

Holzwege, p. 301: 'All historical study calculates what is to come from its pictures of the past, which are determined by the present. Historical study is the continual destruction of the future and of the relation of the true historical past to the coming of what is destined.'

55. Bloch, *Das Prinzip Hoffnung*, Pt. II: 'The Anticipating Consciousness', pp. 49–394.

56. Rosenzweig, *Der Stern der Erlösung*, Heidelberg 1954, Pt. II, Book III, p. 170.

57. I mean this in the sense of a 'hermeneutics of danger' (J. B. Metz), which W. Benjamin (op. cit., p. 270), expressed as follows: 'It is essential to lay hold of a recollection which flashes through the mind in the moment of danger.'

58. Cf. here, with extensive evidence, W. Leiss, *The Domination of Nature*, New York 1972.

59. J. E. Lovelock, *Gaia*, Oxford and New York 1979, has shown in the so-called 'Gaia hypothesis' that the planet earth has to be viewed as a single living organism. He expounds scientifically what K. Löwith put forward philosophically in the name of a rediscovery of nature; see his critical attitude towards historical existence (Stuttgart 1960) and towards Christian existence (Stuttgart 1966).

VI The Space of Creation

1. A. Koyré, *From the Closed World to the Infinite Universe*, Baltimore 1957.

2. B. Pascal, *Pensées*, no. 206, ET (Everyman's Library) London and New York 1908, p. 61.

3. Ibid., no. 72, p. 17.

4. F. Nietzsche, *The Joyful Wisdom*, §125. *Werke*, ed. K. Schlechta, II, Munich 1955, p. 127; cf. ET, *Works* 10, London 1910, p. 168.

5. M. Eliade, *The Sacred and the Profane*, ET New York and Evanston, 1959, p. 20. I am following Eliade's account here.

6. Ibid., p. 32ff.

7. O. F. Bollnow, *Mensch und Raum*, Stuttgart 1963; H. Schmitz, 'Das Göttliche und der Raum' in *System der Philosophie* III/4, Bonn 1977.

8. Linguistically the topological terms 'neighbouring region' and 'way' should be introduced into the concepts of space. Cf. D. Wunderlich, 'Sprache und Raum' in *Studien der Linguistik* 12, 1982, pp. 1–19 and 37–59, esp. pp. 5f.

9. Topological, projective and Euclidean characteristics of space emerge in the course of the development of a child's concept of space. Cf. J. Piaget and B. Inhelder, *Die Entwicklung des räumlichen Denkens beim Kind*, Stuttgart 1975.

10. W. Capelle, *Die Vorsokratiker*, Berlin 1958, p. 72.

11. Parmenides, fragment 8, lines 22–25.

12. Ibid., lines 42ff.

13. Plato, *Timaeus*, 51a. Cf. also M. Jammer, *Concepts of Space*, Cambridge, Mass., 1954, Oxford 1955, pp. 12ff.

14. Plato, *Timaeus*, 50a. Cf. also R. Arnheim, *Die Dynamik der architektonischen Form*, Cologne 1980, pp. 17ff.

15. Cf. Jammer, op. cit., pp. 15ff.

16. So Jammer, op. cit. p. 20.

17. J. v. Uexküll, 'A Stroll through the Worlds of Animals and Men' in C. H. Schiller, *Instinctive Behaviour*, New York 1957.

18. I am here following Steck, *World and Environment*.

19. Ibid., p. 84.

20. Midrash Rabbah Genesis II, LXVIII, 9, quoted in M. Jammer, op. cit., p. 28.

21. Cf. here Moltmann, *The Trinity and the Kingdom of God*, pp. 108ff.

22. Cf. below ch. XI: 'The Sabbath: the Feast of Creation.'

23. Scheler, *Stellung des Menschen*, pp. 40f.; cf. ET, pp. 38f.

24. Ibid., p. 46; ET, p. 44.

25. In response to W. Pannenberg, *What is Man?* ET Philadelphia 1970, p. 12.

26. Koyré, *From the Closed World to the Infinite Universe*; J. J. C. Smart, *Problems of Space and Time*, New York 1964, offers an excellent collection of philosophical and scientific contributions on the concepts of space and time.

27. I am following the accounts of Max Jammer and Alexandre Koyré but draw different conclusions from the findings. Cf. also K.-D. Buchholtz, *Isaak Newton als Theologe*, Witten 1965, esp. pp. 69ff.

28. Koyré, op. cit., p. 106.

29. Jammer, *Concepts of Space*, pp. 26ff.; Koyré, op. cit., pp. 147f.

30. Koyré, op. cit., pp. 148f.

31. Ibid., pp. 153f.

32. Jammer, op. cit., pp. 93ff.; Koyré, op. cit., pp. 155ff.

33. Quoted by Jammer, op. cit., p. 112. F. Oetinger took up Newton's view of space and linked it deliberately with the kabbalistic idea about the *spatium*: God is not merely omnipresent; he himself constitutes space. In his space God 'feels' all things and events. Cf. E. Zinn, *Die Theologie des Friedrich Oetinger*, Gütersloh 1932, pp. 58ff.

34. Jammer, op. cit., p. 35.

35. A. Safran, *Die Kabbala*, Bern 1966, p. 281. The image of the *zimsum* 'illustrates the idea of creation and of God's activity'.

VII Heaven and Earth

1. B. Jacob, *Das erste Buch der Tora Genesis*, p. 23. It is only Gen. 2.4 which has the reverse order: 'In the day that Lord God made the earth and the heavens . . .' But here the difference between 'making' and 'creating' should be noted. B. Jacob, *op. cit.*, pp. 77ff. Cf. ch. IV §1.

2. Cf. Ps. 104; Gen. 1.

3. Cf. J. Nelis, 'God and Heaven in the Old Testament', *Concilium* (ET) 123, 1979, pp. 22–33. Nelis distinguishes five different categories in which heaven is talked about. This whole number of *Concilium* is devoted to the subject of heaven.

4. The threefold division is dogmatic tradition; cf. F. Diekamp, *Katholische Dogmatik nach den Grundsätzen des Hl. Thomas*, III, Münster 1922, pp. 406ff.; D. Tilenus (Calvinist), *Syntagma tripertitum Disputationum theologicarum in academia Sedanensi habitarum*, Geneva 1618, p. 455, says that 'coelum trifariam in scriptura sumitur'. See the other examples cited in Heppe and Bizer, *Dogmatik der evangelisch-reformierten Kirche*, pp. 390ff.

5. M. Welker explicitly draws attention to this in *Universalität Gottes und Relativität der Welt*, Neukirchen 1981, pp. 203ff.

6. Cf. ch. II, §2.

7. Plato, *Timaeus*, 34 b. ET by F. M. Cornford (altered).

8. Barth, *CD* III/3, p. 419. Also M. Schmaus, *Katholische Dogmatik*, I, Munich 1938, considers heaven to be 'a parable of God's mode of existence', i.e., his sublimity (p. 287).

9. Barth, *CD* III/3, pp. 421, 422, 433.

10. Ibid., p. 422.

11. Barth (ibid., p. 426) talks explicitly about the 'hierarchy in the relationship between heaven and earth'.

12. Barth, *CD* III/2, pp. 418ff. and III/4, pp. 170ff.

13. Barth, *CD* III/3, p. 422: 'The Dialectic of the Contrast between Heaven and Earth'; (p. 423): 'the superiority of heaven to earth'. J. T. Beck, *Die Vollendung des Reiches*, Gütersloh 1887, pp. 6ff., on the other hand, uses the metaphor of 'the organism', and talks about creation's 'heavenly, earthly and bodily organism'.

14. I have taken over this distinction from Johann Gerhard, *Loci theologici*, ed. H. Preuss, Berlin 1863 ff., Loc. XXXI, tract. 6, §8 (vol. IX, pp. 293f.), but I am applying it in my own way.

15. J. Gerhard, loc. cit. (p. 293): 'tum aereum, videlicet totae aereae regionis ab aquis et terra ad lunae usque orbem expansio; tum aethereum, videlicet firmamentum omnes sphaeras coelestes comprehendens . . .'

16. P. Evdokimov, 'Nature', *SJT* 18, 1965, pp. 1–22, esp. pp. 8ff.; P. Gregorius, *The Human Presence. An Orthodox View of Nature*, Geneva 1977, ch. V: 'God's Activity in the World. Gregory of Nyssa and the classical Christian alternative', pp. 54ff. Whitehead's idea that certain 'eternal objects' serve as 'potentiality for actual entities' (*Process and Reality*, pp. 40ff.) must undoubtedly be seen as 'a footnote to Plato', but as a modern and relevant one.

17. Cf. Diekamp, *Katholische Dogmatik*, III, pp. 436ff.; M. Schmaus, *Der Glaube der Kirche*, II, Munich 1970, pp. 799f.; Gerhard, *Loci theol.*, XXXI, tract. 6. Typical of the general Christian understanding is also 'the

heaven of our longing'. Cf. H. Häring, *Was bedeutet Himmel?* Theologische Meditationen 55, Einsiedeln 1980.

18. Gerhard, *Loci theol.*, XXXI, tract. 6. §9 (p. 294): '*Coelum spirituale* est vel *gratiae*, quod ecclesiae in terris militanti, vel *gloriae*, quod vel Deo creatori, vel creaturis, beatis scil. angelis et hominibus, puta ecclesiae in coeli triumphanti, tribuitur.'

19. Cf. *Hutterus redivivus oder Dogmatik der ev.-luth. Kirche*, ed. K. Hase, 2nd ed., Leipzig 1836, p. 352.

20. Schmaus, op. cit., p. 799.

21. Ibid.

22. G. Ebeling, *The Lord's Prayer in Today's World*, ET London 1966 (= *On Prayer*, Philadelphia 1966), p. 55.

23. Welker, *Universitalität Gottes*, p. 205.

24. Luther *Vom Abendmahl Christi. Bekenntnis.* WA p. 26; BoA 3, p. 408.

25. BoA 3, p. 389.

26. Gerhard, *Loci theol.* XXI, §89 (Preuss, vol. V, p. 85): 'Christus ita adscendit in coelum, ut adscenderit etiam super omnes coelos et consederit ad dextram Dei . . . Ubi observa, adscendionem Christi ad coelos in sacris literis non tantum describi abstracte et distincte, ut sit solus adscendionis motus, quo corpus Christi locali metastasei e terra evectum ac subinde ad coelos altius elevatum (qua ratione adscensio et exaltatio Christi distinguuntur), sed etiam concrete et conjuncte, ut adscensio simul complectatur exaltationem Christi ad dextram Dei.' On the Calvinistic interpretation of Christ's ascension and his sitting at the right hand of God, cf. Heppe-Bizer, pp. 390f., and esp. p. 399; Rijssen: 'Nos Christum localiter, visibiliter et corporaliter e terra in coelum tertium supra coelos adspectabilis evectum fuisse statuimus; non per praesentiae visibilis et familiaris conversationis tantum subductionem, sed per veram et localem naturae suae humanae translationem, ubi mansura sit usque ad diem iudicii, ut licet praesens semper sit nobiscum gratia sua et spiritu ac divinitate, non amplius sit tamen nobiscum praesentia corporali carnis suae.'

27. K. Stock, *Annihilatio mundi. Johann Gerhards Eschatologie der Welt*, Munich 1971, p. 113. For a critical view of this concentration of heaven on God, see already P. Althaus, *Die letzten Dinge*, 6th ed., Gütersloh 1957, pp. 358ff.

28. Gerhard, *Loci theol.* XXXI, tract. 6. §8 (p. 293): '*Coelum gloriae*, quod Deo tribuitur, non significat locum aliquam creatum, sed increatam, aeternam, invisibilem, infinitam et omnipotentam Dei majestatem.'

29. W. Elert, *Morphologie des Luthertums* I, Munich 1931, reprint 1952, pp. 220f.

30. L. Feuerbach, *The Essence of Christianity*, ch. 18, ET by George Eliot, London 1854, New York 1855, p. 172. On Feuerbach's religious and theological roots, cf. R. Lorenz, 'Zum Ursprung der Religionstheorie Feuerbachs', *EvTh* 17, 1957, pp. 171ff.

31. Feuerbach, op. cit., p. 173.

32. Ibid., p. 174.

33. Feuerbach, *Das Wesen der Religion* (1845), Berlin 1913, p. 308. It was quite in line with Feuerbach's thinking when R. M. Rilke wrote: 'God, the now ineffable One, is relieved of his attributes, which revert to creation – to love and death . . . Everything that belongs profoundly and intimately to this world – everything which the church has misappropriated to the world beyond – returns again; and all the angels, with hymns of praise, decide for the earth.' Quoted by R. Guardini, *Zu R. M. Rilkes Deutung des Daseins*, Bern 1946, p. 21.

34. K. Marx, 'Critique of Hegel's *Philosophy of Right*: Introduction', ET in *Early Writings* (Pelican Marx Library), Harmondsworth 1975, p. 244.

35. Ibid., p. 251.

36. Bloch, *Das Prinzip Hoffnung*, pp. 1524ff.

37. Ibid., p. 1404.

38. Ibid., p. 1416.

39. Ibid., p. 1520.

40. Ibid., p. 1529. Cf. also, even earlier, Tillich, *Systematic Theology* I, p. 212: 'The realm against which the divine images are projected is not itself a projection. It is the experienced ultimacy of being and meaning. It is the realm of ultimate concern.'

41. Bloch, op. cit., p. 1530f.

42. Ibid., p. 1534. Cf. also J. R. de la Pena, 'The Element of Projection and Belief in Heaven', *Concilium* (ET) 123, 1979, pp. 72–81.

43. My *Theology of Hope* was directed against this reduction.

VIII The Evolution of Creation

1. Where German anthropology is concerned, J. G. Herder's *Über die Ursprung der Sprache* (1770) established the approach and pegged out the boundaries of anthropological enquiry in a way which exerted a profound influence well into the twentieth century.

2. P. Teilhard de Chardin, *The Appearance of Man*, ET London 1965, New York 1966, p. 268.

3. Pastoral Constitution on the Church in the Modern World, *Gaudium et Spes*, Art. 14 (ET, *The Documents of Vatican II*, ed W. M. Abbott, London and Dublin 1966, p. 212).

4. Whether a 'development' in the modern sense can already be seen here is a matter of dispute. C. Westermann, *Schöpfungsbericht*, Stuttgart 1960, p. 20, writes: 'Here the concept of development has been introduced into the process of creation in an astonishing way.' W. H. Schmidt, *Die Schöpfungsgeschichte*, 2nd ed., Neukirchen 1967, p. 186, takes a different view: 'A "development" is unknown to Genesis 1.'

5. I have taken over this translation of "Adam" from Phyllis Trible, *God and the Rhetoric of Sexuality*, Philadelphia 1978, pp. 18ff.

6. This was pointed out by O. Weber, *Foundations of Dogmatics* I, ET Grand Rapids, Mich., 1981, p. 561.

7. H. Denzinger, *Enchiridion Symbolorum*, 30th ed., Fribourg 1955, §§2094ff.

8. Cf. the Holy Office's decretal of 6 December 1957, and its monitory of 30 June 1962.

9. G. Altner, ed., *Der Darwinismus. Die Geschichte einer Theorie*, Wege der Forschung 449, Darmstadt 1981; A. Montagu (ed.), *Science and Creationism*, Oxford 1984, with essays by I. Asimov, K. Boulding, St.J. Gould, G. Hardin, G. Marsden, G. Stent *et al.*

10. J. S. Huxley, 'Darwin und der Gedanke der Evolution' in Altner, op. cit., p. 489.

11. Cf. Altner, op. cit., pp. 95ff.

12. I am indebted to Margaret Kohl for drawing my attention to a very popular poem of the era which gives expression to this existential feeling: Tennyson's *In Memoriam* (published 1850), stanzas LV and LVI:

LV

....

Are God and Nature then at strife,
That Nature lends such evil dreams?
So careful of the type she seems,
So careless of the single life;

that I, considering everywhere
Her secret meaning in her deeds,
And finding that of fifty seeds
She often brings but one to bear,

I falter where I firmly trod,
And falling with my weight of cares
Upon the great world's altar-stairs
That slope thro' darkness up to God,

I stretch lame hands of faith, and grope,
And gather dust and chaff, and call
To what I feel is Lord of all,
And faintly trust the larger hope.

LVI

'So careful of the type?' but no.
From scarped cliff and quarried stone
She cries, 'A thousand types are gone:
I care for nothing, all shall go.

'Thou makest thine appeal to me:
I bring to life, I bring to death:
The spirit does but mean the breath:
I know no more.' And he, shall he,

Man, her last work, who seem'd so fair,
Such splendid purpose in his eyes,
Who roll'd the psalm to wintry skies,
Who built him fanes of fruitless prayer,

Who trusted God was love indeed
And love Creation's final law –
Tho' Nature, red in tooth and claw
With ravine, shriek'd against his creed –

Who loved, who suffer'd countless ills,
Who battled for the True, the Just,
Be blown about the desert dust,
Or seal'd within the iron hills?

No more? A monster, then, a dream,
A discord. Dragons of the prime,
That tare each other in their slime,
Were mellow music match'd with him.

O life as futile, then, as frail!
O for thy voice to soothe and bless!
What hope of answer, or redress?
Behind the veil, behind the veil.'

13. G. Altner, *Schöpfungsglaube und Entwicklungsgedanke in der protestantischen Theologie zwischen Ernst Haeckel und Teilhard de Chardin*, Zürich 1965. Altner's account is very informative, but his declaration of incompatibility can no longer be maintained. For another view, even then, see S. M. Daecke, *Teilhard de Chardin und die evangelische Theologie*, Göttingen 1967. For Altner's view now, cf. his *Grammatik der Schöpfung. Theologische Inhalte der Biologie*, Stuttgart 1971, and 'Evolution und "Evolution" ' in Rudolph and Stöve (ed.), *Geschichtsbewusstsein und Rationalität*, Stuttgart 1976.

14. See ch. IV, §1.

15. S. M. Daecke, article 'Entwicklung', *TRE* IX, pp. 705–16, and 'Gott – Opfer oder Schöpfer der Evolution?', *KuD* 28, 1982, pp. 230–247, where he goes in detail (n. 54) into this chapter of my doctrine of creation (read in manuscript).

16. Ibid.

17. E. Haeckel, *The Riddle of the Universe*, ET 2nd ed., London and New York 1901, pp. 295f. For comment cf. O. Hertwig, *Zur Abwehr des ethischen, des sozialen und des politischen Darwinismus*, Jena 1918.

18. M. Eigen and R. Winkler, *Das Spiel. Naturgesetze steuern den Zufall*, 3rd. ed., Munich 1979, p. 192. Cf. also. E. von Weizsäcker (ed.), *Offene Systeme I. Beiträge zur Zeitstruktur von Information, Entropie und Evolution*, Stuttgart 1974.

19. P. Kropotkin, *Mutual Aid: a Factor of Evolution*, London and New

York 1902, reprint 1972; also his *Ethics: Origin and Development*, New York 1924, London 1925, reprint New York 1947. This dispute is still being carried on today, e.g., through K. Lorenz, *On Aggression*, ET London and New York 1966. Lorenz sees 'struggles' between animals even in peaceful environmental situations, because he presupposes that struggle is '*Peaceable Nature*, ET San Francisco 1984, the father of all things'. For the other side in the ongoing dispute, cf. S. Lackner, who shows that evolution achieves its greatest successes, not through 'the struggle for existence', but through symbiosis and co-operation.

20. Cf. ch. IV, §1.

21. Cf. ch. V, §5.

22. Of particular interest here is the combination of genetic information (DNA) and linguistic information (memory). What is inherited and what is acquired by way of experience and tradition? The subject of genetic information is the species; the subject of the linguistic information is the group within a species. How is the information stored in the collective memory bound up with the genetic information? How does the spider know the pattern of its web, or the mother love for her child?

23. Cf. here W. Stegmüller, *Hauptströmungen der Gegenwartsphilosophie* II, 6th ed., Stuttgart 1979, who describes and discusses the philosophical implications of the modern theory of evolution: see ch. IV ('Die Evolution des Kosmos', pp. 497ff.) and ch. V ('Die Evolution des Lebens'). For the general reader, cf. H. von Ditfurth, *Wir sind nicht nur von dieser Welt. Naturwissenschaft, Religion und die Zukunft des Menschen*, Hamburg 1981.

24. C. F. von Weizsäcker, *Die Geschichte der Natur*, 3rd ed., Göttingen 1957, and – in more detail with regard to the problem of time – *Die Einheit der Natur*, Munich 1971. Cf. also G. Picht, 'Die Idee des Fortschritts und das Problem der Zeit' in *Hier und Jetzt* I, Stuttgart 1980, pp. 375ff.

25. Von Weizsäcker, *Geschichte der Natur*, p. 65 (not in ET).

26. Cf. S. Toulmin, *The Discovery of Time*, London and New York 1965, p. 263: 'Are the laws of nature changing?'; Toulmin here appeals to P.A.M. Dirac. Cf. also W. Pannenberg, *Erwägungen zu einer Theologie der Natur*, Gütersloh 1970, pp. 65ff.: 'Kontingenz und Naturgesetz.'

27. We have to thank T. Torrance for his working out of the concept of a 'contingent order' of contigent events. Cf. *Christian Theology and Scientific Culture*, pp. 16ff. He has thereby independently developed M. Polanyi's approaches in *Knowing and Being*, London and Chicago 1969.

28. I. Prigogine and I. Stengers, *Dialog mit der Natur. Neue Wege naturwissenschaftlichen Denkens*, Munich 1980 (German trans. from English MS.), p. 268. Cf. also p. 283: 'The most important result of this discussion is that the future is no longer given. It is no longer contained in the present.' In this section I am following Prigogine's description of the experience of time in dissipative systems. Cf. also I. Prigogine, *From Being to Becoming. Time and Complexity in the Physical Sciences*, San Francisco

1980. On Prigogine's theory of dissipative systems, cf. Peacocke, *Creation and the World of Science*, pp. 97ff.

29. N. Bohr, *Atomic Theory and the Description of Nature*, Cambridge and New York 1934, p. 4. Cf. also W. Heisenberg, *Physics and Beyond*, ET London and New York 1971.

30. M. Eigen, 'Schöpfung oder Offenbarung?' in *Lust am Denken*, ed. K. Piper, Munich 1981, p. 45.

31. Prigogine and Stengers, op. cit., pp. 267ff.

32. The concept of self-transcendence as the principle of the world aligned towards God is also used by Karl Rahner in 'Christology within an Evolutionary View of the World', *Theological Investigations* V, ET London and Baltimore 1966, pp. 157–92.

33. Moltmann, 'Creation as an Open System' in *The Future of Creation*, pp. 115ff.; Peacocke, *Creation and the World of Science*, pp. 154ff.

34. With reference to C. Bresch, 'Vom Würfeln, das kein Glücksspiel war', in *Lust am Denken*, pp. 25–53.

35. Contrary to Thomas Aquinas, *Summa Theologica* I q 90 art. 3 ad-2, for whom time has a circular structure, in which beginning and end correspond.

36. Contrary to R. Bultmann, *Glauben und Verstehen* III, Göttingen 1960, pp. 29, 36, for whom the eschatological revelation is the 'restoration' of the revelation in creation. In contrast, P. Evdokimov, 'Nature', *SJT* 18, 1965, pp. 1–22, gives the Orthodox view as follows: 'The Kingdom is not simply a return back towards paradise, but its forward-moving creative fulfilment which takes in the whole of creation' (p. 8).

37. The scientific principle of the conservation of energy reflects the theological principle of the continuous preservation of the world through God.

38. On the problem of *creatio continua*, cf. Weber, *Foundations of Dogmatics*, I, pp. 503ff.; W. Trillhaas, *Dogmatik*, Berlin 1972, pp. 152f.; H.-G. Fritzsche, *Lehrbuch der Dogmatik* II, Göttingen 1967, pp. 294ff.

39. Athanasius also made a clear distinction between the effortless command at creation and the incarnation, even though he did not integrate the suffering and death of Christ into his conception of the incarnation of the Logos of creation. Cf. *De incarnatione* §44.

40. The deferment of judgment on sin (πάρεσις τῶν ἁμαρτιῶν) contains a promise of the forgiveness of sins (ἄφεσις τῶν ἁμαρτιῶν). Cf. here. Weber, *Foundations of Dogmatics*, I, pp. 515f.

41. Teilhard de Chardin, *The Appearance of Man*, p. 270.

42. Cf. here also Peacocke, *Creation and the World of Science*, pp. 203ff., who restores pan-entheism to favour, in order to link God's transcendence with his immanence.

43. This is critically directed against Bloch's 'ontology of Not-Yet-Being'. Cf. E. Bloch, *Philosophische Grundfragen I. Zur Ontologie des Noch-Nicht-Seins*, Frankfurt 1961. An ontology of this kind only gives

occasion for a temporary hope. Its fulfilment lies in the closed system of 'the home of identity'.

IX *God's Image in Creation: Human Beings*

1. Cf. L. Scheffczyk (ed.), *Der Mensch als Bild Gottes*, Wege der Forschung 124, Darmstadt 1969. Cf. also Bonhoeffer, *Creation and Fall*; Barth, *CD* III/1, pp. 191ff.; Lossky, *In the Image and Likeness of God*.

2. This was pointed out by O. Weber, *Foundation of Dogmatics* I, ET Grand Rapids, Mich., 1981, pp. 558f.

3. Thus already Thomas Aquinas, *STh I* q 93 art. 4: 'Imago Dei tripliciter potest contueri in homine.'

4. W. H. Schmidt, *Die Schöpfungsgeschichte der Priesterschrift*, 2nd ed., Neukirchen 1967; C. Westermann, *Genesis, 1–11: A Commentary*, ET Minneapolis and London 1984; J. J. Stamm, 'Die Gottebenbildlichkeit des Menschen im AT', *Theologische Studien* 54, 1959; Trible, *God and the Rhetoric of Sexuality*; J. Jervell, article 'Bild Gottes I', *TRE* VI, Berlin 1980, pp. 491ff.; H. W. Wolff, *Anthropology of the Old Testament*, ET London and Philadelphia 1974.

5. Cf. here Moltmann, *The Trinity and the Kingdom of God*, pp. 105ff.

6. A list of the possibilities is discussed by Schmidt, op. cit., pp. 129ff., and Westermann, op. cit., pp. 144ff.

7. This has been pointed out by Trible, op. cit., p. 21.

8. In agreement with Schmidt, op. cit., pp. 139, 143, n. 3 contrary to Westermann, op. cit., pp. 153f.

9. Schmidt, op. cit., p. 144.

10. Cf. here §4 of the present chapter.

11. Thus H. Gunkel, *Genesis*, 6th ed., 1922, and E. Jüngel, 'Der gottentsprechende Mensch' in *Neue Anthropologie*, ed. H.-G. Gadamer and P. Vogler, vol. 6, Munich 1975, p. 355.

12. Thus W. Gross, 'Die Gottebenbildlichkeit des Menschen im Kontext der Priesterschrift', *Theol. Quartalschrift* 161, 1981, pp. 244–264.

13. Trible, op. cit., p. 19. However P. A. Bird takes a critical view of this opinion; cf. ' "Male and Female he created them": Gen. 1:27b in the context of the Priestly Account of Creation', *HTR* 74.2, 1981, pp. 129–59.

14. Cf. §4 of the present chapter.

15. Contrary to the presupposition of the Catholic social encyclicals 'Rerum novarum' (1891) and 'Quadragesimo anno' (1931).

16. Cf. here P. A. H. de Boer, *Fatherhood and Motherhood in Israelite and Judean Piety*, Leyden 1974.

17. This is a comment on M. Daly, *Beyond God the Father: toward a philosophy of women's liberation*, Boston 1973; she considers that Tillich's metaphysical theology is non-patriarchal.

18. D. Staniloae, 'Der dreieinige Gott und die Einheit der Menschheit', *EvTh* 41, 1981, pp. 439ff.

19. Cf. here, O. H. Steck, *Der Schöpfungsbericht der Priesterschrift*, Neukirchen 1975; also his *World and Environment*, pp. 102ff.

20. J. Jervell, *Imago Dei. Gen. 1.26f. im Spätjudentum, in der Gnosis und in den paulinischen Briefen*, FRLANT 58, Göttingen 1960; also his article 'Bild Gottes I', *TRE* VI, pp. 491–8, with the further literature there cited.

21. Jervell, TRE VI, p. 497.

22. This is also in line with modern philosophical anthropology when, with Dilthey, it starts from the assumption that the human being is not fixed by nature, but that he has an open history and can only be understood in this light. Cf. M. Landmann, *Philosophische Anthropologie*, Berlin 1955, pp. 251ff.

23. J. M. Lochman, *Reich, Kraft und Herrlichkeit*, Munich 1981, pp. 45ff.

24. Thomas Aquinas, *Summa Theologica* I q 93 art. 4.

25. On the history, cf. the contributions by S. Otto, G. Ladner, L. Hödl, F. Dander, A. Rohner and A. Hoffmann in Scheffczyk, *Der Mensch als Bild Gottes*, pp. 133ff.

26. Cf. Concilium Tridentinum, Sessio VI, cap. 1, Denzinger, *Enchiridion Symbolorum*, §793.

27. E. Brunner, *Man in Revolt*, ET London and New York, 1939, pp. 95ff.

28. Ibid., pp. 140ff.

29. Still important here is H. J. Iwand, *Glaubensgerechtigkeit nach Luthers Lehre*, Theologisches Existenz heute 75, Munich 1941.

30. H. Kropatscheck, *Das Problem der theologischen Anthropologie auf dem Weimarer Gespräch zwischen Flacius Illyricus and Victorinus Strigel*, dissertation, Göttingen 1943; G. Moldaenke, *Schriftverständnis und Schriftdeutung im Zeitalter der Reformation I: Flacius Illyricus*, Stuttgart 1936; H. E. Weber, *Reformation, Orthodoxie und Rationalismus* I/2, Gütersloh 1940, pp. 6ff.

31. *Solid. decl. I, Bekenntnisschriften der Evangelisch-lutherischen Kirche*, 2nd ed., Göttingen 1952, pp. 843ff.

32. Contrary to H. Thielicke, *Wer darf sterben*? Freiburg 1979, who calls a severely handicapped person an 'off-duty image of God' ('Ebenbild Gottes außer Diensten') (p. 63).

33. Greg. Naz. *Or.* 31.11. Cf. also *The Five Theological Orations of Gregory of Nazianzus*, ed. A. J. Mason, Cambridge 1899, pp. 158f. For comment cf. G. Mar Osthathios, *Theology of a Classless Society*, London 1979, pp. 91ff.

34. Augustine, *De Trin.* XII, c. 5 and 6. Cf. also M. Schmaus, *Die psychologische Trinitätslehre des Hl. Augustinus*, Münster 1927.

35. Augustine, op. cit., c. 6.

36. Quoted in Schmaus, op. cit., pp. 222f.

37. Quoted in Thomas Aquinas, *Summa Theologica* I q 93 art. 5. The

translation of this and following passages is taken from the edition of the *Summa* (Latin text and English trans.) published by Blackfriars, London and New York 1964 ff., vol. 13.

38. Quoted ibid., art. 7.

39. Ibid., art. 8.

40. Ibid., art. 4.

41. Ibid., art. 6.

42. Ibid.

43. Ibid.

44. Cf. here F. K. Mayr's great and important essay, 'Trinitätstheologie und theologische Anthropologie', *ZThK* 68, 1971, pp. 427–477. Also K. E. Børresen, *Subordination et équivalence. Nature et rôle de la femme d'après Augustin et Thomas d'Aquin*, Oslo and Paris 1968; Ruether, *New Woman – New Earth. Sexist ideologies and human liberation.*

45. W. Krusche presents this discussion very well in *Das Wirken des Heiligen Geistes nach J. Calvin*, Göttingen 1957, pp. 33ff.

46. Thomas Aquinas, op. cit., art. 4.

47. Cf. Moltmann, *The Trinity and the Kingdom of God*, pp. 94ff.

X *'Embodiment is the End of All God's Works'*

1. Cf. E. Zinn, *Die Theologie des Friedrich Christoph Oetinger*, Gütersloh 1932, pp. 118ff.

2. P.-M. Pflüger (ed.), *Die Wiederentdeckung des Leibes*, Fellbach 1981; D. Kamper and C. Wulf, *Die Wiederkehr des Körpers*, Frankfurt 1982, pp. 9f. Similarly J. Y. Fenton, *Theology and Body*, Philadelphia 1974.

3. R. zur Lippe, 'Am eigenen Leibe' in D. Kamper and C. Wulf, op. cit., p. 28: 'Where definitions are arrived at through separation instead of through particular forms of relationship, degrees of intensity and clarity about a counterpart, violence has already been made the principle.'

4. Kamper and Wulf, op. cit., p. 16.

5. M. Tibon-Cornillot, 'Die transfigurativen Körper. Zur Verflechtung von Techniken und Mythen' in Kamper and Wulf, op. cit., pp. 145ff.; J. Baudrillard, 'Vom zeremoniellen zum geklonten Körper: Der Einbruch des Obszönen', op. cit., pp. 350ff.

6. E. Schweizer, article 'σῶμα', *TDNT* VII, 1024ff.

7. Plato, *Phaedo*, 64c, trans. R. S. Bluck, London 1955.

8. Ibid., 79 c–d.

9. Ibid., 80e, 81a.

10. Bloch, *Das Prinzip Hoffnung*, pp. 1385ff: 'Der Augenblick als Nicht-Da-Sein, Exterritorialität zum Tod.' For critical comment cf. Moltmann, *Theologie der Hoffnung*, p. 326: 'Exterritorialität zum Tod und Auferstehung der Toten.' (From appendix not included in ET.)

11. R. Descartes, *Meditationes*. In the dedication he writes: 'I have always been of the view that the two questions, *God and the soul*, are the most important of those which are to be discussed rather with the help of

philosophy than theology' (*Oeuvres Philosophiques* II, ed. F. Alquié, Paris 1967, p. 383). 'God and the soul' are the two focuses of Augustine's theological ellipse. With this the Pauline theme 'God and the body' (II Cor. 6) is moved out of the centre of theology.

12. 6th Meditation, op. cit., p. 226 [Latin] = p. 488 [French].
13. Ibid., p. 231 = 497.
14. Ibid., p. 228 = 492.
15. Ibid., pp. 232f. = 500.
16. K. Jaspers, *Descartes und die Philosophie*, Berlin 1948, pp. 50f. On space as an essential feature in the human being's experience of his own body, cf. H. Plügge, *Der Mensch und sein Leib*, Tübingen 1967, pp. 1ff.
17. I am restricting myself here solely to Barth's *Church Dogmatics*, III/2 §46: 'Man as Soul and Body'. On Barth's theological anthropology as a whole, cf. K. Stock, *Anthropologie der Verheissung. Karl Barths Lehre vom Menschen als dogmatisches Problem*, Munich 1980.
18. *CD* III/2, p. 325.
19. Ibid., p. 424.
20. Ibid., p. 418.
21. Ibid., p. 332.
22. Ibid.
23. Ibid., p. 341.
24. Ibid., pp. 325, 332, 418.
25. Ibid., p. 364.
26. Ibid., p. 425.
27. Ibid.
28. Ibid., p. 424.
29. Cf. ch. IX §5.
30. The theological model is of course the human being Jesus Christ, about whom Barth says: 'A second point to be noted is that the oneness and wholeness of his human life is fashioned, structured and determined from within, and therefore necessary and of lasting significance. The interconnexion of the soul and body and Word and act of Jesus is not a chaos but a cosmos, a formed and ordered totality. There is in it a higher and a lower, a first and a second, a dominating and a dominated. But the man Jesus Himself is both. He is not only the higher, the first, the dominating, nor is He both in such a way that the lower, the second, the dominated is associated with Him only externally or accidentally. This would again imply the destruction of that oneness and wholeness. He is also the lower, the second, the dominated. He is not only His soul but also His body. But He is both soul and body in an ordered oneness and wholeness. His being is orderly and not disorderly. Nor is He this in such a way that the order is accidental and imposed from without. He is it in an order which derives from Himself. He Himself and from Himself is both the higher and the lower, the first and the second, the dominant and the dominated' (CD III/2, p. 332). But is this 'inner sovereignty' (ibid.) and self-control really the

outstanding characteristic of the human being Jesus? Can the struggle in Gethsemane be interpreted in those terms? One has the impression that in this passage Barth is adopting Schleiermacher's christology, with its thesis about Jesus' 'always dominant consciousness of God'.

31. Ibid., p. 425.

32. Is this not the 'absolutist man' of the Enlightenment, whom Barth describes so aptly and of whom he takes so critical a view? Cf. *Protestant Theology in the Nineteenth Century*, ET London and Philadelphia 1972, ch. 2, pp. 33ff.

33. *CD* III/2, p. 427 (altered). (He expands this further in III/4, § 54.1: 'Man and Woman', esp. pp. 171ff.) Here too Barth applies his hierarchical concept of order: 'A precedes B, and B follows A. Order means succession. It means preceding and following. It means superordination and subordination' (p. 169).

34. *CD* III/2, p. 368: 'The antithesis of soul and body, like that of heaven and earth, is an antithesis within creation and immanent in the world . . . But the soul and body of the human being are a single human being, just as heaven and earth as a whole are one cosmos.'

35. On the following passage cf. H. W. Wolff, *Anthropology of the Old Testament*, ET London and Philadelphia 1974; K. A. Bauer, *Leiblichkeit – das Ende aller Werke Gottes. Die Bedeutung der Leiblichkeit des Menschen bei Paulus*, Gütersloh 1971.

36. See also M. Luther, WA 2, 415,14: 'Caro est, non carnem habet.' 'Soul' and 'flesh' always mean the *totus homo* in different aspects.

37. Cf. Moltmann, *The Trinity and the Kingdom of God*, pp. 148ff.

38. Barth, *CD*, IV/1, pp. 200f.

39. Cf. ch. IV, §5.

40. I am here using terms belonging to Gestalt psychology, because they come very close to the perichoretic interpretation of body and soul which I am putting forward; but I am not thereby making a dogma out of Gestalt therapy itself. Cf. F. S. Perls, R. F. Hefferline and P. Goodman, *Gestalttherapie. Lebensfreude und Persönlichkeitsentfaltung*, Stuttgart 1979; H. Petzold, *Die neuen Körpertherapien*, 2nd ed., Stuttgart 1980; A. Lowen, *Bioenergetics*, New York 1975; J. O. Stevens, *Awareness*, Lafayette, Calif., 1971, New York 1973. Cf. also H. P. Dreitzel, 'Der Körper in der Gestalttherapie' in Kamper and Wulf, *Die Wiederkehr des Körpers*, pp. 52–67. I am using the concept of Gestalt theologically in the same sense as D. Bonhoeffer in his *Ethics*, London 1964, pp. 64ff.: 'Ethics as Formation', and A. A. van Ruler, *Droom en Gestalte*, Amsterdam 1947; *Gestaltwerdung Christi in der Welt*, Neukirchen 1956.

41. H. P. Dreitzel, art. cit., p. 55.

42. Cf. chs. I. 8, and IV §5.

43. C. A. van Peursen, *Leib, Seele, Geist*, Gütersloh 1959, p. 166.

44. G. Picht, 'Ist Humanökologie möglich?' in C. Eisenbart (ed.), *Humanökologie und Frieden*, Stuttgart 1979, pp. 91ff. W. Pannenberg

has also rightly stressed this point, most recently in *Anthropologie in theologischer Perspektive*, Göttingen 1983, pp. 501ff. J. G. Droysen already declared in *Historik* (1868; 4th ed., ed. R. Hübner, Darmstadt 1960, p. 377): 'But where the human spirit runs ahead either of itself or of reality, the idea of God stirs in it.'

45. R. zur Lippe, in Kamper and Wulf, op. cit., p. 31.

46. J. V. Taylor has made this point particularly aptly in *The Go-Between God. The Holy Spirit and the Christian Mission*, London and Philadelphia 1972.

47. F. Hölderlin, *Über Religion*, *Werke* IV, Stuttgart 1961, p. 278.

48. R. zur Lippe, art. cit., p. 36.

49. I have taken this formulation from A. Toffler, *Future Shock*, New York and London 1970, p. 470. Cf. also *The Eco-Spasm Report*, New York and London 1975.

50. Cf. here S. Heine, *Leibhafter Glaube. Ein Beitrag zum Verständnis der theologischen Konzeption des Paulus*, Vienna 1976, esp. pp. 136ff.

51. G. W. F. Hegel, *Phenomenology of Mind*, ET London and New York 1910, pp. 30f.

52. J. C. McGilvray, *The Quest for Health and Wholeness*, Tübingen 1981.

53. P. Lüth, *Kritische Medizin. Zur Theorie-Praxis-Problematik der Medizin und Gesundheitssysteme*, Hamburg 1972.

54. I. Illich, *Medical Nemesis. The Expropriation of Health*, London 1975, New York 1976.

55. Ibid., p. 169.

56. D. Rössler, *Der Arzt zwischen Technik und Humanität*, Munich 1977, p. 119.

57. Barth, *CD* III/4, pp. 356ff., with reference to the psychosomaticist R. Siebeck.

58. This will have to be justified in the *Christology* and further expounded in the *Eschatology*.

XI *The Sabbath: the Feast of Creation*

1. General literature: A. Heschel, *The Sabbath. Its meaning for modern man*, New York 1951; F. Rosenzweig, *Der Stern der Erlösung*, Pt. III, Book I, Heidelberg 1959, pp. 63–69; K. Barth, *Church Dogmatics*, III/1, pp. 213–28; E. Stamm, *Die theologische Begründung des Sabbatgebotes im Alten Testament*, Theologische Studien 46, Zürich 1956; H. W. Wolff, *Anthropology of the Old Testament*, pp. 135–42; N.-E. Andreasen, *Rest and Redemption. A Study of the Biblical Sabbath*, Michigan 1978; A. Szabo, 'Sabbat und Sonntag', *Judaica* 15, 1959, pp. 161ff.; E. Fromm, *You shall be as gods*, New York 1966, London 1967; W. Rordorf, *Sunday: the history of the day of rest and worship in the earliest centuries of the Christian church*, ET London and Philadelphia 1968; W. Grimm, *Der Ruhetag. Sinngehalt einer längst vergessenen Gottesgabe*, Arbeiten zum

Neuen Testament und Judentum 4, Frankfurt 1980; H. Riesenfeld, 'Sabbat et jour du Seigneur' in *New Testament Essays. Studies in Memory of T. W. Manson*, ed. A. J. B. Higgins, Manchester 1959; D. A. Carson, *From Sabbath to Lord's Day. A biblical, historical and theological investigation*, Exeter 1982; J. Moltmann, *Theology and Joy*, ET London and New York 1973, and *The Church in the Power of the Spirit*, ET London and New York 1977, pp. 267ff.: 'The Feast of the History of God.'

2. H. Gese, *Zur biblischen Theologie*, Munich 1977, p. 79.

3. Rosenzweig, op. cit., p. 65; Barth, op. cit., p. 214.

4. R. Schutz, *Ta fête soit san fin*, Taizé 1969; he is echoing a saying of Athanasius.

5. F. Rosenzweig, op. cit., p. 69. Cf. Berakoth 57b: 'Sabbath is one-sixtieth part of the world to come.' Exod. Rabbah XXV, 12: 'If Israel were to celebrate only one sabbath properly, Messiah would immediately come.'

6. G. von Rad, 'There Remains Still a Rest for the People of God: an Investigation of a Biblical Conception', ET in *The Problem of the Hexateuch and Other Essays*, Edinburgh and New York 1966, pp. 79–93, and his *Old Testament Theology* I, p. 148: 'If God blessed this rest, then it is to hand as a kind of third thing between him and the world, provisional, of course, and unperceived by man, but still a good gift of salvation.' This is an interesting comment, but I cannot myself see that God blessed 'rest' and not 'the seventh day' (Gen. 2.3). Did God 'create rest' (*menuha*) on the seventh day? A. Heschel says (*The Sabbath*, p. 22): 'Just as heaven and earth were created in six days, *menuha* was created on the Sabbath.' Like Barth (CD III/I, p. 220), I do not consider that the 'completion' of creation consists in this further creation. God does not 'create' on the seventh day. On the contrary, his *menuha* consists in his Being and presence, and is in this sense 'uncreated'.

7. Barth, *CD* III/1, p. 214.

8. Barth, ibid., pp. 216f.: 'God . . . made himself temporal and human, i.e., He linked Himself in a temporal act with the being and purpose and course of the world, with the history of man . . . His honour is compromised and at stake.' Heschel writes (op. cit., p. 60): 'The Sabbath is the presence of God in the world.'

9. Rosenzweig, op. cit., p. 68.

10. Westermann, *Genesis 1–11: A Commentary*, pp. 167ff.

11. Cf. article 'Heiligung', *RGG*[3] III, cols. 177–82.

12. Heschel, op. cit., p. 8: 'Judaism teaches us to be attached to holiness in time, to be attached to sacred events, to learn how to consecrate sanctuaries that emerge from the magnificent stream of a year . . . The main themes of faith lie in the realm of time. We remember the day of the Exodus from Egypt, the day when Israel stood at Sinai; and our Messianic hope is the expectation of a day, of the end of days.'

13. M. Susman, *Das Buch Hiob und das Schicksal des jüdischen Volkes*, Zürich 1948, p. 16.

14. Von Rad, *Old Testament Theology* II, p. 104n., talks about a 'historicising' of the Canaanite agrarian festivals.

15. Heschel, op. cit.

16. Fromm, *You shall be as gods*, p. 199.

17. Rosenzweig has drawn attention to this dialectic, op. cit., p. 68: 'What else could redemption be but the reconciliation of revelation and creation!'

18. G. W. F. Hegel, Preface to *The Philosophy of Right*, ET London and New York 1896, p. xxx.

19. Rosenzweig, op. cit., p. 68.

20. We may take as examples here J. Jeremias, *New Testament Theology*, vol. 1: *The Proclamation of Jesus*, ET London and New York 1971, pp. 209ff., and L. Goppelt, *Theology of the New Testament.*, ET Grand Rapids, 1981–82, London 1982–3, pp. 91ff.

21. Goppelt, op. cit., p. 92.

22. Jeremias, op. cit., p. 209,

23. Ibid., pp. 204, 211.

24. Goppelt, op. cit., p. 194. One asks oneself whose alternative this is supposed to be.

25. A. Trocmé, *Jésus et la révolution non-violente*, Geneva 1961; J. H. Yoder, *Die Politik Jesu – der Weg des Kreuzes*, Maxdorf 1981, ch. 3: 'Die Bedeutung des Jubeljahres'; cf. also Grimm, *Der Ruhetag*.

26. As H. Braun maintains in his *Jesus*, Stuttgart 1969, p. 84.

27. Goppelt's view, op. cit., p. 95.

28. Rordorf, *Sunday*, pp. 93f.

29. E. Hertzsch, 'Sonntag', *RGG*[3] VI, cols. 104–42. Cf. also W. Nagel, *Geschichte des christlichen Sonntags*, 2nd ed. Berlin 1970.

30. Riesenfeld, 'Sabbat et jour da Seigneur', pp. 210ff.

31. For more detail cf. S. Bacchiocchi, *Antijudaism and the Origin of Sunday*, The Pontifical Gregorian University Press, Rome 1975.

32. Quoted in Rordorf, op. cit., p. 162. The edict continues: 'Farmers indeed should be free and unhindered in their cultivation of the fields, since it frequently occurs that there is no more suitable day for entrusting seeds of corn to the furrows and slips of vine to the holes (prepared for them), lest haply the favourable moment sent by divine providence be lost.' The idea of putting the Christian Sunday in the place of Israel's sabbath is part of the chiliastic character of the *sacrum imperium*: the *politia Moysi* is viewed as a foreshadowing of the kingdom of Christ. The kingdom of Christ is not the Christian church but the Christian 'commonwealth' – the Christian *imperium*. This is shown by the sabbath-Sunday typology which Eusebius of Caesarea puts forward in his *Commentary on the Psalms*, in reference to Psalm 91 (PG 23.1165–84). He transfers the Mosaic law to the Christian *imperium*. In a similar way the regulations of the Aaronic priesthood were transferred to the priesthood of the imperial church under Constantine. In this Christian empire there was no room for an independent

Judaism, either in Israel or in the synagogues. The laws relating to the Jews which were issued by the Christian emperors Theodosius and Justinian make this plain. This is Christian chiliasm.

33. Rosenzweig, op. cit., p. 127.

Appendix: Symbols of the World

1. I am attempting here to work with the symbol concepts developed by Paul Ricoeur. Cf. his *Conflict of Interpretations*.

2. C. G. Jung, *Psychology and Religion*, ET, Collected Works 11, London and Princeton 1958, p. 50 et passim. Cf. also K. Mann, *Schöpfungsmythen. Vom Ursprung und Sinn der Welt*, Stuttgart 1983.

3. J. Macquarrie, *Principles of Christian Theology*, London and New York 1966, pp. 200ff., began to work with two 'models of creation', i.e., 'making' and 'emanation'. Peacocke, *Creation and the World of Science*, pp. 38ff. and 104ff., extended these models further, adding 'play', 'music' and 'dance'. I am developing the attempt to work with several models, in order to overcome the one-sidedness of the model 'the world as God's work'.

4. E. Neumann, *Die grosse Mutter. Eine Phänomenologie der weiblichen Gestaltungen des Unbewussten*, Zürich 1956; J. J. Bachofen, *Das Mutterrecht*, Suhrkamp-Taschenbücher Wissenschaft 175, Frankfurt 1975; E. O. James, *The Cult of the Mother Goddess. An Anthropological and Documentary Study*, New York and London 1959; R. Patai, *The Hebrew Goddess*, New York 1967; H. Göttner-Abendroth, *Die Göttin und ihr Heros*, Munich 1980; D. Wolkstein and S. N. Kramer, *Inanna, Queen of Heaven and Earth. Her stories and hymns from Sumer*, San Francisco 1983.

5. M. Stone, *When God was a Woman*, New York 1978; R. R. Ruether, *New Woman – New Earth. Sexist Ideologies and Human Liberation*, New York 1975.

6. H. Zimmer, *Die indische Weltmutter*, Frankfurt 1980, and *Philosophies of India*, New York 1951, London 1952, pp. 241ff.: 'The Cosmic Man'.

7. H. Schlier, *Die Zeit der Kirche. Exegetische Aufsätze und Vorträge*, Freiburg 1966, pp. 159ff., 299ff. In his own speculative way J. T. Beck developed his own ideas, in the philosophy of science, about 'the purification and new formation of the earth system' in cosmic christology; cf. his *Die Vollendung des Reiches Gottes*, Gütersloh 1887, pp. 68ff.

8. H. Urs von Balthasar, *Kosmische Liturgie*, Freiburg 1941, p. 270. The eschatology of the anakephalaiosis has continually led to protological speculation about the heavenly, pre-worldly archetypal man. The kabbalistic idea of 'Adam Kadmon' influenced Osiander, Böhme, Oetinger and other Protestant theologians.

9. I. E. Lovelock, *Gaia. A New Look at Life on Earth*, Oxford and New York 1979; L. Margulis and D. Sagan, 'Gaia and Philosophy' in L. Rounen (ed.), *On Nature*, Notre Dame 1984, pp. 60–75.

10. A. Dietrich, *Mutter Erde*, 3rd ed., Berlin 1925; M. Eliade, *History of Religious Ideas*/I, ET London and Chicago 1979, pp. 40ff.: 'Woman and Vegetation'.

11. Dietrich, op. cit., p. 32.

12. Stone, *When God was a Woman*, pp. 11ff.: 'Who was she?'

13. Eliade, *The Sacred and the Profane*, pp. 135ff.: 'Terra Mater'; pp. 144ff.: 'Woman, Earth, and Fecundity.'

14. This is shown by Phyllis Trible's exegesis in *God and the Rhetoric of Sexuality*, pp. 75ff.

15. Zeno, PL 11, 479: 'Fontanum semper virginis matris dulcem ad uterum convolate . . .'

16. Dietrich, op. cit., p. 114.

17. Cyprian, *De unitate ecclesiae* c. 6: 'Habere iam non potest deum patrem, qui ecclesiam non habet matrem'. Ibid., c. 5.: 'illius foetu nascimur, illius lacte nutrimur, spiritu ejus animamur.'

18. F. Nietzsche, *The Will to Power*, §916, new ET New York 1967, London 1968, p. 484.

19. E. Hornung, *Geschichte als Fest*, Darmstadt 1966.

20. Eliade, *The Myth of the Eternal Return*, and *The Sacred and the Profane*, pp. 20ff.

21. Eliade; *The Sacred and the Profane*, p. 98.

22. Ibid., p. 146.

23. See ch. XI.

24. J. Moltmann, 'The Liberating Feast', *Concilium* (ET) vol. 2 no. 10, *Politics and Liturgy*, February 1974, pp. 74–84.

25. A. K. Coomaraswamy, *The Dance of Shiva*, 2nd ed., New York 1957, London 1958; H. Zimmer, *Myths and Symbols in Indian Art and Civilization*, New York 1953, pp. 151ff.; Peacocke, *Creation and the World of Science*, pp. 106ff.: 'The dance of creation'; Capra, *The Tao of Physics*. Capra links the energy-based world view of modern physics with the symbol of 'the cosmic dance' found in eastern mysticism and in Indian and Chinese philosophy.

26. H. Zimmer, op. cit., p. 153.

27. A. K. Coomaraswamy, op. cit., p. 71.

28. Ibid., p. 72.

29. Sri Aurobindo, quoted by Coomaraswamy.

30. H. Rahner, *Man at Play*, ET London 1965, New York 1967, p. 66.

31. Ibid.

32. Quoted in Rahner, op. cit., pp. 89f.

33. Ibid., p. 86 (slightly altered).

34. E. R. Curtius, *European Literature and the Latin Middle Ages*, ET London 1953, pp. 138ff.: 'Theatrical Metaphors'; R. Dahrendorf, *Homo sociologicus. On the History, Significance and Limits of the Category of Social Role* (London 1973; trans. by the author and first published in *Essays on the Theory of Society*, London 1968), pp. 8ff.

35. Plato, *Leges*, 644d; *Philebus*, 50b.

36. M. Luther, WA 40 I, 463: 'Omnes ordinationes creatae sunt dei larvae, allegoriae, quibus rethorice pingit suam theologiam: sol alls Christum in sich fassen.' Similarly also WA 31 I, 436; WA *Briefe* 9, 610.

37. For these various perspectives cf. J. Huizinga, *Homo ludens. Vom Ursprung der Kultur im Spiel*, Hamburg 1956; E. Fink, *Spiel als Weltsymbol*, Stuttgart 1960; G. Gilg, *Das Spiel Gottes mit der Welt. Aspekte zum naturwissenschaftlichen Weltbild*, Stuttgart 1960; Moltmann, *Theology and Joy*; M. Eigen and R. Winkler, *Das Spiel. Naturgesetze steuern den Zufall*, Munich 1975.

38. See ch. II §3.

39. Heraclitus, Fragment 52 (Diehls), ET from *Art and Thought of Heraclitus. An edition of the fragments* by C. H. Kahn, Cambridge and New York 1979, p. 71, XCIV.

40. E. Fink, op. cit., p. 237.

41. Rahner, *Man at Play*, p. 11.

42. J. Habermas shows how difficult this is: in *Legitimation Crisis*, ET London 1976, he equates contingency with chaos (p. 118) and says of all the things that do not 'overmaster contingency' that 'we must in principle live disconsolately with them' (p. 120). At this point he makes no distinction between contingency in 'controllable' natural events and the existential risks to which human beings are exposed in birth, illness and death.

43. F. J. J. Buytendijk, *Das Menschliche*, Stuttgart 1958, p. 229.

44. A. Rodriguez, SJ, 'Juegos de Dios con el Alma' (God's Play with the Soul), *Obras Spirituales* II, Barcelona 1886, pp. 222–32.

45. F. Kluge, *Etymologisches Wörterbuch der deutschen Sprache*, 19th ed., Berlin 1963, p. 864.

46. Cf. here G. Freudenthal, *Atom und Individuum im Zeitalter Newtons. Zur Genese der mechanistischen Natur- und Sozialphilosophie*, Frankfurt 1982; C. Merchant, *The Death of Nature. Women, Ecology and the Scientific Revolution*, San Francisco 1980.

47. Quoted in W. Philipp, *Das Zeitalter der Aufklärung*, Bremen 1963, pp. 35f. On Wolff's obsession with the machine cf. W. Philipp, *Das Werden der Aufklärung in theologiegeschichtlicher Sicht*, Göttingen 1957, pp. 128ff.

48. W. Heisenberg, *Physics and Beyond*, p. 214; similarly C.F. von Weizsäcker, *Die Einheit der Natur*, Munich 1971, p. 16.

49. Bloch, *Das Prinzip Hoffnung*; *Experimentum mundi*, Frankfurt 1975.

50. Bloch, *Das Prinzip Hoffnung*, p. 17.

51. A. Gehlen, *Urmensch und Spätkultur*, Bonn 1956, p. 285.

52. This was the direction which Bloch indicated when, contrary to Feuerbach, he demanded a 'new eschatology of religion', instead of an 'anthropology of religion' (*Das Prinzip Hoffnung*, p. 1416) and saw in Christianity the appearance of 'the essence of religion: 'That is to say, not

an apologetic, and hence static, myth, but an inherent humane-eschatological and hence explosive messianism' (p. 1404).

53. Cf. T. W. Adorno, *Minima Moralia. Reflexions from Dangerous Life*, ET London 1974, p. 247; 'Knowledge has no light but that shed on the world by redemption: all else is reconstruction, mere technique. Perspectives must be fashioned that displace and estrange the world, reveal it to be, with its rifts and crevices, as indigent and distorted as it will appear one day in the messianic light.'

INDEX OF NAMES

Harper & Row is proud to present other important books by Jürgen Moltmann:

THE POWER AND THE POWERLESS

"Theologians who can truly preach are rare. Jürgen Moltmann is one of those who can proclaim his faith not only from the podium but from the pulpit. In these sermons, the radical urgency of the gospel is related to things as apparently disparate as food, peace, justice, resistance, solidarity, death, new life, and a host of other arenas where life is daily being lived and where new light from Scripture is always desperately needed. The reader is empowered."—Robert McAfee Brown

THE THEOLOGY OF HOPE

"This is a stimulating and important book, a 'must' for every theological student and every preacher who wishes to become acquainted with the most significant movement in contemporary continental theology. Nowhere else is the present departure from neo-orthodoxy . . . more clearly spelled out, except possibly in the writings of Pannenberg."—*Christian Century*

THE CRUCIFIED GOD

"This book makes it clear that an authentic theology of hope must take seriously the perennial wretchedness of the earth. It is a timely reminder to disillusioned visionaries—who too quickly abandon the struggles for personal and political liberation—that the risen Christ reigns from the cross. Moltmann follows the path of crucifixion into the Godhead itself, reaching a profundity of interpretation that is rare in trinitarian thought."—*The Christian Century*

THE CHURCH IN THE POWER OF THE SPIRIT

"Moltmann represents the theology of liberation at its best, and those who wish to know more about this theology would do well to study this creative and searching theologian."—*Christianity Today*

CAMROSE LUTHERAN COLLEGE
LIBRARY